Wiltshire Record Society

(formerly the Records Branch of the Wiltshire Archaeological and Natural History Society)

VOLUME 57

Impression of 400 copies

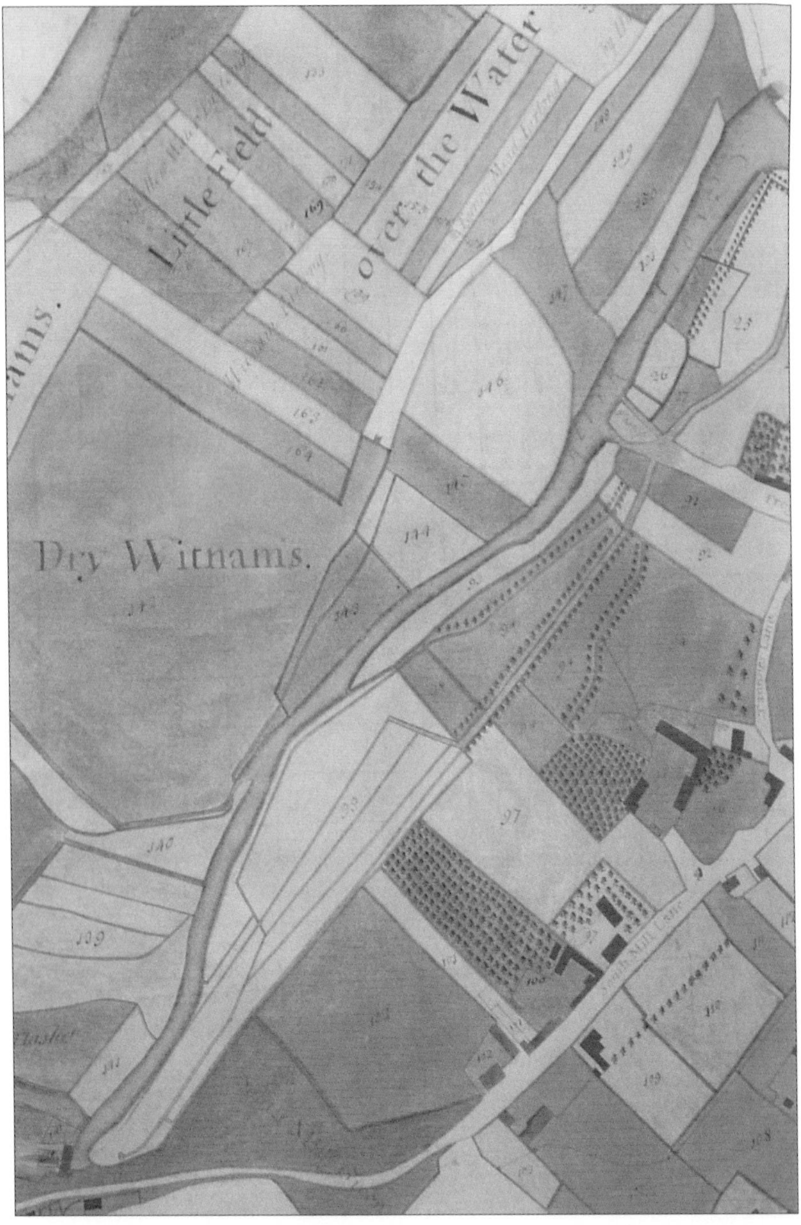

Detail from Henry Flitcroft's book of maps of Amesbury, 1726, showing part of a 17th-century water meadow system constructed on the River Avon above South Mill to the west of the town (WSRO 944/1)

WILTSHIRE FARMING IN THE SEVENTEENTH CENTURY

EDITED BY

JOSEPH BETTEY

TROWBRIDGE

2005

c/o Wiltshire and Swindon Record Office,
Bythesea Road, Trowbridge BA14 8BS

ISBN 0 901333 34 4

Typeset by John Chandler
Produced for the Society by
Salisbury Printing Company Ltd, Salisbury
Printed in Great Britain

CONTENTS

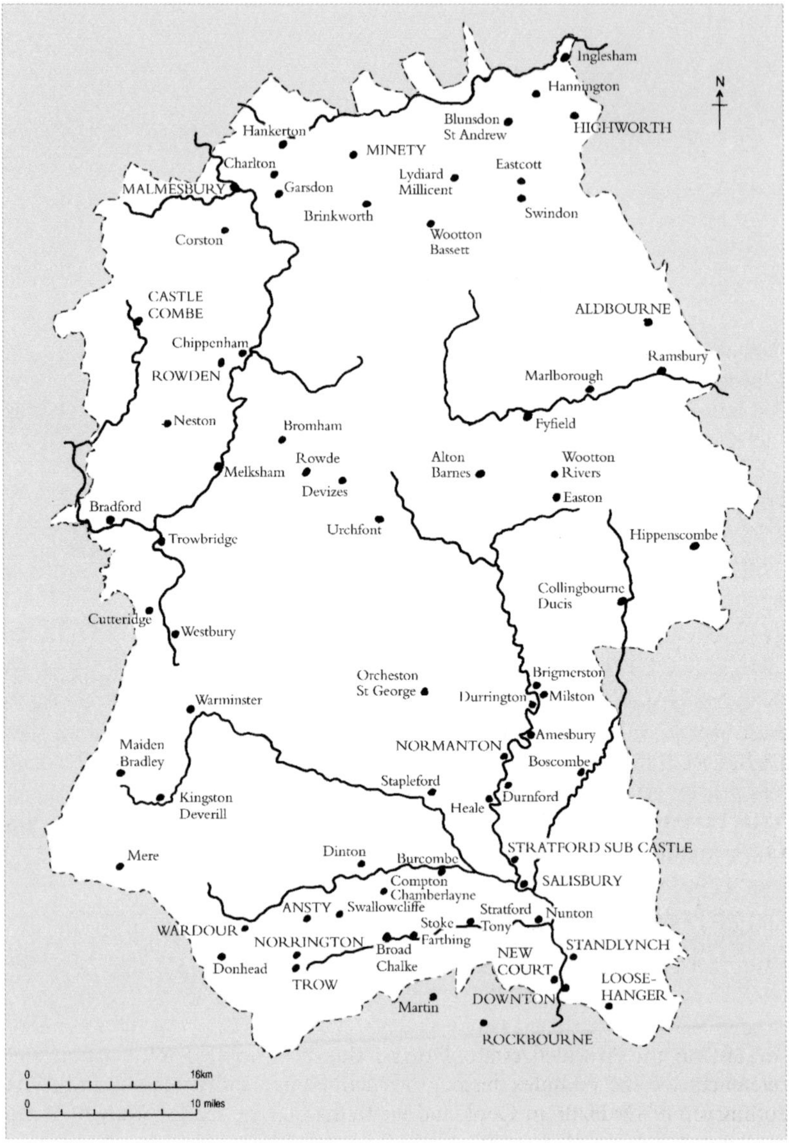

Location map showing the principal places to which the documents refer. Those printed in capitals figure largely in the text.

ACKNOWLEDGEMENTS

The help received in the preparation of this volume is gratefully acknowledged. The General Editor, Dr John Chandler, and the Committee of the Wiltshire Record Society welcomed and supported the proposal for a volume on this subject and in this format; Dr Chandler has been involved in all aspects of the production. Steven Hobbs has provided encouragement, as well as assistance and advice on sources; his colleagues at the Wiltshire & Swindon Record Office have been unfailingly helpful. Historical research on any topic in Wiltshire is assisted by the scholarly information contained in the *Victoria County History of Wiltshire*; the guidance provided by the work of the present Editor, Dr Douglas Crowley, his colleagues and their predecessors has been invaluable. Michael Marshman and his colleagues in the Wiltshire Local Studies Library provide a superb source on all aspects of Wiltshire history. The earlier work of Dr Eric Kerridge on early-modern farming in Wiltshire has pointed the way to many aspects of the subject. The assistance of archivists at The National Archives (Public Record Office), Hampshire Record Office, Somerset Record Office and the University of Bristol is acknowledged with thanks. Material from the Wyndham collection in the Somerset Record Office is reproduced by permission of the estate of the late Dr Catherine Wyndham, and extracts from the Sherfield papers in the Hampshire Record Office have been used by courtesy of the Jervoise-Herriard estate.

Many other people have helped on specific topics. The former Wiltshire County Archivist, Kenneth Rogers, has provided information and suggestions on sources over many years. Robert Moody has shared his detailed knowledge of the history of the Benett family, in particular on the career of John Bennett, steward on the Arundell estate. Donald Box has supplied information and references on the complex history of Malmesbury and its town lands. The enthusiasm of Dr Hadrian Cook and Dr Kathy Stearne for the study of water meadows has been of great assistance. Dr Cook also advised on the map of Downton water meadows and arranged for it to be drawn by Phillip Judge. James and Tina Bond produced the map showing the location of many Wiltshire rabbit warrens. The location map and illustrations were supplied by Dr Chandler.

JOSEPH BETTEY

EDITORIAL NOTE

Introductory material and editorial commentary are printed in italics. The original spelling and capitalisation of documents have been kept, but abbreviations, including ampersands, have been extended. The symbol 'þ' (thorn) in words such as 'þe' and 'þt' has been printed as 'the' and 'that'; 'w^{ch}' has been extended to 'which'. Some punctuation has been added for the sake of clarity. Wherever possible, the meaning of obsolete words or terms, the modern form of aberrant place-names, and the dates of saints' days have been added within square brackets. Uncertain readings are followed by (?). Dates are given as they appear in the documents, with the year beginning on 25th March. References for the location of each source appear at the beginning of the entry.

ABBREVIATIONS

APC	*Acts of the Privy Council*
Aubrey	John Aubrey, *Natural History of Wiltshire*, 1969 edn.
BL	British Library
BRO	Bristol Record Office
Cal. S P Dom	*Calendar of State Papers, Domestic*
DRO	Dorset Record Office
HRO	Hampshire Record Office
PRO	Public Record Office (The National Archives)
SRO	Somerset Record Office
VCH	*Victoria County History of Wiltshire*
WAM	*Wiltshire Archaeological & Natural History Magazine*
WN & Q	*Wiltshire Notes & Queries*
WRS	Wiltshire Record Society (formerly the Records Branch of the Wiltshire Archaeological and Natural History Society)
WSRO	Wiltshire & Swindon Record Office

Weights, measures, and sums of money occurring throughout the volume are as follows:

1 statute acre = 4840 sq. yards
1 rood = ¼acre = 1210 sq. yards
1 perch = 30¼ sq. yards
1 rod, pole or perch = 5½ yards = 16½ feet
1 chain = 22 yards = 66 feet
1 bushell = 8 gallons
1 peck = ¼ bushell = 2 gallons
1 quarter = 28 lbs
1 cwt. = 112 lbs.
1 groat = 4d
1 noble = 6s 8d
1 angel = 10s
1 mark = 13s 4d

LIST OF MAPS AND ILLUSTRATIONS

INTRODUCTION

This volume makes available a collection of farm accounts and other documents which illustrate the husbandry, crops, livestock, labour, and farming methods of Wiltshire during the 17th century. The extracts printed in the following pages include material from manorial court rolls, surveys, stewards' accounts, enclosure agreements, correspondence, tithe dues and market records. Probate inventories are another major source for agrarian history. The many hundreds of Wiltshire inventories which survive make it impossible to choose a representative selection, although lists of livestock, crops, tools and equipment from a small sample of inventories have been included in this volume. They illustrate many features of farming in the county; in particular they show the marked differences between the husbandry of the various regions. Throughout the 17th century the major characteristic of farming in the county continued to be the marked contrast between the sheep–corn agriculture of the chalk downlands and the dairy-farming, cattle-raising husbandry of the clay vales. The two regions were certainly as different as chalk and cheese. Together the downland and the 'cheese country' occupied most of the county. Intruding into the low-lying pasture lands of the cheese country is the narrow strip of the Corallian ridge, low hills rising in places to 400 feet, and extending north-east from Calne through Wootton Bassett to Highworth and beyond into the Vale of White Horse. Here there was some arable as well as livestock farming, and malting barley was despatched along the Thames to brewers in Oxford, Reading and London. Along the north-west fringe, the light lands of the southern Cotswolds supported another district of sheep and corn; in the south-west corner of the county, the rich pastures and extensive commons around the Vale of Wardour were noted for the production of butter.[1]

Writing during the 1670s, the Wiltshire antiquary, John Aubrey, was well aware of the differences in the landscape, farming and people of the two regions of the county. He was born in 1626 at Easton Piercy, near Kington St Michael, in north Wiltshire and lived for a time at Broad Chalke in the Ebble valley, so he knew both parts well. In a famous passage, he described the people of the cheese country as 'slow and dull, heavy of spirit: here about is but little tillage or hard labour; they only milk cows and make cheese; they feed chiefly on milk meats,

1 J. Thirsk, ed., *The Agrarian History of England & Wales*, IV, 1500-1640, 1967; E. Kerridge, *The Agricultural Revolution*, 1967, 42-51, 117-20, 123-6; J.H. Bettey, *Wessex from AD1000*, 1986, 121-30; *V.C.H. Wilts.*, IV, 1959, 43-64.

which cools their brains too much and hurts their inventions'. He also suggested that the people of north Wiltshire were quarrelsome, litigious and nonconformist ('apt to be fanatics'). Whereas on the downs the arable land meant that people worked hard, 'and being weary after hard labour, they have no leisure to read and contemplate religion'.[2]

THE CHALK DOWNLANDS

The downlands of Wiltshire occupy more than half the county. The distinctive landscape, with smoothly-contoured hills, free-draining soil and deeply-cut river valleys, including both Salisbury Plain and the Marlborough Downs, divided by the Vale of Pewsey, remains the largest expanse of unbroken downland in England. The underlying chalk gives a unity to the topography, farming and settlement pattern of this region, although there are considerable variations in the geology. In some parts the chalk is mantled with deposits of flints, gravel, loam and clay-with-flints. Below the chalk and appearing around the edges of the escarpments and in the valleys are fertile bands of greensand from which many of the springs or streams emerge and where most of the settlements are to be found. Although much of the downland presents an aspect of bare hills with occasional plantations or shelter belts of beech and yew, in some parts the soil, particularly clay-with-flints, provides support for extensive tree cover. This verdant woodland of beech, oak, hazel, yew, hornbeam and holly, to be found, for example, in Savernake Forest and Cranborne Chase, gives an unwarranted appearance of fertility. In fact the woodland generally survives only on the poorest or most difficult ground.

The particular character of the chalk downlands gave rise to distinctive features in its farming, land tenure, settlement patterns and society. The region was dominated by great estates and major landowners, manorial control over the tenant farmers remained strong, and there were numerous large farms dependent upon the work of landless labourers. Common field agriculture continued in many manors, as did a farming system based on 'sheep and corn'. Grain production on the light soils depended upon the land being enriched by the folding of large numbers of sheep upon the arable. It was the numerous flocks of sheep which so impressed 17th-century travellers, and it was the effect of the close grazing by sheep that maintained the characteristic downland turf and plant-rich sward.[3]

Early in the 18th century, Daniel Defoe described a journey across the Plain, from Shaftesbury to Salisbury:

> It has neither house nor town in view all the way, and the road which often lyes very broad, and branches off insensibly, might easily cause a traveller to loose his way, but there is a certain never failing assistance upon all these downs for telling a stranger his way, and that is the number of shepherds feeding, or keeping their

2 J. Aubrey, *Natural History of Wiltshire*, 1969 edn., 11.
3 J.H. Bettey, 'Downlands' in J. Thirsk, ed., *Rural England*, 2002, 27-49.

> vast flocks of sheep, which are every where in the way, and who, with a very little pains, a traveller may always speak with.[4]

Typical of many chalkland manors was Compton Chamberlayne where a detailed Survey of 1597 listed 2,055 acres, including 516 acres of 'old enclosures' which were mostly farmsteads, cottages and adjacent paddocks; 305 acres of 'new enclosures', mostly small areas of pasture and 34 acres of 'common meadow'. The 846 acres of arable land were in two fields divided into numerous furlongs and strips; and finally there were some 300 acres of downland grazing.[5] At Collingbourne Ducis in 1607 there were 27 acres of meadow, 300 acres of arable, and more than 800 acres of common grazing for sheep shared between the farmer of the demesne lands and 15 copyhold tenants.[6]

The noted surveyor, John Norden, who had experience of the royal estates throughout the chalklands, praised the sheep-fold for its effect on crops of wheat and barley. He wrote in 1607:

> . . . in Dorset, Wiltshire, Hampshire, Berkshire, and other places champion, the farmers do much enrich their land indeed with the sheepfold. A most easy, and a most profitable course: and who so neglecteth it, having means, may be condemned for an ill husband; nay, I know it is good husbandry to drive a flock of sheep over a field of wheat, rye or barley newly sown, especially if the ground be light and dry, for the trampling of the sheep and their treading doth settle the couth about the corn, keeping it the more moist and warm, and causeth it to stand the faster, that the wind shake it not so easily, as it will do when the root lieth too hollow'.[7]

The farm accounts which are included in this volume show that it was wheat and barley which were the principal sources of profit for downland farmers. The sheep-fold was vital for enriching the soil, and the profit derived from the sale of wool, lambs and mutton was welcome, but was a secondary consideration. The notebook of Robert Wansborough who farmed at Shrewton during the 1630s shows clearly that his major concern was his corn crops, and that his flock of some 800 sheep was valued mainly as an essential element in the production of grain.[8] In 1665 Robert Seymer of Hanford near Blandford Forum in Dorset produced a description of downland farming in Dorset and south Wiltshire for the recently established Royal Society. He concentrated almost entirely upon arable farming and methods of cultivation, but also wrote: '. . .the chiefest help that the hill country hath for their corne grounds is their great flocks of Sheep which they constantly fold upon their Land'.[9] Wheat and barley, the two main crops of the chalkland, could most efficiently be produced by large-scale farming. The 17th century saw an increase in large farms, with

4 D. Defoe, *A Tour Through England & Wales*, Everyman Edn., I, 218.

5 WSRO 332/252 Survey of Compton Chamberlayne 1597.

6 WSRO 9/9/371 Survey of Collingbourne Ducis 1607.

7 J. Norden, *Surveyor's Dialogue*, 1618.

8 E. Kerridge, 'The Notebook of a Wiltshire Farmer in the Early Seventeenth Century', *WANHM*, 54, 1951-2, 416-28.

9 Royal Society MSS, Classified Papers 1660-1740, 10/3/10.

considerable capital investment and often with their own sheep flock at the expense of the smaller tenant farmers.

For an efficient sheep-fold it was essential to have a large number of sheep, and flocks of several hundred were common on chalkland manors. In many places the sheep of all the farmers were kept in a single common flock, with a shepherd or shepherds employed by the whole manor. Only landowners or those farming large separate areas, such as those leasing demesne lands, could keep sufficiently large numbers of sheep to fold their own land. The need for a common sheep flock to manure the ground was one of the main reasons why the communal organization of agriculture survived, with common arable fields divided into strips where the tenants had their dispersed holdings. At Brigmerston and Milston in 1608 the manorial custom stated that 'the fould course oughte to begynne one season att one end of the feilde and the other season att the other end of the feilde'. Likewise at Stratford Tony in 1627 it was ordered that the fold 'shall beginne this yeare att one end of the feild and the next yeare att the other end, and where it is taken off to be set down againe and soe to contynue'. The glebe terrier compiled at Orcheston St Mary in 1677 shows that as well as the right of grazing for his sheep, lambs, cattle and pigs, the rector possessed 38 acres of arable land, 'the said land to be folded according to the custom of the place or else the parson is to have the fold upon every eighth night or every eighth acre'.[10] Co-operation among tenants in the chalklands also included the provision of hurdles for the fold, winter hay for the sheep, and the employment of a cowherd, hogward, hayward and even a want (mole) catcher for the manor. The tightly packed, nucleated villages along the chalkland streams, the shape of the manors which were long and narrow, stretching from the river valleys up on to the high downland, the continuing dominance of great estates and above all, the common sheep flock, all helped to preserve the power of the manor and the manorial courts. The careful regulations for the employment and conduct of the manorial shepherd at Heale which are included in this volume show the importance attached to his work. The presentments at the manorial court of Heale also illustrate how tight control over tenants could be maintained within a manor. The threat of losing the benefit of the sheep fold on his strips within the arable fields was enough to bring the most recalcitrant tenant into line and would ensure that the orders of the manorial court were obeyed. The flocks kept on chalkland manors were very large. Tenants at Charlton in the Avon valley south of Salisbury had 1,800 sheep in 1628; at Alton Barnes in 1659 there were 2,300. A survey of Sutton Veny in 1613 listed grazing rights for 1,100 sheep; and at Bishopstone, east of Swindon in 1647 the tenants had pasture for 1,260 sheep on the downs. At Tilshead in 1623 the demesne farmer had grazing rights for 1,300 sheep on the downs, and the tenants had a flock of more than 1,000 sheep. The farmer of the demesne at Broad Chalke in 1631 had the right to pasture 800 sheep on the South Down and 400 on the North Down. Even with these numbers, there were constant attempts to exceed the permitted numbers, and regular warnings

10 WSRO 2/1 6 September 1608; HRO 44M 69 A8/3/5 4 January 1627; S. Hobbs, ed., *Wiltshire Glebe Terriers 1588-1827*, Wiltshire Record Society, 56, 2003, 321-2.

occur in manorial court records. At Bemerton and Quidhampton there were frequent complaints about over-stocking with sheep, and in 1625 the 'Surveyor of the Fold' was ordered to enforce new 'stints' or limitations on numbers. Similar restrictions on sheep were ordered at Wylye, Alvediston and Stoke Farthing in 1663-4. At Shrewton in 1599 it was decreed that lambs were to count as sheep after St Luke's Day (18 October). In the court rolls of East Overton and Fyfield during the 1670s there are constant orders about 'stints' or restrictions on grazing rights, and many complaints of over-stocking. In 1679 it was decreed that 'the Lambs to goe for sheepe after Lammas Day (1 August)'. In a dispute at Compton Chamberlayne in 1597 over downland claimed as common by the tenants, the manorial surveyor argued that it was not common land on the grounds that there was no record that the tenants had ever been rebuked for over-stocking it, 'which would have been many times ere this yf they had any right of common there'. There were few definite boundaries on the downs, and this led to frequent complaints over encroachments by sheep from adjacent manors. Disputes between neighbouring manors even extended into disagreement about water for the flocks. For the most part the sheep flocks on the downland depended on the so-called 'dew-ponds', which in fact were carefully constructed and were fed by rainfall. During drought the flocks had to drink from chalkland streams, which led to problems. In 1620, for example, the tenants of Baverstock complained at the manorial court that:

> Henrie Weeke the shipard [shepherd] of Dinton hath brought his shippe [sheep] to water in this manner and likewise Mr Earthe's shippard in like manner to the prigidies [prejudice] of the Lorde of this manner and his tenantes[11]

Farmers with cornland but no sheep were obliged to rent the services of a flock in order to dung and tread their land. At Amesbury in 1586 tenants with arable but no sheep were ordered to pay 12*d.* an acre each year towards the costs of the common sheep flock. In *c.*1600 Thomas Bennett of Tisbury complained that his father, John Bennett, had let a flock of 80 sheep to William Cyfrewast of Toller, Dorset 'to no other commoditie or intent but onely to compost and dunge the land of the said William aforesaid'. Cyfrewast had refused to pay the £13 6*s.* 8*d.* for both the sheep fold and the wool which he had taken.[12]

A few cows were kept on the chalklands to supply domestic needs, and some butter and cheese was made. This is evident from the accounts for Norrington in 1669-70. They include references to cows and calves, the employment of a dairy maid and an income from the sale of cheese and butter. Chalkland cheese was not of high quality, however, and was intended for immediate consumption. It is noteworthy that when the steward at Downton, John Snow, bought cheese to send to Sir Joseph Ashe at Twickenham, he sought

11 WSRO 2/1; 332/252; 549/42; 2057/M3; 2057/M63; 2057/M12; 332/249; *VCH Wilts.*, VIII, 1965, 25-31, 52, 68, 167, 244; XI, 1980, 57-8, 194-7; XII, 1983, 7; XV, 1995, 270-1; E. Kerridge, ed., *Surveys of Philip, First Earl of Pembroke and Montgomery 1631-2*, WANHS Records Branch, 9, 1953, *passim*; Canon Bennett, 'Orders of Shrewton 1599', *WANHM*, 23, 1887, 33-9.

12 P.R.O. C3/18/92.

supplies from Somerset and north Wiltshire. On most chalkland manors the arable lands were divided into several large fields, sub-divided into furlongs and into the strips of land held by each tenant. The arrangement remained the same as it was when so clearly described by William Cobbett in 1826. During his journey down the Avon from Milton Lilbourne to Salisbury, Cobbett gave a description of the landscape which can hardly be bettered:

> The shape of the thing is this: on each side *downs*, very lofty and steep in some places, and sloping miles back in other places; but each *out-side* of the valley are downs. From the edge of the downs begin capital *arable fields* generally of very great dimensions, and in some places running a mile or two back into little *cross-valleys*, formed by hills of downs. After the corn-fields come *meadows* on each side, down to the *brook* or *river*. The farm-houses, mansions, villages, and hamlets are generally situated in that part of the arable land which comes nearest the meadows.[13]

The way in which chalkland farming integrated arable and meadow on the lower land with downland sheep walks above is clear all around Salisbury Plain. The shape of each parish or tithing was designed to ensure that each had a share of the fertile soil in the valleys and access to downland. For example, along the northern escarpment of the Plain from Westbury through Bratton and Edington to West Lavington, each of the long narrow parishes runs from the clay vale, through the fertile greensand to the high chalk downland. East Coulston, for instance, is half a mile wide and nearly five miles long, rising from 150 feet above sea level to 700 feet on the downs.

The complex manner in which the arable lands of individual tenants were scattered through the multitude of furlongs in the common fields can be seen in the glebe terriers, where the arable belonging to the incumbent of each parish is listed in detail. Many incumbents had a bewildering number of strips dispersed throughout the arable fields; manorial surveys show that leasehold and copyhold tenants had similarly complicated property holdings. On those manors with three fields it was customary for one field to be fallow each year. On poorer land such as at Mere or some parts of Amesbury there were two fields, one of which was fallow each year; elsewhere in Amesbury there was a complex system involving ten fields. A 1574 custumal of Winterbourne Stoke recorded that

> Our custom is to divide the arable into three fields: to sow two fields and Leave one Sommer fallow—TheTennants Fould goeth all over two of the tennants fields every year —.[14]

Other manors had four, five or more common fields. For example, the arable lands belonging to the parish church at Warminster in 1649 were dispersed among eight separate fields. In a description of Great Cheverell written by the rector about 1695, he commended the fertility and variety of soil in the parish, listing sand, clay, white land (chalk loam) and hill ground. He

13 W. Cobbett, *Rural Rides*, Everyman Edn., 1912, 35.
14 S. Hobbs, ed., *op. cit, passim. VCH Wilts.*, IV, 1959, 43-64.

wrote that 'greate part of the arable Lands never or seldom lye still [i.e. fallow], but are sowne every yeare. But nevertheless it very well answers the Husbandman's expectations'. At New Court Farm in Downton a survey of 1709 shows that of the 346 acres of arable, three-fifths were sown with corn each year, while two-fifths were fallow, although the fallow ground was sown with grass seed. During the same period the tenants of the Earl of Pembroke's manors of Burcombe and Ugford agreed 'for the Improvement of their Summer [i.e. fallow] field' to sow grass in it 'and that there be a Continuance of such Soweing of Grass yearly'.[15]

Increasing demand for wheat and barley from the rising populations of London and towns such as Bristol and Southampton meant that corn-growing brought the highest returns for farmers. Writing in 1651 the agricultural commentator Walter Blith noted: 'Now Tillage yeeldeth the greatest profit to the Land-lord or Occupier'. Consequently many chalkland manors saw an increase in the cultivated area by gradual inroads into the downland grazing. Mostly this was on a small scale, but in a few places new common arable fields were created. More than 70 acres of former sheep pasture were ploughed at Bulbridge and were described in a survey of 1631 as 'newe broke arrable ground'. At Fugglestone and Stratford-sub-Castle new fields were ploughed in *c.*1670 and incorporated into the common arable of each manor.[16]

The wheat and barley produced on the chalklands were sold at the markets such as Warminster, Hindon, Salisbury, Wilton and Shaftesbury. John Aubrey wrote of Warminster that: 'It is held to be the greatest corn-market by much in the west of England'. He also described Hindon as 'perhaps the second best market after Warminster in this county'.[17] Shaftesbury was also an important corn market. Evidence given in a dispute over tolls at the market in 1632 tells of carts loaded with corn from Wiltshire and Dorset arriving at Shaftesbury market for sale 'into Blackmore and some parts of Somersetshire – for that this town standeth in the midway between the hill and the vale'.[18] The accounts for Norrington 1669-70 show the numerous markets to which corn was sent, as well as the considerable amount sold in small quantities to individuals or to bakers and maltsters. Much of the corn grown in Wiltshire was purchased by 'badgers' or small-scale dealers for transport to towns. There are numerous references in the Wiltshire Quarter Sessions Accounts to the licensing of badgers, and the Somerset justices also issued many licences for transporting corn from Wiltshire markets.[19]

15. H.C. Brentnall, 'A Document from Great Cheverell', *WANHM*, 53, 1949-50, 430-40; *WANHM*, 41, 1920-2, 117; WSRO 490/788; 2057/M23.
16 Walter Blith, *The English Improver, Improved*, 1652, 82; WSRO 2057/S5 Vol. I, f2; *VCH Wilts.*, IV, 1959, 51.
17 J. Aubrey, *op. cit.*, 114.
18 PRO E178/5256; SP16/188/67; E134/5 Jas I H22; E134/18 Jas I E1; E134/22 Chas I E9.
19 H.C. Johnson, ed., 'Minutes of Proceedings in Sessions 1563-92', WRS, IV, 1949, 1-13, 124, 134, 140-9; N.J. Williams, ed., 'Tradesmen in Early Stuart Wiltshire', *WRS*, XV, 1960, *passim*; Somerset Record Society, 23, 1907; 24, 1908; 28, 1912; 34, 1919; E. Kerridge, *Trade & Banking in Early Modern England*, 1988, 26-9.

THE CHEESE COUNTRY

The claylands of north and west Wiltshire were predominantly occupied by small family farms concentrating on the production of butter, cheese, pigs and beef cattle, and consequently manorial control was much weaker. Many manors in north and west Wiltshire ceased to operate at all, or exercised few powers. One clayland manor where the manorial court continued to function was Hannington, but the manorial accounts are quite different from those of chalkland manors. There are no references to communal farming, and apart from recording changes of tenancies, the entries are concerned with ditches, water courses, land drainage, flooded roads or impassable footways. There are also regular reports of impounded livestock which had strayed into the manor, a consequence of the large areas of unenclosed rough grazing where livestock could easily wander for several miles.[20] Farms in the clay vales of north and west Wiltshire remained small. Dairy farming, the production and sale of cheese, and the raising of livestock could most conveniently be carried out on family farms using little outside labour. The land produced good grass without expensive drainage work, but much of it was unsuited to arable. The large estates and close manorial control on the downlands produced many written records, such as court books, orders, common-field regulations, stewards' accounts, correspondence and notes. Several examples are included in this volume. Dairy farming and cattle raising, on the other hand, produced far fewer written records. The business of these small farms was conducted along time-honoured lines, with little need for a written record. Moreover, many small farmers would have found writing difficult. The antiquarian John Britton recalled that as a boy in the 1770s he spent time on a dairy farm in north Wiltshire, and he '. . . never saw either a book or newspaper in the house; nor were any accounts of the farming kept'.[21] Documentary evidence of farming practice is inevitably more plentiful for the chalklands, and this is reflected in the records selected for this volume. It has been particularly difficult to find any documents which illustrate the trade in livestock brought annually from Wales by drovers to be fattened on the pastures of north Wiltshire. Of the importance of this trade there can be no doubt, as is evident from occasional references, but no detailed account of the trade has been found. An example of an incidental reference occurs in a suit before the Court of Star Chamber in 1623. William Brounker of Whaddon, grazier, had purchased fifty cattle in Shropshire and the Welsh border and brought them back to Wiltshire. Unfortunately, one black cow had been stolen and Brounker found himself charged with stealing it. In his evidence he stated he had gone:

> . . . to certain fayers in Shropshire and the county of Radnor to buye Rother beasts [cattle] there to stock his grounds as the Grasiers dwellinge neare your Subjecte in the said county of Wilts use to doe.[22]

20 Bristol University Library, Special Collections DM 31 A, Court Book of Hannington 1629-83.

21 John Britton, Note on Aubrey's *Natural History of Wiltshire*, 1847 edn., Part II Chapter VII.

22 PRO STAC 8/54/10.

Clearly this was a common practice among farmers in that district, but without the dispute over the stolen cow no record of it would survive. The tithe account for Minety and the account from Rowden Farm in 1671-3 which are reproduced in this volume give an indication of the large-scale movement of cattle in and out of the pastures and commons of north Wiltshire. The glebe terrier for Stratton St Margaret compiled in 1705 makes specific mention of the vicar's right to the tithe of 'Welch beasts'. In 1729 the vicar of Wanborough, which is on the Ridgeway along which droves of cattle passed, noted in the Register of Baptisms that the land in the parish was increasingly stocked for short periods with cattle from other places, yielding nothing to the parson 'either by plough or pail'.[23] These accounts also show the number and importance of the local markets and fairs at which livestock changed hands. An indication of the extent of the trade in fat cattle is provided by the long list of farmers and drovers from north and west Wiltshire who are recorded as falling foul of the regulations at Smithfield market during the early decades of the 17th century. During the 22 year reign of James I there were more than 100 men from Wiltshire accused of offences at Smithfield market. Many were obviously dealers engaged in a regular trade and were reported more than once. Almost all came from the cattle-raising area, including Malmesbury, Castle Eaton, Wootton Bassett, Quemerford, Liddington, Swindon, Cricklade, Minety and Chippenham.[24]

Many farmers, especially in north and west Wiltshire, also bred horses, although since they kept few records, only occasional references to their activities survive. Horse breeders from Wiltshire are listed among the dealers at Shrewsbury and other Midland horse fairs. Wiltshire dealers also visited the Taunton horse fair and Devizes became a noted market for horses. The best source of evidence concerning Wiltshire horse dealers is the record of trading at Magdalen Hill fair, just outside Winchester. The fair, held in July each year, specialised in horse trading. Many of the horses sold were bred in Wiltshire. Wiltshire farmers also bought brood mares and stallions at the fair. During the 1620s John and Thomas Barrett of Warminster, Henry Marcham and Nicholas Knight of Heddington, Thomas Tacker of Potterne, Matthew Pole of Westbury, Thomas Alford of Minety and John Walsh of Chute were regular dealers in horses at the fair. Later there are references to other dealers from Burbage, Potterne, Beechingstoke, Pewsey, Idmiston, Everleigh and Warminster.[25] In south Wiltshire several members of the Gorges family of Longford Castle were active horse breeders, possessing imported Barbary horses and racehorses, some of which they sold to members of the royal court during the visits of Charles I to Wilton. They were also involved in breeding nags, coach horses, amblers and other specialised horses.[26] In 1692 John Snow, steward at Downton, bought two

23 S. Hobbs, ed., *op. cit.*, 413. *VCH Wilts.*, IX, 1970, 180.

24 WRS, XV, 1960, 52-99.

25 P.E. Edwards, 'The Horse Trade in Tudor & Stuart England', in F.M.L. Thompson, ed., *Horses in European Economic History, 1983, 113-131;* Winchester Cathedral Archives, *Magdalen Hill Fair Accounts*, I am grateful to Dr Peter Edwards for his transcript of these accounts.

26 J.H. Bettey, ed., *Correspondence of the Smyth Family of Ashton Court*, Bristol Record Society, 35, 1982, 49, 78.

high-quality black horses for Lady Mary Ashe's coach – one came from Nicholas Moore of Durrington, the other from Henry Haitter of Witherington Farm, Downton. Each horse cost £18.[27]

As with the trade in livestock, it is difficult to find illustrative material for the very large trade in butter and cheese which was conducted in local markets and especially in Marlborough, where there was an important cheese market. John Aubrey described Marlborough as 'one of the greatest markets for cheese in the west of England. Here doe reside factors for the cheesemongers of London'.[28] Writing in *c.*1720, Daniel Defoe commented upon the amount of cheese which was produced in north Wiltshire and sent to London, Bath, Bristol, and even exported to the West Indies. Defoe also noted another product which was to continue to be important in the economy of the county. He wrote '. . . the farmers of Wiltshire . . . send a very great quantity of bacon up to London, which is esteemed as the best bacon in England, Hampshire only excepted. The bacon is raised in such quantities here, by reason of the great dairies, . . . the hogs being fed with the vast quantity of whey, and skim'd milk, which so many farmers have to spare, and which must otherwise, be thrown away'.[29] Notwithstanding its importance, nothing can be found concerning the cheese market at Marlborough. In this respect, the accounts listing the sales of livestock at Castle Combe fair which are reproduced in the volume are particularly valuable. Not only do they show the local importance of such a fair for trade in livestock, but they also confirm John Aubrey's statement that 'The most celebrated faire in North Wiltshire for sheep is at Castle Combe, on St George's Day (23 April), whither sheep-masters doe come as far as from Northamptonshire'.[30] Markets and fairs for the sale of sheep and cattle at Malmesbury, Highworth, Marlborough and Devizes were similarly important in north Wiltshire. The accounts from Norrington illustrate the scale of the livestock trade at fairs such as Yarnbury, Wilton, Weyhill, Shaftesbury and Chilmark in south Wiltshire.

SHEEP SALES

The sheep kept in Wiltshire were the forerunners of the west-country horned breeds, the Wiltshire and Dorset Horns. The main concerns for farmers were the agility of the sheep and their readiness to be close folded at night on the arable. They were large, hardy animals, slow to fatten and with a light fleece. Their chief value was in the fertility they brought to the soil for corn crops, although they did produce early lambs which provided a useful extra income for farmers. There was a large annual turnover of sheep from the folding flocks. This was because the daily round of being driven long distances to downland grazing and back again to the fold made heavy demands on the sheep. There was

27 WSRO 490/909-12.
28 J. Aubrey, *Natural History of Wiltshire*, 1969 edn., 15.
29 D. Defoe, *A Tour Through England & Wales*, Everyman Edn., I, 1927, 284.
30 B.L. Add. MSS 28, 211, Courts & Rentals of Castle Combe & Oxendon 1416-1664; J. Aubrey, *op. cit.*, 114.

a constant need for new stock, especially wethers (castrated rams), to replenish the flocks. Sheep bred in north and west Wiltshire, west Dorset and Somerset were regularly purchased by chalkland farmers, and many thousands of sheep changed hands each year at the west-country sheep fairs or were sold by dealers. Except when some dispute arose, it is rarely possible to find evidence of these deals, although the accounts printed in this volume give an indication of the extent of the trade.

Evidence for the activities of sheep dealers is found in the Wiltshire Quarter Sessions Rolls for 1634. Several men were presented for marketing offences in Wiltshire and Dorset. It was alleged that:

> . . . they continually go from Faire to Faire, and from Market to Market, from Sheepfould to Sheepfould, from one man to another, where they buye continually great numbers of sheepe; as for example one Saterday to the market at Blandford Forum, the Wensday following sell the same againe at Wilton. Nay, they and most of them will buye one day and sell the same the next, nay, buy and sell in one and the same day, insomuch that our Fayres and Markets are generally and for the most part furnished by these sort of jobbers and Ingrossers who take up all the cobs and pens [i.e. stalls in the market] there that other men viz. Farmers and Yeomen who doe not trade as they doe must sell their sheep in common fields abroad in regard they cannot gett penns for them. Some of the before named have not been ashamed to brage and boast that they have sould this yeare last past 6,000, 5,000,4,000 and 3,000 sheepe, some more some lesse . . .'[31]

When purchasing sheep bred on the heavy lands of Somerset and west Dorset buyers often demanded a warranty that the sheep were free from diseases such as liver rot or coath, and these warranties gave rise to many legal disputes and court actions, providing some evidence of the extent of the trade. John Clym of Plush near Buckland Newton in the Blackmore Vale, for instance, sold 160 ewes at Hindon fair in 1635 at £5 13*s.* 4*d.* per score, he warranted them 'free from Rott & Coath'; a claim which later proved to be false. At Stoford fair near Yeovil in 1649 John and William Luckeys, graziers who were 'buyinge and selling several sorts of cattle and sheep' purchased 120 sheep to take to Wiltshire. John Dawe, who sold them the sheep, warranted the animals to be sound and even produced the healthy livers of two recently killed sheep which were said to be from the same flock. Nearly all 120 sheep died from liver rot shortly after the deal was made.[32] The account books of John and Leonard Snow of Downton show that they bought large numbers of sheep at local fairs on behalf of dealers in the Home Counties. For example, in the 1690s they bought flocks at Weyhill, Britford, Chilmark, Wilton and other fairs; they also purchased sheep for John Robinson of Ham in Middlesex, John Gilles of Kempton Park, John Pavey of London, as well as for other dealers. At Britford in 1690, for example, John Snow bought 20 ewes from John Doore of Stalbridge all 'warranted sound' for 6s 10d each, and 14 more ewes not warranted at 5s 0d each.[33]

31 WSRO A1/110/1635 H No. 205, Quarter Sessions Rolls, New Sarum, 8 January 1635.
32 PRO C8/111/105; C6/523/97; C21/P21/11; CP40/261/342.
33 WSRO 490/842.

FARMERS' TOOLS, IMPLEMENTS AND TECHNIQUES

Probate inventories provide evidence of the equipment used by Wiltshire farmers during the 17th century, although many home-made articles were of low value and were no doubt ignored by the appraisers. Most important for arable farmers was the plough known as a 'sull' or 'sullowe'. This generally consisted of a beam, usually made of ash, a coulter, share and mould board, although some richer farmers possessed a wheeled plough. Horses were mostly employed to pull the plough, although oxen continued to be used especially on heavier land; in each case yokes or harnesses were required. Teams of horses or oxen were known as a 'plow'. Other implements included a light harrow, known as an 'eythe', or a heavier version known as a 'drag'. These were made of wood, with iron tines. Few inventories mention a roller, and on the chalkland the feet of the folded sheep consolidated the land. The contracts for breaking up downland to grow woad, which are quoted in this volume, however, specify that the husbandmen should 'eare, till and plowe', all of which involved the use of a plough; also the contract required the farmer to 'harrowe, dragge, rowle and sowe . . . '. The most expensive item of equipment was the cart or 'putt'. Wagons were rare among smaller farmers and John Aubrey claimed that the wagon was not introduced into south Wiltshire until after the Civil War. The inventories of many farmers do not list any wheeled vehicle.

Farmers growing corn needed a flail and winnowing sheet for threshing, also sacks, scales, sieves and hurdles for the sheep fold. Dairy farmers required buckets, bowls, butter- and cheese-making equipment, including a cheese-press. Inventories seldom list hand-tools separately, referring merely to 'tools of husbandry' or 'other lumber', although occasionally a hatchet, mattock, fork or 'prong', spade, rake and axe are mentioned. It is evident from the accounts in this volume that at harvest, barley, oats and rye, as well as hay, were cut with a scythe; while wheat, with its more valuable straw for thatching, was cut with a sickle, or with a bagging or 'greping' hook. Wheat was bound into sheaves and allowed to stand in stooks or 'shocks' for some days before being carried and stored in a rick. Hay and barley could be left for a time in 'pooks' or 'hand-mows' in the field if the weather was unsuitable for carrying it to the rick Threshed corn was stored in granaries, often raised on staddle stones to prevent rats and mice from entering, and several examples survive in the county. The slow and laborious process of threshing with a flail went on throughout the winter.

The usual course of cultivation and cropping in the common arable fields was to sow wheat after a fallow. On the chalk the land was left unploughed during the summer fallow and had the benefit of the sheep fold and of any dung that could be obtained and transported. On the clayland the fallow field was stirred two or three times during the summer to loosen the soil and prevent the heavy growth of weed which would otherwise occur on that rich ground. In late summer the land was prepared for the wheat crop which was sown in September, being broadcast at about three bushells to the acre. In the following year peas or beans were sown in March or barley, oats or vetches in April. Barley was broadcast in April at three or four bushells to the acre. Beans were sown in March, often set singly with a dibber. Weeding the arable crops employed many women and children during the early summer. Wherever common field arable survived and manorial control remained strong, any attempt to alter the regular course of cultivation was strongly resisted by the majority of tenants, since this deprived them of grazing rights on the fallow field. This is evident from the manorial regulations reproduced in this volume. The very precise manorial orders concerning the time of breach of the fields for grazing by livestock made any divergence from ancient custom impossible without wholesale enclosure.

In his Report to the Georgical Committee of the Royal Society on the agriculture of the Dorset and Wiltshire chalklands written in 1665, which has already been cited, Robert Seymer gave a good account of arable techniques. This is worth quoting in detail:

> The soyle for the most part is a shallow mould mixter with an abundance of Flints, and somewhere the Chalk. The graine they generally sow is either Red Wheat, Barley, Oats, Pease or Vetches.
>
> For their Red Wheat they let their land lye without fallowing [shallow ploughing] it all the summer, and soyle [dung] it, or fold their sheep on it, that it may gaine a Greensward, and plough it, sow it, and harrow it in about ten peck [2½ bushells] to an acre, the beginning of August. They account the earliest sowing the best for their Land, that the Corne may take good rooting before the hard winter approaches.
>
> For their Barley they give their land a winter fallow [ploughing] as soone as conveniently they can after the dispatch of their wheat sowing, that the frosts coming upon it, may mellow their ground and make it dust; then about the beginning of Aprill they plough it, sow it, drag it, and harrow it in, about four bushells to an Acre. Afterwards they tread it with their Sheep, and fold them on it, which is their chief improvement, both for this and likewise their Wheat.

Seymer went on to report that Oats were sown 'about the latter end of February' at 4 bushells to the acre. Peas and Vetches were sown in March at 2 bushells to the acre.[34]

IMPROVEMENT AND INNOVATION

A notable feature of Wiltshire agriculture during the 17th century was the way in which farmers grasped new methods, new techniques and new crops. By its nature, most farming continued to be conducted along traditional lines, but improvements were eagerly pursued. Much open and unimproved common pasture survived in the cheese country, as well as large areas of rough wood-pasture in the royal forests of Pewsham, Savernake, Braydon and Melksham. Many of these commons were over-stocked, ill-drained, overgrown and unprofitable. The common at Dauntsey in 1579 was described as 'voidable,

34 Royal Society MSS, Classified Papers 1660-1740, 10/3/10.

unprofitable and overgrown with brambles and briars, not worth twelve pence an acre'. Later, after enclosure with ditches, pales and quickset hedges it was said to be worth thirteen shillings an acre. At Hannington in 1632 the commons were said to be 'in a deep, watrye part of the cuntrye, [and] subjecte oftentymes to overfloweing with water and thereby to rott and hungerbane suche sheepe and cattle as were put to feede thereon; and by reason of such moystures and rottennes of the soyle ... were most commonlye soe stocked and trodden downe with the cattle thereon goeing that all the grasse was spoyled'. [35] The 17th century witnessed a transformation of this region by enclosure and drainage, much of it accomplished by agreement among commoners, urged on by landlords desiring the higher rents improvement would bring. The disafforestation of the royal forests, although deeply unpopular with those who had enjoyed rights of common, and accompanied by major riots, nonetheless resulted in much enclosure and improvement of pasture. In this low-lying land arable farming was of secondary importance, and many of the small family-run farms were almost entirely grassland.

John Aubrey provides a vivid account of change in the appearance of north-west Wiltshire during his lifetime.

> The country was then [c1550] a lovely *campania* as that about Sherston and Cotswold. Very few enclosures unless near houses. My grandfather Lyte did remember when all between the Cromhalls and Castle Combe was so, when Easton, Yatton and Combe did intercommon together. In my remembrance much hath been enclosed and every year more and more is taken in.[36]

Before enclosure livestock could roam at will over large areas of woodland and common. Innumerable hours must have been spent in searching for stray sheep and cattle. For example, in a case of alleged rape at Purton, tried before the Ecclesiastical Court in 1616, the accused, John Frye, came from Brinkworth, some five miles away. He stated that he was passing through Purton 'to look for some cattle which were strayed'. Many enclosures were small scale and involved only exchanges of land among tenants with the approval of the landlord. The records of Bromham, Stanley, Rowden and Chittoe contain numerous references to exchanges and enclosures by agreement. In 1619-20 it was agreed by the lord, Sir Henry Baynton, that the tenants should have their lands:

> laid together in equall proportion by the generall consent and agreement of all the parties aforesaid, to the intent that as well as the said Lord as every of the said Tennantes may enjoy from henceforth the plotts of grounde allotted unto him in severaltye according to their former estates formerly granted unto them.[37]

The process of enclosure by agreement is illustrated in this volume by examples from Brinkworth, Charlton, Hankerton and Hannington. Not all the so-called 'enclosures by agreement' were achieved without controversy or

35 G.M. Young, 'Some Wiltshire Cases in Star Chamber' *WANHM*, 50, 1942-44, 446-51; WSRO 1033/42 Enclosure Agreement for Hannington 1632.

36 J. Aubrey, *Miscellanies on Severall Curious Subjects*, ed., E. Curll, 1714, 31-2.

37 WSRO D1/39/2/8; 122/1 25 Sept 16 Jas I; *VCH Wilts*, VII, 1953, 185.

dissent. It was difficult for small holders to resist pressure from the lord, freeholders and larger farmers, even though enclosures might deprive them of access to common grazing and be against their best interests. At Bremhill in 1610 the common was enclosed by an agreement in the manorial court, but some tenants later complained that their acquiescence had been obtained by threats and they were 'very hardly drawn to give their consents'.[38] Further examples of the pressure which could be exerted on tenants are included in the text.

'IMPROVING' LANDLORDS

A notable feature of many of the advances in Wiltshire agriculture during the 17th century is the way in which farmers were encouraged by landlords to adopt new methods. The Earl of Berkshire of Charlton Park was responsible for much of the progress in enclosure on his estates in north Wiltshire; the St John family of Lydiard Tregoze encouraged drainage work on their estates; the spread of water meadows along the chalkland valleys owed much to the encouragement of the Earl of Pembroke and his steward, and to John Snow, steward to Sir Joseph Ashe. The Earl of Arundell's steward, John Bennett, actively encouraged drainage work, forestry and the introduction of new crops.. The Danvers family of Dauntsey, Sir Henry Baynton of Bromham, the Thynnes at Longleat, the Seymour family at Savernake and the Hydes at Heale were all active in encouraging improved agricultural methods. Even amid the pressing concerns and controversies of his political career, Anthony Ashley Cooper, first Earl of Shaftesbury, was keen to encourage agricultural improvements on his estates. When Parliament was dismissed in 1675 and he was able to spend time at Wimborne St Giles, he brought with him from London several books on agriculture and estate management. These included Walter Blith's *English Improver or a New Survey of Husbandry* (1649), Gervase Markham's *English Husbandry* (1616) and John Evelyn's *Sylva and Calendarium Hortense or Gardener's Almanac* (1664).[39]

INNOVATION ON THE DOWNLANDS

During his journey through the Wiltshire downlands, Defoe noted the way in which the area of arable land had been greatly increased. He described '. . . many thousand acres of the carpet ground being of late years, turned into arable and sowed with wheat'.[40] The response to the rising profitability of corn-growing by the extension of arable at the expense of waste, woodland, rabbit warrens and downland pasture was a common theme of chalkland farming during the second half of the 17th century. This is illustrated in many of the documents which follow. Much of this extension of arable was achieved by 'burnbaking' or 'denshiring', that is stripping, drying and burning the turf and spreading the ash

38 PRO Chanc. Proc. Ser I, 8/9.
39 WSRO 750/1 John Bennett's Accounts; PRO 30/24/5 Part 293 Shaftesbury Papers.
40 D. Defoe, *op. cit.*, 285.

before ploughing, and cultivating the land. John Aubrey claimed that the practice was first introduced into Wiltshire in 1639 by 'Mr Bishop of Marton [Martin]'. This is confirmed by the records of the Earl of Shaftesbury concerning John Bishop's tenure of Horsey Farm at Martin. In 1639 Bishop was said to have spent £230 'in bringing Earth and Chalke to the Land and in Rootinge parte of the grounde and in burning of Beete' in order to improve the extremely barren land. The accounts of Richard Osgood in this volume have references to burn-baking land at Normanton, and part of the downland at Allington had been burnbaked in 1674. There are also references to burnbaking parts of the downland at Maddington, Newton Tony, Durnford and Durrington.[41] After centuries of close grazing by sheep flocks, the virgin downland was extremely fertile. Stripping and burning the turf had the effect of destroying at least some of the insect pests such as wireworms and leatherjackets which were present, and, initially, good crops of corn could be grown. Without the advantage of artificial fertilisers, however, it was difficult to maintain this early fertility, and many farmers were sceptical about the wisdom of destroying ancient grassland. John Aubrey wrote '. . . they say 'tis good for the father, but naught for the son, by reason it does so weare out the heart of the land'. In a law suit over the ploughing up of ancient pasture at Milton Abbas, Dorset, in 1672 a witness used identical words 'Such husbandry was good for the Father, but naught for the Son'. Other witnesses declared that it was 'against all Ancient Husbandry'. Nonetheless the extension of arable on parts of the Wiltshire downs continued, and early in the 18th century Defoe was impressed by the farming he saw during his journey across Salisbury Plain.

> One thing here is worth while to mention, for the observation of those counties in England, where they are not yet arrived to that perfection of husbandry, as in this county, and I have purposely reserved it to this place: The case is this, The downs or plains, which are generally called Salisbury Plain; but, particularly, extend themselves over the counties of Southampton, Wilts, and Dorset, were formerly all left open to be fed by the large flocks of sheep so often mentioned; but now, so much of these downs are plowed up, as has increased the quantity of corn produced in this county, in a prodigious manner, and lessened their quantity of wooll, as above; all which has been done by folding their sheep upon the plow'd lands, removing the fold every night to a fresh place, 'till the whole piece of ground has been folded on; this, and this alone, has made these lands, which in themselves are poor, and where, in some places, the earth is not above six inches above the solid chalk rock, able to bear as good wheat, as any of the richer lands in the vales, though not quite so much: I say this alone; for many of these lands lie so remote from the farmers houses, and up such high hills, for the farmers live always in the valleys, and by the rivers, that it could not be worth their while to carry dung from those farm-houses, to those remote lands; besides, the draught up hill would be so heavy, and the ways so bad, that it would kill all their cattle [oxen and horses].[42]

41 J. Aubrey, *op. cit.*, 103; PRO 30/24/32/7; C22/716/58; *VCH Wilts.*, XV, 1995, 10.
42 J. Aubrey, *Natural History of Wiltshire*, 1969 edn., 103; PRO C22/716/58; D. Defoe, *op.cit., I, 284–5.*

Dressings of marl, chalk and lime were applied to the soil in an attempt to promote fertility and increase yields. At Compton Chamberlayne in 1597 the surveyor noted that, '. . . there is a chaulk pytt at the south-west corner of Compton arable fields neere the bottom of the Downe, where the tenants doe fetche Chaulk for manuringe theyr Lands, to the great enryching of theyr grounds'. In his Report to the Royal Society in 1665 Robert Seymer commented: 'Of late yeares in the hilly parts some have covered their ground over somewhat thick with chalk, and find it to be a very lasting improvement'. Also on the chalklands new fodder crops such as sainfoin, rye grass, vetches and different varieties of clover were introduced, especially on the great estates, as is shown by the accounts for the Arundell's farm at Ansty which are printed here. Sainfoin or French Grass was introduced as a fodder crop on the chalkland during the 1650s and rapidly became an established part of arable rotations. The earliest reference is found at Maddington in 1651. When Michael Woodward, Warden of New College, Oxford, visited the college estate at Colerne in 1668 and 1669, he commented on the sainfoin being grown there by Thomas Harris, a college tenant. With such a new crop, the Warden was uncertain of the spelling but settled for 'quinque folia, cinque foile'. He noted that 'it thrives very well'. Thomas Harris asked for timber 'to build him a loft to lay his St Foile in'. Sainfoin was being grown on the Downton estate in 1671. In a letter to the steward, John Snow, the lord of the manor, Sir Joseph Ashe, wrote on 5 February 1671: 'I approve of sowing the St Foine seed in the ground you mention, but let the fences be wel kept up, or the sheep wil come in and destroy it'. In a Chancery dispute over the demesne land at Teffont Evias in 1692 it was recorded that 38 acres had been sown with a crop described as 'cinquefoil' or 'sainfoin'. [43] Hops were grown around Salisbury and Wilton to supply the numerous brewers there. There are many references to hop-yards and hop-gardens in south Wiltshire. Two men were described as 'hop-gardeners' at Bromham in 1636, and in the same year a man at Colerne was accused of cutting 'hopp-poles' in a coppice. Since the crop was generally grown in small plots it seldom appears in probate inventories or other records.[44]

Tobacco was grown in several places during the early 17th century, and was a profitable though labour intensive crop. Its cultivation was suppressed by the government during the 1620s in order to protect the trade from Virginia. In the Proclamation of 1627 ordering the destruction of all tobacco planted in England, it was alleged that great quantities were being grown in Wiltshire, although only Wootton Bassett is specifically mentioned.[45]

The cultivation of cabbages as a field crop was said by John Aubrey to have been introduced from Holland by Sir Anthony Ashley of Wimborne St Giles (d.1627) who had lived for a time in the Netherlands. Aubrey also refers to

43 WSRO 332/252 Survey of Compton Chamberlayne 1597; Royal Society MSS, Classified Papers 1660-1740, 10/3/10; J. Thirsk, ed., *The Agrarian History of England & Wales*, IV, 1500-1640, 1967, 566; W.R.S., XIII, 1957, 29, 56; WSRO 490/910, Letter of Sir Joseph Ashe to John Snow 5 February 1671. PRO C5/307/14. *VCH Wilts.*, XIII, 1987, 189-90.

44 *WN & Q*, VIII, 1915, 383.

45 *APC*, 1627, 409-10.

the field cultivation of both cabbages and carrots in Wiltshire, and carrots were certainly being grown at Stratford sub Castle in 1624.[46]

During the late 16th century woad, which had previously been imported in large quantities to supply the needs of dyers, was introduced on the chalklands, especially on newly-cultivated downland. A Government enquiry of 1585 found that 338 acres of woad were being grown in Wiltshire. A total of 59 growers were listed from all parts of the county. Most had plots of one or two acres, but a few were growing woad on a much larger scale. John Bayliss, a Salisbury clothier, had 43 acres, John Dowse of Collingbourne Ducis was growing 25 acres, and Robert Green of Urchfont had 17 acres.[47] Because woad was such a hungry crop, grown only for two or three years in the same place, often by contractors or by the dyers themselves, few written records of its cultivation have survived. Even the mills for crushing and processing the woad, and the sheds for drying and storing it were temporary structures. At Amesbury the tenants were specifically forbidden from growing woad. This was because it was believed to exhaust the ground, and its cultivation led to the ploughing up of downland grazing to the detriment of the sheep flocks. The recusant lord of the manor of Norrington, Thomas Gawen, alleged in *c.*1610 that his tenant, Richard Kennell, had impoverished the land by ploughing up 25 acres of meadow and pasture to grow woad. The wealthy Salisbury clothier, George Bedford, produced large quantities of woad on Cranborne Chase and especially on newly-broken arable land at Martin. His accounts contain many agreements with husbandmen to plough and cultivate virgin downland, to sow woad on his behalf and to supply woad to his four woad mills. An inventory of his possessions at the time of his death in 1607 lists 18 tons of processed woad worth £400, leases of land for growing woad at Martin, Blagdon, Pentridge and Handley; 'an olde woade house and fower woade mylles whereof two are at Martin and two at Blagdon', worth £10. Some of the woad was used at his own cloth mill at Laverstock, and he also supplied woad to clothiers in several parts of Wiltshire and Somerset. In his will he left bequests to the poor of the parishes of Damerham, Martin, Pentridge and Cranborne, 'in remembrance of my good will for theire labours and worke bestowed on my business'.[48]

Bedford's widow married the prominent Salisbury lawyer and member of Parliament, Henry Sherfield. His accounts include many references to large-scale woad cultivation on his land at Winterbourne Earls, and at Blagdon and Boveridge on Cranborne Chase. In 1610 for example, Sherfield leased for four

46 Bodleian Library MS Aubrey 2 f88; HRO (Jervoise of Herriard Collection), 44M69/L25/7; J. Thirsk, *Alternative Agriculture*, 1997, 277.

47 PRO E163/14/9; E163/15/1. I am grateful to Prof. Richard Hoyle for information on the 1585 Enquiry.

48 PRO E163/15/1; E163/14/9; STAC Jas I 1/6; 154/4; E. Kerridge, *The Agricultural Revolution*, 1967, 218-9; HRO, (Jervoise of Herriard Collection), 44M69/L28/1-3; 44M69/L44/17; 44M69 L57/1-3. I am grateful for permission to consult and quote from this collection. R.B. Pugh, ed., *Calendar of Antrobus Deeds before 1625*, WANHS Records Branch, 3, 1947, 128, 134. J.B. Hurry, *The Woad Plant*, 1930, 11, 16-18, 65; J. Thirsk, *Alternative Agriculture*, 1997, 79-96; J.H. Bettey, 'The Cultivation of Woad in the Salisbury Area', *Textile History*, 9, 1978, 112-117.

years 120 acres of pasture land and rabbit warren at Boveridge. The lease gave Sherfield the right to plough up the land and destroy the rabbit warren for the purpose of growing woad. A few months later he leased a further 22 acres at Tidpit in the parish of Martin. His account book shows that he sold large quantities of woad to clothiers and dyers from Frome, Lacock, Salisbury, Andover, Newbury, Hungerford and London. Although heavily involved with his legal practice, Sherfield took a close personal interest in his farm at Winterbourne Earls and in his woad trade. In February 1626, for example, while Sherfield was at his office in Lincoln's Inn, he received a letter from a Salisbury dyer, Henry Cabbell, who was processing some of his woad. Cabbell wrote: 'I have set your woad, it is very fyne woad to work . . . it is coming on well'. Enclosed with the letter is a small sample of woollen cloth dyed with the woad; the cloth retains its attractive deep blue colour.[49]

Sherfield also entered into partnership with his step-son, George Bedford, to import and grow madder, cole and oil-seed rape from Holland and extract oil, 'for procuring Madder from beyond the Seas and in plantinge and husbandinge thereof, and also in the trade of Growing and husbanding of Cole and Rape and makinge the same into oyle . . . '. The madder plants he obtained were grown at Appledore in Kent, but Sherfield certainly grew rape on his land in Wiltshire. An entry in his account book for September 1624 records 2s 6d 'Paid for cutting of the Rape seed at Stratford and threshing of it and winnowing'. There are also references to rape being grown on land Sherfield leased at Amesbury.[50]

Further evidence of concern for increased productivity is found in the trouble farmers took over selection of seed and seed dressings. For his farm at Winterbourne Earls in 1599, Henry Sherfield ordered seed from the poorer land at Martin and specified that it should be 'good, sweete, clene, dry and wel-wynoed seed wheate'. During the 1630s Robert Wansborough of Shrewton bought seed corn from Easterton, Imber, Market Lavington, West Lavington, Corton, Urchfont, Wilsford, Langford, Chalke, Stert and Salisbury. He also possessed a mill to clean the seed corn and remove weed seeds. The Earl of Shaftesbury instructed his bailiff at Wimborne St Giles to spare no pains in obtaining the best seed in 1675, and suggested that the barley seed should come from 'shady places and north side hills as from Bemerton by Salisbury'. In his Report to the Royal Society in 1665 Robert Seymer described the care chalkland farmers, took 'to make choyce of the best and cleanest [seed], and of that for the most part which was grown in a poorer soyle, and at least different from the nature of that ground where they intend to sow it'. Seymer also described '. . . an Engine (called a Mill) made with small wires which are placed so neare together that the Corne cannot run thorow them unless small and dwinling; thorow this Instrument they cast their seed, which separates the good from the bad, and all those smaller seeds, as cockle and other which are very injurious to corne'. Writing in *c.*1695, the rector of Great Cheverell said of his parish 'The Husbandman needs not fetch his seed from other parts (as usually

49 HRO 44M69/L30/76.
50 HRO 44M69/L25/7; L30/68.

others doe) for that the Seed growne on one of these sort of Lands is a good exchange for the other'. Various dressings were used in an attempt to improve germination and resist blight. Most involved mixing the seed with lime, although each farmer appears to have used his own recipe, using additions such as brine, eggs, urine and red lead.[51]

WATER MEADOWS

The most important improvement, and the major west-country contribution to agricultural progress was the introduction and rapid spread of water-meadows. By providing an efficient method of producing an early growth of grass, the water meadows enabled farmers to overcome the age-old barrier to progress caused by 'the hungry gap'. This was the period in the spring before the natural growth of grass occurred, and when the previous year's hay crop had been eaten. It was this gap which restricted the number of livestock which could be kept. The limitation on sheep numbers meant that the amount of arable land which could be folded was restricted, and corn production could not be increased. The water meadows also produced abundant and reliable crops of hay.

Many riverside meadows had always been occasionally inundated by naturally-occurring floods, but the earliest references to the complex process of watering by artificial means are not found until the early 17th century. It was in the chalkland valleys of southern England that the production of early grass by covering the surface of a meadow by a shallow rapidly-moving sheet of water began and reached its fullest extent. The system demanded an elaborate arrangement of hatches, sluices, channels and drains. The clear, fast-flowing chalk streams of Wiltshire, Dorset and Hampshire, with their constant temperature, valuable nutrients and calcareous nature were ideal for the purpose, and the water meadows became an indispensable element of chalkland farming.[52]

The idea of creating meadows that could be watered at will by artificial means was first published by Rowland Vaughan in his book *The Most Approved and Long Experienced Water Workes*, (1610). This described Vaughan's work in the Golden Valley, Herefordshire. Vaughan had family and business connections with the Herberts, Earls of Pembroke, whose widespread Wiltshire lands included many chalkland manors, and Vaughan dedicated his book to William, first Earl of Pembroke. It is probable that it was through this connection that the earliest water meadows were developed in Wiltshire, and certainly the process owed much to the encouragement by energetic landlords. The initial expense of installing hatches and adapting the surface of a meadow with carefully graded channels, ridges, and drains was inevitably heavy. For this reason the first water

51 HRO 44M69/L33/10; L25/1-4; L57/1; Bristol University, Shrewton MSS, 76/68; PRO 30/24/5 Part 293 Lord Shaftesbury's Notebook 1675; Royal Society MSS, Classified Papers 1660-1740, 10/3/10; *WANHM*, 53, 1949-50, 430-40.

52 J.H. Bettey, 'The Development of Water Meadows in the Southern Counties', in H. Cook & T. Williamson, eds., *Water Management in the English Countryside*, 1999, 179-195.

meadows were essentially manorial rather than individual enterprises. During the early years of the 17th century there are several references in manorial accounts to what appear to be early attempts at watering. 'Wet Meads' and 'Water Closes' were mentioned at Netherhampton, Broadchalke, Chilmark, Dinton and Teffont, but it is not clear whether these were naturally wet or were the result of controlled flooding. Similarly, references to water-courses at Stanton St Bernard and Mildenhall may refer to drainage work rather than watering. At Baverstock on the river Nadder in 1620 there was a complaint in the manorial court that, 'the water at Stonie Bridge is turned out of Course by William Allenes over into John Greenes and John Mesoles freeholds to water the Meads'.

A year later it was said that John Greene of neighbouring Barford St Martin 'turneth the water out of his course into his own grounde'. A remarkable early water-meadow experiment was made on the Avon at Amesbury in 1624. The Salisbury lawyer, Henry Sherfield, considered bringing an action 'against Mr Newdigate for drowning my grounds at Amesbury'. He complained that Newdigate, 'did sett up hatches on the River to drowne his meadowes at West Ambrosbury whereby my grounds are hurt, . . . the lands where my flocke feedeth are drowned and soe my sheepe [are] banned'. At Bremhill in 1630-1 there was a complaint at the manorial court that, 'Vincent Smith of Kellwayes in the parish of Bremhill maketh a baye at the lower end of Dreycotts meade over into Ivy meade a thwart a water course whereby Dolemeade belonging to the Lord of the mannor is overflowed and halfe Dreycotts meade also'. By 1632 some form of watering was already established on the Earl of Pembroke's land at Charlow Mead, Ramsbury, on a tributary of the river Kennet. An agreement was made between Roger Bankes of Crowood in the parish of Ramsbury, yeoman, and the owners of How Mill, Hugh and John Cooke, whereby in return for an annual payment of 2s 6d Bankes was permitted to dig a water course and take water from How Mill pond:

> as before it was wont to be conveyed out, to water and flot one mead called Charelow Meade when and as often as the aforesayd Roger will thinke fitte always provided that the aforesayd Roger convey the water thither at his own charge.

This agreement was repeated in a grant from the Earl of Pembroke's agents in 1656, giving liberty to 'flote and drowne out of the Mill pond of how Mill . . . one parcell of meadow ground commonly called Charlow Meade.[53]

One of the first definite and full-scale schemes in Wiltshire was at Wylye in 1632. The Earl of Pembroke's steward presided over a meeting of the manorial court when the tenants agreed to share the costs of watering the common meadow. Water meadows had already been constructed at Puddletown and Affpuddle in Dorset, and evidently the process and method of construction was well understood. The tenants at Wylye agreed to employ John Knight of nearby Stockton to, 'drawe a sufficient and competant quantitie of

53 WSRO 332/249 3 April 1621; 19 April 1629; 122/1; HRO 44M69/L25/3; WSRO 3397/5.

water of the River of Wylye, out of the same River, sufficiently to water and flott all the said groundes or soe much thereof as by industry and art may be watered or flotted'. Knight was to be paid 14s 0d for every acre of water meadow created, and thereafter 2s 0d per annum for each acre maintained. Clearly the methods and work involved were already well understood at Wylye; and landlord, steward and tenants were all convinced of the benefits to be gained. Another early example can be found in the Manorial Court Book of Britford in 1634 where: 'It is agreed that the Common Meade shall be drowned before this nexte yeare followinge att a season convenient'. In the following year there are references to an 'undertaker' being appointed to manage the watering of the meadow. As in Dorset, water meadows were soon created along many of the Wiltshire chalkland valleys. Again John Aubrey is proved to be a reliable witness, for writing in *c.*1680 he recalled, 'the improvement of watering meadows began at Wylye about 1635, at which time we began to use them at Chalke'. Aubrey also mentioned the creation of water meadows on the Kennet between Marlborough and Hungerford in about 1646, 'and Mr John Bayley, of Bishop's Down, near Salisbury, about the same time made his great improvements by watering there by St Thomas's Bridge'. At Shalbourne in 1639 Richard Clifford was reported by the parish constable for making a hatch in his meadow, 'whereby the water is bayed back in such wise that the King's leige [liege] people cannot passe to the Church without danger'.[54] The early grass and abundant hay produced by the water meadows were so valuable that the idea spread along the chalkland valleys around Salisbury and along the Kennet in eastern Wiltshire. An extensive area of water meadows was developed along the Avon at Amesbury during the 1650s, and at Damerham in 1661 there was 'a meadow taken out of the farmes and improved by water'. At the same time on the Avon south of Salisbury there were 70 acres of meadow 'drowned by art'. Seven acres of water-meadow on the river Kennet at Ramsbury were leased for £11 a year in 1667, 'with the water theare to come and be drawn into the said meadow for the bettering and ymproving thereof'. In the same year the manorial court at Netherhampton ordered the regulation of the meadows by 'the Supervisors of the Waters for flowinge the Moores and Marshes'. Watering of meadows was already well established on the river Nadder at Sutton Mandeville by the 1650s. The greatly increased value of the watered meadows there is evident from an agreement recorded in the churchwardens' accounts on 21 June 1656. Dry or unwatered meadows were to be charged a parish rate of 12s 0d per acre, whereas watered meadows were to be rated at 24s 0d per acre.[55]

Some of the problems and costs of operating and maintaining the water meadows can be seen from the accounts of Richard Osgood which are included in this volume. In particular, Osgood's notes reveal his concern about the difficult task of installing a hatch in the fast-flowing river Avon in order to divert some of the water into his meadow. Osgood's accounts show the heavy

54 E. Kerridge, 'The Floating of the Wiltshire Watermeadows', *WANHM*, 55, 1953, 105-118; Aubrey, *op. cit.*, 104; HRO 44M69/A8/1/16 Court Book of Britford 1629-52.

55 WSRO 283/4 14 Sept 1658; 84/47; 212A/27/27; 2057/M8; A1/110/1642 Quarter Sessions Rolls, Hilary , 1642; 2219/1 Churchwardens' Accounts of Sutton Mandeville, 1602-93.

on-going costs of maintaining the water meadows. The constant repair of weirs and hatches, the labour of clearing water courses, and the carriage of stone and timber was costly. It is an indication of the value of water meadows that so many manorial lords and their tenants were prepared to invest in them. Also included in this volume are details of the elaborate scheme for watering the meadows on the Avon south of Salisbury during the period 1665-1690, from the notebooks and correspondence of John and Leonard Snow, stewards of the wealthy London merchant, Sir Joseph Ashe. Although he lived at Twickenham, Middlesex, Joseph Ashe leased the manor of Downton and adjacent land along the Avon from the bishops of Winchester. The property was managed on his behalf by John Snow and later by his son, Leonard. The scheme for creating water meadows along the valley involved digging two long main 'carriages' or water-courses from Alderbury, more than three miles upstream. This could supply water for a series of meadows down the valley, enabling water meadows to be constructed for the manorial farms at Witherington, Standlynch, Barford, New Court and Wick. The construction involved 41 agreements with landowners, farmers and millers, the construction of numerous bridges and all the costs of hatches, weirs and ground work for the meadows. The eventual cost of the whole scheme cannot have been much less than £5,000.

When in 1677 Sir Joseph Ashe complained about the costs, which were double John Snow's original estimate, the steward pointed out the complexity of the scheme but also emphasised its value. He reminded his employer that the early grass and the increased supply of hay for winter feed were extremely valuable, and the fact that 194 acres of meadow which had previously been let for £218 per annum were now worth £428; if they could not be let for this sum, John Snow undertook to rent them himself.

In spite of his protestations about costs, Joseph Ashe was an extremely wealthy man. As well as his business interests in London, he had estates at Twickenham and Yorkshire and the highly lucrative lease of the manor of Downton. It is an indication of his wealth that in addition to these estates which he left to his son, James, he provided each of his two daughters with a dowry of £10,000. His daughter Katherine married William Windham of Felbrigg, Norfolk, and Mary married Horatio, Viscount Townshend of Raynham, Norfolk. Mary was the mother of the agricultural 'improver' Charles 'Turnip' Townshend.[56]

By the 1660s water meadows had already become an established feature in many chalkland manors. Robert Seymer in his Report on chalkland farming to the Royal Society in 1665 wrote that: 'the greatest improvement they have for their ground is by winter watering of it, if it lye convenient for a River or lesser streame to run over it'. Water meadows had also been created in the river valleys of Hampshire, and John Worlidge who farmed near Petersfield commented in 1669 that the water meadows were, 'one of the most universal and advantageous improvements in England within these few years'.[57] By providing a lush growth

56 WSRO 490/842-910; Elizabeth Griffiths, ed., *William Windham's Green Book 1673-1688*, Norfolk Record Society, 66, 2002, 1, 26.

57 Royal Society MS CP10/3/10; J. Worlidge, *Systema Agriculturae*, 1869.

of early grass and an ample hay crop, the water meadows made the first breach in the age-old barrier to agricultural progress. On most manors the primary purpose of the water meadows was to provide early feed for the ewes and lambs during the 'hungry gap' of March and April, and to produce hay for feeding the sheep flock during the winter. Thus more sheep could be kept, more arable land could be folded and heavier crops of wheat and barley could be produced. At Downton, however, there was a ready market for milk and butter from nearby Salisbury, and the meadows there were equally valued for producing feed for milking cows. In order to persuade both landlord and tenants of the advantages they would derive from water meadows, John Snow produced a list of arguments . These may be summarised as follows:

1. There would be a great increase in crops of hay
2. Men could keep more sheep and cattle and thus their arable land would be improved
3. There would be an increase in corn and grass for fattening cattle and for butter and cheese
4. 'That there will be a greater increase of Hay by wateringe of Meadowes is knowne by common experience'
5. Disturbance or damage caused by the work would be properly compensated.[58]

During the 18th century numerous observers commented on the crucial rôle of the water meadows in the farming system of the downlands. As usual, however, it was William Cobbett writing in 1828, who described their value most succinctly. Describing the Avon valley he wrote

> The farms are all large, and generally speaking, they were always large, I dare say; because *sheep* is one of the great things here; and sheep, in a country like this, must be kept in *flocks*, to be of any profit. The sheep principally manure the land. This is to be done only by *folding*; and to fold, you must have a *flock*. Every farm has its portion of down, arable, and meadow; and, in many places, the latter are watered meadows, which is a great resource where sheep are kept in flocks; because these meadows furnish grass for the suckling ewes early in the spring; and indeed, because they have always food in them for sheep and cattle of all sorts.[59]

TENURE AND MANORIAL CUSTOM

Most land in Wiltshire during the 17th century was part of one or other of the great estates which occupied so much of the county. Copyhold tenure for lives, generally three lives, was by far the commonest form of tenure. Writing in 1634, Samuel Stillingfleet, steward for Lord Salisbury, wrote: 'heere with us, lives are estimed better than leases'. Except for demesne farms, leases for term of years did not become common until the 18th century. Copyhold tenure meant that

58 WSRO 490/903-12; *VCH Wilts.*, XI, 1980, 71-7.
59 W. Cobbett, *Rural Rides*, Everyman Edn., Vol. II, 1912, 40.

the rights of both landlord and tenant were subject to traditional practice 'according to the custom of the manor'. Rents were generally low and landlords depended upon entry fines for the bulk of their income. Manorial custom had the force of law within each manor, and was the guiding principle in the decisions of manorial courts. It is clear from the dispute over husbandry practice at Corston which is included in this volume that manorial custom observed from 'time out of mind' was of crucial importance. Customs varied widely from manor to manor. It was manorial custom enforced by the manorial court which regulated the pattern of tenants' daily lives, especially on the chalkland where manorial control remained strong throughout the century. Custom prescribed the conditions of tenure, the rights of transfer, inheritance, rents, fines, heriots, methods of cultivation, grazing rights and entitlement to timber, fuel and stone.

The variation in manorial custom between different manors can be illustrated from the different rights accorded to widows. This was a matter of great importance for landlords, for in some manors a young widow could retain possession of a tenement for many years, and thus deprive the lord of entry fines. It also greatly affected a widow's prospects of remarriage. Widow's rights ranged from retaining full possession of the property, to the right to a part, or loss of the estate upon remarriage or for unchaste life. In manors where the custom was beneficial to widows, the landlord was powerless to regain possession of a tenement, even if an elderly tenant, close to death, married a young woman. She could retain possession for many years. At Amesbury, for example, the manorial custom allowed a widow to keep the estate held by her late husband, 'as well if she marry as if she marry not'. At Brigmerston and Milston a widow could retain possession of her late husband's estate, but upon her death the lord was entitled to take her best possession as a heriot. At Collingbourne Ducis the custom was that, 'yf anie widowe take a husband or commit fornicacon she shall presentlye forfeyt her widow's estate'. At Purton, however, if a widow 'doe marry or live incontinently unmarried and that incontinencye be publiquely proved . . . she shall forfeit her estate'. In contrast, the manorial custom of Christian Malford was more liberal and stated: 'Our Custom is that when a widow Doth live unchaste that appertaineth unto the Ecclesiastical Court for that our Custom have not to Do with it, but for her Living She shall Injoy it by Our Custom'.[60]

A further problem for landlords and stewards on large estates could arise when there was confusion over whose name had been used when the grant of copyhold was made. At a time when large families were common, if a child was one of the 'lives' in a copyhold, and that child died, a sibling might be substituted without the landlord's knowledge. For this reason it was not unknown for two children in a family to be given the same Christian name. It was this possibility which led to the presentment by the homage at the manorial court at Stratford Tony in 1664:

> Wee present to our knowledge there was never any man that have twoe Children Christened by one name whereby the lord was or may bee deprived

60 Salisbury MSS, Hatfield House, General 89/20; WSRO 2/1; 9/9/371; *WANHM*, 40, 1919, 118; 41, 1922, 174–6; 47, 1935–7, 524.

of his right by the keepinge any tenement longer than hee ought to hould the same.[61]

MANORIAL STEWARDS

Many of the large landowners of Wiltshire were frequently absent from their estates, and depended upon reliable stewards for the efficient management of their affairs. Several of the accounts in this volume illustrate the importance of stewards; in particular, the variety and crucial nature of their work is shown by the extracts from the records of two remarkable stewards. John Snow was steward on the Downton estate of Sir Joseph Ashe, who lived at Twickenham (Middlesex), and John Bennett who managed the widespread lands of the Arundells of Wardour. John Snow came from Winterbourne Stoke where he paid hearth tax on a three-hearth house during the years 1676-89; he moved to Downton with his wife and family in 1662. The extracts from his accounts which are printed in this volume reveal how indispensable he was to his employer. Not only did he manage the estate and exploit all its resources, deal with tenants, collect rents and fines, and create more than 200 acres of water meadow, he also undertook many other tasks, personal and political, for the Ashe family. Sir Joseph Ashe was MP for the borough of Downton from 1662-81, and it was John Snow who fostered good relations with the electors, managed the elections and arranged lavish entertainment for the voters. He carried the rental income to Twickenham, engaged servants from Downton to work in the household there, and supplied foodstuff and livestock. He also made several visits to an estate which Sir Joseph possessed at Wawne, near Beverley in Yorkshire, to advise on drainage schemes, tenancies and farming activities. When John Snow died in 1698 he was succeeded as steward at Downton by his son Leonard.

John Bennett was likewise invaluable to the Arundell family. He lived at Motcombe, near Shaftesbury and managed the Arundell manors in Wiltshire, Somerset, Devon and Dorset. His remarkably busy career included serving as one of the MPs for the borough of Shaftesbury. He was responsible for the conduct of manorial courts, collecting rents and fines, and for all other aspects of estate business. His accounts show other duties, such as caring for the ruined castle and parkland at Wardour and supervising the demesne farm at Ansty. Bennett's accounts also reveal another aspect of his life. He was evidently a wealthy man and not dependent upon the £50 a year paid to him by Lord Arundell. His accounts show that he was lending large sums of money at 6% interest to clients from Bristol to the south coast. He lent more than £1,000 to Lord Arundell, and sums ranging from £800 to £20 to others, including several loans to his own relatives. His financial dealings were extremely complex and his notebook contains long lists of those who had borrowed from him and the interest they owed.

Trustworthy stewards like John Snow and John Bennett, taking personal care of all the business of their employers, were essential for the efficient

61 HRO 44M69/A8/3/5; J.H. Bettey, 'Manorial Custom and Widows' Estate', *Archives*, XX, 1992, 208-16.

functioning of the great estates which dominated so much of Wiltshire. For tenants, the ever present, vigilant steward was often a much more formidable figure than the non-resident landlord.[62]

RABBIT WARRENS

On many parts of the downland the production of rabbits or 'coneys' remained a profitable activity throughout the 17th century. Rabbits were not then the pests which they later became, but were prized for their flesh and fur which both commanded good prices. The number of 'warren' or 'conygre' place-names across the downland bears witness to this widespread use of poorer soils or steep hillsides. Within warrens the rabbits were carefully nurtured; artificial burrows were provided and they were fed during the harsh 17th-century winters. In return, the rabbits produced remarkably large numbers of progeny, so that warren-keeping was highly profitable. John Aubrey commended the rabbits produced in the large warren at Aldbourne, 'our famous coney-warren; . . . the coneys there are the best, sweetest, and fattest of any in England; a short thick coney, and exceeding fatt.' The warren on Aldbourne Chase continued to be profitable throughout the 17th century, and the glebe terrier compiled in 1671 includes the vicar's right to 'a composition of £3 per annum to be paid on Quarterdays for the tithe of conies belonging to the North Walk of Aldbourne chase'. Rabbit warrens declined in the later 17th century as rising corn prices meant that, wherever practicable, arable farming provided a more profitable use for the land. In addition, the price of rabbit fur and skins was reduced as large quantities of different furs and skins were imported from north America. Extracts are included here giving details of the warrens at Aldbourne, Clarendon Park, Durley, Easton Royal, Hippenscombe and Mildenhall.[63]

THE LABOURING POOR

Finally, although it is not directly related to agriculture, some evidence has been included in this volume regarding the poverty and living conditions of the landless labourers upon whom so much of the regular round of farming tasks depended. The figures for the size and flimsy nature of the cottages erected on the waste are a reminder of the sharp social gradations within rural society. There was a great contrast between the affluent life-style of the wealthy landowners and those who leased the demesne farms, and the few possessions or absolute poverty of those at the base of the social pyramid. On the chalklands especially, the large farms depended upon seasonal labour; this is evident from

62 J.H. Bettey, 'The Eyes and Ears of the Lord: Seventeenth-Century Manorial Stewards in South Wiltshire', *WANHM*, 96, 2003, 19-35.

63 J. Aubrey, *op.cit.*, 59; J. Sheail, 'Rabbits and Agriculture in Post-Medieval England', *Journal of Historical Geography*, 4, 1978, 343-55. S. Hobbs, ed., *Wiltshire Glebe Terriers 1588-1827*, Wiltshire Record Society, 56, 2003, 321-2.

the accounts for both Norrington and Ansty included in this volume. There are many references to labourers, both men and women, being employed for cultivation, weeding and harvest work; these workers inevitably had long periods of unemployment when their services were not required. The well-known problems of poverty, beggars, illicit settlement on waste land and the burden of parochial poor relief which became so pressing during the 17th century are reflected in the extracts included here. In particular, the tiny and insubstantial hovels, erected overnight in the widespread but mistaken belief that this gave some legal right, seem hardly adequate to sustain life, let alone bring up a family. It was upon the labour of the inhabitants of these hovels that much of the progress and improvement made by Wiltshire agriculture during the 17th century rested.

'A Wiltshire Ram', from Thomas Davis, General View of the Agriculture of Wiltshire, 1811 ed.

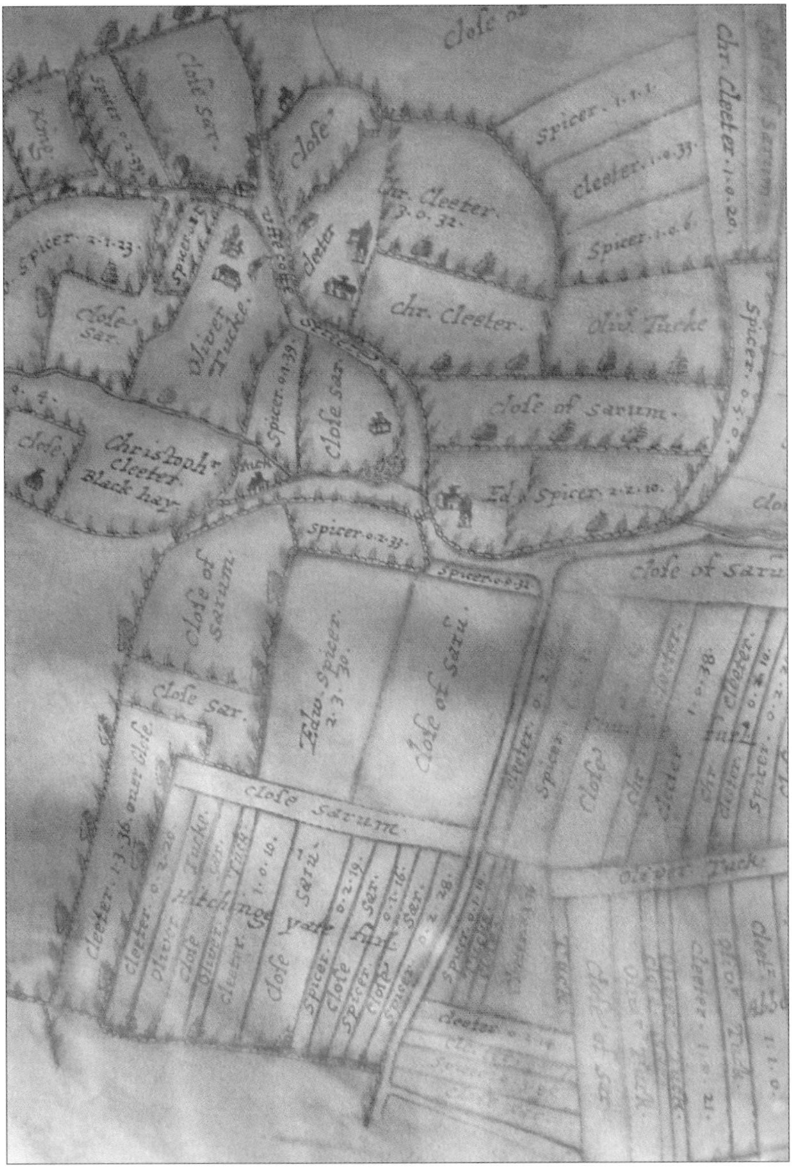

Uffcott in Broad Hinton, on the Marlborough Downs. Detail from an estate map of Charterhouse lands, 1616 (WSRO 631/1/1/5). The chalkland hamlet's buildings and associated crofts are depicted, as well as individual strips and consolidated groups of strips in openfield furlongs.

Part of Stockton's West Field, from an untitled map by Edward May, 1640 (WSRO 153/1). Strips follow the curving contours of a chalkland coombe, and lynchets are depicted on the steepest parts of the hillside.

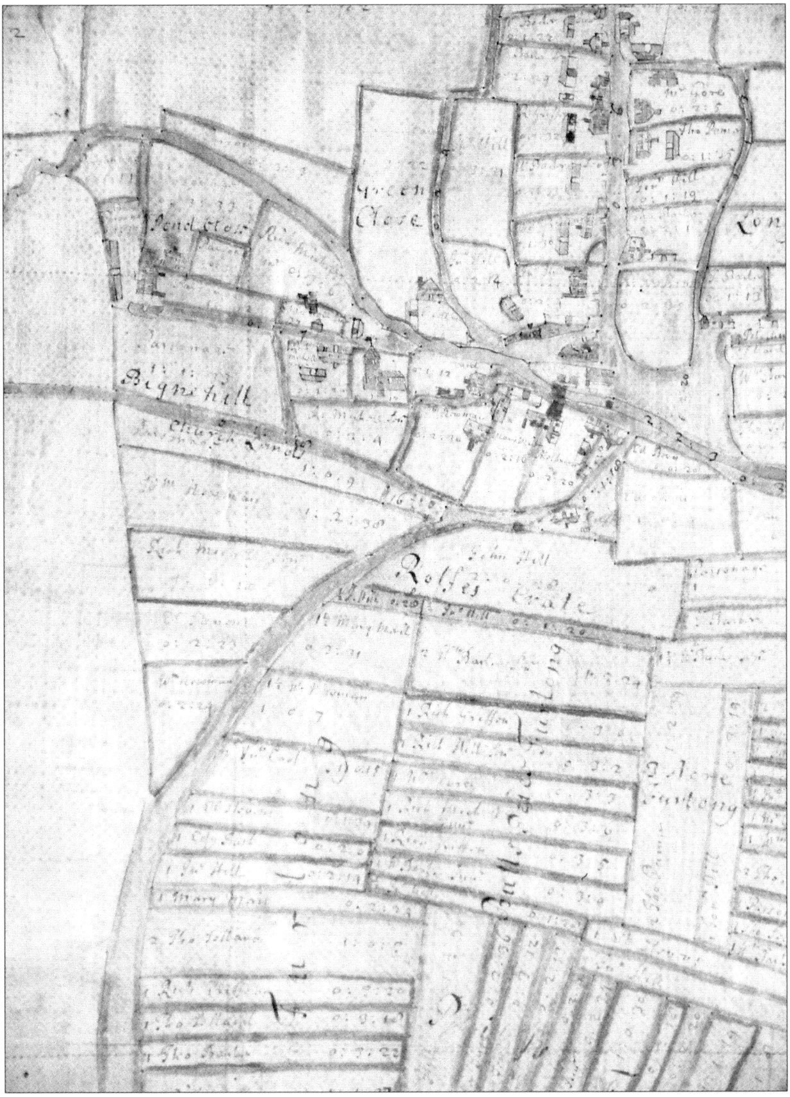

Detail from 'The Mannor of Stratford Toney in the County of Wilts, survey'd for Thomas Jervoise Esq by William Naish, 1706' (WSRO 776/922). The elongated parish and its settlement's irregular plan straddle the River Ebble, so that the community's open fields occupied both sides of the valley. The map's orientation has south at the top, so part of the North Field is seen here abutting the village crofts.

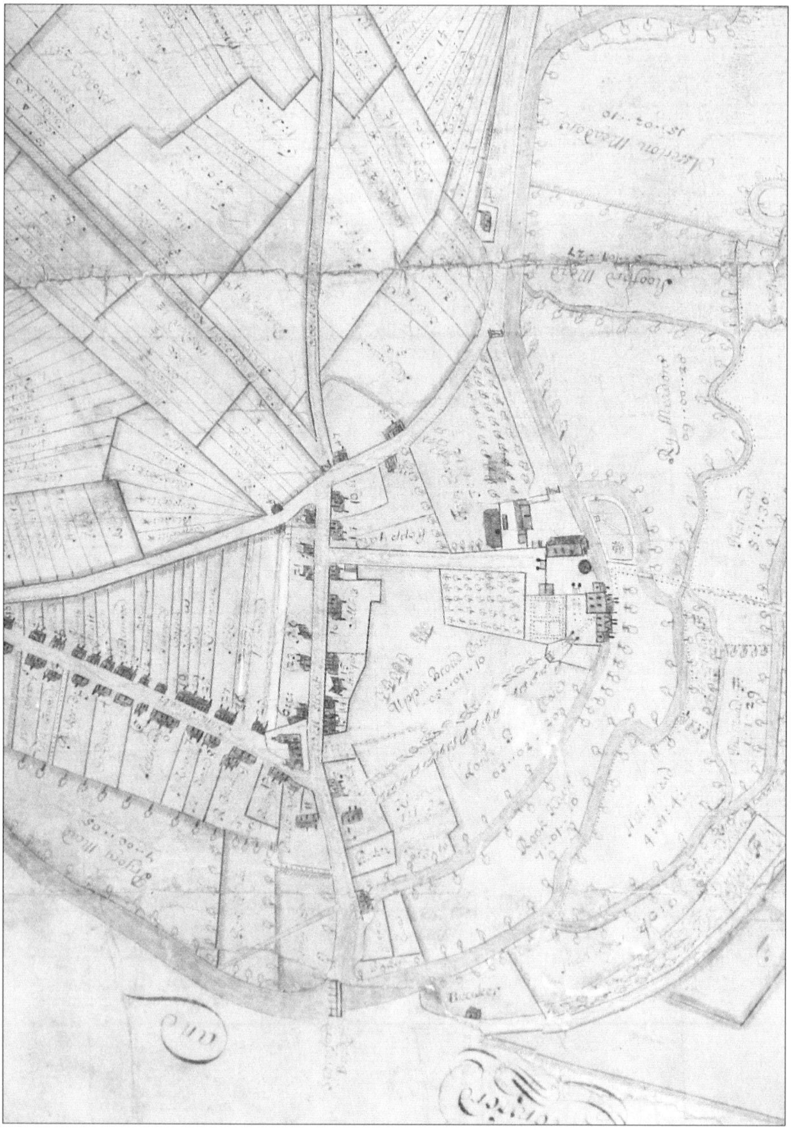

Detail from 'Map of the manor of Great Wishford, by David Oland jr, 1698' (WSRO 1096/1). The River Wylye demarcates the southern parish boundary, and the village, with its very regular plan, occupies a large meander, surrounded by meadows and openfield arable.

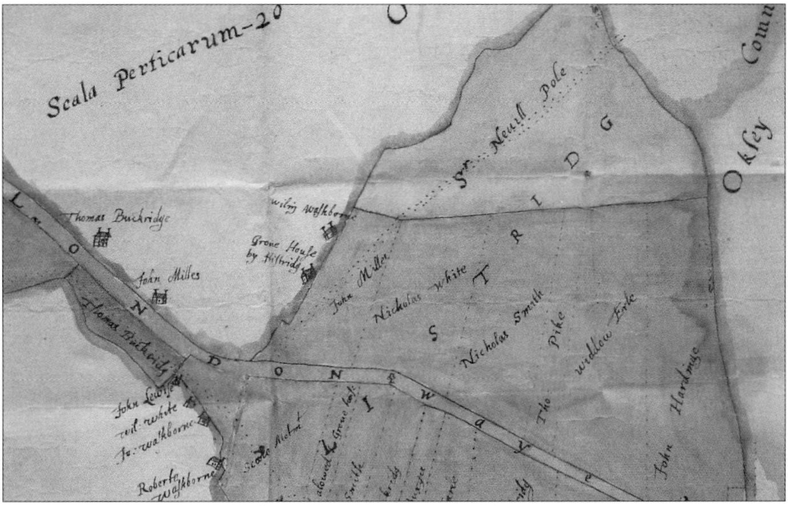

Seventeenth-century enclosures in north Wiltshire clayland parishes. Above: Flisteridge in Crudwell, 'as first enclosed', 1638 (WSRO 374/1). Below: 'The mappe of Rowden Down in the parish of Chippenham as it is now devided for inclosure', a plan of 1669 by John Maye (WSRO 1259/36).

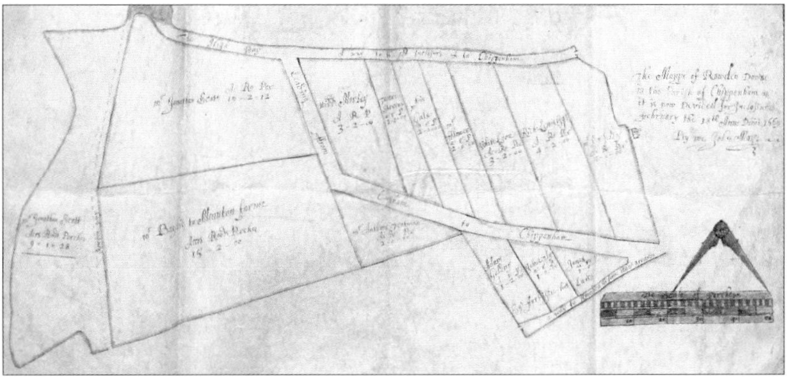

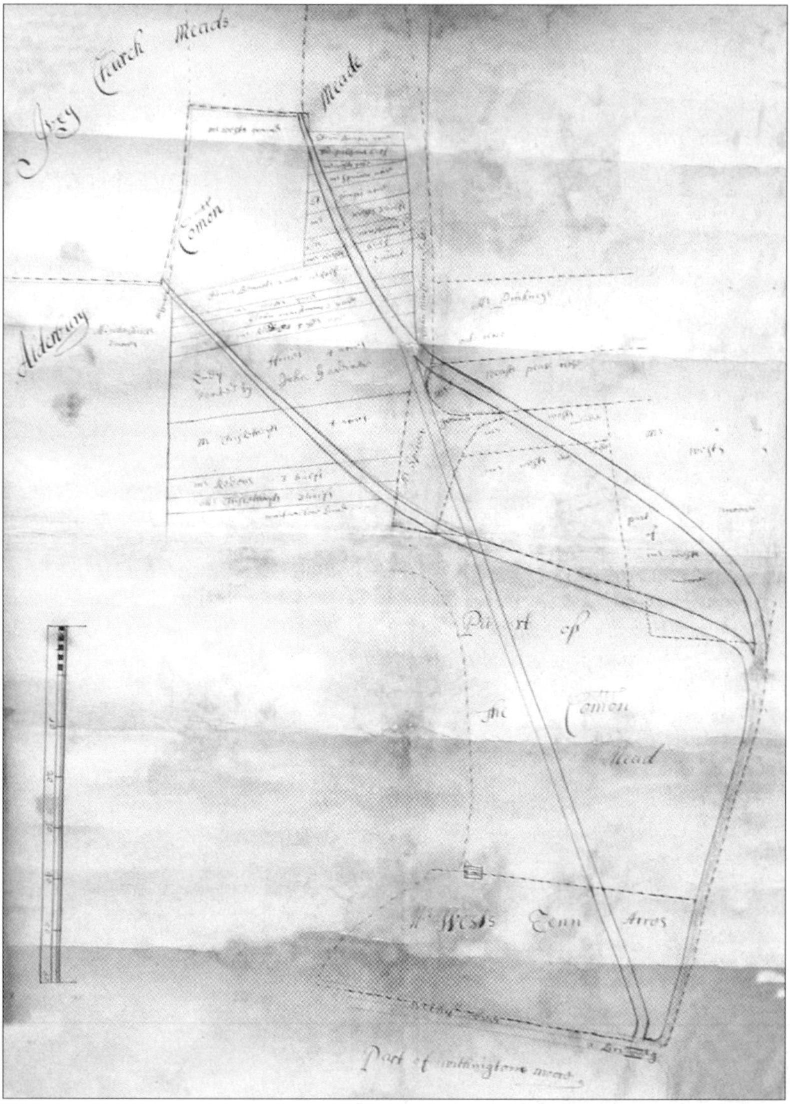

Water management on the Radnor estate at Downton: 'A map of a drayne intended between Withington [Witherington] moore through Alderbury meads to Ivychurch grounds, made August the 5 and 6, 1692.'

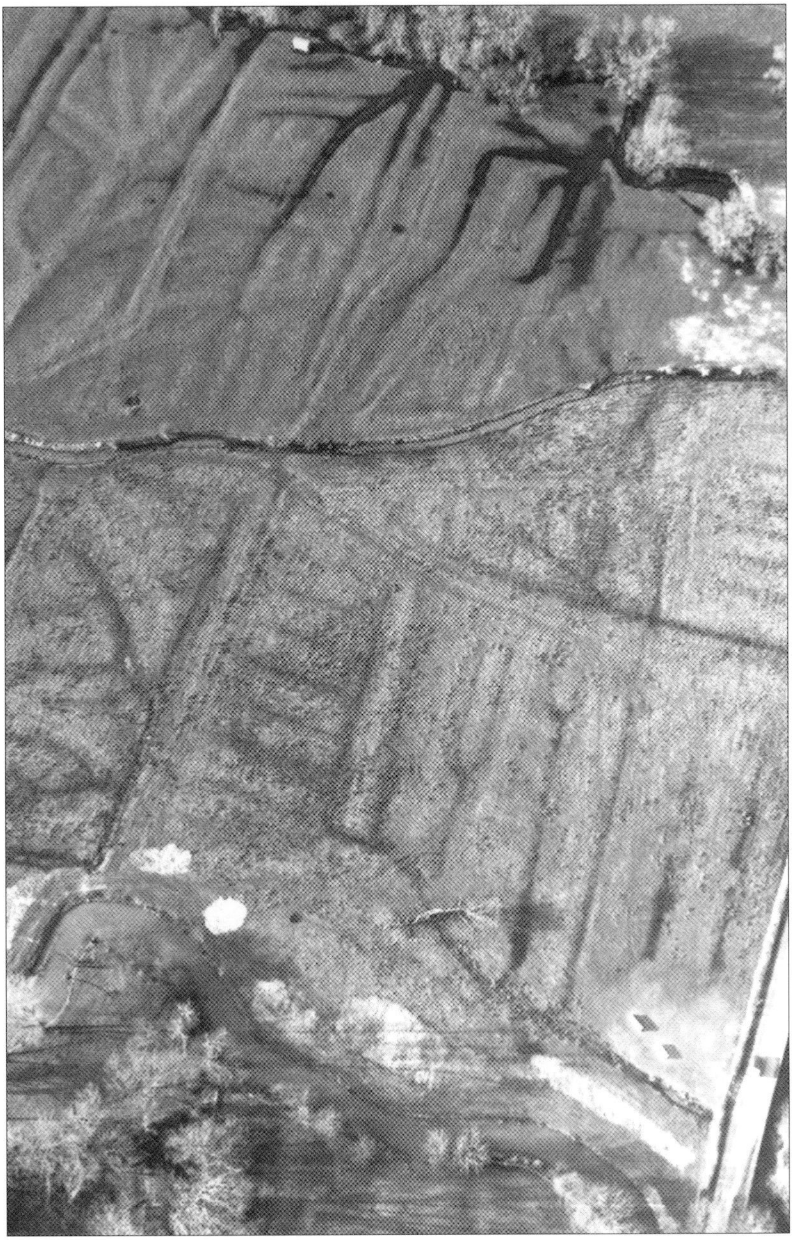

Aerial photograph, taken in 1982, of the remains of a water meadow system on the River Ebble, north of Homington village (WCC AER 1628, reproduced by kind permission of Roy Canham, County Archaeologist).

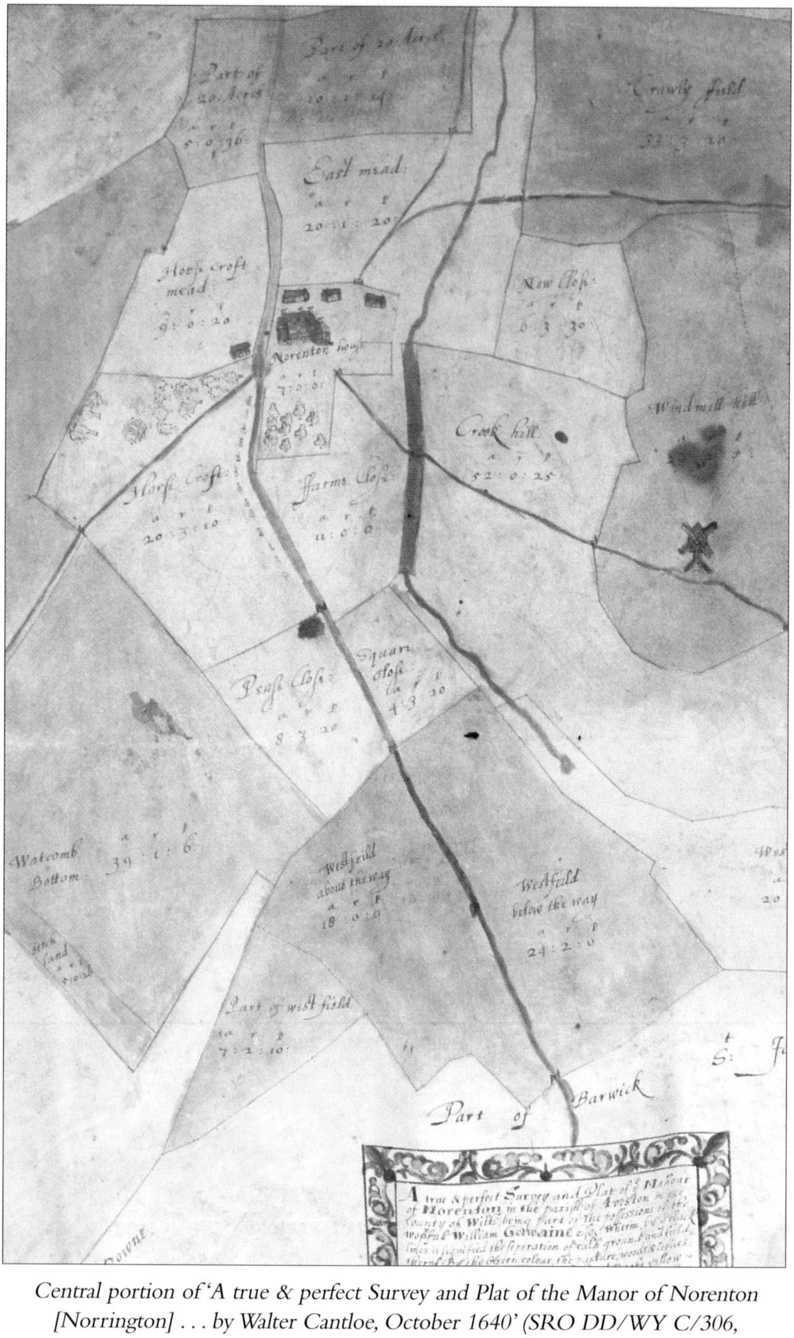

Central portion of 'A true & perfect Survey and Plat of the Manor of Norenton [Norrington] . . . by Walter Cantloe, October 1640' (SRO DD/WY C/306, reproduced by kind permission of the Somerset Record Office, and estate of the late Dr Catherine Wyndham).

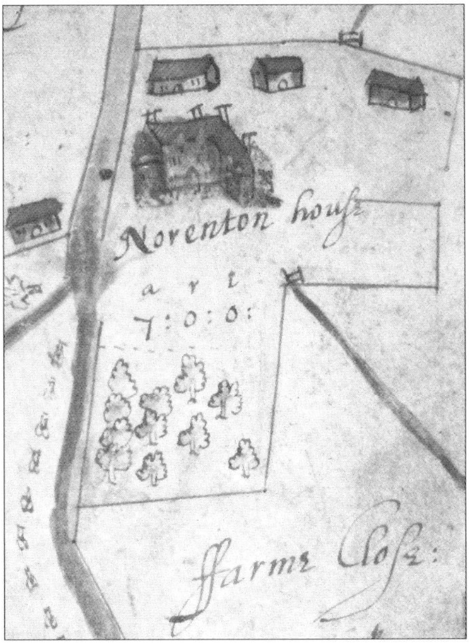

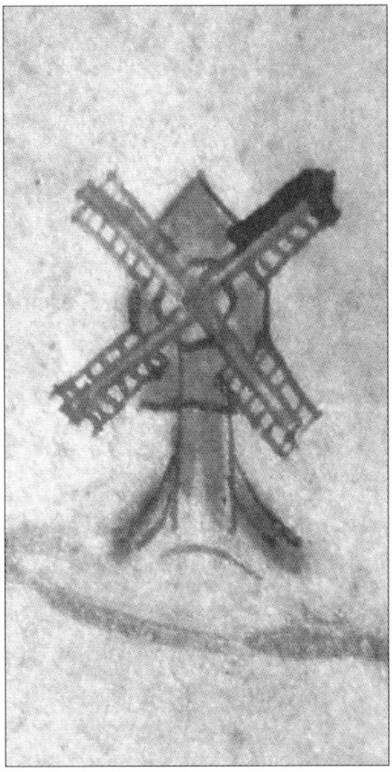

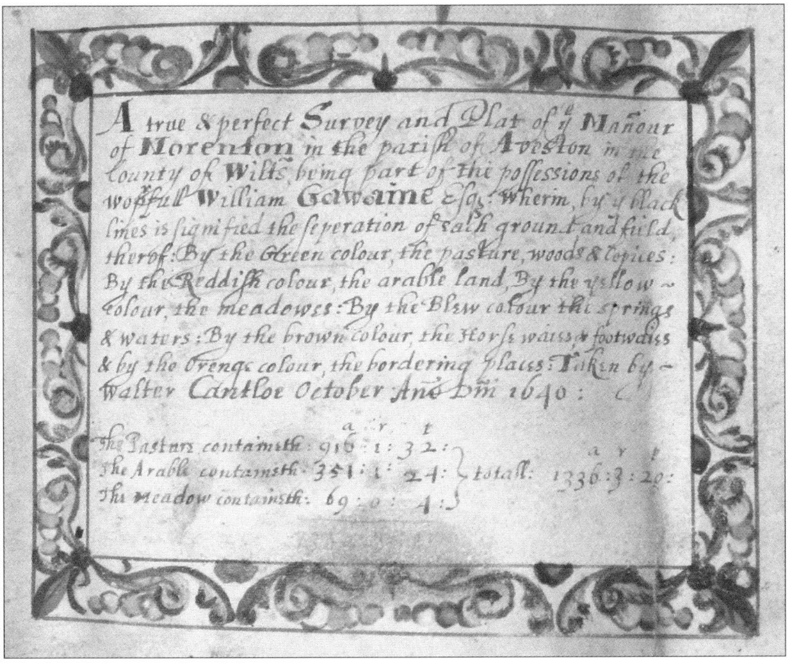

Enlarged details, of Norrington manor house, windmill and legend, from Walter Cantloe's 1640 Norrington estate map (see previous page).

A granary raised on staddle stones to prevent rats and mice gaining entry. This was formerly in the Longleat estate, and has been moved to Lackham Museum of Agriculture and Rural Life, Wiltshire College Lackham.

NORRINGTON AND TROW FARMS IN THE PARISH OF ALVEDISTON 1664-70

The manor of Norrington, together with the adjacent farm of Trow, was held by the Gawen or Gawaine family from 1377 to 1659. After the Reformation more and more of the Gawen wealth and property was seized by the Crown because of the resolute attachment of successive members of the family to the Catholic faith. Norrington manor consisted of a 14th century house, farm buildings, pigeon house, gardens and orchards. A map drawn for William Gawen in 1640 shows a total of 1336 acres consisting of 916 acres of pasture, 315 acres arable and 69 acres meadow, 7 acres house and garden, 29 acres woodland. A manorial windmill is shown on the top of Windmill Hill. The estate covered most of the western part of Alvediston parish, extending from the valley of the Ebble up on to the downland on either side (SRO DD/WY Map of Norrington 1640).

In 1659 William Gawen was obliged to sell his remaining property, and after a complex legal dispute, it was purchased by Wadham Wyndham, sergeant at law (SRO DD/WY Box 178). At the Restoration in 1660, Wadham Wyndham was appointed a judge of the King's Bench and received a knighthood. The survey of Norrington printed below, now in the Somerset Record Office, was made for Sir Wadham in 1664. Sir Wadham Wyndham lived at Norrington with his wife, Barbara, from 1660 until his death on 25 December 1668, aged 59. An ornate monument was erected to his memory in Alvediston church. The eldest son, John Wyndham, who inherited Norrington, was a barrister-at-law in London, and for a year after her husband's death the estate was managed by his mother, Lady Barbara Wyndham. It was no doubt for her benefit that the accounts printed below were compiled by the steward, Luke Dyer. Lady Wyndham evidently moved to Salisbury, and the references in the accounts to 'my Lady Wyndham's booke' indicate that she kept a corresponding record of the management of the estate. She lived until 26 December 1704 and was buried in Alvediston church. The accounts covering her year as executor of the Norrington estate during 1669-70 provide a remarkably detailed record of farming, markets, labour and household expenses. [R. Hoare, Modern Wiltshire, *IV, Part II, 1833, 80-94; H.A. Wyndham,* A Family History 1688-1837: The Wyndhams of Somerset, Sussex and Wiltshire, *1950, 13: G.M. Young, 'Some Wiltshire Cases in Star Chamber',* WANHM, *50, 1942-44, 450.]*

SRO DD/WY Box 108

A Survey of the Farme of Norington 12 August 1664

	A	R	P
Imprimis, The Capitall Messuage, The Stable & Outhouses with the ponds & Backsids & Gardens	7 acres		
Meadow & Pasture			
One Close of pasture cald Farm Close lying west of the Said Messuage	11	0	6
One Close cald Horsecraft lying north of the said Messuage	9	0	0
One Close cald East Mead lying East of the said Messuage	20	1	20
One Close cald Crookhill pasture lying Southwest of the said Messuage	52	0	25
One Close pasture cald New Close lying South East of the said Messuage	6	3	30
One Close pasture cald Pease Close lying north west of the said Messuage	8	3	20
One Close pasture cald Square Close lying west of the said Messuage	4	3	20
One Close pasture cald Bushie Close lying North the high waye leading to Trow	4	0	20
One Mead cald West mead lying west the said Messuage	2	2	24
One Mead cald Whisly mead lying Southwest the high way leading from Barwick to Trow	7	3	20
One Mead cald Hay house mead lying west of the said highway	6	3	0
One Close pasture cald Bushie Gaston adjoining now converted to arrable	13	2	11
One Meadow cald Morgan & Whites Mead lying also Southwest of the said highway	4	1	0
Trow Farm			
One Messuage cald Trow with Barnes & Stables thereto belonging	1	0	0
One Close of pasture adjoining to the said Messuage calld Trow Close	39	2	0
One Downe cald the North Downe with the warren & Watcome Lodge lying North Norington house	297	2	0
One sheep downe cald the South downe & Pincombe lying the South of Trow house	400	0	0
Arrable			
One Close cald 20 acres lying North East Norington house, divided into two parts			
Whereof one contains	10	1	14
The other contains	5	0	36
All that Bottome cald Norington bottom & Whatcom			

	A	R	P
bottom with severall other parcels adjoining lying North the other Messuage containing 100 acres or thereabouts	100	0	0
All that Feild cald Prest Feild lying west the said Messuage lying on both sides the foote way leading to Barwick	49	4	10
One Close cald Crawley feild lying Southwest Norington house	33	3	20
One Close cald Windmill hill wherron the windmill stands	29	2	9
One parcell of Ground adjoining now lying in Comon with the last mentioned Close cald Maudlyn furlonge	19	3	0
One Close cald Trow feild lying Southwest the said Messuage cald Trow	39	2	0
One Close cald Gascomb feild lying South of Trow house	33	3	20
One Close cald Whisly Hill lying towards Bridmore farme	37	1	0
Severall other parcells lying dispersed in Bridmore feilds			
Coppice & Woodland			
One parcell of Wood cald Marshwood where sometime stood a Lodge house to keepe Deere	35	2	27
One Coppice cald Gascomb Copice	5	2	31
One little parcell of Copice lying towards Bridmore cald Pincomb		3	0
One little parcell of Copice between Gascome & Trow feild cald Gascom Ditch	1	0	39
Copices lying in Wiltes and near to Cranborne Chase			
One Copice cald Stapleford Copice	1	0	0
One other Copice cald Cokers Copice	6	0	0
One other Copice cald Crawleys	15	0	0
One other cald Daniels Cops	7	0	0
One other called Cabin Cops	2	0	0
One other cald Grandly way Cops	1	0	0
One other cald Gawen's plot	5	0	0
One other cald Gawen's higher cops	20	0	0
One other cald Gawen's Lower cops	20	0	0

One cottage lately biuld neere the high way By one Adlam which he holdeth at will

Ther is payable to the Mannor of Norington the Rent of ten shillings yeerly out of Mr Golds Farme in Alvediston

Also the liberty of a warren on the North Downe & a purleiu & plase for Deere on the South Downe

Accounts of Norrington and Trow Farms in the parish of Alvediston for Lady Barbara Wyndham, kept by Luke Dyer, Steward, May 1669–July 1670

This account book was kept by the Steward in order to provide Lady Wyndham with a complete record of income and expenditure on the demesne farm. It is, therefore, unusually full and informative. As well as recording the taxes, poor law payments, and parochial tithes paid, the Steward gives a complete picture of the work, crops, stock and dairy produce of a large chalkland farm. The accounts show the importance of the flock of more than 800 sheep; the sheep were divided into North and South flocks the profit from cereal crops, wool, butter and cheese, the number of markets and fairs at which produce was sold, the expenses for labour, horses, implements and the running of the manorial household. Numerous men and some women were employed, almost all of them on an irregular basis. Payments to the porter or carrier were presumably for taking the produce to Lady Wyndham who was living in Salisbury. The meaning of a few entries is obscure. Of particular interest are the growing of hops, the profit from pigeons and from the dairy, the purchase of tobacco, pitch and tar which were used as dressings for ailments of sheep, and work on cleaning out the pond ('riding the pond'). The 'plows' referred to are the teams of horses or oxen used to pull carts, ploughs or other implements, as well as ploughs for turning the soil. Law-day, lady or lade silver was a due paid to the lord of the manor. The accounts show the regular purchases of sheep for the fold, and the numerous markets and fairs at which sheep were bought and sold. According to these accounts the income for the year was £442 11s 7d. The expenditure was £365 9s 8d, most of which was for labour and household expenses. This gave a profit that year of £77 1s 11d.

SRO DD/WY Box 185

An Account of Taxes

	£	s	d
July 18 1669			
Paid Mr Fry Collector for the poore of the parish of Alvediston	3	6	8
Paid Richard Mullens of tieth [tithe] more		3	4
October 6 1669			
Paid George Brothers of Gent(?)- fine		5	4
October 25			
Paid Thomas Scamel of Barweke Collector for the poore 4 rats [rates]		4	0
Paid Samuel Coomb tithing man of the parish of Alvediston of Lady Silver		2	8
Paid Samuel Coomb for the discharge of the tithing offis		2	8
Paid Robert Toomer Churchwarden for the use of the Church of Alvediston	1	0	0

	£	s	d
February 25 1669			
Paid Mr Frye for the use of the poore of Alvediston	2	13	4
April 9 1670			
Paid George Toomer Churchwarden of Alvediston 2 rates	1	0	0
Paid Mr Toomer tithingman of Alvediston of lade silver		2	8
Paid Mr Toomer for the discharg of the tithing offis		2	8
April 23			
Paid Mr Frye for the use of the poore of Alvediston one rate	1	13	4
Sum	2	18	8
June 24 1670			
Paid Jo Brine of Shasbury half a years rent for a lofte a stable and a penthous		12	0
June 29			
Paid Rich Mullens of Brode Chalke 20 fleses [fleeces] out of the vicars tith		[blank]	
Paid Rich Mullens of tieth monie due to Sir Jo Penruddock		3	4
		15	4
July 2 1670			
Payd John Monk Churchwarden of Berick St John 2 rates		2	0
July 7			
Paid Samuell Combe Church warden of Alvediston		1	0
July 30			
Payd Mr Georg Stillingfleet £6-15-0 for Eight yeares Rent in Arreares due Michaelmas last past to the right Honerable James, Earle of Salsbury for a mead called Whishley mead within the manor of Berrick St John	6	15	0
	7	17	0

An Account of what Beasts Bought and Sold upon the farm of Norrington and Trowe Sence May 5 1669

	Folio
An Account	
of Pease	8
of what Sheepe Sold or Bought	10
of Ots	19
of beanes sold	18
of what horses Sold or bought	20
of barle sold	24
of pigges	30
of weat sowne and sold	32

	Folio
of what made by the dairy	36
of worke done by the Smith in showinge [shoeing] horses and other workes	48
of nesecaries bought in	74
of workemens wagges in Tillage upon the farme	52
of Hedginge worke	70
of houshold expenses	75

An Account of Pigeons Sold

	£	s	d
August 12 1669			
Sold 2 dozen of pigeons for		2	0
August 27 1669			
Sold 2 dozen of pigeones for		2	0
September 29			
Sold 7 doszen and halfe of pigeones for		7	6
October 19			
Sold 1 doszen of pigeones for		1	0
May 30 1670			
Rec. for 10 doz and half of pigeons		10	0
July 30			
Sould 11 dozen & ½ of pigeones for		11	6

An Account of Bese [Beasts] Soueld

	£	s	d
July 8 1669			
Sold Brothers 4 Calfes for	1	18	0
October 17 1669			
Rece of George Sanders for 1 Calves lease In Trow Close 16 weeks	4	4	0
Dec 13 1669			
Sold Rich. Coomb one bull for	2	10	0
March 12 1669			
Sold one cow & calfe for	2	11	4
Then one Cow dyed & the skin sold for		9	4
April 16 1670			
Rec for one bull sold	1	15	0
Rec of Jo Bankes for 7 Calves	2	0	0
May 16 1670			
Rec of Rich. Burge of Marnel in Hindon Faire for 6 oxen	32	0	0
The same day & place rec. for 2 oxen	11	0	0
The same day & place rec. for 2 sters	8	15	0
May 21			
Rec. for Mr Molton for 2 Sters	9	15	0
Rec.for one Cowe sold	3	8	0
Rec of Laurance Brothers for 3 calves	1	0	0
Sum	67	8	0

An Account of Beasts bought and what theare Stands Charged upon my Lady Windhams Booke

May 5 1669			
Brought from Southy of Cowes			19
Brought from Sarum of Cowes			1
Bought of Mr Coxe of Cowes			2
Tottall of what Cowes			22
Brought from Southy of young beasts			11
Of the abovesayd Cowes that were brought from Southy & Sarum of Calves fallen there and since Caulfed 17 wherof stands charged upon my Lady Windhams booke May 5 1669			15
Soe tottall of Cowes upon Norrinton & Trow Farmes May 5 1669			22
Of yearlings			11
Of this yeares Calves			15
Of oxen for the Plowes			12
June 5	£	s	d
Since bought by mee one Cowe & Caulf of Tho Brittel of Motcum [Motcombe] at Shaftesbury market for	3	19	0
June 7			
Bought of Henry Gerrand at Gillingame faire one bull for	2	0	6
Totall	5	19	6
April 21 1670			
Bought of Mr South of Duned [Donhead] one Cowe & calf pris paid	3	17	0
May 21 1670			
Bought in Mere faire one Cowe & calfe pris paid	4	10	0
The same daye & plase bought one cowe pris paid	3	13	0
Sum	8	3	0

An Account of Pease Sold

Dec 18 1669			
Sold Steven Haylock 2 bushells of pease for		5	0
Feb 12			
Sold Rich. Coomb 3 bs. of pese for		7	6
March 5			
Rec of Mr Gauntlet for 3 qts of pese	3	0	0
Rec of John Ges for 12 bs of pese	1	10	0
Rec of Tho. Brite for 3 bs of pese		8	0
Rec. of Will Scamel for 2 bs of pese		5	0
Rec. of Ralf Skinner for half a bs of pese		1	6

	£	s	d
March 26			
Rec of Mr Young for 5 bs of pese		13	0
Rec for one bs & half		4	0
Totall	6	1	6
April 16			
Rec for 18 bs of pese	2	5	0
Rec of My Lady Wyndham for 5 bs & a peck		11	4
Rec for one qt of pese		18	8
Rec for 8 bs & half of pese		18	6
Totall	4	13	6

An Account of What Sheape Sold or Bought

	£	s	d
Sold 10 Sheepe Skyns for & 4 Lambs Skyns for		13	4
Nov 6 1669			
Sold Edward Cooper at Barweks faire 20 ewes for	5	10	0
Sold Will Clemant at Barwek faire 20 wethers for	9	4	0
	15	7	4
Sold Suzan Lambord 30 pound of lokes [locks] for		13	9
Sold Tho. Trowbroge 30 pound of lokes for		13	9
October 9 1669			
Recd of Joyles [?Gyles]Gervase for 28 sheepe in Lesfeld at one shilling per pese	1	8	0
October 12			
Recd of Robert King for 11 Copples in Lesfeld at 2s 2d per copple	1	3	0
October 17			
Recd of George Sanders for 4 copples in Lesfeld at 2s 2d per coppel		8	8
October 29			
Recd of Charles Laves for 11 sheepe in Lesfeld at 1s 2d per sheepe		12	10
	5	13	0
November 1			
Sold to Tho. Trobrege 2 wayte of lokes [locks]	1	7	6
November 15			
Sold to Tho. Trobrege 1 wayte of lokes		13	9
November 29			
Sold Michael Down of Tisbury 5 black fleeces wayt 9 pounds for		9	0
	2	10	3

	£	s	d
November 6 1669 [*The entries for this date are crossed out*]			
Recd of Edward Cooper of —? for 20 ewes at Barrek [Barwick] fair	5	10	0
Recd of Will Clemant of Shasbury for 20 wethers At Barrek faire	9	15	0
	15	5	0
Dec 1 1669			
Sold Tho Trobrig one wayt of lokes [locks]		13	9
Dec 7			
Sold Tho Pottell 50 pound of lokes	1	13	1
March 12			
Recd of Tho Pottell for 18 pound of lokes		8	3
The total of lokes is 6 wayt & 8 pounds			
Sum	4	6	4

There stands Charged upon my Lady Wyndhams Booke of Sheepe upon the Farmes of Norrington & Trowe May 5 1669

May 5 1669

Of wethers in number	456
Of Ewes in number	314
Of Lambes in number	252
Of Rams in Number	4
Totall	785 besides Lambs

	£	s	d
Bought Sence the 5 May by Luke Dier May 24 1669 of Mr Robert Shephard at Hindon fayre 100 hogs for	61	15	10
May 24 1669			
Bought of Will Rake of Est Stowre [East Stour] in the County of Dorset 37 Cupples prise 14s 6d the cupple paid	26	16	6
	88	12	4
October 19 1669			
Bought of Tho Bright of Chicklad [Chicklade] at Hindon faire 20 ewes for	6	12	0
Feb 23 1669			
Paid Richard Mullens of Chalke 20 Custom fleeces due out of the vicars tieth at Norrington	[blank]		
November 6 1669			
Paid Francis Baster for Sheepe pens and sheepe lese		3	6
Feb 21 1669			
Paid Mr Frye for tieth hay	7	1	4

An Account of Wool Sold

	£	s	d
May 21 1670			
Recd of Ralf Dyer of Corston for 51 wayt [weight] of wool at £1 12 0 the wayt	81	12	0
Recd for one pound of black wool		1	0
Recd of Andrew Alford for 13 sheepe skins and 4 lambs skins		14	0
	82	7	0
June 4			
Rec of Walt Alford for 3 sheep skins		3	0
July 30			
Sould 11 pound of black wooll		11	0

An account of Beanes Sould

	£	s	d
July 30th 1670			
Sould to Rich Coombe 3 pecks of beanes kides [kidney]			9
Sould to Ralph Skinner ½ bushell for			6
Sould to Rich Toomer ½ bushell for			6
July 30th 1670			
Sould 4 pound & ½ of hoppes [hops] for		3	4

An Account of Ots [Oats] Sold

	£	s	d
March 12 1669			
Rec of Walter Scamel for 4 qts of ots	2	18	0
Rec of Rich. Coomb for 6 bs of ots		10	0
Rec of Tho Brat for 5 qts of ots	3	3	4
Rec of Mr Markes for 6 qts of ots	3	15	11
Rec of El Dyer for one qt of ots		12	8
	11	0	7
May 21 1670			
Sold 5 qts & 4 bs of otes for	3	6	0
Sold 5 qts of dust [chaff] for		10	0
	3	16	0

An Account of Horses Sould

	£	s	d
July 19 1669			
Sould to John Little Field at Chilmarke faire one horse for	2	18	0

An Account of horses bought and what theare did stand Charged upon my Lady Wyndhams Booke May 5 1669

Of horses for the plow 7

	£	s	d
July 13th			
Sins bought by mee of John Ellen of Worle in Chilmarke's faire one Stone Colt for	7	14	0
Bought 3 bushells and half of Otes, paid		6	5
September 29th			
Paid Mr Fry for the hire of his mare		9	0
Paid Mr Fry for the Carreage of a lode of plankes		2	0
March 19th 1669			
Bought 3 bushells of fetches [vetches] for		7	6
Bought one bushell of beans for		4	6
May 16th 1670			
Bought of Walter Kingman of Winterborn Stoke at Hindon faire too horses pris paid	11	4	0
The same daye and place bought of Jo Dyer of Hatchbury one gray hors pris paid	6	0	0
May 24th			
Bought of Jo Samwell of Market Laventon at Salsbury faire one rone hors pris paid	5	15	0
The same daye and place bought of Mr Will Sodwell of Burford one gray hors pris payd	5	10	0
	28	10	0

An account of barle [barley] sold

	£	s	d
October 17th 1669			
Sold Mr William Hurman of Shasbury 4 quarters and 6 bushels of barle for	4	15	0
October 28th 1669			
Sold George Cerly of Bradle 5 quarters of barle in Hindon market for	4	16	8
Nov 2nd 1669			
Sold Mr Will Ledlo of Salbury 5 quarters & 4 bushells of barle for	5	4	6
Sold Tho Croker half a bushel for		1	2
Nov 9th 1669			
Sold John Lavrons of Salsbury 5 quarters & 4 bushels of barle for	4	15	4
Nov 13th 1669			
Sold Mr Will Hurman of Shasbury 5 quarters of barle for	5	3	4
Nov 20th 1669			
Sold Mr Will Hurman of Shasbury 5 quarters of barle for	5	6	8
Sold Tho Pool of Shasbury 5 quarters of barle for	5	5	0
Nov 25th 1669			
Sold Mr Will Hurman of Shasbury 5 quarters of barle for	5	6	8
Nov 27th 1669			
Sold Mr Evens of Shasbury 5 quarters of barle for	5	6	8

	£	s	d
Nov 30th 1669			
Delivered unto Mr Brody of Salsbury for My Lady Wyndhams use 10 quarters of barle prise	9	0	0
	45	9	4
Dec 4th 1669			
Sold Mr Will Hurman 5 quarters for	5	6	8
Dec 11th			
Sold Mr Will Hurman 5 quarters for	5	6	8
& 5 quarters for	5	6	0
Dec 18th			
Sold Mr Will Hurman 5 quarters for	5	4	0
Dec 22nd			
Sold Mr Hurman 5 quarters for	5	3	4
Dec 24th			
Sold Mr Will Hurman 5 quarters for	5	3	4
January 8th 1669			
Sold Mr Evens of Shasbury 5 quarters of barle for	5	1	8
Sold Tho Pool of Shasbury 5 quarters of barle for	5	1	8
January 15th			
Sold Mr Evens of Shasbury 5 quarters & 2 bushels of barle for	5	6	0
Sold Tho Croker 2 bs of barle for		5	0
Sold Ralf Skinner half a bushel		1	3
Jan 29th			
Sold Mr Evens of Shasbury 10 quarters & 4 bs of barle for	10	2	0
	25	18	4
Feb 5th			
Sold Mr Hurman of Shasbury 4 quarters of barle for	3	18	8
Sold James Toomer 5 quarters of barle for	4	18	4
Feb 12th			
Sold John Pery one bs of barle		2	5
Sold Mr Hurman 5 quarters & 2 bs of barle for	5	5	0
Sold Tho Croker half bs of barle		1	2
Feb 27th			
Sold Mr Hurman 5 quarters & 2 bs of barle for	5	7	0
Sold Mr Evens of Shasbury 10 quarters & 2 bs of barle for	10	6	0
	29	18	7
March 12th 1669			
Rec of Walter Scamel for 3 qtrs of barle	3	2	0
Rec of Tho Croker for half a bs of barle		1	3
Rec of Mr Evens for 5 qtrs & 5 bs of barle	5	11	3
Rec of Mr Hurman for 5 qtrs & 2 bs	5	1	6
Rec for 2 qtrs & 6 bs	2	12	1
	16	8	1

	£	s	d
April 2nd 1670			
Rec of Mr Hurman for 6 qtrs & 2 bs	6	3	0
Rec for one qtr of barle		19	8
April 9th			
Rec of Mr Cox for 5 qtrs & 3 bs	5	11	1
Rec of Mr Harris for 4 qtrs 6 bs & half	4	8	6
April 16th			
Rec of Jo Witt for 5 qtrs of barle	5	3	4
Rec of Jo Vinsent for 7 bs of barle		19	1
Rec of Henry King [for] 10 bs of barle	1	5	10
	24	10	6
April 23rd 1670			
Bought 10 qtrs of barle for seed	10	4	1
May 14th			
Sold Tho Pool 5 qtrs of barle for	4	13	4
Sold Mr Harris 5 qtrs of barle for	4	17	8
Sold Mr Evens 5 qtrs of barle for	4	6	8
Sold Mr Hurman 5 qtrs of barle for	4	0	0
Sold 7 bs of barle for		14	4
	18	2	0
June 4th 1670			
Sold Ed Tise 6 qtrs of barle for	4	16	0
Sold 14 bs of barle for	1	8	0
June 11th			
Sold Ed Tise 6 qtrs of barle	4	16	0
June 18th			
Sold Mr Evens 4 qtrs & one bs of barle for	4	13	4
	15	13	4
July 2nd			
Sould Mr Hurman 4 qtrs of barley for	4	18	0
July 7th			
Sould Edward Tise 4 qtrs of barley for	4	10	8
July 14th			
Sould Edward Tise 4 qtrs of barley for	4	10	8
July 23			
Sould 6 bushells of barley for		18	0
	14	17	4

An account of What pigges are sould, Slain or dead upon the farms of Norrington & Trow

August 1st 1669

Dyed in haye harvest one of those Slipes [piglets] bought by Charles Lanes

	£	s	d
May 14th 1670			
Sold 4 slipes for	1	16	0

An account of pigges bought

	£	s	d
August 21st 1669			
Bought of Richard Morgen of Melbro one Sowe and 4 pigges for	1	8	6
So there stands Charged upon my Lady Windhams booke 2 Sowes & 17 slipes			
Nov 20th 1669			
Paid the Sowe giller for spaing 4 sowes		1	0
Feb 27th 1669			
Paid John Parkens for Spaying 3 sows and cutting 5 boars		1	0

An account of weat soune [sown] in the year 1669

34 quarters, 6 bushels & half

An account of weat sold

	£	s	d
October 25th 1669			
Sold Steven Haylock 1 bushel of weat		4	8
Sold Richard Coomb half a bushel of weat		2	4
Nov 9th 1669			
Sold Rich Coomb half a bushel of weat for		1	11
Sold Steven Haylock 1 bushell of weat		3	8
Nov 29th 1669			
Sold Tho Croker 1 bushell of weat		3	8
Sold Rich Coomb 1 bushel of weat for		3	8
		12	11
Dec 11th 1669			
Sold Tho Croker one bushel of weat		3	8
Dec 22nd			
Sold Tho Croker one bushel of weat		4	0
Sold Mr Will Herman 3 bushells of weat		12	0
Dec 24th			
Sold in Shasbury market 3 bushels of weat		12	0
	1	11	8
January 29 1669			
Sold Rich Coomb one bs of weat		4	0
Sold Steven Haylock 2 bs of weat		8	0
		12	0

	£	s	d
Feb 5th			
Sold in Shasbury market 8 bs of weat	1	13	0
Sold Steven Haylock one bs of weat		4	0
Sold Rich Coomb one bs of weat		4	0
Sold Tho Croker 2 bs of weat		8	0
Feb 17th			
Sold Ellen Sander Measer [?measure] 3 bs for		12	9
	3	1	9
March 12th 1669			
Rec of Steven Haylock for 2 bs of weat		8	0
Rec of Rich Coomb for one bs of weat		4	0
March 19th			
Rec of Tho Croker for 3 bs of weat		12	0
Rec for 3 bs of weat		13	0
March 29th			
Rec for 7 bs of weat	1	10	4
	3	7	4
April 9th			
Rec of Joh Pery for 3 bs of weat		13	0
April 15			
Rec for 3 bs of weat		13	6
Rec of Tho Croker for 3 bs of weat		13	0
Rec of Rich Coomb for 2 bs of weat		8	4
	2	7	10

An account of what is mad by the dary [dairy]

	£	s	d
August 24th 1669			
Rese of Elizabeth Bradle for butter	1	14	11
Rese of John Card for 3 Cheeses		5	7
Rese of John Pery for 3 Cheeses		5	7
Sept 13			
Rese of Nicholas Toomer for 4 Cheeses		6	3
Rese of Robert Toomer for 2 Cheses		2	11
October 19th			
Rese of Nicholas Toomer for 1 Chese		2	4
Rese of Tho Croker for 1 Chese		2	4
Sold Robert Toomer 1 cheese for		1	0
November 9th			
Sold Nicholas Toomer 1 cheese for		2	1
Sold Robert Toomer 1 cheese for		1	0
Sold Will Toomer 1 Cheese for		1	7
Sold Ellen Dyer 2 Cheeses for		3	2
Nov 29th			
Delivered unto my Lady Wyndham at Salsbury 4 doszen & 7 pound of butter		18	4

	£	s	d
Delivered unto my Lady Wyndham at Salsbury 6 doszen of butter pris	1	4	0
Delivered unto my Lady Wyndham at Salsbury 42 Cheeses wayt 200 pris	2	0	0
Delivered unto my Lady Wyndham at Salsbury 14 Cheeses wayt 100 pris		18	0
	3	8	2
January 4th 1669			
Sold Will Snooke of Tisbury 124 Cheses waying 800 wayeght [8 cwt.] for	9	6	8
March 12th 1669			
Rec of Ed Allen for 7 Cheeses waying half a hundred		11	8
May 30th 1670			
Rec of the Widd Perry for 4 doz and 11 pound of Butter by her sold		19	4½
Rec for 2 ould cheses		3	1
	1	2	5½
June 4th 1670			
Sold Jo Pery 3 ould cheses for		1	8
Sold Samuel Coomb one ould chese		1	0
Sold Nicho Toomer one ould chese		1	9
July 7th			
Sould ould cheese for		1	6
Sould Nich Toomer 1 ould Chese for		1	6
Sould George Sanders 2 ould cheeses for		2	7
Sould Rich. Coombs 2 ould cheeses for		2	3
Sould 5 Skimed Cheeses for		4	2
Sould 84 Raw milk cheeses waying 5 cwt for	5	11	0
	6	3	0
July 30th			
Sould by the Widd Perry 6 duzen & 11 pound of wheay butter for	1	4	11
Recd of the widd Perry for 19 pound of Lard		6	1
	1	11	0

An account of worke doune by the Smith in Shooing & other workes

	£	s	d
June 28th 1669			
Paid Samuel Foote of Barweke for 31 Shooes & 30 Removes & other iron worke	1	10	2
August 9			
Paid Samuel Foote for 14 shoose & other iron workes		1	4
Paid Micael Doone of Tisburi for the Ier [iron] worke of a new plow		14	0
Paid Micael Doone for a new plow whele		3	8

	£	s	d
Paid Micael Doone for mending a paire of plow Ierns [irons]		4	0
August 19th			
Paid Umphry Cotton of Tisburie for 15 shooses & 100 of nailes		5	0
Paid for Shooing the baye nagge			6
Paid Will May for Cuering & Shooing the little nagg		4	0
Sept 23rd			
Paid for a Scoureing rod		1	0
Paid for shoeing the little nagg			6
Then paid Micael Doune for mending a share & Ier worke for a vann		6	0
Sept 24th			
Paid Humphry Cotton for bord nailes, hors nailes & late [lathe] nailes		1	1
Sept 29th			
Paid Samuel Foote for 10 Shoose & 6 removes & other ier worke as his biles [bills] duth wittnes		10	4
	4	19	9
October 25th 1669			
Paid Miciel Douen for mending to paire of plow ierones		5	0
Paid Humphy Cotton for bord nailes			6
October 29th			
Paid Samuel Fote for 8 Shoose & 2 removes and other ierworke about the plow		6	6
		12	0
Dec 13th 1669			
Paid Micael Doun for making six paire of iron harness	2	4	0
Paid for a hors comb			6
Feb 5th 1669			
Paid John Scamel for Shooing of 7 horses for one quarter		8	9
Paid the same to Scamel for other ier worke about the plows		11	0
	3	4	3

An account of worke dun by the Smith

	£	s	d
May 28th 1670			
Paid to Jo Scamel for Shoing & other Iron worke about the plow		14	5
June 8th 1670			
Bought 2 paire of fetters paid		2	6
Paid for a padlock			6
Paid Humphrey Cotton of Tisbury for 3 paire iron Harnes wayte 45 pound	1	2	6
Sum total	1	5	6

	£	s	d
July 19th			
Payd John Scamell Smith for Shooing 7 horses from March 25th to June 24th & other Iron work as by his bills doth more Largely appeare	1	4	6
July 30th			
Paid Humphry Cotton Smith for one halter Reins and A payer of Thill Harrins & 5 pickprongs		7	0
	1	11	6

An account of worke mens wages in tilage upon the farmes of Norrington & Trowe

	£	s	d
June 12th 1669			
Paid Tho Croker for 6 dayes workes		4	0
Paid Will Small for 6 dayes worke		3	0
Paid John Abbott for 4 dayes worke		4	6
June 23rd			
Paid Hinery Warom for 12 dayes worke		4	0
Paid Richard Coomb for 5 dayes worke		4	2
July 1st			
Paid Nicholas Young for 12 dayes worke		5	0
Paid John Adlom for makeing 5 doszen and 4 hurdles		6	2
July 2nd			
Paid John Adlom mowing in the orchard		2	0
Paid John Adlom for making a flake [wattle hurdle] for Trow barnn		2	6
Paid Steven Haylock for 4 dayes worke		3	4
Paid Tho Haylock for 2 dayes worke		4	6
Paid Tho Croker for 3 wekes worke		14	0
Paid Will Sandres for 1 month		8	0
Paid George Sandres for 2 dayes worke			8
Paid Francis Sandres for 2 dayes worke			8
Paid George Sandres Senior for 1 daye		1	4
Paid George Sandres for 2 dayes mowing in the orchard		2	0
	3	7	4

An Account of cutting and making of haye upon the farms of Norrington & Trowe

	£	s	d
July 24th 1669			
Paid John Adlom & Robert Adlom George Sandres & Richard Coomb for Cutting and making 62 akers of haye	8	5	4
Paid Steven Haylock for Cutting of 16 akers & half of gras	1	8	8
Paid Elizabeth Pery for 4 dayes haymaking in the orchard		1	4
Then paid Elizabeth Adlom for 4 dayes		1	4

	£	s	d
July 29th			
Paid Jane Toomer for 7 dayes		4	8
Then paid Elizabeth Pery for 8 dayes		5	6

An account of Cutting of pese and fetches[peas & vetches] by Estemation 23 akers

	£	s	d
July 30th			
Paid Elizabeth Croker for 2 dayes		1	4
Paid Cathern Hiscock for 2 dayes		1	2
Paid Jane Hiscock for 2 dayes		1	4
Paid Steven Haylock for 4 dayes		4	0
Paid Richard Coomb for 4 dayes		4	0
His wife for 2 dayes		1	4
Paid Samuel Coomb for 2 dayes		2	0
Paid John Adlom for 4 dayes		4	0
Paid George Sanders for 3 dayes		3	0
Paid George Sanders for his 2 dafters [daughters] 4 dayes		4	4
Paid John Adlom's wife for 2 dayes		1	4
Paid Sarah Lonn for 4 dayes		2	8
	11	11	4

An account for greping [reaping with a light sickle] of barle & otes

	£	s	d
August 27 1669			
Paid Elizabeth Pery for 18 dayes worke		12	0
Paid Sara Sandres for 16 dayes worke		12	0
Paid Mare Poulden for 10 dayes worke		7	1
Paid Sara Lond for 16 dayes worke		12	0
Paid Roger Coomb for 2 dayes worke		2	0
Paid John Abbott for 11 dayes worke		12	0
Paid Jone Abbott for 10 dayes worke		7	6
Paid Francis Sanders for 13 dayes worke		9	9
Paid George Sanders for 2 dayes worke		2	0
August 29th			
Paid Samuel Coomb for 3 dayes worke		3	0
	3	19	4

An account for Cutting weate in the North feeld

August 1st 1669

	A	R	P	£	s	d
Paid George Sanders for cutting	6	1	3	1	5	6
Paid John Adlom for cutting	3	2	0		14	0
Paid Robert Adlom for cutting	6	2	24	1	6	6
Paid Will Staples for cutting	2	2	10		10	3

	A	R	P	£	s	d
Paid Steven Haylock for cutting	3	3	13		15	10
Paid Richard Coomb for cutting	3	2	34		14	10
Paid John Hiscoke for cutting	4	0	31		16	0
Paid Roger Coomb for cutting	2	0	37		10	0
Paid John Sanger for cutting	4	1	8		17	3
				7	17	2

	£	s	d
Dec 17th 1669			
Paid John Cool for a dayes worke			9
Paid Richard Coomb for 24 dayes work		18	0
Paid Steven Haylock for 24 dayes work		18	0
Paid Tho Croker for a month		16	0
Paid Ed Croker for a month		4	0
Paid Hen Warren for 21 dayes		6	8
Paid Sara Lond for 2 dayes worke			8
Paid Will Sandres for a month		8	0
Paid George Sandres Sr for 2 dayes worke		1	6
Paid the porter for car. Of 2 lode of bar		1	0
Paid John Smith half a yeres wages	1	15	0
Dec 27th			
Paid Ralf Skinner for 12 dayes work		9	0
	6	19	5

An account of cutting weate in the South feild

August 4th 1669

	A	R	P	£	s	d
John Adlom for Cutting	3	3	10		15	3
Paid George Sanders for Cutting	2	1	0		8	6
Paid Robert Adlom for Cutting	4	1	23		17	6
Paid Tho Alford for Cutting	1	2	30		6	9
Paid Will Gutch for Cutting	1	2	4		6	1
Paid Joyse Cotton for Cutting	1	2	30		6	9
Paid Will Staples for Cutting	2	1	24		8	7
Paid John Card for Cutting	6	0	0	1	4	0
Paid Roger Coomb for Cutting	[blank]			[blank]		
Paid Steven Haylock for Cutting	2	2	18		11	0
Paid Richard Coomb for Cutting	[blank]			[blank]		
Paid John Sanger for Cutting	[blank]			[blank]		
Paid John Hiscoke for Cutting	[blank]			[blank]		
				5	4	2

October 11th 1669

An account for riding [cleaning out] the pond at Norrington

	£	s	d
Paid Simeon Witte for 3 dayes worke with his plow		9	0
Paid James Toomer for 7 dayes worke with his plow	1	8	0

	£	s	d
Paid Robertt Toomer for 8 dayes worke with his plow	2	8	0
Paid Daved Long for 10 dayes worke with his plow	3	3	0
Paid John Adlom for 20 dayes worke		15	0
Paid George Sanders for 19 dayes worke		14	3
	8	17	3

An account of worke mens wages

	£	s	d
Nov 6th 1669			
Paid the porter			6
Bought a Sherch [small strainer] bottom paid			8
Bought a new seve [sieve] paid			6
Paid Nicho Brite for 9 days worke		10	0
Paid the porter			6
Paid the porter			6
Paid the osler [ostler] for the plow stan [standing, i.e. stabling for the horses]			8
Paid the porter			6
November 20th			
Paid Steven Haylock for 23 dayes		17	3
Paid Rich Coomb for 24 dayes		18	0
Paid the porter			6
Paid Hen Warren for a month		8	0
Paid Tho Croker for a month		16	0
Paid Ed Croker for a month		4	0
Paid George Sandres for 1 month		8	0
Nov 27th 1669			
Paid the porter			6
Paid the Bucher for dresing two fat piggs			8
Nov. 30th 1669			
Paid the porter			6
	4	17	9
Dec 11th 1669			
Paid John Abbot for 3 dayes worke		3	6
Paid the porter for car [carriage] of 2 lode of barle		1	0
Paid Robert Davis for bring the fat bese [beasts] from Elton [Ilton, Somerset] to Norington		6	4
Dec 17th 1669			
Paid John Cool for a dayes worke			9
Paid Richard Coomb for 24 dayes work		18	0
Paid Steven Haylock for 24 dayes work		18	0
Paid Tho Croker for a month		16	0
Paid Ed Croker for a month		4	0
Paid Hen Warren for 21 dayes		6	8
Paid Sara Lond for 2 dayes worke			8
Paid Will Sandres for a month		8	0

	£	s	d
Paid George Sandres Sr for 2 dayes worke		1	6
Paid the porter for car[riage]. of 2 lode of bar[ley]		1	0
Paid John Small half a yeres wages	1	15	0
Dec 27th			
Paid Ralf Skinner for 12 dayes work		9	0
	6	19	5

An Account of Hedging Worke

	£	s	d
December 13th 1669			
Paid John Adlom for making 179 perch of quick hedg	2	3	9
Paid John Adlom for making 75 perch of dead		15	0
March 10th 1669	2	18	9
Paid John Adlom, George Sandres & Robert Adlom for making 110 perch of quick hedg	1	18	4
April 16th 1670			
Paid Jo Adlom for makeing 37 perch of dead hedg		6	4
Paid Jo Adlom for makeing 11 perch of quick hedg		2	9
Paid Jo Adlom for making 3 duezen of hurdles		3	6
Sum		12	7
May 17th 1670			
Paid Jo Adlom for makeing 47 perch of dead hedg		6	9
Paid Jo Adlom for making too dz of hurdles		2	4
Sum		9	1

An Account of Nesecaries Bought

	£	s	d
April 9th 1670			
Paid for a bottel		1	6
For a dusen of Crookes paid		1	2
For 2 milk renges [?] paid		1	0
For a quier of paper paid			6
		4	2
May 28th 1670			
Paid for a gert [girth?]			3
Paid for a paire of Shoods [shoes] for Tho Haylock		2	8
Paid for Stockings for Tho Haylock		1	10
Paid for 2 wood straps		6	4
Paid for 2 strainers			9
Paid for 2 pudden baggs			8
Paid for thred			2
Paid for a hors lock		1	6
Paid for half a dus of Crooks			7

	£	s	d
Paid for a pound of Sope			4
Sum		15	1
June 4 1670			
Paid the Collormaker for 3 halters		7	6
For 4 Collors		6	8
For 3 paire of pipes		4	6
For 3 backties		3	6
For 4 paire of hames [part of harness]		3	4
Paid for broomes			6
Paid for 45 pound of readdel [ruddle for marking sheep]		1	6
Paid for 5 rakes		1	8
Paid for a dust seve [chaff sieve]			7
Paid for 7 yards of Cloth for Chees Cloths		5	2
Paid for a pich Cettel [pitch kettle i.e. small cauldron]		5	0
Paid for 22 pound of pich		4	6
Paid for 3 qts of tarr		2	6
Paid for half a du of pick stems [½ dozen pick handles]		4	0
Paid for a Shovel		1	4
Paid for 7 hemp halters		3	0
Sum total	2	15	3
July 2nd 1670			
Payd for 100 of Lafts [laths] & 250 Laft nayles		1	10
Payd for ½ a pound of powder			8
Payd for 2 pound of Shott			4
Paid for 5 Else of Corse doulese [coarse dowlais cloth] to make Changes for Tho Halocke		5	5
July 9th			
Paid for a huchmuck [wicker strainer used in brewing]			6
Payd for a board nayles			2
Paid Fording of Hindon for a brewing fate [vat]	1	9	0
Payd for ½ a dozen of Sope		1	8

Houshould Expence

	£	s	d
1669			
Bought meat and Seuet [suet] paid		4	0
Paid Tho Pool for 18 bushells of malt	2	8	0
February 12th			
Paid for meat & seuet		11	0
Paid for half a pound of piper			9
For half a pound of ginger			5
For half a pound of Starch			3
For a paire of shooes for Thos Haylock		2	6
For 4 pesomes			2
For half a dozen of Sope		1	9

	£	s	d
For Stockings for Tho Haylock		1	3
For one El and 3 quarters of Canvais for Tho Haylock		2	1
For tyen [laces]			4
For one bushell and half of planten beanes		7	0
For half a bushell of pese		1	10
For 200 of plants		1	0
February 24th			
For sedes			4
For meat		1	9
For thread			2
For one hundred of plants			6
For powder & shot			2
Paid Mr Frye for one bushell of weat		5	2
Paid Mr Frye for half a bushell of barle		1	5
Totall	4	12	4
March 5th 1669			
Paid for one pound of raisons			4
For one pound of sand			1
For half a hundred of plants			4
For meat & seuet		2	10
For a pound of frut			4
For 2 hundred of plants		1	6
For sedes			4
For half a doesen of Sope		1	8
For half a peck of garden pese			4
For one hun[dred] & half of plants		1	2
March 26th 1670			
For one pound of frut			4
Paid for 2 pound of frute			7
For 2 pound of seuet		1	0
For half a dozen of Candles		2	0
Totall		13	0
April 2nd 1670			
Bought meat paid		4	0
April 9th			
For 2 pound of seut paid			7
For a qt of vele & 2 pound of seuet		4	0
April 16th			
For a pound of seut paid			4
For meat & seuet		3	10
April 23rd			
For frut & spice paid			5
For meat & seuet paid		2	4
For half a dozen of Sope paid		1	8

	£	s	d
April 30th			
For a pound of frut paid			4
For meat & seuet paid		2	3
For a pound of frut paid			4
Sum	1	0	1
May 14 1670			
Paid for meat & seuet		5	0
Paid Tho Pool for 16 bushells of malt	2	0	0
May 21st			
Paid for meat		3	6
For a pound of frute			5
For half a pound of Steeck			3
May 24th			
Paid for a legg of mutton and seut		2	4
May 28th			
Paid for meat		2	6
Sum	2	14	0
June 4th 1670			
Paid for 2 pound of frute			6
June 8th			
Paid for one pound of frute			3
June 11th			
Paid for meat seuet		6	4
For sand			1
June 18th			
Paid for meat & seuet		3	0
June 24th			
Paid for meat & seuet		3	9
Paid for one pound of frute			6
Paid for 9 bushells of salt		13	6
Paid for a pound of Sope			4
Paid for half an C of Sope		1	8
Sum total	1	2	11

Household Expences

	£	s	d
July 2nd			
Paid for meat & suett		4	0
July 9th			
Paid for meat & suett		3	6
Paid for a pound of Carrots			6
July 14th			
Payd for a pound of Suett			10
Paid for meat and suett		6	6

	£	s	d
Paid for a pound of currants			6
		15	10

Emplements

	£	s	d
October 17th 1669			
Paid John Bundy of Chalke, collor-maker For half a hors hide 4 Collers & other worke about the plase		19	0
Paid Daved Prant thresher for 3 dayes		3	0
Paid for a wryting booke		1	6
Paid for a tar box			8
Bought 3 els of canvais for hopbags		2	6
Paid for sack tires [ties]			3
Paid for tyen [?twine] to mend sakes			3
Paid for brimstone			5
Paid for 3 halters		1	0
	1	8	7
November 17th 1669			
Paid the Coller maker for 5 paire of hames and 5 paire of backties & 5 paire of pipes		16	0
November 27th			
Bought half a dozen of Sakes		19	0
Paid for 4 Caving [?calving] Cords		2	0
Paid for an earthen pot			4
Paid for half a hors hide		4	0
	2	1	4
January 18 1669			
Paid for 2 ox boes [bowes or yokes]		1	2
Paid for mending a seve			6
Paid for 200 of latnailes			6
Paid for mending a Casment		1	0
Paid for Spekes			6
Paid for 2 skoops		2	4
Paid for a new Saddle		11	6
		17	6
February 17th 1669			
Paid the Collermaker for 4 Collers, 5 paire of small pipes and 2 halters		10	8
Paid for half a hors hide		4	6
Paid for mending a Collor			10
Paid for 2 new pits			8
Totall		16	8

	£	s	d
March 10th 1669			
Paid John Pery for tar		2	6
For mending 2 ren seves [sieve for rennet]			10
March 19th			
For 4 Hemp halters		2	0
Bought 4 yards of woollen cloth for Tho Haylock		13	0
For buttons & thread			10
For draarsh [drawers] for Tho Haylock		1	6
Half a dozen of besomes			5
15 Els of Cloth for Chese Clouts		7	9
[line illegible]			6
Paid for turnopes [turnips]			2
For half a pecke of otemel			8
October 9th			
Bought one [?round] of befe & seuet		5	0
October 17th			
Paid for turnopes			2
Laid out in meat		3	0
In starch			1
October 25th			
Laid out in meat		4	0
In turnops			2
In Sope and Candles		4	0
October 29th			
Laid out in meat		2	6
	1	14	11
November 5th 1669			
Bought of Will Bagle 9 bushells of Salt		13	6
November 6th			
Laid out in meat		3	6
In tapes [taps] for barels			3
In a Shepes bell		1	0
November 13			
Laid out in meat & seuet		3	6
In turnepes			2
November 20th			
Laid out in meat & Otemeal		3	10
Paid Tho Poole of Shafsbury for 18 bushels of malt		10	8
Paid for half a doszen of Candles		2	4
November 27th			
Paid for meat & seuet		3	2
Paid for making 3 bushels of Otes into Otemeal			8
Paid for powder & shot			11
Paid for frute & spice			8
	4	4	0

	£	s	d
December 5th 1669			
Paid for meat		2	7
Paid for besomes [brooms]			4
Laid out in meat		3	10
In Sope & Candles		6	6
Paid for an Erthen butter pott			10
December 24th			
Laid out in meat		11	6
In frut		2	0
In half an El of Canvais			8
Paid Tho Pool for 6 bushels of malt		16	0
Paid for sterch & Corke			2
Laid out in smal pots & pans		1	0
For half a pound of powder & 2 pound of shot		1	0
	2	5	9
June 24th 1669			
Bought of Tho Collenes of Dunned [Donhead] 1 wagon pris paid is	5	1	0
June 27th 1669			
Bought of Robert King at tro [Trow] 1 rick staddel, 1 mill, 2 troes, [troughs] 1 bucket & Chaine & 13 rakes to serve bese [beasts]	2	5	0
Bought 3 rakes pris paid		1	0
Bought a rope for Trow well		4	0
Bought a paire of hemp thil lugs[loop supporting shaft] paid			9
Bought 3 prongs & a long rake paid		2	4
Paid John Abbott for 3 gretbords and 2 Spendles		2	0
	7	16	1
July 7th			
Paid for a bridle		1	4
For powder & shot			8
For a wallet		1	6
For a erthen butter pott			5
For 3 ox boes & a Jacke line		2	2
For 2 Cartlines		10	4
For a picking pick		2	8
		17	1
For 2 forkes		1	8
August 1st			
Paid for 3 halters & pick Stem [handle]		1	9
For half an El of Canvais & thread			9
August 9th			
Nicholas Cave for a waine		9	0

	£	s	d
Bought 3 dishes and a mouse trap			11
Paid for half a doszen of Seves		2	6
For 16 Els of Canvaies for a winnling [winnowing] Sheet		16	0
August 21st			
Bought 2 Candle Stekes & 3 lockes for		3	2
Paid the Cooper		2	0
September 8th			
Paid the Cooper for hooping 2 Coulets [barrels] & other vesel		3	8
September 9th			
Paid Mr Matthews of Shasbury for 300 foot of plankes for the weat barne	4	7	0
Paid Richard Coomb for 2000 of Spekes		3	0
Paid the Cooper by Mr Golsboro		8	0
September 14th 1669			
Paid the Widdow Laves for 4 harroes	1	0	0
Paid the Widdow Laves for the hire of 2 horses at 6d the day		10	0
September 19th 1669			
Bought one dozen of Sakes pris paid	1	19	0
Bought a welrope for Norrinton wel paid		2	0
Bought a bed cord		1	0
	8	10	4

An Account of House hould Expenses

	£	s	d
July 3rd 1669			
Imprimis, bought 2 bead of befe		14	10
Bought 1 bushel of weate for		5	4
July 18th 1669			
Bought 1 bushell of weate for		5	2
Laid out in meat		5	4
In Sallet Oyl			4
Paid James Toomer for 11 bushels and half of malt		18	0
Laid out in Sope Otmel & Bromes		1	1½
July 24th			
Laid out in befe and suet		10	0
July 31st			
Laid out in meat		8	6
	3	18	7½
August 7th 1669			
Laid out in meat		3	10
In carrots			4
One bushel of weat paid		5	0
Half a duszen of Soope		1	6

	£	s	d
August 10th			
Bought 3 bushells & half of Salt for		4	11
1 Pound of Sand & 2 earthen platters			5
August 21			
Laid out in meat		5	4
For [?] corke & broomes			3
In a duszen of Candles		4	4
For bonding the four plants & broomes		1	0
August 26th			
Laid out in meat		5	0
Paid Thomas Poole for 7 bushels of malt	1	1	0
Paid for Chicking [chicken]		3	2
Bought 1 bushel of weat paid		4	4
Paid for Otmel			4
For 1 pound of Sope			3
For 1 bushel of weat		4	8
For meat		6	6
August 29th			
Bought 1 bushel of weat paid		4	4
	3	10	6
September 4th			
Paid John Willes for meat		3	2
Laid out in tobacko for Sheepe			4
September 11th			
Bought half a duszen of Sope paid		1	10
For 2 pound of Seuet			8
[recte 6s 0d]		7	0
January 15th 1669			
Paid meate		4	0
Paid for 6 pound of Sope		1	8
Paid for tobacko for the Sheepe			7
January 29th			
Paid for meat & seuet		8	10
Paid for half a dus of Candles		2	4
Paid for paper			4
		17	9

An Account of House Hould Expensce

	£	s	d
May 7 1669			
Imprimis, bought of John Willes 1 hinder quarter of mutton		3	6
1 bead of befe wayde 21 pound & half		4	5
1 hinder quarter of veale pris paid		2	0
1 Cavleses [calves] heing [??] pris paid			6

	£	s	d
1 neatshroud of befe wayd 28 pound			10
May 28th 1669			
Bought a peck of Salt pris paid			6
June 4th			
Bought of Mr West of Sarum 2 Seves paid		1	2
June 5th			
Bought of John Willes 1 pese of befe paid		4	0
Paid Mr Cox for 2 bushels of weate		10	8
Bought 1 Cord for the cheese pres & gert web			8
Paid Mr Cox for 1 peck of barle & 4 pound of hops and a butter pot		3	10
Paid for 1 quier of paper		1	0
Totall	1	18	11
June 12th			
Bought 1 quarter of veale pris paid		2	2
Bought 1 peck of Salt & half a quarter of Otmel			8
Bought half a bead of befe paid		2	2
Bought half a bushel of Salt paid			10
June 24th			
Bought of Jasper Arnall 1 netshroud of befe		4	0
Bought 1 bushel of weate		5	4
Bought 1 pound of Sope & 1 peny worth of starch			4½
June 30th			
Bought 1 pese of befe & Seuet paid		3	8
		19	2½

An Account of Workmens Wages

	£	s	d
June 29 1670			
Paid George Sandres for making 200 & half of faggots		2	4
Paid Simmeon Read one quarter's wages ending the 24th of this moneth	1	10	0
Paid Jo Small one quarter's wages ending the 24th of this moneth		17	6
Paid to Jo Acten Shepard of the North flock one quarter's wages ending the 24th of this moneth	2	7	6
Paid Elias Juggrem Shepard of the South flock one quarter's wages ending the 24th of this moneth	2	7	6
Paid Ralf Skinner for 10 dayes		7	6
Paid porter			6
Sum Total	17	9	3
July 2nd 1670			
Payd the porter			6
Paid Henry Warren 10 day's worke		3	4
Payd Sarra Lowe for 10 day's worke		3	4

	£	s	d
Payd Stephen Haliock for 17 days worke		12	9
Payd Rich Combe for 17 day's worke		12	9
Payd Tho Crocke for one month		18	0
Payd Tho Crocke Junr for one month		8	0
July 7th			
Paid the porter			6
July 9th			
Payd the porter			6
July 14th			
Payd the porter			6
July 19th			
Payd Ralph Skiner for 14 day's worke		10	6
Payd Theson, gelder, for Spaying one Sowe			4
Payd Henry Worram for 12 day's worke		4	0
July 27th			
Payd John Adlam for cutting and making of 53 acres of grass att 2s 6d per acre	6	12	6
Payd John Adlam for cutting of 24 acres of Grass	2	10	0
Payd John Adlam for 3 day's worke		2	8
Payd John Adlam for cutting the orchard		1	4
Payd Tho Croker for one month	1	2	0
July 30th			
Payd Tho Croker his wife for 10 days		5	0
Payd him for his 2 sons a month		12	0
Payd Nicholas Britt for 11 day's worke		12	0
Payd Henry Warram for 6 days worke		2	0
Payd Richard Comb & his wife for 3 days		5	6
Payd John Adlam & his wife for 3 days		5	6
Payd Will Sanders for 3 days worke		2	0
Payd George Sanders & his dafter for 3 days		5	6
Payd George Sanders Junr for 2 days worke			9
Payd Stephen Halock for 3 days worke		3	6
Payd his Sonn for 3 days worke		1	0
Payd John Perry for 3 days worke		2	6
Paid Elizab. Perry for 3 days worke		1	6
Paid Richard Combe for 2 days mowing in West Field		2	0
Paid Ralph Skinner for 10 days worke		7	8
Paid Elizab. Perry for 7 days worke		3	6
Payd John Pery for 1 days worke			10
Paid Rich. Combe for 1 days worke			6
	16	17	10
January 14 1669			
Paid the porter		1	0
Paid Jerard for 6 dayes worke		6	0
Paid the wanter for 2 doz of wants [moles]		3	0
Paid Tho Croker for one month		16	0

	£	s	d
Paid Ed Croker for one month		4	0
Paid Richard Coomb for 21 dayes work		15	9
Paid Ralph Skinner for 20 dayes work		15	6
Paid Stephen Haylock for 20 dayes		15	0
Paid Will Sanders for one month		10	0
Paid George Sanders for one month		8	0
January 29th			
Paid porter		1	0
	4	15	3
February 2nd 1669			
Paid Henry Warren for 15 dayes		5	0
Paid Ellenor Briddel one quarters wages		13	9
Paid porter			6
Paid Steven Haylock for 23 dayes		13	3
February 12th			
Paid Ralf Skinner for 20 dayes		15	0
Paid Rich Coomb for 23 dayes		17	3
Paid Will Sanders for one month		10	0
Paid George Sanders for one month		8	0
Paid Tho Croker for one month		16	0
Paid Ed Croker for 12 dayes		2	0
February 24th			
Paid porter		1	0
Paid Nicho Brite, Carpenter, for 7 dayes		8	4
Paid mee Luke Dyer by my Lady Windham for half a yeares wages	7	0	0
Allowed mee by my Lady Windham for markets & faire expenses		13	4
Total	12	17	5
March 12th 1669			
Paid Steven Haylock for 23 dayes		17	3
Paid Rich Coomb for 24 dayes		18	0
Paid Ralf Skinner for 24 dayes		18	0
Paid Tho Croker for one month		16	0
Paid the porter		1	6
Paid Tho Croker Junior for one month		8	0
Paid Will Sandres for one month		10	0
Paid George Sanders for 18 dayes		6	0
Paid Ed Croker for 6 dayes		1	0
March 25th			
Paid Simeon Read half a years wages	3	0	0
Paid Ell. Briddell one quarters wages		13	9
Paid Nicholas Foel half a yeares wages	2	5	0
Paid John Small one quarters wages		17	6
Paid for Cutting the boore			8

	£	s	d
Paid the wanter for killing wants or moles	1	9	0
Totall	13	2	2
Paid Rich Coomb for 23 dayes worke		17	3
Paid Ralf Skinner for 23 dayes		17	3
Paid Tho Croker for 24 dayes		17	0
Paid Ralf Skinner for 6 dayes		4	6
Paid Tho Croker for his 2 Sonns		14	0
Paid Will Sandres for 24 dayes		10	0
George Sandres for 24 dayes		8	0
Paid the porter for the carig of 5 lode		2	6
Totall	5	7	6
May 4th 1670			
Paid Stev Haylock for 23 dayes worke		17	3
Paid Nicholas Brite for 3 dayes worke		3	6
Paid the porter		1	6
Paid Tho Croker for one month		18	0
Paid him for his two Sonns		14	0
Paid Rich Coomb for one month		18	0
Paid Will Sandres for 18 dayes		7	6
Paid George Sandres for 18 dayes		6	0
Paid the porter			6
Paid for drenching the baye nagg		1	0
Paid Sara Lane for weding the Close			10
Paid for cutting the little piggs		1	0
Paid mee Luke Dyer by my Lady Wyndham half yeares wages	7	0	0
Allowed mee for markets Expence		6	8
Sum	11	16	5
June 4th 1670			
Paid the glazeer for mending the windows		1	6
Paid Tho Croker for a month		18	0
Paid him for his 2 Sonns for 18 dayes		6	0
Paid Rich Coomb for 21 dayes worke		15	0
Paid the porter		1	6
Paid to Jo Adlam for making 30 doz of hurdles	1	15	0
Paid Jo Adlam for making 4 flakes [wattle hurdles]		4	0
Paid George Sandres for washing Norrington & Trow flockes of Sheep		18	0
Paid Jo Adlam for shereing Norrington & Trow flockes of Sheep	1	17	0
Paid for berring, printing & realing and mending [preparing fleeces for sale]		4	5
Paid for winding up the wool		6	0

	£	s	d
Paid Ellenor her Last quarters Wages		13	9
Paid the mason for one dayes work		1	6
Paid Henry Waren for 14 dayes worke		4	8
Paid Sara Lane for 14 dayes worke		4	8
The weeding account			
Paid Elizabeth Croker for 14 dayes		4	8
Paid Mara Polden for 15 dayes worke		5	0
Paid Rich Coombs wife for 14 dayes		4	0
Paid Will Sandres for 16 dayes		5	0
Paid George Sandres for 16 dayes		5	0
	9	16	8

ANSTY FARM ACCOUNTS 1693–1706

Ansty Farm was part of the estates of the Arundell family of Wardour. It was used as the demesne or home farm to supply produce to the family who lived at Breamore House (Bremer), following the destruction of Wardour Castle during the Civil War. There was a farm house at Wardour (Warder) which was also used by the family. Lord Henry Arundell died in 1694 and was succeeded by his son, Thomas, who died in 1712. These accounts were evidently compiled by the steward on the basis of information supplied by the farmer, Peter Wilson. They show the crops and livestock produced on the farm, divided between those sold for cash, 'the Reall Proceed' and those supplied to the households at Breamore and Wardour which were also given a monetary value, 'the Valuable Proceed'. Considerable quantities of provisions were supplied to 'Mrs Jenkins' who was evidently the cook to the household at Breamore. In addition, the accounts show the income received for work done by the 'plough', that is the team of horses or oxen which was hired to local farmers. The sheep flock was also occasionally hired for folding on neighbours' arable land.

Particularly interesting are the annual lists of expenses. These show the heavy costs of labour, and the large number of labourers. Only a few men, including the shepherd, carter, thresher and a boy were employed regularly. The rest were hired for sheep-shearing and harvest or were employed at piece work for hedging and ditching. Women and children were employed for weeding the corn or at harvest time. A flock of 300 or more sheep was kept on the farm and the relatively new fodder crops of sainfoin (French grass), rye-grass, clover and vetches (fetches) were grown. Part of the crop of sainfoin and clover was threshed and the seed sold; during the 12 year period the sale of this seed brought the large sum of £19 6s 6d. The annual profit from the sale of wool and surplus sheep was considerable. Some cattle were kept, but there are no references to milk and dairy produce; presumably there was a dairy at Breamore. Wheat and barley were the main cereals grown, with an emphasis on barley, but there is also mention of oats and rye. The oats were used to feed the horses. Barley was used for malting and as feed for pigs and poultry. Some wheat was charitably provided for the parish poor. Seed corn was supplied to other Arundell estates. Large quantities of peas were grown each year and 19 acres of hay were mown.

The precise acreage of the farm is uncertain, but a Survey of 1698 indicates that it included 150 acres of arable, as well as pasture, meadow and grazing rights on the downs south of the village as far as the Ridgeway route from Shaftesbury to Salisbury. Woodland covered more than 100 acres. The *other farms in the parish were all much smaller. There were four of 30-60 acres, and a further 35 tenants held only a few acres or cottages. It was these tenants who supplied the irregular needs for labour on the demesne farm. Two of the principal tenant farmers (Best and Rebeck) appear to have been involved in the running of Ansty farm and their names appear frequently in the accounts. (*VCH Wilts., *13, 1987, 96)*

These accounts provide a good indication of the income, costs and profits from a large demesne farm and of the sort of husbandry to be found there during the late 17th century. The final section also contains information on the amount of seed corn sown and the yield received, showing an average increase of nearly five-fold for wheat and three and a half-fold for barley.

WSRO 2667/12/97

Yr	Bushells	Goods Sold	Rate	For	Value
1694	235	Wheat	4s 1¼d	£ 48 3 4	
	578	Barley	1s 10d	£ 43 3 10	
	191	Pease	1s 11d	£ 18 7 7	£ 109 14 9
	58	Sheep & Lambs		£ 31 18 0	
	21	Weight of Wool att 30 pound per weight		£ 21 0 0	£ 52 18 0
1695	173	Wheat	3s 0¼d	£ 26 2 10	
	367	Barley	2s 3¾d	£ 44 2 10	
	456	Pease	3s 1½ d	£ 71 6 9	£ 141 12 5
1696	114½	Wheat	6s 5½d	£ 36 18 5	
		Barly	2s 5½d	£ 33 3 11	£ 70 2 4½
1697	28	Wheat	6s 0¼d	£ 8 8 10	
	1144	Barly	2s 9d	£ 19 6 3	
	272	Pease	2s 8¾d	£ 37 2 4	
	19	Ansty House	6s 2d	£ 5 17 0	
		Hoggs 19	18s 11d	£ 18 18 0	
		Wool 2690L		£ 114 2 6	
		Aftermath		£ 3 0 0	£ 207 4 11
1698	63	Wheat	5s 0d	£ 15 15 3	
	244½	Barly	3s 3d	£ 39 13 0	
	114	Pease	2s 0d	£ 11 8 4	
		Sheep 70	11s 1d	£ 38 15 0	£ 105 11 7

Yr	Bushells	Goods Sold	Rate	For	Value
1699	206½	Wheat	3s 9¾d	£ 39 9 5	
	60½	Barly	2s 11¾d	£ 8 17 7	£ 52 10 0
	24	Pease	3s 7d	£ 4 6 8	
		Hoggs 6		£ 6 4 0	
		Hoggs 2		£ 6 0 0	£ 12 4 0
		Sheep 60	11s 4d	£ 34 0 0	
		Wool 1176 pound		£ 60 11 0	£ 94 11 0
		Oxen 2		£ 11 0 0	£ 11 0 0
		Timber		£ 6 2 6	£ 6 2 6
1700	185	Wheat	3s 1d	£ 29 1 4	
	44	Barly	2s 0d	£ 4 8 0	
	47½	Pease	2s 3d	£ 5 6 4	£ 38 15 8
		Hoggs 10	20s 0d	£ 10 0 0	
		Hoggs 2	52s 6d	£ 5 5 0	£ 15 5 0
		Sheep 40	11s 0d	£ 22 0 0	
		Ditto 20	9s 0d	£ 9 0 0	
		Ditto 7	8s 0d	£ 2 16 0	£ 33 16 0
		Wagon Loan 8 days		£ 2 8 0	
		Shepherd Hyr 23 days		17 3	£ 3 5 3
1701	217	Wheat	2s 8d	£ 29 6 5	
	187	Barly	2s 3¼d	£ 19 7 6	
	64	Pease	2s 3d	£ 7 2 6	
	141	Fetches	2s 0d	£ 14 1 4	£ 69 17 9
		Sheep 40	11s 0d	£ 22 0 0	£ 22 0 0
		Ditto 50	7s 2d	£ 17 18 4	£ 17 18 4
		Wool 607 £	11¾d	£ 29 6 5	
		Hoggs 10		£ 10 0 0	
		Ditto 2		£ 4 0 0	£ 14 0 0
		Wagon Loan 7 days		£ 2 2 0	
		Shepherd hyr 25 days		18 9	
		Willsons Contack		£ 1 0 0	
		Boy 15 days		5 0	£ 4 5 9
1702	157	Wheat	2s 8d	£ 20 17 4	
	82.2	Barly	1s 2½d	£ 5 0 7	
	51.3	Pease	2s 1d	£ 5 6 2	
	24	Fetches	1s 8d	£ 2 0 0	£ 33 4 1
		French Grass		£ 2 0 0	
		72 lb Clover Seed		£ 5 17 0	£ 7 17 0
		Loan Cart & Servants		£ 2 11 0	£ 2 11 0

Yr	Bushells	Goods Sold	Rate	For	Value
		Tack Wills. Conr [?]		£ 1 15 0	£ 1 15 0
		Sheep 9	8s od	£ 3 12 0	
		Weathers 40	8s od	£ 16 0 0	£ 19 12 0
		Hoggs 2	42s 6d	£ 4 5 0	
		Porkers 10	16s od	£ 8 0 0	£ 12 5 0
1703	123½	Wheat	3s 1½d	£ 20 14 2	
	8	Barly	2s 3d	18 0	£ 21 12 2
		Pease	—		
	32	French Grasse	2s 1½d	£ 3 8 0	£ 3 8 0
	60	Sheep	8s od	£ 24 0 0	
	9	Weathers	8s od	£ 3 12 0	
	2	Hoggs	17s od	£ 1 14 0	
	8	Hoggs	14s od	£ 5 12 0	£ 34 18 0
	1	Porker	8s od	8 0	
	2	Porkers	12s od	£ 1 4 0	
	1	Bacon Hogg		£ 2 1 0	£ 10 19 0
		For 1 Cow Keeping		£ 1 15 0	£ 1 15 0
		Butt & Boy		£ 1 7 6	£ 1 7 6
1704	176½	Wheat	2s 11½d	£ 26 4 1	
	4½	Barley	1s 6d	6 9	
	?100½	Pease	8s 8d	£ 9 15 7	£ 36 6 5
		Hog Sheep 5	7s od	£ 1 15 0	
		More 40	8s od	£ 16 0 0	£ 17 15 0
		Piggs 9	14s od	£ 6 6 0	£ 6 6 0
		1 Cow Keeping		£ 1 15 0	£ 1 15 0
		74 weight wool	23s od	£ 89 14 0	£ 89 14 0
1705	206½	Wheat	2s 7½d	£ 27 3 8	
	110	Pease	3s 0½d	£ 16 12 6	
	84½	Vetches	2s 11¾d	£ 12 12 3½	£ 56 8 5½
	?40	Weather Hoggs	7s 6d	£ 15 10 0	
	10	Sheep	6s od	£ 3 0 0	£ 18 10 0
	9	Piggs Kild	12s od	£ 5 8 0	£ 5 8 0
		2 Cows Keeping	30s od	£ 3 0 0	£ 3 0 0
1706	393	Wheat	2s 10¼d	£ 56 2 11	
	485	Barley	2s 4¾d	£ 49 10 0	
	100	Pease	2s 6d	£ 12 10 0	£ 118 2 11
	86	French Grasse	21d	£ 7 0 0	£ 7 0 0
		Sheep 60	6s od	£ 18 0 0	£ 18 0 0

Porkers 7	17s od	£ 5 19 0	£ 5 19 0
Wool 39 weight	22s od	£ 42 18 0	£ 42 18 0
Keep 2 Cows		£ 3 0 0	
4 Boult [?bullocks]		£ 1 9 4	£ 4 9 4
Ergrasse [?]		£ 2 0 0	£ 2 0 0

The Total Sumes of each Particular Year for the Reall Proceed

Year	£	s	d
1694	162	12	9
1695	141	12	5
1696	70	2	4
1697	207	4	11
1698	105	11	7
1699	176	7	6
1700	91	1	11
1701	166	8	3
1702	77	4	1
1703	66	13	8
1704	151	16	5
1705	83	6	5½
1706	198	9	3
Total	1698	1	6½

The Valuable Proceed of Ansty Farme

Year	Bush	How Dispos'd	Rate	Value
1694	98	Wheat to Seed	3s 6¼d	£ 17 5 2
	113	Barly to Seed	1s 6d	£ 8 9 6
	132	Pease to Seed	2s 3d	£ 14 17 0
		Hay of 19 acres	20s od	£ 19 0 0
			Total	£ 59 11 8
1695	18	Wheat to Seed	4s 1d	£ 3 13 6
	196	Barly to Seed	2s 8d	£ 26 2 8
		Hay of 19 acres	20s od	£ 19 0 0
			Total	£ 48 16 2
1696	22	Wheat to Ansty Housekeeper	6s 5½d	£ 7 3 2
	36	Wheat to Bremer		£ 11 12 6

Year	Bush	How Dispos'd	Rate	Value
	90	Wheat to Warder		£ 29 7 8
	73	Ansty Seed [wheat]		£ 13 15 8
	240	Barly to Warder Malting	2s 5½d	£ 29 10 0
	19	Barly to Warder Poultry		£ 2 6 8½
	92	Barly to Bremer		£ 11 6 2
	92	Ansty Seed [barley]		£ 11 6 2
	144	Oats Ansty Carthorses	1s 10d	£ 13 4 0
		Hay of 19 acres		£ 19 0 0
			Total	£ 161 16 0½
1697	36	Wheat to Bremer	6s 0¼d	£ 10 16 9
	92	Wheat to Warder		£ 27 13 11
	81	Ansty Seed [wheat]		£ 24 7 8
	276	Barly to Warder Malting	2s 9d	£ 37 19 0
	60	Barly to Warder Poultry		£ 8 5 0
	112	Barly to Bremer poultry		£ 15 8 0
	92	Ansty Seed Barly		£ 12 13 0
	23¼	Ansty Hogs Pease	2s 8¾d	£ 3 2 5
	59¼	Ansty Seed [pease]		£ 7 13 3
		Hay of 19 acres		£ 19 0 0
		42 Beasts 11 weeks at 4d per week		£ 7 14 0
			Total	£ 182 12 9
1698	4	Wheat to Ansty Poor	5s 0d	£ 1 0 0
	58	Wheat to Warder		£ 14 10 0
	32	Ansty Seed [wheat]		£ 8 0 0
	194	Barly to Warder	3s 3d	£ 31 4 0
	144	Barly to Bremer		£ 23 8 0
	164	Ansty Seed [barley]		£ 26 13 0
	30	Pease to Bremer Hogs	2s 0d	£ 3 0 0
		Hay of 19 acres		£ 19 0 0
			Total	£ 126 15 0
1699	4	Wheat to Ansty Poor	3s 9¾d	15 3
	39	Wheat sent to Warder		£ 7 8 8
	124	Barly to Bremer	2s 11¾d	£ 18 9 5
	2	Barly to Warder		5 11
	240	Barly to Bremer Malting		£ 35 15 0
	19	Pease to Warder	3s 7d	£ 3 8 1
	20	Ansty Hoggs		£ 3 11 8
		Hay of 19 acres		£ 19 0 0
			Total	£ 88 14 0

Year	Bush	How Dispos'd	Rate	Value
1700	4	Wheat to Ansty Poor	3s 0d	12 0
	5½	[illegible]		16 6
	192	Barly to Bremer	2s 0d	£ 19 4 0
	148½	Barley to Warder		£ 14 17 0
	121	More [to Warder]		£ 12 2 0
	11	Barly to Ansty Piggs		£ 1 2 0
	38	Pease	2s 4d	£ 4 8 0
	21½	Pease [for] the fatt Hoggs		£ 2 10 2
		Ansty Team to Plow at Warder 36 days	6s 0d	£ 10 16 0
		Caring [carrying] Oats to Bremer 9 days	4s 6d	£ 2 0 6
		Hay of 19 acres		£ 19 0 0
			Total	£ 75 6 10
			Add	£ 12 2 0
1701	111	Wheat to Ansty Poor	2s 7d	£ 14 6 9
	4	Wheat [to] Poor of Ansty		10 4
	288	Barly to Bremer	2s 0½d	£ 29 8 0
	110	Barly to Warder		£ 11 2 11
	13½	Barly [for] Hoggs, Piggs & Pidg.[pigeons]		£ 1 6 6½
	32	Pease to Warder	2s 3d	£ 3 12 0
	167	Oats [for] Ansty Horses	1s 6d	£ 12 10 6
		Rye Grass 10lb	16s 0d	£ 8 0 0
		Hay of 19 acres		£ 19 0 0
		Straw omitted 6 Load		[blank]
			Total	£ 99 17 0½
1702	4	Wheat to Ansty Poor	2s 8d	10 8
	160	Wheat to sent to Warder		£ 21 6 8
	45	Barly sent to Warder	1s 2½d	£ 2 14 4½
	192	Barly to Bremer for Malting		£ 15 12 0
	304	Barly [for] Doggs & Pultry [to] Bremer		£ 24 14 0
	7	Barly to the Piggs at Ansty		9 9
	6½	Pease to Warder	2s 1d	£ 4 4 0
	132	Barly [for] Ansty Hoggs		£ 1 8 1
	296	Oats to the Cart Horses	1s 5d	£ 20 19 4
		Teemes [teams] Loan 10 days to Bremer		£ 2 5 0
		Hay 19 acres	20s 0d	£ 19 0 0
		Straw 5 load omitted		[blank]
			Total	£ 113 18 3½

Year	Bush	Goods Sold	Rate	Value
1703	4	Wheat to the Poor	3s 1½d	12 6
	160	Wheat to Warder	3s 2½d	£ 25 0 0
	268	Barly to Bremer	2s 3d	£ 30 3 0
	240	Barly to Fordingbridge	2s 3d	£ 27 0 0
	26	Wheat to Warder		£ 2 18 6
	160	Oats to Bremer	1s 6d	£ 12 0 0
	138	Oats Ansty Cart Horses	1s 6d	£ 10 7 0
	14	French Grass Seed	2s 1½d	£ 1 9 6
	14	Fatt Hoggs Pease	2s 4d	£ 1 12 8
		Hay of 19 Acres		£ 19 0 0
		Omitted Straw 3½ load		[blank]
			Total	£ 130 3 2
1704 (without Hay)				
	4	Wheat to the Poore	2s 11½d	
	179	Wheat to Warder	£ 27 1 4½	
	252	Barly to Bremer		
	240	Barly to Fordinbridge		
	40½	Barly to Jenkins	2s 0d	£ 53 ?18 0
	7	Ansty Piggs [oats]		
	60	Oats to Bremer		
	150	Ansty Cart Horses	1s 6d	£ 7 5 0
			Total	£ 80 19 4½
1705 (without Hay)				
	10	Fetches for Seed	2s 11¾d	£ 1 9 9½
	21	Pease for Seed	3s 6d	£ 3 13 6
	4	Wheat to the Poor		
	156	To Warder Poor [wheat]		
	3½	To Jenkins Bredd [wheat]		£ 24 10 6
	264	To Bremer Barly	2s 2d	£ 44 4 0
	144	For seed [barley]		
	48	Oates for Seed	1s 6d	£ 3 12 0
			Total	£ 77 9 9½
1706	4	Wheat for Poor		11 5
	4	Wheat to Bremer	2s 10¼d	11 5
	288	Barly to Bremer	2s 4¾d	£ 34 10 0
	246	Oates to Bremer	2s 6d	£ 30 15 0
			Total	£ 66 7 10

Ansty Farme Expence as per Willsons Annuall Account ending Michaelmas 1694 Including the Stock

	Rate	Value
For 174 Weather Sheep at	11s 6d	£ 100 1 0
For 50 Ewes going upon the Farme	9s 6d	£ 23 15 0
Weather Hogg Sheep 113 at	11s 6d	£ 50 17 0
5 More at	11s 0d	£ 2 15 0
For 50 Weather Sheep at	10s 0d	£ 25 0 0
For 10 more ditto at	9s 0d	£ 4 10 0
Two Yoake of Oxen		£ 20 10 0
Horses 6 at £ 7		£ 42 0 0
A new Wagon & Wheels	£ 10 10 0	
Two pair of Wheels for another	£ 9 10 0	
Last harness 4 pair & 2 pair Thrills	£ 2 10 0	
A Dragg & harrow	£ 2 0 0	
Shovells, Fann & ½ Bushell	£ 1 2 0	
4 Dung Potts with the Wheels	£ 4 0 0	
An Iron Barr for the Fold	4 0	
Bushell, Sives, Ropes & Rudrs	19 6	
The Collar Maker's Bill	£ 1 10 0	
The Smith's Bill for Shoeing	£ 7 9 0	
For Halters to Carry Corne	4 0	
For 6 doz. Of hurdles to pen Sheep	18 0	£ 40 17 9
For 6 small Piggs		£ 1 10 0
For an old Rick of Hay 6 Tunn	£ 6 0 0	
Mowing 19 Acres of Grass	£ 1 8 6	
60 days hay(making) at 5d per day	£ 1 5 0	£ 8 13 6
Wheat to sow 108 Bushells	£ 37 16 0	
Barly to sow 136 Bushells	£ 23 7 6	
Pease to sow 48 Bushells	£ 10 8 0	£ 71 11 6
For Sowing & plowing 12 Acres	£ 13 4 0	
Sowing & single plowing 6 Acres	£ 2 5 0	
Barly Doub [?], Worke 28 Acres	£ 15 8 0	
Sowing 12 acres of Pease at 6s 8d	£ 4 0 0	
For 110 Load of Soyle at 8d	£ 3 13 4	
Washing sheering of Sheep etc.	£ 1 10 0	£ 40 0 4
To Wm Moores the Thracher Wages	£ 11 2 9	
To Math. Butt Sheppard	£ 12 0 0	
Cecill Willson's wages	£ 14 0 0	
Holly's Boy ½ year's wages ending Michaelmas	£ 2 12 0	
To Carrington the Carter ½ year's wages	£ 5 10 0	£ 45 4 9
For 42 dayes weeding the Corne at 4d per day	14 0	
Harvesting the Corne as per Bill	£ 17 2 1½	£ 17 16 1½
	Total	£ 495 1 11½

Willson's Annual Account ending Michaelmas 1695

	Rate	Value
Matthew Butt, Sheppard year's wages	£ 12 0 0	
Cecill Willsons year's wages	£ 14 0 0	
Holly's Boy with the Plow for a year	£ 5 5 0	
To Robt Dalton for Wages	£ 3 10 0	
To W m Moore for a year's thrashing	£ 11 2 9	
To Perry for 10 days at 9d ditto	7 6	
To the Sheppard's Boy 111 days at 3d	£ 1 7 9	
Carrington with the Plow 86 days at 9d per day	£ 3 4 6	
Tho. Bower 11½ days at 9d	8 3	
To Perry's Boy with the Plow 17 days at 4d per day	5 8	£ 46 5 3
Harvesting the Corne for the Year 1695	£ 12 10 5½	
2 Maids 9 days Cleansing of Seed at 8d per day	6 0	£ 12 16 5½
For Hay Making of 19 Acres	£ 1 7 0	
Mowing the same at 18d per acre	£ 1 8 6	£ 2 15 6
Waching & sheering 360 sheep with Bread & Beere	£ 1 10 0	£ 1 10 0
Mending the Horses' Geares		9 0
For 4 piggs to eat up the wast corn		£ 2 8 0
To Farmer Horder for 64 bushells of Oats for the Cart Horses at 15d		£ 4 0 0
	Total	£ 75 10 4½

Ansty Farme Expence ending Michaelmas 1696

To the Thrasher Wm Moore	£ 10 17 6	
Butt the Sheppard's Wages	£ 12 0 0	
Holly's Boy ditto	£ 6 0 0	
To Cecill Willson the same	£ 12 0 0	£ 40 17 6
To Thatching the Long Stable	£ 3 12 0	
To Scamell 10 days at 5d	5 06	
To the Carpenter there	17 8	£ 4 15 6
To Tho. Perry Sowing 34 days at 6d	17 0	
To Scamell for the same	£ 1 7 0	
For Mowing	£ 1 9 0	
40 days Haymaking at 5d	16 8	
Reaping Binding & Setting the Tyth	£ 3 14 3	
Weeding Corne 68 days at 4d	£ 1 8	
Bringing Corne home	£ 6 4 11	£ 15 13 6
50 Sheep bought at 10s per sheep	£ 25 0 0	
Butt's Boy tending sheep at 3d	£ 2 1 0	£ 27 1 0

	Rate	Value
Washing 307 sheep and Sheering		£ 1 12 9
The Smith's Bill for the Cart Horses	£ 7 16 4	
The Corn Sacks 10 at 3d 4d per sack	£ 1 13 4	
For 6 plow traces, halters etc	9 8	
For two last Pannells	13 2	£ 10 12 6
	Total	£ 100 12 9

Ansty Farme Expence ending Michaelmas 1697

To Matthew Butt Sheppard per annum	£ 12 0 0	
John Holly's wages per annum	£ 10 0 0	
To Wm Moore Thrasher	£ 10 10 0	
To Butts Boy	£ 5 10 0	
To Cecill Wilson his wages	£ 12 0 0	£ 50 6 0
Bills of Harvesting	£ 22 1 4	
To Haymaking		
Ditching Hedging & husbandry Bills	£ 16 16 1½	
The Court Stable	£ 15 16 1	
To Plow Tackle & Cart Implements	£ 13 7 1	
Buying of Cattle	£ 4 16 0	£ 75 7 3½
	Total	£ 125 13 3½

Ansty Farme Expence ending Michaelmas 1698

To Cecill Willson his year's wages	£ 12 0 0	
To Wm Moore Thrasher per annum	£ 10 18 0	
To John Holly	£ 9 0 0	
To Matthew Butt Sheppard per annum	£ 12 0 0	
To his Boy	£ 5 0 0	
Washing sheering etc of 300 Sheep		£ 1 15 6
Paid 96 days weeding the Corn at 4d	£ 1 12 10	
For 135 days harvest work at 15d	£ 8 8 7	
Cutting 42½ acres of Barly at 12d	£ 2 2 0	
Wheat 17 acres reaping at 4s per acre Bring 130 Perch	£ 3 13 3	£ 22 1 8
6 days Reaping wheat at 22d per day	11 0	
John James his Bill for harvest	£ 1 16 0	
For 36 Bushells of seed wheat	£ 12 12 0	
For 20 bushells of seed pease at 3s 9d	£ 3 15 0	
For 8 bushells of seed Fetches at 3s 10d	£ 1 10 0	
For 48 bushells of seed Oats at 1s 9d	£ 4 4 0	
Incident Charges of Husbandry	10 8	
Tho. King's Bill	£ 5 9 6	
Robert Scamell's ditto	£ 3 7 0	

	Rate	Value
Edw. Moors & Jerrard's Bill	13 2	£ 11 18 8
John James two bills	£ 1 18 4	
Tho Smith's years Bill	£ 7 3 0	
For 80 bushells of Oats for the Carthorses	£ 6 0 0	£ 13 3 0
Mowing & haymaking of 19 Acres	£ 2 3 1	£ 2 3 1
	Total	£ 118 2 9

Ansty Farme Expence 1699

Mowing 19 acres of meadow at 18d	£ 1 8 6	
Hay making the same	£ 1 0 8	£ 2 9 2
Reaping 48 acres at 1s per acre	£ 2 8 0	
5 Acres 28 perch at 4s and 2½ at 2s	£ 1 5 9	
24½ days at 20s & 5days at 2s	£ 2 10 10	
4 Acres more Reaping at 4s	16 0	
Harvesting 17 days at 1s per day	17 0	
88 days at 8d per day	£ 2 18 9	
33½ ditto at 18d per day	£ 2 10 6	£ 13 6 10
Wm Moore Thrasher a year's wages	£ 10 18 0	
Math Butt Sheppard the same	£ 12 0 0	
Ditto Boy for worke £ 5 John Holly £ 10	£ 15 0 0	£ 37 18 0
Bought 64 sheep	£ 34 6 0	
Sheep washing 300 at 4d per score	5 0	
Shearing at 10d per score with meat & drink	£ 1 10 6	£ 36 1 6
Paid the Smith's Bill for the Carthorses		£ 9 9 2
For 5 pair of plow harness etc	£ 1 4 10	
Two Wood Ropes 31 weight at 6d per pound	15 6	
For a pair of Cart wheels	£ 1 3 0	
Sives & 7 doz hurdles at 3d	£ 1 5 8	£ 4 9 0
Seed Wheat 16 bushells at 4s 10½d	£ 3 18 0	
Seed Oats 47 bushells at 2s	£ 4 14 0	
For Fetches 18 bushells at 3s 9d	£ 1 10 0	£ 10 2 0
For a Cart Colt	£ 7 0 0	
For 4 steers	£ 14 10 0	£ 21 10 0
To Cecill Willson is Year's Sallary		£ 12 0 0
Ditching 342 perches at 3½	£ 4 19 9	
38 days at 23d hedging	£ 1 14 6	
33 days at 6d & 511 days at 3d	£ 5 19 5	£ 12 13 8
	Total	£ 159 19 4

Ansty Farme Expence 1700

To Wm Moore Thrasher a year's wages	£ 10 18 0	
To Matthew Butt Sheppard ditto	£ 12 0 0	

	Rate	Value
To John Holly the same	£ 10 0 0	
To Bull's (?Butt's) Boy ditto	£ 5 0 0	
To Cecill Willson ditto	£ 12 0 0	£ 49 18 0
To James Butts for Tending the Sheep	£ 2 12 6	
Looking to the Sheep in seed time	17 0	
Washing & shearing etc	£ 1 5 0	£ 4 14 6
Edw. Moore for Ditching & Planting	£ 3 16 0	
Ditto a Bill for more Ditching	£ 4 4 11	
Ditto a Bill that was forgot	3 0	
John James as per Bill	7 0	£ 8 10 11
For 32 Bushells of Seed Wheat	£ 6 4 0	
For 22 Bushells more at Bremer at 4s 9d	£ 5 5 3	
For 30 Bushells of Fetches at 2s 9d	£ 4 2 6	£ 15 11 9
James's Boy going to Plow	1 6	
Six dozen of hurdles at 3s 6d	£ 1 1 0	£ 1 2 6
For 72 Bushells of hop clover and Rye grass at 22½d per Bushell	£ 6 15 0	£ 6 15 0
Marketing etc	18 10	18 10
Harvesting 48 days at 20d	£ 4 0 0	
Greeping [reaping] 35 days at 8d per day	£ 1 3 4	
Two days ditto at 12d per day	2 0	
22 Weeders of Corne that year	£ 1 12 5	£ 6 17 9
Reaping 36 acres of Barly at 12d	£ 1 16 0	
5 days Reaping of Wheat at 2s 0d	£ 10 0	
Reaping 7½ Acres at 4s 0d	£ 1 12 2	
Reaping 4 Acres at 6s 6d	18 0	£ 5 16 2
Reaping of 3 Acres 105 perches	17 6	
Reaping 9 days at 23d per day	17 0	
Reaping 10 days at 2s 0d per day	£ 1 0 0	£ 7 10 8
Mowing of 19 Acres Medow	£ 1 8 6	
For making hay	£ 1 5 9	£ 2 14 3
The Smith's Bill for the Cart Horses etc	£ 11 1 5	
Oats 40 Bushells for the Coach horse at 21½d per Bushell	£ 3 12 6	£ 14 13 11
For 32 Sheep at 11s 6d		£ 18 8 6
	Total	£ 137 11 7

Ansty Farme Expence per Willson's Annual Account ending Michaelmas 1701

To Wm Moore Thrasher per annum	£ 10 5 6	
To Matthew Butt Sheepard ditto	£ 12 0 0	
John Holly £ 10 Cecill Willson £ 12	£ 22 0 0	
To Matthew Butt's Boys	£ 5 0 0	£ 49 5 6
To Wm Coole for 75 days at 5¾d	£ 1 16 0	

	Rate	Value
John James for Thrashing Clover etc	£ 1 12 10	
To Matthew Butts Boy Matt	£ 2 14 0	
Ditto another boy Wm	18 3	
For Marketing	£ 1 3 0	
Moores & John Jerrard's hedging etc	£ 3 12 4	
Washing 260 Sheep at 4d per score dyet 20d and also Sheering at 10d per score	£ 1 15 0	
Seed Oats 56 Wheat 16 Pease 28 Bushells	£ 10 18 0	£ 24 9 5
8 Corn Sacks £ 1 6s 8d, a haire wind [winnowing]sheet 18s 0d	£ 2 4 8	
For 5 dozen of hurdles	17 6	£ 16 16 9
Plow Tackle as per Bill	£ 13 14 7	
Weeding of Corn 30s 9d Mowing 35 acres Barly	£ 3 5 1	
For Mowing 9 Acres of Oats	9 0	
A Bill for Harvesting	£ 10 10 4	£ 14 4 5
To Several women for Hay making	17 3	
Mowing 18 Acres of Rye Grass & 19 Medow	£ 2 9 6	£ 3 6 9
Smith's Bill for shoeing etc per annum	£ 10 4 7	
For a Cart Colt	£ 6 0 0	£ 16 4 7
For 168 Bushells of Oats for the Cart Horses		£ 11 10 0
For 50 Weathers at 8s 2d per Weather	£ 20 8 2	
For 60 Weathers at 5s 0d per Weather	£ 15 0 0	
To Bremer 24 Bushells of Barly at 2s 0d	£ 2 8 0	£ 2 8 0
	Total	£ 173 13 7

Ansty Farme Expence per Willson's Annuall Account 1702

To Wm Moore Thrasher	£ 10 5 6	
To Matt Butt Shepard Wages	£ 12 0 0	
Ditto Boy Wm 110 days	£ 2 13 4	
John Holly's wages	£ 10 0 0	
To Cecill Willson's Wages	£ 12 0 0	£ 46 19 10
Matt. Butt's Boy James 30 days	10 0	
To Wm Cook 22 days at 9d	16 0	
To Matt Butt's Boy Matt	£ 5 0 0	
John James Plowing etc	17 6	
Moore & Jerrard's Bill	£ 3 17 8	
To severall Children picking Stones	6 5	
For Plowing 39 days at 4d	13 0	
Pepin 9 days	6 9	
For Making Rick, Thatching	4 6	
Washing etc 160 sheep	15 2	
Bread etc to	£ 1 0 0	£ 14 7 9
To Women Weeding as per Bill	£ 1 7 10	

	Rate	Value
Cutting 18 Acres of Barly in Farm Field	£ 1 15 0	
Mowing of 18 Acres of Oats	18 0	
Reaping 21 Acres at 4s 0d	£ 4 4 0	
Reaping 10 Acres of Rye	9 0	
Reaping of Wheat	£ 2 0 0	
John Jerrard cutting of Fetches	£ 1 7 4	
For Gathering of Barly	9 4	
Baker 3½ Acres	7 6	
To Judith James 8d Harvest 12s 0d	12 8	£ 13 10 8
To Hay Making Rye Grass 18 acres		
Meadow Grass 11 acres 59 days per Bill	£ 1 9 11	
Hop and Rye Grass 11 acres	£ 2 3 6	
For Mowing 6 Acres of Tare Grass in Farme Feild	9 0	£ 4 2 5
For Sives and Riders [?riddles]	1 6	
Collar Makers Bill	£ 1 8 4	
Dung Pott & Wheels	£ 1 8 0	
The Smiths Bill for that year	£ 8 2 0	
The Carpenter's Bill ditto	17 4	
Six dozen of hurdles	£ 1 1 0	£ 12 18 10
For 50 weather Hoggs at 9d per hogg		£ 19 7 6
3 Quarters of Oats at 12s and 5½ Quarts at 10s 6d		£ 4 13 9
	Total	£ 116 8

Ansty Farme Expence per Willson's Annual Account 1703

To Matt Butt his Year's Wages	£ 12 0 0	
Paid Wm Butt for Keeping of Sheep that Yeare	£ 5 0 0	
To Matt Butt Junr for going with the Plow	£ 9 0 0	
To Cecill Willson his Wages for that yeare	£ 12 0 0	
To Wm Moores for Thrashing that Yeare	£ 10 6 6	£ 48 6 6
To Wm Pipping For Thrashing & other work 16 days at 9d	12 0	
To John Holly for—[blank] days at [blank]	£ 5 7 3	
To John Newport for Plowing etc 39 days at 4d	13 0	
To John Jeanes for [blank] days at—	£ 1 17 0	
To Edw Moores & John Jerrard for —days hedging that Year	£ 3 8 3½	£ 12 15 6½
For Weeding the Corne —Days at—	18 0	
For Mowing 19 Acres of Grass at 18d	£ 1 8 6	
For Mowing 6 Acres of French Grass	9 0	
For Haymaking	£ 1 3 6	
To a Woman for Leazing Wheat & Cockling		

	Rate	Value
Barly 13 days at 4d [weeding]	4 4	
For Moweing 36 Acres of Barly at 12d	£ 1 16 0	
For Moweing 18 Acres of Oats at 12d	18 0	
To Wm King for Reeping of — 4 dayes at 2s od	8 0	
To Wm Lawrence for Harvest Work by Agreement	£ 2 0 0	
To Edw Moores & John Jerrard for Reeping 5 days at 2s od and cutting of Pease 2 days at 12d	12 0	
To John Jeanes for Reeping etc 11 Days at 1s 6d	16 0	
Ditto wife for Harvest work 6 days at 8d	4 0	
John Newport for the Like 21 days at 8d	14 0	
To Israel Targett for 2 days at 1s 4d	2 8	
To John Harwood for the Like 4 days at 12d	4 0	
To Roger Perry for 10 days harvest work at 8d	6 8	
To Edw Alford for Reepeing 11 Acres of Wheat at 4s od	£ 2 4 0	
To John Scamell & Wm Butt for Reepeing 5 acres & 39 perches of Wheat at 4s od	£ 1 1 0	
To the Widow Boyter's 3 maids for Harvesting	9 4	
To Wm Coole for Harvesting 18 days at 1s 4d	£ 1 4 0	£ 16 3 6
To Wm Pippin for Harvesting 2 days at 1s 4d	2 8	
For Washing & Shearing 270 sheep at 1s 2d per score	15 0	
For bread and Cheese etc for the Shearers and a Great many Children	£ 1 0 0	
To John Holly for Harvesting 10½ days at 1s 4d	14 0	£ 2 11 8
To the Coller maker his Bill for Mending the Plow Harness	7 8	
The Smith's Bill for that yeare	£ 8 15 0	£ 10 15 2
The Carpenter's Bill for Plow worke	11 6	
For 6 dozen of hurdles to Fold the Sheep at 3s 6d per dozen	£ 1 1 0	
Wheat Bought 16 Bushells at 4s od per Bushell	£ 3 4 0	
Pease 28 Bushells at 2s 4d per Bushell	£ 3 5 4	
Sheep bought 20 at 6s 6d per sheep	£ 6 10 0	
Weathers 67 at 7s 6d	£ 25 2 6	
For Store Piggs 14 at 5s 5d & 2d over	£ 2 16 0	£ 41 17 10
	Total	£ 132 13 2½

Ansty Farm Expence per Peter Willson's Annuall Account 1704

Payd Cecill Willson his yeare's wages	£ 12 0 0
To Matthew Butt his yeare's wages	£ 12 0 0

	Rate	Value
His boy's dyett, wages and attending plow	£9 0 0	
His Matt attending the sheep	£5 0 0	
Wm Moore Thrashing	£10 6 6	£48 6 6
To Wm Peppin thrashing & other work	15 0	
James Butts boy thirteen days plowing	13 4	
Ditto¼ year's work from Midsummer	£1 15 0	
To John Jeanes for work	11 8	
Paid his boy for 15 days plowing 5d	6 3	
To Edw Moore & John Jerrard at the Hedging	£2 16 2	
John Holly for 23 days work at 9d	17 3	
To Edw Moore & John Jerrard more	£1 17 6	
Paid for Haymaking	£1 4 6	£7 19 2
For weeding corne	19 0	
For Leazing of seed [removing weed seed]	5 0	
Mowing 35 Acres of Barley	£1 15 0	
Mowing 14 Acres of Oats at 12d	14 0	
Reaping 8 acres 45 perches	£1 13 1½	
Wheat 4 acres & 15 perches	16 6	
Will. Cob for harvest work	£1 10 9	
Will. Pepin reaping & other harvest work	£1 2 8	
John James for the same	18 0	
Edw Moor for the same	10 6	
Will Lawrence	£2 0 0	
John Newport for the same	18 0	£18 14 3½
Roger Perry nine days harvesting	6 0	
John Horwood 5 days	5 0	
John Holly 3 days	3 0	
Washing & shearing 270 sheep at 1s 2d per score	15 9	
Bread & Beere for the shearers	£1 0 0	£10 11 5
The Collar maker's Bill	£1 0 3	
The Smith's Bill	£7 13 6	
The Carpenter for plow worke	16 8	
For 6 dozen of Hurdles at 3s 6d per dozen	£1 1 0	
Wheat bought 24 Bushells to sow in Heath at 3s 7½d	£4 7 0	
Wheat bought 24 bushells sow'd in Farme Feild	£4 18 0	
Barly bought 39 bushells sow'd in Farme Feild, Upper Rye Acre, Dry Close	£2 18 6	
Oates bought for the Horses 27 bushells at 1s 0½d	£1 8 2	
Pease bought 64 bushells at 3s 0d	£9 17 0	£25 13 8
Fetches 26 bushells at 1s 11d	£2 10 0	
Hog sheep 61 at 7s 6d	£22 7 6	
More 12 at & 7s 0d	£4 4 0	
Piggs 9 at 3s 0d	£1 7 0	

	Rate	Value
For 1 cowe keeping upon the farme	£ 1 15 0	
For wool sold 78 weight	£ 89 14 0	
Total		£ 139 13 6

Ansty Farme Expence per Willson's Account 1705

Paid Cecill Wilsons wages for the yeare	£ 12 0 0	
Matthew Butt the same	£ 12 0 0	
Tho. Bradly the same	£ 11 0 0	
Math Butt's boy minding the sheep	£ 5 0 0	
Will Moore thrashing a yeare	£ 10 6 6	£ 50 6 6
William Pepin for thrashing & other work	17 3	
To his boy with the plough 45 days at 3d	12 0	
Jo Newport going to plough & other work	11 8	
James Butt's boy with the plow 8 days at 4d	2 8	
Jo James threshing & other work 5 days at 10d	4 2	
His boy 40 days at 4d sowing graine	13 4	
Edw Moore & Jo Jerrard Hedging	£ 4 4 1	£ 7 5 2
Moor & Jo Jerrard mowing 35 acres at 1s 8d	£ 2 12 6	
For Haymaking	£ 1 18 0	
For Weeding Corne	14 6	
Louzing [weeding] Corne for seed	4 4	
Picking stones in Dry Close	4 6	
For Seves to winnow corne	5 3	
Mowing 30 acres of Barley at 12d per acre	£ 1 10 0	
Reaping 6 acres of wheat at 4s per acre	£ 1 4 0	
10 Acres more of wheat at 4s	£ 2 0 0	
3 Acres ½ and 19 Lug	14 6	
Jo Holly 2 days harvesting at 18d	3 0	
Jo Newport Harvesting 24 days at 10d	£ 1 0 0	
Jo Perry 3 days for the same at 10d	3 0	
Will Butt for the same 14 days at 10d	18 8	
Will Lawrence for the same	17 0	
His boy harvesting at 10d per 20 days	16 8	
Wm Cole Harvesting at 18d per 18 days	£ 1 7 0	
Wm Baker cutting 3 acres pease at 2s 0d	6 0	
Edw Moore & Jo Jerrard fetches cutting at 3d 0d	9 0	
To Pepin Underhill & a boy Harvesting	£ 2 3 4	
Washing etc 270 sheep at 1s 2d per score	15 9	
Bread, Cheese etc	£ 1 0 0	£ 24 0 6
The Collar Maker's Bill	£ 1 5 0	[recte £ 16 18 5]
The Smith's Bill	£ 7 9 9	
The Carpenter's Bill for work plow	£ 1 3 8	
For 5 dozen hurdles at 3s 6d	£ 1 1 0	
For a journey carrying Barley	8 4	£ 11 7 9

	Rate	Value
For wheat bought 48 bushells at 3s 9d seed	£ 9 0 0	
Oates bought 48 bushells at 2s 0d seed	£ 4 16 0	£ 21 13 0
Oates bought 96 bushells at 19½d Horses	£ 7 17 0	
Weather Hoggs 69 at 7s 6d	£ 25 17 6	
Piggs, Ten bought at 3s 0d	£ 1 10 0	£ 27 7 6
Eight Rates to the poore and half a rate to the clerk at 16s 2d	£ 6 17 5	£ 6 17 5
Improperly placed heere is to be deducted		[blank]

Total Sum of Payments £ 145 17 10

Ansty Farme Expence per Wilson's Account 1706

To Cecill Wilson a yeares wages Mich. 1706	£ 12 0 0	
Ditto 10 months ending July 29th 1707	£ 10 0 0	
Math Butt shepherd to Michaelmas 1706	£ 12 0 0	
Ditto 10 months to July 29th 1707	£ 10 0 0	
Brady plowman a yeare ending 1706	£ 11 0 0	
Ditto ½ year ending Lady Day 1707	£ 5 10 0	
Math Butt's boy a yeare's wages etc	£ 7 10 0	£ 68 0 0
Will Moore for thrashing 22 months	£ 18 18 0	
Witt 21 days threshing etc at 9d	15 9	
His boy plowing 35 days at 5d, 39 days at 3d	£ 1 5 7	
Jo James 3 days thrashing at 10d	2 6	
His boys 22 days plowing at 5d	9 2	
To severall Thrashers of French Grass & Carrying	11 3	
To Moor & Jo Jerrard for Hedging etc	£ 4 9 7	
To Jo Best plowing 16 days at 9d	12 0	
Widdow Watt's boy 64 days at 3d	16 0	
To Edward Moor & Jo Jerrard 35 Acres at 18d	£ 2 12 6	
For Haymaking 1706	£ 1 6 6	
Weeding Corne 1 12 10 Picking stones 9d	£ 1 13 7	
For seves in that yeare	2 8	
Mowing 36 acres of Barly 12 acres Oates at 1s 0d	£ 2 8 0	
Reaping wheat 14¾ acres at 4s 0d	£ 2 19 0	
Reaping 10 days at 2s 0d per day	£ 1 0 0	
Harvest Worke 31 days at 13d	£ 1 13 0	
62 days at 14d	£ 3 12 0	
25 days at 10d	£ 1 3 4	
8 days at 18d	12 0	£ 7 0 4
Making a wheat Rick	2 6	
Washing & shearing 270 sheep at 14d per 20	15 9	
Dinner for the sheep shearers etc	£ 1 0 0	
The collar maker's bill	19 6	
The Smith's bills £ 7 16 8 + £ 3 15 7	£ 11 12 3	

	Rate	Value
Ditto for Iron work to the wagon	£ 6 11 0	
Carpenter's work about the wagon	£ 1 18 8	
For splaying & cutting the piggs	2 0	
For 6 doz of Hurdles at 3s 6d per doz	£ 1 1 0	
For markett expence	9 0	
Wheat bought 48 bushells at 3s 6d	£ 8 8 0	
Oats for the Cart Horses 76 bushells at 1s 3d	£ 4 15 0	
Weather Sheep 60 at 7s od	£ 21 0 0	
68 at 6s od	£ 20 8 0	
Porkers bought at 2s 6d	17 6	£ 55 8 6
Totall Sum of Payments		£ 195 2 7

An Account of Ansty Farme of All Payments relating to it from 1694 including the Stock

Hinds wages payd per annum in toto	£ 583 5 5
The Severall Bills of Harvesting	£ 214 18 0
For Ditching & Hedging in the Farme	£ 95 14 5½
Bills of Haymaking for the 19 Acres	£ 46 9 3
Sheep shearing & their meate & drinke	£ 16 17 11
Sheep bought to stock the ground with	£ 379 16 2
Young Cattle with some Oxen bought	£ 39 16 0
Cart stable smith's Bills	£ 74 8 4
Plow tackle with Horse Geeres etc	£ 79 12 5
Small Hoggs to eat up	£ 10 1 6
Cart Horses bought	£ 55 0 0
Wheat Barley pease & oates to sow	£ 201 2 10
Soyle Bought of Wilson 110 load at 8d	£ 13 13 4
Repaires to the Farme House	£ 4 15 6
Total Expence in 12½ yeares	£ 1805 11 1½

An Account of all the Reall Receipts being Goods Sold of the Farme of Ansty Since 1694

Wheat sold 2287 Bushells	£ 384 4 4
Barley sold 2239½ Bushells	£ 267 18 3
Pease sold 1449¾ Bushells	£ 205 1 9
Sheep & Lambs 635	£ 288 16 4
Wool 8613 pounds	£ 357 11 11
Hoggs sold £ 101 Oxen sold £ 11	£ 112 0 0
Fetches sold 249¾ Bushells	£ 28 13 7½
Severall pecies of Decayed Timber	£ 6 2 6

Clover seed & French Grass seed sold		£ 19 6 6
Wagon Loan & Hyre as per bill		£ 39 10 6
Straw 15 load £ 7 10 0		
Beasts Tack at 4d £ 7 14 0		£ 15 4 0
Wheat sent to Warder 1060 Bushells		
	Bremer 72 Bushells	
	Ansty House 42 Bushells	
	For seed 302 Bushells	
	Total being 1476 Bushells	£ 293 3 6½
Barley to Warder 1150 Bushells		
	Bremer 3192 Bushells	
	Ansty 137 "	
	For seed 801 "	
	The Totall Being 5280 Bushells	£ 621 1 8
Pease to Warder 210 Bushells		
	Bremer 30 "	
	Ansty 71 "	
	To sow 211 "	
	The Totall being 522 "	£ 65 2 1
Oats to	Warder 144 Bushells	
	Bremer 486 "	
	Ansty & Hrses 895 "	
	To Sow 48 "	
	The Totall Being 1573 "	£ 132 16 10
Stock Sold to Farmer Rebeck & Best		
	& others	£ 229 3 9
Total of Real & Valewble Receipts		£ 3072 7 7

Inserted into the volume of Ansty farm accounts are some loose sheets containing additional lists and calculations. These are printed below. Most are neatly written and carefully set out; they provide interesting information about crops, sowing rates, yields and livestock. The quantities of grain are listed in bushells [B] and pounds [p]There are also some rough calculations headed 'Ansty Payments from 1694' and 'Ansty Valuable Provision from 1694'. The latter must be incomplete, since the total given is wildly inaccurate. These accounts are included at the end of this section.

It appears that in 1706 Ansty farm ceased to be run directly by the Arundell estate as a demesne or home farm. In 1707 the horses, oxen, sheep and equipment were sold. Much of the livestock and equipment was purchased by the tenant farmers Best and Rebeck who took over the running of the farm.

The Account of Peter Wilson for Ansty Farme for the year ending Michaelmas 1704

Quality of Grayn	Names of Ground Sowed	Acres Sowed	Bushells Sowed	Bushells Received	
				Bushells	pecks
Wheat	Ground called Heath Furlong	17	55		
	Part of Farme feild	12	38		
	Totals	29	93	359	02
Barly	Part of Farme Feild	20	85		
	Upper Rye Close	5	21		
	Dry Close hole	10	42		
	Totals	35	148	544	02
Oats	Ground called Inner Cholden	14	70	230	00
Pease	Lower Rye Close	6	24	100	02

Quality of Grayne	Bought Bushells B p	Value	Sold Bushells B p	Value	Disposed of B
Wheat	24 00	£4 7 0	176 02	£26 4 1	179 to Warder 4 to Poore
Barly	39 00	£2 18 6	4 02	6 9	252 to Bremer 240 to Fordingbridge 40 to Warder 7 to the Pigs
Oats for the Horses	27	£1 8 2			80 to Bremer 150 for the Plough horses
Pease	28	£4 4 0	100 02	£9 15 7	
	36	£5 8 0			
Fetches	14	£1 8 0			
	12	£1 2 0			
	No	**Value**	**No**		**Value**
Hogg Sheep					
att 7s 6d	61	£22 17 6	5 att 7s 6d		£1 15 0
att 7s od	12	£4 4 0	40 att 8s od		£16 0 0

Piggs					
att 3s 0d	9	£ 1 7 0	9 att 14s 0d		£ 6 6 0
Cow Keeping	1				£ 1 15 0
Wool					
78 weight att £ 1 3 0					£ 89 14 0
				Total	£ 151 16 5

Other Disbursements

	£	s	d
Graine bought as above	54	2	2
Paid for wages in the year	38	0	0
Paid Dayes worke in the year	18	5	8
Paid Haymaking, Harvest and sheep shearing	18	14	3½
Paid Workmen's wages in the year	10	11	5
	139	13	6½

The State of the Proceeding Account

Received as per Proceeding particulars	151	16	5
Disbursed as per Proceeding particulars	139	13	6½
Soe due from the Accompt	12	2	10½

The Account of Peter Wilson for Ansty Farme for the year ending Michaelmas 1705

Quality of Grayn	Names of Ground Sowed	Acres Sowed	Bushells Sowed	Bushells Received
				Bushells pecks
Wheat	Lower Ryclos	6	19	370 already measured out
	Part of Eight Acres	12	38	
	Ramshill part of Farme feild	10	31	120 or there-abouts by computation in Recke and Barne Unthreshed
	Totals	28	88	
Barly	Part of Farme field	12	48	
	Part of Heath furlong	17	69	408 00
	Totals	29	117	
Pease	Ground called Cheldon	18	67	131 00
Fetches	Other part of Eight Acres	8	32	94 03

Quality of Grayne	Bought Bushell	Value	Sold Bushell B p	Value	Disposed of B p
Wheat	48 att 3s 9d	£ 9 0 0	206 02	£ 27 3 8	156 for the Poore att Warder 3 02 To Mrs Jenkins 4 To the Poore at Ansty 264 To Bremer 144 For Seed sowne for 1706
Barly					264 To Bremer 144 For seed sowne for 1706
Oats for seed for 1706	48 att 2s 0d	£ 4 16 0			
for the plough horses	96 att severall prices	£ 7 17 0			
Pease			110	£ 16 12 6	21 for seed sowne for 1706
Fetches			84 03	£ 12 12 3½	10 seed sowne for 1706
Sheep Weather hoggs	69 att 7s 6d			£ 25 17 6	
	40 att 7s 9d			£ 15 10 0	
	10 att 6s 0d			£ 3 0 0	
Piggs	10 att 3s 0d			£ 1 10 0	
	9 att 12s 0d			£ 5 8 0	(1 killed by Bullock)
Cow Keeping	2			£ 3 0 0	
			Total	£ 83 6 3½	

Disbursements

	£	s	d
Graine bought	£ 49	0	6
Payd for Wages	£ 40	0	0
Paid for days worke	£ 17	11	8
Paid Haymaking, harvesting and sheep shearing	£ 21	0	6
Paid workmens Bills	£ 11	7	9
Paid Rates to the Poore and half a rate to the Clerke att 16s 2d for Ansty being forgott to be charg'd in Ansty Bill for Taxes as appears	£ 6	17	5
	£ 145	17	10

The State of the Proceeding Account

Disburst as per Proceeding particulars	£ 145	17	10
Received as per Proceeding particulars	£ 83	6	5½
Soe due to the Accompt on this Account	£ 62	11	4½

Also included in the neatly written accounts is the following list of work done and livestock and equipment sold in 1706 7. It is headed 'A Note of what was Received for the stock when Rebeck and Best took Ansty Farme 1707'.

An Account of work done by his lordshipp's plough and stock sold of from Ansty Farm to Farmer Rebeck and Farmer Best and others in the year 1706

For Carrying Soyle upon the wheat the summer	£ 2	10	0
For fallowing [ploughing] & sowing 18 acres of wheat ground in heath furlong at 7s 6d per acre	£ 6	15	0
For fallowing & sowing of 5 acres of wheat ground in Upper Ryeclose at 5s od per acre	£ 1	5	0
For fallowing 20 acres for Barly in the Ground called Eight acres at 3s 6d per acre	£ 3	10	0
For fallowing 18 acres for Barly in Cort Chorden at 3s 6d per acre	£ 3	3	0
For fallowing 5 acres for Barly in part of Farm feild at 3s 6d per acre		17	0
For ploughing & sowing 6 acres of pease ground at 6s od per acre in Farmfeild	£ 1	16	0
For ploughing onely 11 acres of pease ground at 4s od in part of Farmfeild	£ 2	4	0
For ploughing and sowing 12 acres of oat ground in heath furlong at 6s od per acre	£ 3	12	0
For 7 qtrs 7 bushells of seed wheat at the price of 3s 6d per Bushell	£ 11	1	9
For 220 weather sheep at the price of (In margin: Sold to Farmer Rebeck & Farmer Best)	£ 91	0	0
For Quantity of Fetches in the Tallet [loft] at	£ 1	0	0
For 2 wagons	£ 10	10	0
For 2 dung pots at £ 3 and 3 old ploughs at 7s 6d	£ 5	7	6
For a drag and 5 harrows at £ 1 18s & 2 woodropes with one corn line 10s	£ 2	8	0
For 20 qtrs of dust [chaff] at 2s per qtrs	£ 2	0	0
For Barly Straw being the product of 46 qts and 6 bushells of Barly at 1s 9d	£ 2	6	0
For an Iron Bar for the Fold		5	0

For a Skreen for dressing corn [a screen to separate dust & weed seed from seed corn]		7	0
For 6 pair of Cart harness	£ 2	10	0
For an old furnace	£ 1	10	0
For 10 old Sacks at 1d per Sack		10	0
For Keeping 4 beasts at straw the winter 1706 22 weeks at 4d a peice	£ 1	9	0
For 4 Crebs to Serve beasts in		10	0
For part of an Old Hay rick	£ 4	0	0
For 2 carthorses	£ 14	0	0

Sold to other persons

For 3 carthorses	£ 9	5	0
For 4 plough oxen	£ 16	0	0
For 60 weather hogs at 7s 6d a peice	£ 28	10	0
For a very old wagon	£ 2	0	0
For 3 old plough chains with crooks to them weighing 28 lb at 2d per pound		4	0
	£ 229	3	9
Whereof			
Allowed by abatement to Farmers Rebeck and Best being promised by Mr Chester £ 1 11s 6d And for 11 journeys to Bremore and elsewhere with their teames £ 5 9s 0d	£ 7	0	6
So remains	£ 222	3	3

Three small sheets of rough and obviously incomplete calculations are also included loose at front of volume as follows:

Ansty Payments from 1694

Hinds Wages	£ 583	5	5
Harvest	£ 214	18	0
Ditching	£ 95	14	5½
Haymaking	£ 46	9	3
Sheep shearing	£ 16	17	11
Sheep Bought	£ 379	16	2
Cattle Bought	£ 39	16	0
Stable Bills	£ 74	8	4
Plow Tackle	£ 79	12	5
Hoggs	£ 10	1	6

Coach Horses Bought	£ 55	0	0
Corne to Sow	£ 201	2	10
Soyle Bought	£ 3	13	4
Repaires	£ 4	15	6
	£ 1805	11	1½

Another version of the above

Hinds Wages	£ 642	12	3
Harvesting	£ 195	19	7½
Husbandry	£ 186	6	10
Sheep Shearing	£ 24	5	4
Stock Bought	£ 374	9	2
Cattle Bought	£ 181	0	1
Plow Tackle	£ 201	3	1
Haymaking	£ 44	13	6
Corne to Sow	£ 213	7	10
Oates to Coach Horses	£ 29	13	8
Total Ansty Expences from 1694 to 1706	£ 2093	11	4½

Ansty Valuable provision from 1694

1694	£ 59	11	8
95	£ 48	16	2
96	£ 161	16	0½
97	£ 282	12	9
98	£ 126	15	0
99	£ 88	14	0
1700	£ 75	6	10
01	£ 99	17	0½
02	£ 113	18	3½
03	£ 130	3	2
04	£ 80	19	4½
05	£ 77	9	9½
06	£ 66	7	10
Total	**£ 3010**	**9**	**6**

[recte £ 1412 7 11½]

FROM THE ACCOUNTS OF RICHARD OSGOOD 1677-81

Richard Osgood was the tenant of a farm at Normanton in Wilsford south of Amesbury. The farm belonged to William Trenchard of Cutteridge in North Bradley. Trenchard (c1643-1713) was member of Parliament for Westbury 1679-81, Heytesbury 1690-95 and Westbury 1702. He acquired Cutteridge, Normanton and Durnford through an uncle who was declared a lunatic in 1655. At Cutteridge he rebuilt the house on a grand scale, second only to Longleat within Wiltshire. (E. Cruickshank et al., eds., The House of Commons 1690-1715, *History of Parliament Trust, 2002, 680-1). The precise relationship between Osgood and Trenchard is not clear from these accounts. Osgood charged his landlord for work done on the house, fishpond, pigeon house and for digging a well. He also charged for taxes, implements, work on the water meadows and for provisions bought for the house, possibly for consumption by Trenchard. There are also separate bills from William Hayward for installing new hatches in the water meadows and for repairing and stocking the pigeon house. From the 31 papers of receipts and accounts, many undated and others containing receipts written on scraps of paper, the following have been selected to illustrate Osgood's farming activities and work on the water meadows. These brief accounts provide information about the fishpond, pigeons, turkeys, cultivation of sainfoin and clover, the purchase of a wheeled plough; and contain a reference to burn-baking. Above all, they show the cost of the water meadows, including keeping the weirs and hatches on the river Avon in repair; and making secure foundations in the fast-flowing river with stone from the Chilmark quarries. This was especially difficult, and Osgood was evidently keen to obtain advice on the best methods.*

WSRO 91/1

(a) Farmer Osgood's Account since his Comeing to Normanton

		£	s	d
	The Summe due to Mr Trenchard for three years Rent is	624	0	0
	Whereof he hath desburst as follows:			
	Uppon the first Reckoning Mr Trenchard received in Money & Account	252	2	6
Oct 13 1677	He received by Henry Greenhill	50	0	0

	£	s	d
Jan 16 1677/78			
He received of Mr Barton Jones	50	0	0
He received by Tom Attwood for 18 Quarters of Barley	22	4	0
He received from Mr Blatch	25	18	0
He received at Normanton	36	0	0
In Money	10	0	0
For 17 months Pay	11	8	3
For Mending of Wilsford Bridge		4	4
Pd Chimney Money [i.e. hearth tax] for One Yeare		10	0
For the Hake for the fishpond		13	6
Pd Coles for Mending the Tumbling Bay & putting in the Hake		6	0
Pd for Trophee Money [rate levied for the local militia]		5	0
Pd for Chimney Money		10	0
For 2 Locks to the Inside Doores		5	0
For Carriage of the Withey to the fishpond		10	0
Pd Mr Gauntlet		1	0
Pd for the Wood & Carriage to the Snt Foine [sainfoin]	2	0	0
Pd for Picking the Stones in the Snt Foine	2	0	0
Pd Philip Dawkins	7	4	0
Pd for Piles and Hurdles & Worke at the Moore Hatches		15	0
Pd John Bedford for Nineteen Dayes Worke	1	0	0
Pd Mr Gauntlet & Gentleman Fins [fines]		3	0
Pd Gaole Money		6	8
Pd for Digging the Well	5	0	0
Pd for Six Kine	18	0	0
Pd for One quarter of Malt	1	4	0
Pd for Hay for the Horses and a Bill of 4s	1	0	0
In a Bill for things Spent in the House	2	3	3
Pd for 3 Bed Matts [mattress]		7	6
	500	1	0

(b) William Trenchard Esq his Bill 1680, May 10th

	s	d
For macking a new sheep brige and putting in 2 braces in the haches	9	4
For putting in a new pear of haches hath Coust to the rapyerer [repairer]	10	8
For nailes to do it 3s, and for saing [sawing] it out 6 shilen [6s], in all	9	0
Payed to William Fine for helping do the haches 5 dayes work	6	8
Payed to John Saning for Jentel man fine	2	0
Payed to William Smart for 65 dousen of seter [hedging plants]	5	0
For one dayes work to form it up	5	0
Payed for seting the 65 dousen	6	6
Payed to Jorge Pyel for 30 dosen of seter and 14 boundel		

	£	s	d
[bundles] of Withy	2	4	0
Payed John Sanig for trofel [i.e. trophy money] mony		8	2
Payed Henery Good's Boy the 3 months pay	1	1	0
	18	7	4

(c) A bill for Sqier Trencher

	£	s	d
For 61 fote of Oacking timber at 40s a tone	3	1	0
For carpenders worke to maeke the troncks and poting in troncks in	2	19	0
Paide to the saiers [sawyers] for saeing of all the timber	1	14	0
Paid to the smethe for all sorts of nailes		10	0
Paid to the labrers for doing of all the worke to bring the water to the med [mead]	3	6	0
For the repaier of the hacches to Squier Trencher part is		15	0
Mr Haperd hayth paid for his part for the repaier of the hacches all rede		15	0
Soe of this bill I have reserved of farmer Osgood in part	6	17	6
So thare remaines due upon this bill	5	8	6

(d) William Hayward's Account to William Trenchard Esqr concerninge Normanton in October 1680

24 October 1680

	£	s	d
Repairing the greate wyre and wyre houses & fish pond hatches viz. Imprimis, Wm Viney 18 days @1s 6d per diem	1	7	0
Paid Thomas Alderidge 10 days		10	0
Paid Jno Bedford 10 days		15	0
Pd Robert Deere & Isaac 4 days and the boy 3 days		15	0
Pd Wm Viney for 35 Piles which will serve for the Moore Wyre		7	4
Pd Farmer Osgood one Dozen hurdles		3	0
Pd Robert Deere for 140 foote of Plancke & Square Oake at 3d per foote	1	15	0
Pd Nailes about the Wyre from Longs the Smith		1	0
Pd Robert Deere for 4 hatch posts	1	10	0
Pd Geo. Piles for his Oake Sull [plough] at 40d per tun		5	0
Pd Viney, Bedford & Tho Alderidge up to the Arme Pitts in Water pullinge up the bay ½ a day		2	6
Pd Jno Dickman & his son sawinge the hatch posts		1	6
Pd Jno Dickman & his son 5 days for sawing out of Elme for the wyre under water, and slittinge other stuff for uses		11	8
Summe	8	6	4

(e) Pigeon House account viz.

	£	s	d
Paid Wm Viney & Jno Dickman 6 days each of them cuttinge downe and the sawinge out of Elme about the pigeon house at 14d per diem	1	4	0
Pd Robert Deere 2 dayes, Isaac 3 dayes & the boy one day		7	4
Pd Isaac Deere one day about the barne		1	4
Pd Jno Munday 5 doz Pigeons at 2d per dozen beinge chosen out of 15 or 16 dozen			10
Pd a Messenger to procure the pigeons			4
	1	13	0

(f) Concerninge the Moore Hatches viz

	£	s	d
Pd my expenses one night at the Choppinge Knife at Amsbury with my farmer Cozen and my Cozen Hayward discoursing about the Stone Wyre and agreeing upon the same, and how to gett out the old wyre		2	9
Pd my Expenses once more to Amsbury to meete the partyes afforesaid & to meete the quarre man when we drew a plott of the Wyre & tooke order for the stone		2	0
Pd one halfe towards a Messenger to send to the quarreman		1	0
Pd Mrs Nalder for ½ a dozen of Turkeyes		10	0
Pd my Expenses once more havinge made 2 or 3 journeys to Amsbury about partinge or securinge the staff of the old Wyre which lay soe confusedly about the ground		1	0
		16	9
Pd a messenger to send the maid from Sr Richards			3
Pd given the Carter to be careful of the turkeyes			6
			9
Wyre account	8	6	4
Pigeon house account	1	13	0
Total Summe	10	16	10

(g) Account for blacksmith's work on ploughs etc. 1681

	s	d
Wm Trenchard Esquire his Bill		
29 September		
For a print for Sheepe [for marking]	2	6
13 October		
For a Drowning Spade	3	6
For fasting horse shoes		2

	£	s	d
17 October			
For ½ C of board nails			5
For a share & coulter & dole chaine and plow chaine, 2 Tayle Ires, 2 Rings for the plow wheels & spindle & crook for the weldrons way	1	8	0
For 2 Tacks & nails & rench & nails for the plow		2	2
For 2 plates & Rings behind on the plow			6
For 2 boxes & 2 stock bonds for the smale plow wheele & duble key for the spindle		1	0
For 2 plates and nails to hold the spindles in the weldrons			4
For a old Line pinne to hold the dole chaine to the plow			1
For 1 share			4
For 11 ferralls & sprigs to the spokes of the wheels			11
	1	19	11

2 December 1681

Recd in full of this bill £1 –19 –0 of Edward King for the use of Wm Trenchard Esq, I say Received by me John Martin

(h) Hatches

		£	s	d
	Moore Hatches			
1st	Pd for Piles & Hurdles & worke		15	0
	Pd John Bedford	4	0	0
	Pd the Joiner for Mending the Hatches		2	6
	3 day Worke for 3 Men about the Hatches		11	6
2nd	Osgood's Bill	2	18	4
	Pd the Sawyer		10	0
	The Bill for repairing the Hatches	11	14	6
3rd	Pd to Carpenters & Mason at the Wire		10	8
	Pd Wm Dawkins at times	12	8	6
	Carrying Timber to the Trunk		10	0
	Pd Old Dawkins	1	0	0
	-? Hatches	1	15	8
	Mr Hayward's Bill	10	16	0
		45	0	0
		[recte £ 47	12	8]

(i) Undated Account

		£	s	d
1st	17 Monthes Pay to the King	11	8	3
2nd	The King's Pay	2	11	0
3rd	Six Monthes Pay	7	2	0
	For the Tax	2	1	0
	More	2	1	0

		£	s	d
1st	Chimney Money [i.e. Hearth Tax]		10	0
	Chimney Money		10	0
	Chimney Money		5	0
	More		5	0
2nd	More		5	0
3rd	More		5	0
	More		10	0
	More		5	0
1st	Wood Carraige to the Snt Foine	2	0	0
	Picking of Stones in the Snt Foine	2	0	0
	Pd for digging a Well	5	0	0
	Snt Foine seed	2	4	0
	Left to pay the Church & Poore by Mr C		10	0
	Hedging the Fish Pond & the Snt Foine	2	4	6
2nd	Paid to the King's Armes in the Church		10	0
	* Pd the Carpenters & Masons at the Wire		10	0
3rd	For Wood & Plough Boot [manorial right to timber]	25	0	0
	Pd to the Tithing Man		6	0
	Pd Carpenters and Smithes Bill	4	0	0
·	Hop Clover Sow'd in the Burnt Beak [burn-bake]	1	1	0
	Sowing the Wheat Crop	9	0	0
	For the Fold & the Barre	1	0	0
	For Carrying up to the Moore Timber Piles and Hurdles		15	0
	4 Douzen of Hurdles		14	0
	3 Load of Stones from Chilmark	1	15	0
	3 Load of Wood etc	5	0	0
	Forgot the King's Pay [i.e. tax]	2	1	0
	Wm Viney for takeing up the Moore Hatches		10	0
	10 Load of Stones	6	0	0
	Carrying of Cleats (?)		12	0

*crossed out

FROM THE ACCOUNT BOOK OF NICHOLAS ELLIOTT 1685-86

Several members of the Elliott family were clothiers in Salisbury. They also possessed properties in the city and estates in the surrounding area, including land at Winterbourne Gunner, Winterbourne Earls, Stratford-sub-Castle and Laverstock. The detailed account book kept by Nicholas Elliott covers the years 1663 to 1726 and contains much on his dealings in cloth, as well as records of rents, tenancies, credits, debts and his farming activities. There are numerous cross-references to other account books which have not survived. The volume contains a long description of a legal suit in which he was involved in London in 1658 concerning cloth sales to merchants in Morlaix. Elliott's accounts show his concern for the sheep flock which was folded on his arable land, the costs of shepherding, the frequent purchases and sales of sheep at the fairs held at Amesbury, Stockbridge and Weyhill. There are also references to water meadows, the cultivation of wheat, barley, oats, vetches and clover and to the keeping of cows and pigs.

The following accounts refer to the farming on his lands at Swainsfield and Stratford which he had inherited in 1675.

WSRO 1162/3

1685 Account of Sheepe is Dr [debtor] viz.

		£	s	d
October 6				
	Unto cash Roger Nichols for 30 sheepe bought of him to put into Stratford flock as by my old cash book in folio 56 appears & is	7	17	0
May -				
	Unto ditto pd for 40 more hoggs at Amesbury faire as by as by my said book folio 65 cost	9	8	6
	Unto ditto bringing them to Swainsfields			6
8	Unto ditto given another man about them			6
	Unto ditto paid for 20 hoggs more to put into Swainsfields as by said book 65	6	5	0
11	Unto Ditto paid for a score of couples I say 15 couples Gab. Hutfield bought for mee att Stockbridge faire is 30 in number cost as by said book 65	6	9	0
15	Unto Ditto charges at tith of my sheepe in said folio		9	10

		£	s	d
			3	0
25	Unto Ditto paid for a score more ewes and Lambes is 40 as by my said Cash book folio 66 cost mee	7	17	6
June				
4	Unto Ditto sundry charges in said folio sherringe etc	1	0	9½
	Unto Ditto given Baish omitted October 85 as per Cash 57			6
December				
7	Unto Ditto paid the widow Elliott for hurdles 59		1	2
28	Unto Ditto paid the Shepherd his Xmas quarters wages		4	2
1686				
April				
2	Unto Ditto paid Stratford boy looking to my ewes & lambs		1	6
10	Unto Ditto paid Baish his Xmas ¼ given his sonn		4	6
	Unto the Boy another weeks looking to the Ewes etc		1	6
12	Unto Ditto a double Trophy rate to Stratford			11
July				
5	To Baish paid him by 3 articles in said cash folio 67		6	2
13	To Ditto paid my shepherd's Mother 3 weeks pay		5	6
August				
	To Ditto paid ditto his 3 weeks pay keeping		5	6
22	To Ditto paid ditto his 3 weekes wages folio 70		5	6
October				
5	To Ditto paid Gab. Hutfield for 26 Lambs hee bought for me, I had then about mee but	4	0	0
	To Ditto on account with him paid him the rest for them	1	0	8
	To Ditto in 3 articles in 72 more charges amounting to		16	0
26	To Ditto paid the shepherd 3 weeks wages		5	6
30	To Ditto the cost of 3 cowes put to this account	8	0	0
November				
15	To Ditto in 2 articles in folio 75		6	0
	To the worth of hay furnished as by the account 76	3	2	6
December				
6	To Cash in 3 articles as in folio 77		6	2
20	To Ditto in 2 articles as in folio 78		8	1
28	To Ditto his 3 weeks pay & 6d given to his father as in 79		6	0

There follows at the bottom of the page several unspecified payments for 1687. The next page returns to recording payments for 1686

1686				
June				
7	Per cash received of Mr Sutton for the wool as in folio 66	5	10	6
	Paid the trophy rate per Contra ought not to be charged to this account debit but to Stratford and Swainsfield account is			11

		£ s d
September		
28	Per Cash received for 40 Ewes sold by G H at Wayhill faire	11 15 0
November		
17	Per Gabriel Hutfield on account for 20 Chilver 2 teeth [sheep]	6 5 0
26	For cash received for a calfe sold prise	8 0
	For a pigg kill'd worth more than when bought atte least	10 0
May		
14	For 2 cows sold Roger Nicholls	7 6 0
	Soe that my sheepe being now in Stratford flock 30 with 13 lambs increased and 95 att Swainsfield to make good this account currant on the next yeare is	31 15 5
		34 5 2½
		66 0 7½

Now that I may make out my Loss or gaines on the account of Swainsfields and Stratford suppose must value these sheepe now remaining because if sold of that is stock on them for their feeding and increasing being still to helpe soe that what they are more worth than will balance this account is and ought to be to the Credit of that account which as nearest as cann judge is viz 30 with 18 lambs in Stratford flock worth according as they sold last Amsbury Faire at the least 15 0 0

The worst score att Swainsfields	6 10 0
The next worst score worth	7 0 0
The 55 Best worth	22 0 0
	50 10 0
The balance on this account you see is	34 5 0
Price to be carried to the Credit said account	16 4 10
Besides I ought to credit this account of sheepe for the wooll sold Baish the shepherd and Mr Sutton of Sarum clothier	5 19 3

[*Note at bottom of page evidently written later notes –'Mistake & ought to goe to the next yeares account'*]

1685

Swainsfields & Stratford the L[ordship] in my Lands Dr

June		
19	Pd cash pd RN for hatches drowneing mill mead	7 6

		£	s	d
August				
22	Unto ditto pd 2 bus[hells] wheate sowne as in folio 55		8	6
September				
12	Unto ditto given in said folio att twise		1	0
15	Unto ditto pd 3 qtrs wheate sowne in the 6 akers said folio	5	0	0
17	Unto ditto to the shepherd to drive the ground			6
October				
5	Unto ditto pd a quarter wheate more sown	1	13	0
6	Unto ditto pd for 3 bus[hells] Vetches sowne [in] Baish [?] furlong		17	3
8	Unto ditto pd Snook for dung & carriage to the 6 akers	4	0	0
December				
1	Unto Ditto pd Baish a rate for the poore as by Cash 59		1	0
5	Unto ditto pd in full of Snooks note dung pd cash		11	0
January				
9	Unto ditto pd hedging at Swainsfields	2	4	6
February				
20	Unto ditto pd for barley to sow as by Cash	7	7	0
24	Unto ditto pd Nichols his boy beginning of sowing			6
27	Unto ditto pd a poore rate for Laverstock		2	7½
March				
2	Unto ditto pd for Oates sowen this yeare	2	8	0
6	Unto ditto for hedging at Stratford		2	6
	Unto Ditto for Nichols his Littel maid for my Lambes			6
12	Unto Ditto pd 6 quarters Oates more sowen	4	16	0
16	Unto ditto pd 14 bushells Clover sowne att severall fields	2	16	0
	Unto ditto given Nichols his boy			6

1686

		£	s	d
March				
29	Unto ditto for Freemantle for Swainsfields rates		4	3½
April				
12	Unto ditto pd a double trophy rate for Stratford			11
20	Unto ditto pd 3 quarters of barley more sowne	3	13	6
May				
1	Unto ditto pd Mr Phillips rate to Stratford poore		1	6
15	Unto ditto pd another rate to the miller		1	5
June				
11	Unto ditto pd cutting the home ground		4	0
17	Pd my shepherd 3 weekes pay		5	6
24	Pd R Nichols in part his plowing and sowing	5	0	0
	Unto Roger Nichols his account plowing and sowing etc of my this yeare's crop because I say pd him the £5 article above must abate this out of his whole note and then must debit this account	14	0	5

		£	s	d
July				
7	Unto ditto Makeing my hay att Blackwel Mead		4	6
13	Unto ditto Pd moweing said meade		3	6
	Unto dittoMoweing Mill meade		4	0
15	Unto ditto To a Labourer etc about said hay		2	6
19	Unto ditto in 5 articles sundry things		6	3
31	Unto ditto Charges in 5 severalls		15	3
August				
22	Unto ditto reapers in 9 articles	4	14	2
September				
9	Unto ditto Charges in 7 articles	1	9	9½
24	Unto ditto for a shovele in the barne		2	3
29	Unto ditto to a yeare's rent [—?] to debit the account what it did usually yeald mee per Annum, the yeare being now up	30	0	0
October				
17	To Gabriell Hutfield accompting with him this day allowed him for vallowing [ploughing] and carrieing corne for mee belonging to this yeare's account	1	4	10
	To ditto for Row hedging	2	1	8
	To ditto in two articles paid Nichols		12	2
	To ditto in 3 articles threshing	1	8	6
	To ditto in 2 articles	2	0	6
November				
12	To ditto in 3 articles	1	2	6
26	To ditto in 5 articles	1	3	6
December				
6	To ditto in 2 articles		16	6
20	To ditto	4	4	11½
March				
3	To ditto in two articles		11	8
		109	17	5

Per Contra Credit 1686

		£	s	d
October				
6	17 bushells sowen this yeare in the hither craft of Swainsfields suppose about 4½ akers perhaps a little more or less at the price wheate then sold att for seed 4-0 per bushell is	3	8	0
	Per bushells vetches sowen more in said craft suppose 3 akers or thereabouts att 4-0 is		7	0
	Per 12 bushells wheate sowen more in the 3 halves in the North field of Stratford this season as by a note of the particulars on the folio of this on the foregoing articles at said rate is	2	8	0

		£	s	d
	Per 2 bushells more to house att said rate is		8	0
	Per 2 bushells more since to house att said rate is		8	0
15	Per wheate sowen more in Stratfield south field in 3 akers & ½ is 10 bushells & ½ at said rate makes	2	2	0
	Per bushells sowen vetches att Swainsfields which I charge Att 4-0 and 3½ bushells more sowne in the two halves by Hangman's Bushes in Stratford Field makes in all of vetches sowen 15 bushells att said rate is	2	4	0
	Per ½ bushell left which Gabriel Hutfield which because he bought for 3 0 per bushell I charge this account but		1	9
30	A bushell of wheate more to house att		3	8
November				
17	Two potts of Dust [cartloads of chaff] to Gabriell Hutfield on account att		5	0
	A quarter of wheate more winnowed as by my almanake	1	10	8
	On account for the Lease of Swainsfields of Hutfield	1	10	0
December				
19	Per cash received for 5 quarters Barley of Mr Hillery att 17-6	4	0	6
January				
13	Per ditto and left in said hands for mault 7 quarters and ½ bushell sold rate 30-0	6	10	2
	Per ditto per hay furnished in this month and before to Swainsfields and Stratford fold suppose 2½ tonns which I sett att 25-0 per tonn is	3	2	6
21	Per 3 quarters of oates as yett marled sold Madam Earle for	1	15	0
25	Per 1 quarter and 1 bushell wheate sold to the thresher the [blank] House is	1	12	0
March				
15	Per cash received for a quarter of oates		11	0
30	Ditto received of Sutton for 14 bushells more		19	0
		33	6	3
	Per sheepe account the rest of my hay growne thereon furnished both to Swainsfield and Stratford Flocke is in my particular book in the months of January and February att twise to the value of	2	10	0
	Per a pigg, 2 bushells of barley had extraordinary from this account to fatt it and then what the said pig was worth more than when I bought it is 14-0 at Least and 2 bushells of barley is 4-4 in all		18	4½
	Per 3 quarters & a bushell of oates sowen at Swainsfields and Stratford this yeare which would now yealde 15-0 per quarter which this account ought to have credit for £2-7-9 & 1 bushell to Jack's horse which with taileinges [poor quality corn] about 3 bushells both worth 5-0 is in all	2	7	9

		£	s	d
	Per 5 quarters Barley I say per 10 quarters 3 bushells sowne in all this yeare att Swainsfields and Stratford which would yeald in the markett att the Common price 22s 6d per quarter and amounts to	11	15	8
	Per the taileing in all doe beleeve had I not mill'd it would have made a good quarter more tollerable barly with which the worst taileinge together with my piggs Jack's nagg and his pigeons & poultry was worth		12	2
	Per 5 quarters sold R Nichols at 12s 6d per quarter	3	2	6
May				
2	Per rent and milk of Burbaige & a pigg sold him	1	3	0
June				
4	Per 12 bushells of oates sold	1	1	0
6	Ditto Barly sold and put into Mr Hillary	3	12	0
13	Ditto for 2 bushells oates sold the gardner at Stratford		3	6
		64	19	5½

THE MANAGEMENT OF LOOSEHANGER PARK, DOWNTON 1662-83

Loosehanger Park on the high ground some 2½ miles south east of Downton was part of the estate leased from the bishop of Winchester by Sir Joseph Ashe in 1662. Details concerning Sir Joseph Ashe, his lease of the manor of Downton, his estates at Twickenham and in Yorkshire, and the career of his steward, John Snow, will be found in the introductions to the sections on manorial stewards and water meadows in this volume. The Park was on the edge of the New Forest, and consisted of a wooded park, enclosed by a fence, covering more than 300 acres. Within the park was a Lodge originally intended for a keeper. John Snow moved into the Lodge with his family in 1662 and in addition to all his other duties, he immediately began to use all the resources of the Park to produce a profit for his employer. The Park, together with the Lodge and its gardens, had evidently been greatly neglected, and Snow's first task was to make the Lodge habitable and to restore the garden and orchard. His account book records expenditure on repairing windows, doors and floors, installing a new oven and attention to walls, roof, drainage and paths. The garden had clearly become overgrown and men were paid for cutting brambles and clearing the ground. Fruit trees were purchased from 'a gardener of Westbury' including peach, plum, pear and 'Apricocke'. There are also references to 'wall trees' which were presumably espaliers, to 'pruninge of the Vine and for setinge of 3 apltrees and for making and sitinge of one Quadlinge [Codling] hedge, two dayes att 14d per day – 2s 4d'. A large area of the garden was taken up with the cultivation of 2000 hop plants.

In the Park itself John Snow's accounts record an energetic programme of work on repairing the fence and replacing the pales, cutting ferns and brambles, killing moles and scattering molehills, levelling ant hills or 'emmett heaps', and planting many hundreds of young trees. This expenditure was matched by an equally energetic campaign to exploit all the sources of income which the Park could provide. One convenient way of doing this was to let the grazing in the Park to neighbouring farmers. The accounts show that large numbers of cows and heifers were allowed to graze in the Park for 4d or 6d per week, while 18d per week was charged for horses. Even more profitable were the numerous pigs which were allowed in to the Park during the autumn to feed on acorns and beech mast. Owners were charged from 6d to 1s 0d per week for each pig, although as much as 1s 6d per week was demanded for some 'great pigges'. It is a remarkable tribute to the rich nutrition provided for the pigs that owners were prepared to pay so much in order to fatten their pigs before the onset of winter. The seventeenth-century author, Thomas Fuller, commented upon this important feature of farming in the New Forest, and described how the pigs belonging to those with common rights 'feed in the Forest on plenty of acorns — which going out lean, return home fat, without either care or cost to their owners' [T. Fuller, Worthies of England, *1952 edn., 201] For Downton farmers who did not enjoy rights of common, the benefits of the autumnal abundance of the Forest did not come without considerable cost. The charges made for pigs during autumn 1669 are listed below; most pigs appear to have stayed for 1 week.*

The other major source of income from Loosehanger Park was from timber sales, faggots of underwood sold for firing, oak bark used in the tanning of leather, and the manufacture and sale of charcoal or 'cole'. All these profitable resources were fully exploited by John Snow on behalf of his employer. There are numerous references in his accounts to charcoal sales, and he evidently developed a lucrative trade in several specialised timber products such as barrel staves, the bottoms and sides for wooden buckets, wheel spokes and the shaped parts for carts and wagons. Further details of timber products and sales from the Park can be found in PRO E134/18 Charles II/ Trinity 9 and PRO E134/18 Charles II/ Michaelmas 6.

The other way in which John Snow exploited the resources of Loosehanger Park was by converting part of it to arable. This was not done until some years after his arrival, and the following accounts for 1678 and 1683 show the expenses involved. Interesting features of these accounts include evidence of the laborious task of clearing the ground, grubbing up tree stumps and roots or 'mores', ploughing or 'earing' and cultivation or 'breaking'. An account of 'Land Inclosed in Loosehanger Park' dated 28 October 1681 lists 37 acres already under cultivation. [WSRO 490/1063]. Part of the land was evidently burn-baked and the subsequent ploughing was thus much cheaper. Large quantities of chalk and charcoal dust were used to sweeten this ancient forest soil, and the recently-introduced crops of sainfoin ('sankefoyle'), broad clover and hop clover were used as 'break crops' to help in destroying soil pests before cereals were sown. It is notable that John Snow evidently thought it worth paying as much as 3s 6d a bushel for sainfoin seed; no doubt the crop could be sold for fodder to neighbouring farmers.

At the end of this section John Snow appears to seize the opportunity provided by the death of Sir Joseph Ashe in 1686, to present to Sir Joseph's widow, Lady Mary Ashe, a list of his expenses, including numerous visits to the Ashe estates in Yorkshire, going back over several years.

WSRO 1946/Box 12 (10)

Expenses in making the garden, orchard and hop-yard at Loosehanger 1670

	£	s	d
July the 29th			
More disbursted by John Snow which he is to be allowed in tim to come as aforesaid about Emprovinge the Parke in the yeare 1670			
July the 29th			
Paid Robert Moore and John Bownd for Cutinge of fearne and Brambles in the out sides of the Brakes twice that yeare to save the younge trees	2	5	0
January the 31st			
Paid Thomas Tutt senior and Tho. Tutt junior for filling of the pot cart with Cole [charcoal] doust carryed out out of the parke into the garden to Millow [mellow] the ground for the trees 5 dayes att 10d per day		8	4
Paid Richard Hill for helpinge 4 dayes		4	0
Paid John Chalke for the Lent of his horse for too helpe carry the Cole doust for five dayes		5	0
March the 8th			
Paid William Chalke for diginge and Grubinge up of all the Mores [roots] in the Lower side of the garden three dayes		4	0
Paid John Thomas for helpinge 4 dayes		2	0
Paid John Hooker for 9 Apltrees to sett in the garden		6	9
Paid William Davis for 10 Apltrees att 8d a peece		6	8
Paid Thomas Tutt for 3 Apltrees and one Peartree		2	8
Paid Jolliff Hill for helpinge sett the aforesaid Apltrees and for Levellinge of the two plotts of Ground in Lower Sid of the Garden for plantinge of hops there 13 days at 16d per day		17	4
Paid him for 13 dayes for his son Jolliff Hill att 8d per day		8	8
Paid him for his son Roger for 13 dayes att 4d per day		4	4
Paid James Gandy and his Mare for Carryinge in of Swile [dung] to set the Apltrees 6 dayes a peece		9	0
Aprill the first and before Paid Augustin Hollaway for killinge of Want [moles] and Spurlinge [spreading] hills for one whole yeare ending att Lady Day 1671	2	5	0
	8	13	9

For the carridge of Wood for to make a dead hedg about the garden and 28 Lugs more of dead hedge about the East sid of the ground next the younge wood and 23 Lugs ofdead hedge made between the howse and the young wood for to Save the plants. For carridge of the wood too the above said places 6 dayes and for carridg of Bushes to amend the pales that yeare 4 dayes, my

	£	s	d
Mare and Man as appears in the Accompt booke in folio 13-14	1	0	0
	9	13	9
More disbursted as aforsaid in the yeare 1671			
July the 31st			
Paid John Bownd for Cuttinge of the fearne and Brambles in out sid of the Brakes twice	2	0	0
October 21st			
Paid Jolliff Hill that he payd the Widow Noats of Rockbourne Brickkills for Twelve Apltrees and two Cheritrees at 9d a peece		9	0
Paid Jolliff Hill for fetchinge them one daye		1	4
Paid him for helpinge Sett them in the places of those Apltrees that was dead for two dayes		2	0
Paid William Musell for fetchinge of Swile and Layinge it about them and helpinge too dayes		2	0
Aprill the 10th 1672			
Paid Augustine Hollaway for killing of Wants and Spurlinge of the hills for one yeare endinge att Lady Day 1672	2	0	0
	4	5	0
More disbursted as aforesaid in the yeare 1672			
July the 18th			
Paid Thomas [Tutt] senior and Thomas Tutt junior for cutinge the fearne twice	2	0	0
March the 12th			
Paid Roger Jones and Roger Pitts and theire partners for Sinkinge of one Banke in the South and West side of the plott of ground designed too make a hopgarden befor it was taken in, being in length 9 Lugs and in breadth one Lug and in depth one foot 6 Inches at 2s 0d per Lug		18	0
Paid them for Makinge a ditch of 12 Lugs in Length 2d per Lug		2	0
Paid Jolliff Hill senior for Setinge out all the hophills and makinge of them and plantinge 4 dayes		5	4
Paid him for his son Jolliff 4 dayes 2s 8d			
Paid him for two thousand of hop plants 2s 6d		5	2
Paid John Rooke for Carridge of Dung to put about the Apltrees and Cole doust and greate [?ashes] to helpe make up the hophills for 3 dayes at 3s 0d per day		9	0
Paid John Bownd for helpinge fill the pot cart and other worke for six dayes		6	0
Paid John Rooke for Carridge of Dunge to put about Apltrees and peartrees brought from Jolliff's orchard att Downton and other apltrees there for 3 dayes at 3s 0d			

	£	s	d
per day		9	0
Paid John Rooke for carridge of Gravell with his plow and layinge of it in the hole before the Backside gate and in the Backside and about the palls for 6 dayes at 3s 0d per day		18	0
Paid John Bownd for helpinge fill the pot cart for six dayes		6	0
Aprill the 5th			
Paid Augustin Hollaway for killinge of the wants and spurlinge of the hills for one whole yeare ending at Lady Day 1673	1	15	0
	7	13	6

An accompt of the Extraordinary Charges & Disburstments that John Snow have been att in Earinge and Breakinge up over and besides the grubinge of the Severall plotts and parcells of Land taken in of Loosehanger parke in the severall years about the Breakinge and plowinge of it att cost att a fast cost for the doinge of it

	£	s	d
In the yeare 1678 for ploughinge and breakinge up of one Acre and Tenn Luggs of ground tooke in att the west end of the Baren [barn] called the uper Cloose Cost me the Breakinge it up besides the Swile [dung] Carryed in to the said ground	1	0	0
In the year 1678 for plowinge and breakinge up Two Acres below the garden next the younge wood cost mee besides the Swill Carryed into the said ground at 20s per Acre the plowinge and Breakinge of it up	2	0	0
In the yeare 1679 for plowinge and Breakinge up the two Acres tooke in at the west side of the parke Called Stew plot hole cost 10s per Acre	1	0	0
In the yeare 1679 and in the yeare 1680 for plowinge and Breakinge up one ground tucke in about the Midel of the parke containinge nine Acres att 20s per Acre	9	0	0
In the yeare 1679 and 1681 for plowinge and Breakinge up of Seaven Acres one ½ and 20 Lugs of ground tucke in at the west end of the Burchen Copse cost me 20s per Acre	7	12	6
In the yeare 1679 and in the yeare 1680 for the plowinge and Breakinge up of one ground Called Walton's Close below the younge wood which cost me but 10s per Acre because it was burn beaked the said ground beinge six Acres one ½ and 20 Lugs	3	6	0
In the yeare 1681 for plowinge and Breakinge up of one ground tucke in at the East side of the parke next Blacke Lane beinge Two Acres one ½ att 20s per Acre	2	10	0
	26	13	6

Was payed John Chalke for Grubinge and Clensinge of the Mores

	£	s	d
and Roots in one ground of meadow or pasture at the East Corner of the parke at Black Lane and besides the mores grubed up in Clensinge it had in money		15	0
Pd Jolliffe Hill and his partners for diginge of the plot of ground in the South sid of the well beinge 44 Lugs at the first Breakinge it up where the younge orchard is now planted		10	0
	27	13	6

More Disbursted as Aforesaid in the Improvement of the parke in the yeare 1683 and not placed to the Accompt of Sir Joseph Ashe Barronett in the yeare 1683

	£	s	d
August 4th			
Paid Thomas Tutt for Cutting the fearnes 16 0		16	0
April 1683			
paid Thomas Tutt for Cutting of the fearnes and bramble in the parke		16	0
November the first			
Paid Richard Chalke for Killinge of the wants and spurlinge [spreading] of the hills for one halfe yeare to Michaelmas 1683		8	0
November the 14, 15, 16, 17, 18, 19, 20, 21, 22, 23, 24, 26, 28, 29, 30 December the first			
Carryed 30 loads of Chalke from Salt Lane in to the uper part of the Burchen Copes Broken up for 8 oxen and one horse and Rich Prince and Will Gost for goinge with them at 3s per load	4	10	0
December the 31st			
fetched by the plow 3 Loads att 2s 6d per Load for Carridge		7	6
Paid John Wiltt for diginge of the said 33 loads of Chalke and throwinge it out of the Pitt at 3d per Load		8	3
Paid John Pearry for Spurlinge of the said 33 loads of Chalke att 1d ½ per load		4	0
February the 6 1683			
Paid John Wiltt for diginge of 2 Loads moore of Chalke and helpinge fill it at 3d per Load		6	6
3-23 January			
10 days at fetched by my plow 6 Loads of chalke at 2s 6d per Load	3	5	0
Paid James Gandy for Spurlinge of it at 1d per Load		3	3
March the 16th			
Paid Ralph Mounteray for 7 bushells of Sankefoyle [sainfoin] seed att 3s 6d a Bushell and 6d for carridge of it which was Sowen in the Parke	1	5	0
Paid Mr Longe for 54 pounds of Broad Clover att 6½d a pound	1	9	3
Paid James Saunders for 8 bushells of Hop Clover at 3s 4d a			

	£	s	d
Bushell	1	6	8
	13	5	5

Disbursted about the Improvement of the Parke as it apears by this book in folios

		£	s	d
Layd out in the year	1665	5	5	0
	1666	9	10	2
	1667	4	6	0
	1668	7	19	0
	1669	6	4	6
	1670	9	13	9
	1671	4	15	0
	1672	7	13	6
	1673	7	0	2
	1674	3	6	0
	1675	3	8	0
	1676	5	2	4
	1677	7	6	0
	1678	1	1	10
	1679	16	14	6
	1680	4	3	0
	1681	1	12	4
About plowinge and Breakinge up of the ground about the parke In the year 1678 to 81		27	13	6
Layd out about Chalkinge sum part of the ground in the parke In the yeare 1682 and 1683. Layd out more for grass seed sowed in the parke in 1685 and 1686		13	5	5
		151	0	0

Then there ought in all Reson to be Thought fitt to allow Snow for his care in Saving the 8 acres or thereabouts of Burchen copes in the north sid of the parke that was Layd up by Snow November 20 1667, beinge the yeare that is Lost to Snow he being granted all the Earbige without any Exception Besides to consider what Snow have Lost by his Industry in Suckeringe the Tenn Thousand Oakes and Ashes and other Small Trees in the Parke and keepinge the Cattell from that have been a great hindrance too Snow in his Earbige which he ought to have as his promise was to have it without any preservinge of Trees by feedinge of the parke att any time in the yeare the Savinge of the Young Trees hath been a great hindrance to the pasture and by that a Lost too Snow.

An Accompt of the major part of the particulars of the journeys Sir Joseph Ash Barronett required and desired John Snow to Rid[e] with him and without him in his business and Imploy which was no parte of Snow's bargain [without] or runnent [?rent] to do and was forced to hire severall men at the severall absents to Looke to the parke and others Sir Joseph Ashe's Concernes but to be payd for his own time in it and horse as the said Snow was paid of other men for his time and Judgement in Imploy for so much of his time as he was Required and desired out of his Willsheer and was So Imployed by Sir Joseph in any of the following particulars from August 1667 to January 1679.

	Weeks	Days
August the 23rd 1667 was Required by Sir Joseph Ash to Yorksheere and was not Suffered to Return by reason of Extraordinary business to Willsheer until September 21st 1667, beinge	4	2
February the 18th 1669 he was Required by Sir Joseph Ash To drowninge att Twittenham warren and was not Suffered To returne to Willsheer until Aprill 13th	7	4
Aprill the 18th 1670 he was Required by Sir Joseph Ash to Drowninge again to Twittenham warren again and was not Suffered to return to Willsheer untill May the 27th 1670 beinge	6	0
September the 5th 1670 he was required by Sir Joseph too Yorksheer and was not Suffered to Return untill October the 18 beinge 6 weekes	6	0
August the 22nd 1671 was Required to Yorksheere and was not Suffered to Return untill October 3rd 1671	6	0
August the 16th 1672 was Required too Yorksheer and was not Suffered to Return untill October the 12th	8	0
August the 15th 1673 was Required too Yorksheer and was not Suffered to Return untill September the 20th beinge	5	0
March the 12th 1674 was Required to Yorksheer and was not Suffered to Return untill May the first	7	0
June the 18th 1675 was Required to Yorksheer by Sir Joseph Ash and was not Suffered to return untill October the 23rd 1675 beinge	18	0
July the 21st 1676 was Required to Yorksheer and was not Suffered to Return untill October the 21st	13	0
July the 27th [1677] was Required by Sir Joseph Ash too Yorksheer and was not Suffered to return untill September the 11th beinge	6	5
August the 23rd 1678 was Required by Sir Joseph Ash to Yorksheer and was not Suffered to return untill September the 23rd beinge	5	0
July the 10th 1679 was Required to Yorksheer and Returned home again August 19th	6	0
November the 5th 1679 was Required by Sir Joseph Ash to Yorksheer and was not Suffered to return by reason of Extraordinary business untill January the 3rd 1679	8	0
	106	0

John Snow have and did Receive usually for his owne Judgmente and Skill only his own Time of those Several gentelmen, Knights and Lords that have and would at the Severall times as Aforesaid then Imployed Snow, many of them and others as followeth:

Mr John Sadler, Walter Sharpe, Mr Roger Langley, Esq. Bassett, Mr Harwood, Edward Froud, Nicholas Froud, Edward Ward, John Rooke, the Lady Lyle of Moyles Cort, John Chamn Esqr, the Earle of Shaftesbury, and Severall others that have paid John Snow 5s 0d per day, which is thirty Shillings per week, and his meat and drinke and Lodginge for himselfe and his horses for all the time that he was goinge of and ontoo them, and they have Severall of them have gave Snow two guineas a peece and moore over and besides his wages, and the said Snow might have had so much for all or the most part of his Spare time aforesaid of Sir Joseph Ashe's other Business and Concernes that the said Snow was Employed on, and all the rest of Snow's time he was to have to himselfe for his own benefitt, had he not been desired at the Severall times as aforesaid from his hom which was not part of Snow's promise to do, There was and are Severall times as above mentioned and others which he have not Mentioned, the whole beinge one hundred and six weeks time in Jurneys and other business don as aforesaid att one pound Tenn shilling the weeke as Snow received of others Cometh to one hundred fifty nine pounds due from Sir Joseph Ash Barronett to John Snow £159.

Pigs in Loosehanger Park, 1669

These hastily-written accounts appear to have been compiled by John Snow's servant or perhaps by one of his sons. They are difficult to decipher and are not in any chronological order. They do, however, provide an indication of the number of pigs being taken in to Loosehanger Park for fattening on the mast (beech mast) and acorns, and show the large sums which were paid for this privilege. Other account books provide details of the number of people who paid for their cattle and horses to graze in the Park. The strays mentioned in the accounts came from the manorial pound at Downton and were a perquisite of Sir Joseph Ashe as lord of the manor. One stray pig apparently came from as far away as Harnham. Most pigs stayed in the Park for only one week; a few stayed for much longer.

WSRO 1946/Box 12 (10)

An accounte of what Peiggs was tooke in to mast in to Looshanger Parke 1669 and from houme [whom] as fowlleth [followeth]

	£	s	d
September the 22nd day 1669			
Came in Hinary Bowles 3 great peiggs to keping at 1s 6d the weeke a peece for the three		4	6
Then came in two shoutes [litters of pigs] of Henary Bowles to keeping at 9d the week a peece		1	6

	£	s	d
October the first day			
Came inn John Gooles his 6 peiggs to keeping one of them at 1s 6d a peece a weeke for keeping		9	0
Then came in two sowes peiggs more of his to keeping one of them at 6d the weeke			6
Gooles other sowe peigg at 1s 0d the weeke		1	0
October the 6th day			
Came in William Alloway and John Silendes two pigges to keeping at 1s 8d the weeke a peece		3	4
October the 8th day			
Came on two peigges of Richard Curttesros at 1s 6d the weeke a peece		3	0
Then came in on shout [one litter] of Jone Boundeyes at 6d the week	blank		
October the 9th day			
Came in one stray sowe peigge at 1s 8d the weeke		1	8
October the 10th day			
Came in one Peigge of John Courteros to keepinge at 1s 6d the weeke		1	6
October the 14th day			
Came in one Peigge of the widow Barkers of Witherington to keepinge at 1s 6d the weeke		1	6
At the same time came in one Peigge of Edward Snow to keeping at 1s 8d the weeke		1	8
October the 14th day 1669			
Came in John Merriates two Peigges to keeping at 1s 8d the weeke a peece		3	4
October the 15th day			
Came in William Bowles five Peigges to keeping at 1s 6d the weeke a peece		7	6
October the 19th day			
Came in one Peigge that was Cryed [advertised] one strayed at Downton at 1s 10d the weeke for keepinge		1	10
October the 20th day			
Came in John Brewers five Peiggs at 1s 6d the weeke a peece		7	6
Then came in 7 lettel peigges more of John Brewers the keeping at 6d the weeke a peece		3	6
November the 4th day			
Came in Joseph Stoopres four Peigges at 1s 6d the week a peece		6	0
November the 4th day			
Came in John Sanderes four Peiggs at 1s 8d the week a peece for keeping		6	8
November the 6th day			
Came in John Coopears three peigges at 1s 8d the weeke a peece for keeping them		5	0

	£	s	d
November the 8th day			
Came in Geordge Noyes is great peigge at 1s 6d the week		1	6
November the 8th day			
Came in one lettel shout of George Noyes is to keeping at 6d the weeke			6
November 22nd day			
Came in two small pigges of Hinry Bowles and Martin Reanoles to keeping at one shilling the weeke for both of them		2	0
December the 17th day			
Came in 4 peigges small ones of Richard Danneiles at 6d the weeke a peece for the keeping		2	0
December the 18th day			
Came in two great peigges of William Bowles is to keeping at one 1s 0d the weeke a peece		2	0

An account of what peiggs went in Loosehanger Parke at maste and from home [whom] they came and howe long they went in the Parke and when they was foat [fetched] out and by homme in the year 1669 as folloeth

	£	s	d
October the 29th day			
Came in John Browarys (?) five great peigges and hee foat them out againe November the 5th day they being here but one weeke a peece for the keeping Received of him		7	6
Then came in 8 shoutes of John Browens and went out at the same time they being here but one weeke a peece at 3d e weeke a peece Received		2	0
November the 4th day			
came in Robert Bowenans 3 peigges and hee foat them out againe the 6 day of the same instant, they being hear but two dayes a peece at 1s 8d the weeke a peece for the keeping Received it of him		1	0
October the first day			
came in John Gobbes is power (?) sow peigge and hee foat her out againe November the 10th day shee being hear but 6 weekes at 6d the weeke for keeping, Received it		3	0
At the same time came in one power (?) sow peigge more of his and went out at the same time being hear but 6 weekes at one shilling the weeke for the keeping. Received it of him		6	0
November the 4th day			
came in one Peigge of Joseph Stokeses and hee foat him out againe the 15 day of the same instance hee being hear but one weeke and 4 dayes at 1s 6d the weeke for			

	£	s	d
keeping. Received it of him		2	6
October the 8th day			
Came in one small shout of the widow Poundeyes of Charelton and was foat out November the 16th day being hear but 6 weekes and 3 dayes at 2d the weeke for keeping. Received of her in full one shilling		1	0
October the 8th day			
Came in Richard Curttes two great peigges in to the Parke and hee foat them out againe November the 16th day they being hear but 5 weekes and 4 dayes a peece at 1s 6d the weeke a peece for keeping Received it of him in full		17	0
September the 22nd			
Came in three peigges to mast of Hinry Bowles is and he foat them out againe November the 22nd they being hear but 8 weekes and 4 dayes a peece at 1s 6d the weeke a peece for keeping them Received it in full	1	19	0
At the same time Came in two showtes of his to keeping at mast at 9d the weeke a peece the two being hear 6 weekes and 4 dayes at that price. Received it in full		10	0
Then I kept them till November the 22nd day being two weekes more at 6d the weeke a peece for the two shoutes and then they foat them out Received it in full		2	0
October the 9th day			
Came in one strain sow peigge which was cried And strayed at Downton and was chaleinged [challenged i.e. claimed] by Mrs Boende of Aldbury and was foat out by her man November the 22 day being hear but 6 weekes and two dayes at 1s 9d the weeke for keeping		11	0
Received of her for keeping and straing [straying] 3s 0d			
November the 4th day			
came in John Senders two pigges to keeping and hee foat them out againe November the 24th day they being hear but 3 weeks at 1s 8d the week a peece. Received of him		10	0
November the 4th day 1669			
Joseph Stokes is 3 peigges to keeping at mast and hee foat them out againe the 24th day of November they being hear but 3 weekes at 1s 6d the weeke for the keeping a peece Received it of him		13	6
October the 6th day			
Came in William Alloway two pigges and hee foat them out againe November the 25th day being hear but 7 weeks at 1s 6d the week a peece for keeping Received	1	1	0
October the first day			
came in John Gooleis his peiggs one of them went out againe December the 3rd day being hear but 9 weeks at			

	£	s	d
1s 6d the weeke for the keeping at mast		13	6
November the 8th day			
came in one gret peigge of George Noyes is to Mast hee had him out December the 4th day hee being hear but 3 weeks and 5 dayes at 1s 6d the week for keeping Received it of him		5	0
At the same time came in one showt of his to mast and Noyes foat him out at the same time all so hee being hear but 3 weeks and 5 dayes at 1s 6d the week for keeping Received it of him		1	0
October the 10th day			
came in one peigge of John Catores to mast and hee foat him out December the 5th day hee being hear but 8 weekes at 1s 6d the weeke for the keeping Received it of him		12	0
November the 6th day			
Came in 3 peigges of John Crappers and hee foat them out againe December the 6th day they being hear 4 weekes and 1 dayes at 1s 8d the weeke a peece for the keeping Received it in full of him	1	0	0
October the 14th day 1669			
Came in one peigge of the widdow Buckrons of Wetherington and shee foat him out againe December the 10th day hee being hear but 8 weeks and one day at 1s 6d the weeke for the keeping. Received it in full of her man for it		12	8
At the same time Came in two great peigges of John Moriats and hee foat them out December the 10th day they was hear but 8 weekes and 2 dayes a peece at 1s 7d the weeke a peece for the keeping. Received of him for it	1	5	4
October the 19th day			
Came in one strayed great hogge peigge and was Chalenged by Mr Tournor of Harnam and hee foat him out December the 16th day being hear but 8 weeks and 2 dayes at 1s 8d the weeke for the keeping. Received of his man		13	10
October the 15th day			
Came in William Bowles is five peigges and hee foat them out the 18th day of December they being hear but 9 weeks and one day a peece at 1s 6d the weeke a peece for the keeping.	3	7	6
Received of him for Ringing the 5 peigges			6
November the 4th day			
Came in two peigges more of John Sanders and hee foat them out December the 20th day they being hear but 6 weekes and 3 dayes at 1s 8d the weeke for the keeping at mast	1	1	6

	£	s	d
December the 17th day			
Came in 4 small shouts of Richard Dannieles and hee foat them out againe December the 21st day they being hear but 3 dayes at 6d the weeke a peece for the keeping a mast		1	0
October the first day			
Came in John Gooles is 3 peigges and hee foat them out againe December the 10th day they being hear but 10 weekes at 1s 6d the weeke a peece for the keeping at mast. Received it	2	5	0
At the same time came in two peigges of John Gantlates of Cowme [?Combe] and they was foat out December the 10th day they being hear but 10 weeks at 1s 6d the weeke a peece. Received of his man for keeping	1	10	0
November the 22md day			
Came in two small peigges of Hinry Bowles and Markearm Renmales and they foat them out Againe December the 29th day they being hear but 5 weekes a peece for keeping. Received it		5	0
December the 18th day 1669			
Then came in William Bowles is two meidderling [middling] peigges and hee foat them out December the 29th day they being hear but one weeke and 4 dayes a peece at one 1s 0d the weeke a peece Received in full		3	4

AN ACCOUNT OF STOCK AT ROWDEN FARM, CHIPPENHAM 1671-73

Rowden Farm is situated on the west side of the river Avon south of Chippenham. An indenture dated 20 September 1670 records a 99 year lease of Rowden Farm from Sir Edward Hungerford of Farleigh Hungerford to Thomas Long the elder, gentleman, of Mounton in the parish of Broughton *Gifford for the sum of £2,020 and a yearly rent of £10. The property included a capital messuage, barns, stables, orchards, gardens and 340 acres of pasture and meadow. (WSRO 947/1429/1) The farm was occupied by Thomas Long's son, also Thomas, and his wife Katherine. Thomas Long the younger presumably wrote this account, the cover of which has the names of Thomas Long, Katherine Long and Hubert Long written as though by one practising penmanship. The account book has survived among the papers of the Long family of Rood Ashton. These accounts illustrate the lively trade in cattle fattened on the low-lying pastures of Rowden farm, a trade which formed the basis of much of the farming of north and west Wiltshire. The accounts show the number of markets and fairs at which young cattle were purchased for fattening, including a reference to three bought in south Wales. A flock of 250-300 sheep was also kept on the farm.*

WSRO 947/1433

A booke of Account of whatt Stocke I have att Rowden Farme. Anno Dom. 1671

Heifers sold Anno Dom. 1671	**£**	**s**	**d**
Humphery Foord three prise	14	10	0
Francis Lewes one prise	4	2	6
At Chippenham one prise	4	5	0
Humphery Foord one prise	4	10	0
Humphery Foord one prise	4	5	0
Humphery Foord to prise	10	10	0
Humphery Foord prise	3	0	0
Humphery Foord one prise	3	15	0
Humphery Foord 2 prise	11	0	0
Humphery Foord 1 prise	5	0	0
Humphery Foord 1 prise	5	10	0

	£	s	d
Humphery Foord 1 prise	4	0	0
William Powell 2 prise	9	16	8
2 sold to Steeven Clay prise	9	10	0

Whatt heifers I bought in to Rowden Anno Dom 1671 And of whome May the 9th

10 Richard Browne prise	35	0	0
2 of Marshman prise	4	8	0
1 of Thomas Moody prise	3	10	0
1 of Robert Harris prise	2	6	0
1 of Nicholas Jay	2	15	0
1 of Henry Cater	2	10	0
1 of Widdow Harding	3	9	0
1 of Thomas Bartin	2	0	0
1 of Henry Wintworth	3	15	0
1 bull of John Hutton	2	9	0

What Bures [young bullocks] I bought at Rowden Anno Dom 1671

4 August 26th of William Tanner	13	10	0
4 September 13th of Francis Farr	14	10	0
1 at Wootton under Edge	2	2	0
1 cow of William Tanner	3	10	0
1 bur of William Tanner	1	15	0
3 September the 21st at Carleine [?Carleon on Usk]	7	13	6
2 bought the same day	5	13	0
1 bought the same day	2	11	0
4 bought the same day	9	11	0
2 oxen bought September the 30th	12	8	6
4 bought December the 9th cost	23	0	0

What oxen I bought into Stocke Rowden and of whome Anno Dom. 1671 May the 9th

4 John Sparrow prise	19	10	0
2 at Castle Come faier prise	10	5	0
4 of Thomas Selman	19	5	0
1 of John Thatcher	6	10	0
1 John Arnum	6	9	0
2 of Christopher Holloway	13	10	0
1 of Edward Perry	5	10	0
1 of Mr Hipsly	5	8	0
1 of John Harris	5	19	0
1 of Richard Walter	5	12	6
2 of Richard Harvord	13	10	0

	£	s	d
1 of John Lowe	7	2	6
2 of Walter Tiler	11	1	0
4 of William Tanner	16	10	0
1 of Nathanniell Hillio	5	4	0
2 of John Come	13	10	0
1 of old Barrat	6	10	0
2 of William Tanner	11	2	6
1 Free Martin* of William Tanner	5	7	6
1 William Moolas at Wootton under Edge	5	8	0

An account of what my oxen were sold for at Rowden 1672

4 that were bought of Will Tanner were sold for [blank]	[blank]			
1 oxe that was bought at Bathe sold to Steven Clay prise		9	0	0
2 that were bought at Castle Come [blank]	[blank]			

What Sheepe I bought into Stock Rowden Anno Dom. 1671 and of whome May the 9th

38 wethers of Richard Greene prise	23	15	0
20 cupells of Jerram Marshman	10	0	0
9 cupels of Rich. Little	4	10	0
13 cup. & one lambe of Mr Gardner	6	2	6
10 cup of Tho. Willshere	4	0	0
7 cup of Tho. Eyles	2	16	6
6 cupe. of John Hutton	2	12	6
15 cup. of Daniell Doverell and three barren ewes	8	13	0
20 cupells of Will. Player	9	10	0
20 cup. of Misake [?Isaac} Goodren	9	16	6
7 cup. of John Jeffreys	3	3	0

An account of whatt money I have received of Humphery Ford

June the 8th I received of him	10	0	0
June the 17th Received of him	1	0	0
June the 23rd received of him	4	10	0
July the first received of him	4	5	0
Since received of him	10	0	0
August the 23rd received of him	40	0	0

Anno Dom. 1673 what the heifers cost into the ground

March the 17th bought at Malmsbury

The blacke cow cost	3	0	0

An ox-like beast of doubtful sex which never breeds.

	£	s	d
The whery blacke cost	2	12	0
The white heifer cost	2	0	0
March the twentieth at the Devizes			
One yoke of steeres cost	5	10	0
March the 22nd at Chipenham			
One heifer cost	3	9	0
March the 25th at Clacke			
The black heifer with the star in the forehead	3	2	6
The Browne cow cost	2	19	0
The vallow cow cost	2	16	0
The blacke tayled cow	2	10	0
The linded [white backed] heifer coste	2	3	4
The herriot prise	3	10	0
The reed heifer prise	3	0	0
April the 5th at Chipenham			
To heifers prise	4	9	0
April the 21st bought of Mr Weeks			
6 heifers prise	17	10	0
April the 22nd bought of my Cozen Tho. Horne			
7 heifers prise	19	10	0
April the 25th at C[a]lne			
3 heifers prise	8	16	6
April the 24th at the Devizes			
2 heifers prise	5	9	0
At Castle Come faier			
1 heifer prise	3	2	6
1 heifer the same day prise	2	7	0
2 Milch cowes the same day prise	9	5	0
1 Milch cow the 26th of April at Chipenham prise	4	15	0
1 heifer bought of Will. Tanner prise	3	0	0

What every heifer was sold for Anno Domini 1673

My Redd heifer sold for	6	0	0
The herriot sold for	5	17	6
Snellens sold for	4	10	0
The Malmsbury blacke	5	0	0
The Malmsbury Vinny	3	15	0

	£	s	d
The blacke vinny	4	16	0
The Blacke yellow	4	12	0
Tho. Hornes heifer sold for	3	15	0
Tho Hornes little cow	4	0	0
Tho, Hornes red cow	3	13	0
The Whitte heifer sold for	4	12	0
Edw. Beards heifer sold for	3	10	0
Beards cow sold for	4	6	8
Moody sold for	4	17	6
Castle Come heifer sold for	3	16	8
Tho. Clarke heifer	4	0	0
To of Tho. Hornes sold for	9	15	0
To of Mr Wells sold for	9	0	0
One of Mr Jonsenes sold for	3	10	0
To of Tho. Hornes and one of Tanners burrs sold for	13	15	0
The Clake [Clacke] heifer sold for and one of Mr Jonsones and one of Mr Weekes	10	10	0
Mr Jonsons blacke & one of Tanners burrs sold for	9	0	0
The castle combe cow	5	10	0
To little burrs sold for	7	0	6
	109	0	0

What the oxen cost 1673

2 steeres at the Devizes	5	10	0
2 at Chipenham prise	7	1	0
2 at Chipenham prise	9	10	0
2 the same day prise	10	10	0
1 Bull the same day prise	2	3	4
1 oxe prise	6	0	0
2 at Sodbury midsomerday	3	19	0
8 of William Tanner prise	30	0	0
5 of William Tanner prise	24	0	0
6 of Will. Tanner prise	30	10	0

Anno Domini 1673 at our Lady Day What sheepe I had and lambes

March the 28th put into Ladyfeild of Ewes 101 of Lambes 94
At the same time I had of sheepe in Decrits feild 131
Sheepe in the grounds at whome [blank]

The rest of the small notebook contains lists of payments to haymakers, purchases of loads of hay and other unspecified small payments dated 1681–2

EVIDENCE FROM PROBATE INVENTORIES

The following examples of the lists and valuation of livestock, crops, tools and equipment which have been selected from the many hundreds of surviving probate inventories provide more direct evidence about farms and farming than can be found in any other source. In particular, these extracts illustrate the marked differences in farming between the various agricultural regions in the county. The difficulties inherent in attempting to draw general conclusions from probate inventories are well known, and these examples are a random selection which cannot be taken as necessarily representative. Furthermore, it must always be a questionable proposition to assume that wealth and possessions at death accurately reflect the prosperity of individuals at an earlier stage of their lives. The deceased may well have retired from active farming, or have disposed of some parts of his stock and equipment before his death. The extent to which this may have occurred can occasionally be seen by comparing the stock and goods bequeathed in the will with those listed in the inventory. It is also understandable that appraisers varied in their thoroughness and reliability, especially over the listing of old, home-made articles and poultry. Many well-worn tools are no doubt included under the blanket term 'other lumber'.

It is evident, even from this small selection of inventories, that, as usual in rural society, several of the more prosperous farmers had lent part of their accumulated savings at interest to neighbours, either on bonds ('specialties') or without security ('desperate debts'). Farmers on the heavier land continued to use oxen or a mixed team of oxen and horses to pull the 'sullowe' or plough. Sheep and hurdles for the fold figure among the possessions of chalkland farmers, while cheese, pigs and steers were the mainstay of clayland farms. There are several examples of turkeys among the poultry, and some farmers had valuable stocks of bees . On mixed farms in north Wiltshire, such as that of Roger Harris of Swindon (1638), horse breeding provided additional income, as did spinning and weaving. The absence of any mention of a loom suggests that this was provided by one of the clothiers who controlled most of the trade in woollen cloth.

Since copyhold tenure, generally for three lives, was by far the most common form of landholding, farms themselves seldom appear in probate inventories, although occasionally property held by lease is valued. Likewise, a valuation is sometimes given for the profits from a farm during the executors' year specified in some manorial custumals.

The assistance of Robert Jago in the selection of these inventories is gratefully acknowledged.

WSRO P2/K/81

Thomas Kinge of Stoke Verdon (Stoke Farthing), husbandman 8 April 1607

Total wealth £76 10s 10d

	Value
The wheate in the barne unthreshed by estymacon xlviii bushells at iiis the bushell	vii li iiiis
Wheate in the feild in blade xii acres valued at	xii li
An acre of winter fatches [vetches] in blade valued at	xiivis viiid
iii halves [strips of land] of peayes valued at	xviiis
ii acres of barley sowen in the feild valued at	xxvis viiid
iv bushells of barly	vis viiid
vi old sacks, ii small baggs, a peck bagg and a winnowing sheet	xvis
iii old sythes with a snead [handle of scythe] and a cradle [device attached to scythe for laying corn in swathes] therunto	iiis iiiid
iii small ledden weights	xd
iii corne pikes	xiid
Old rakes	iiiid
An old black bill	xiid
Of sheepe of all sorts of weathers, ewes and lambes xxxi prised at	vii li
iiii kine	vi li
iiii horses with the harnesse, one iron bound cart with the furniture	xiii li
belonging, iiii old eythes [light harrows] with tines, one sullowe with	vis
one payer of plough irons	viiid
One Iron barre and three iron wedges	iiis iiiid
An old axe, two hatchetts and a hammer	xxd
A shewing hammer and a paire of pynsers	iiiid
The hay and pease for fodder	xxvis viiid
The wood and lumber in the yard	xxxiiis iiiid
iiii shuttes [litters of pigs]	xxviiis
The poultry about the house of hens, capons & cocks xvi	viiis
An olde dragge for corne	viiid
iii payer of old fetters with ii locks and two cloggs [fetters for horses]	iiiis viiid
An old dung pott	iis
ii dozen of old hurdles	iis
A shovell, a peckaxe and a spade	xvid
An old printe for to printe sheepe [to tag with owner's mark]	viiid

WSRO P3/S/97

Richard Strech of Fyfeild in the parish of Overton, husbandman. 28 February 1613

Hall, Chamber over Hall, Malt loft, Chamber next the Entrie, Little Chamber, New chamber, Inner Chamber, Kitchen

Total wealth £152 11s 14d

	Value
In the Kytchen	
One Malt Querne [mill]	vis viiid
One Furnace	vs
One Malt Stone [for grinding malt]	viiis
Two old Chests	iiis iiiid
A Covell [tub or container] and other stuffe	vs
viii quarters of barley winnowed	vii li
v Kyne and heyfer and two yearlinge bullocks	xvi li
v Geldings, one mare and theire harness	xxii li
One hundred and fower sheepe	xxx li
Corne in the Barne	
Wheate by estymacon v quarters	x li
Barley by estymacon vi quarters	vi li
Two Carts and one dunge pott [small cart]	iiii li
Two Sullowes, iii harrowes with Implements to them and a Seed lypp [for broadcasting seed]	xs
One Grindstone	iis
Wood and Tymber	xxxs
vi Shouts [litters of pigs] or store piggs	xxiiiis
v stocks of Bees	xxs
The lease of a grounde	xls
A Cartlyne and wood ropes	iiis iiiid
ii Ladders	iis vid
Fatches [vetches] and Peason	xxs
Haye	xxs
Wheate and Fatches in the Feilde	xvi li
A Black Jacke [drinking vessel]	xiid
Poultrie of all sorts	iiis

WSRO P3/S/118

William Stone, yeoman Alton Barnes
15 January 1615

Total wealth £116 2s 10d

In the Back syde without

	Value
ii Iron Bound Carts and a Cart Lader	iiii li
ii Plow Sullows with their Irons, two Plow chaines, ii oxe yokes, iiii oxe Bowes, one whippinge iron, iii Eaythes [light harrows], one old borden [wooden] dung Pott	i li
ii ladders	iis
ii spaddes, ii scoopes & v reep hookes	iiiis
one drag Brydle	is vid
The wood and the Tollard [Tallet] or Cart hous	iiii li vs

In the Stable

ii Rackes, one manger & a oxe stall and the mill house and a old tollett over the stable and the plankes	xs

In the Barne

A forme, a Willer [wicker basket], v Rakes, ii forkes, 8 prongs, a planck for a table bord & the carte line	viiis iiiid
It. [Item] the wheatt	xi li iiiis
It. the Barly	xiiii li
It. the Malt	i li
It. Fatches, Peason & hay	v li
It. the wheat in the feeld	xxi li
It. a hundred and xx ti sheepe	xxxvi li
It. one yoak of Oxen	v li
It. v kyne	vii li xs
It. iii two-year bullockes	iii li
It. iiii yearling bullockes	i li vis viiid
It. iii horses & their harnes	v li
It. viii young store piggs	i li
It. the lease of the park ground	iiii li xs

WSRO P2/M/258

Edmund Monday [Munday] of Durrington 20 September 1617

Total wealth £642 4s 0d

Things without doores	**Value**
3 Iron bound cartes & 2 wheel ploughes	v li
4 harrowes, 1 plough hatchet with other implements	vs
Wood & timber	xv li
The wheat	cc li
The Barley	cx li
The Pease, tills [lentils], fetches & hay	xxx li
7 horses & their harnesse, ropes & cart tynes	xxx li
20 rudder beasts & 5 calves	xxvii li
Hoggs & store piggs	viii li
cccclxxx sheepe & lxxx lambes	cxxx li
The Wool liii waightes [1590 lbs.]	lx li
Hens, cockes, gannys [turkeys] & duckes	viiis
Ladders, sackes, hurdells, winsheetes, piggs troughs & collers	i li
Wearing apparell	x li

WSRO P2/R/141

John Rattew of Amesbury, yeoman. 26 November 1619

Total wealth £237 17s 8d

In the Boultinge House [for sifting bran or coarse meal]

One kneading tubb, one searche [sieve] and cleaseene[?], one powdering [salting] Tubb, one cheese vate	vs
Fower shelves	xiid
One measure called a Bushell and two other small measures	iis
One winnowinge sheete, three rudders, fower seeves, one maulte seeve and xiii sacks, Two Willyes [wicker baskets] and one choppinge board	xiid

In the Barnes

At John Streats barne in wheate there viii qtrs at iiis the bushell	ix li xiis
Barlie there xxv quarters at xxd the bushell	xvi li xiiis iiiid
Oates there Eight quarters at xvd the bushell	iiii li

Corne sowed and growinge in the Feeldes

Wheate in the Feeld xxxvi akers and halfe an aker	xxx li
Wheate in the Barnes and in a Reeke by estimacon xvi quarters at iiis the bushell	xix li iiiis
Barlye here alsoe by estimacon xxx qtrs at xxd the bushell	xx li
Pease, Oates, Fetches and thiles [lentils] in the Barnes	vii li

	Value
Haye	iii li
Fower score and six sheepe viz weathers, yewes and weather hoggs	xxi li xs

In the Stables

Fower horses and two geldings	xxv li
Twelve Fatt hogges	vii li xvis
Sixe milche Kyne, three heyfers of ii yeares old and one Bull with two Yearlings	xiiii li
Swyne in the Bartons xvi teene	xlviiis
Turkeys iiii	iiiis
xxx cocks, capons and hennes	xs
Seaven Geese	viis
Tenn Ducks	iiis iiiid
Three Carts	iii li
Three plowes, three payer of Eythes with Plow Timber and other plows and cart tacklinge	xxxiiis iiiid
Six ladders	vis viiid
Boards	vis viiid
Timber and wood	x li
Carte hames, Plowe hames with one corne lyne and fower wood roapes	xls
One Covell [tub or container]	vid
One well buckett with his iron chaine and the horse trough	vs
Five hogg troffes [troughs]	iiis iiiid
Pytche forckes five, fower Rakes, one shovel, Two hatchetts and one wood bill	vis viiid
One barr, two dozen of hurdells and one pickaxe	viiis

WSRO P3/S/201

James Sexton of Awborne [Aldbourne] 29 September 1624

Total wealth £75 13s 8d

In the Butterie

3 Earthen potts, 4 earthen panns, one butter churne	iis vid

In the Siltinge house

5 kives [small barrels], 3 tubbs	xiis
One powdering tubb, three barrells, one salt tubb, one bushell measure, 3 sives, one mault sive	vs

In the Barne

Corne and Fodder in our estymacon	xxx li

	Value
2 pitching prongs, one cutting knife and one Rake	iis

In the Stable

3 horses	vii li xs
The horse harness, halters, one pickaxe & shoovell	xiiiis
The horse rack and skaffold	iiis
2 locks and three paier of Fetters	iis

Cattle and other necessaries in the Barton

2 kien [kine]	iii li
2 paier of cart wheeles, 2 lades [sides or ends for cart], one dung pott, one paier of woodd ropes and the cart lieu and the horse trough	iiii li
One plough, three harrowes, chaine and wheeles	xiiiis
The dunge in the backside	vs
One sowe and three store piggs	xviiis
The wood and timber above the Barton	xxs
The wood and tymber in the close	xs
The benefitt of the coppiehold for this yere to the Administrator as we suppose	xii li
Debts owing	iii li xs

P2/A/141

Ralphe Annerlery of Mayden Bradley, husbandman, 12 July 1626

Total wealth £98 10s 8d

In the chamber over the haull

A hatchett, 2 hookes, 6 iron wedges, a pickaxe, 3 peekes and divers other tools and implements of husbandry and old iron there	xiiis iiiid

In the buttry

4 barrels and 5 trendles	xxs
4 formes, a cupboard, a bushell and other measures, 2 bottles and other woodden vessells and lumber there	xs

In the barne

A mowe of wheate and rye	ls

	Value
2 tubbs a fate and a willie [wicker basket]	vs
A cheese presse	xiid
A yeoatinge stone [for preparing malt or grain]	xiis
3 bundles of lathes	iis
One sullowe, 2 sheares, 2 coulters 3 chaynes, 3 eythes and one dragge,	xxs
A wayne, a paire of wheeles, a dunge draught, a dunge pott, a clavie [beam or shelf], a paire of cart blades and 2 yokes	xls

In the stable

Harnesse for 4 horses, 4 packsaddles, 7 sacks with other implements about the horses	xxs

In the Backside

Certen reede sheaves	vis viiid
A wayne lyne and a wood strapp	iiiis
Wood and poles, tymber and pales with wood and poles over the barne and the stable and the cole house	xxxvs

Catell

2 keene [kine]	v li vis viiid
2 heifers	iii li xiiis iiiid
2 steares	v li vis viiid
1 other steare	iii li
4 mares	ix li
One black [?horse] [hole in manuscript]	ls
One mare and her sucking coult	xxxiiis iiiid
One 2 yere age coult	xls
One pigge	xs

Corne on the ground

3 acres and half of wheate upon his owne ground	vii li
Three acres of wheate upon Mr Haydens land	iiii li xs
Three acres of otes and Barly in Hucklebreache	iiii li xs
One acre of barlie in the west feild	xxxs
2 halfe acres of otes upon Wm Baylies land	xvis

Chattles

One chattle lease [lease for set number of years], for ceten yeres determinable upon 2 lives of 3 acres of ground in Hucklebreache	xvi li
The terme of one yere to come in a ground called Pipeclose	iii li
A piggs troughe, a racke in the stable and a parcell of lambe towe	

	Value
[wool] and some goods unknown	iiis iiiid

Good debts

Oweinge by Sir Henry Ludlowe Knt.	iiii li viiis
Oweinge by Mr Edw. Manninge	xvis

Desperate debts

Oweinge by one Wm Rendall	vs
Oweinge by one Tho. Jarvies	iiis

WSRO P2/K/44

William Kent the elder of Boscombe, gent.
10 January 1633

Total wealth £2,225 7s 2d

Five Hoggsheds, fyve barrells, two coules [large bowls], three payles, one meashing vate, one kyver, one powdring tubb with other woodden vessells	iii li xvis
One butter barrell, one butter churne, sixteene milkpannes with other milke vessells	xvs
One Malt Kerne [mill]	xxs

Cattle

Three horses	xiiii li xs
Fowre Kyne	x li
Fowre great fatt hoggs	vii li
Three small piggs	xxs
Eight hundred and eight sheepe	ccii li
Hay in the backsides and att the downes	x li
240 pounds of Lambs wooll	viii li
Wood and tymber in the backsides	x li
One chattle lease of the parsonage of Durington for xix yeares	mcc li
Money in the house	cii li
Money oweing for lambes sold	xxx li is viiid

WSRO P3/H/306

Leonard Hawkins of Minety, yeoman, 15 March 1637

Total wealth £125 4s 4d

	Value
Six Kine	xviii li
Four Yearlings	v li vis viiid
Two Mares & Colts	ix li
Seven Load of Hay	vii li
Barley & Oates	xviii li
Forty Sheepe	xii li
One Hogg Pigg & Two Store Piggs	iii li

In the Lofte

Five Hundred of Cheese	vi li
Two todd [weight 28 lbs.] of wooll	iii li
Cheese vates, two pailes, two milk bowls & the cheese press	v li
Two ladders, one paire of truckles, one draye with other things	iii li
One payer of harrowes	vis viiid

WSRO P3/H/305

Roger Harris of Escott, Swindon, husbandman, 19 July 1638

Total wealth £108 2s 0d

Eight yeacarse [acres]of wheat & reey [rye]	£13 6s 8d
Three yeacarse and a halfe of barley	£5 0s 0d
Foure yeacarse and a halfe of poulse [pulse]	£6 13s 0d
Five yeacarse and a yarde of grass	£2 13s 0d
A yooke of Oxen & foure Kine	£18 6s 0d
Two mares & a foale	£8 0s 0d
Five & thirtye sheepe & twelve lames	£10 0s 0d
Two hooges	£1 6s 8d
Two geese & poultry	3s 0d
Woole & yearne	£3 6s 8d
Tenn yardes of meadley cloath	£1 13s 4d
Two cartes, one plow with coulter and sheare and chaines and hamiss [hames] and three harowes with other lumberment	£6 0s 0d
For an executors yeare	£10 0s 0d

WSRO P3/H/315

William Heyward of Brinkworth, 6 September 1639

Total wealth £120 18s 4d

13 Kine	xxxx li
4 dry heyfers, 2 weanling [weaning] calves & a mare	xiii li vis viiid

	Value
nine and fiftie sheep	xiii li
1 hoge & 1 sowe & piges	iiii li
All the hay	xvi li
All the wood & timber	ii li xs
The pultrie	iis vid

Household goods

In the cheese loft – all the cheeses	vi li
Bacon	[blank]
Wearing apparel	iii li vis viiid
Money in the House	i li
Money owing & hoped for	
Francis Smith of Brinkworth	v li
Goodman Knap of Broad Somerford	vii li xs
One cheese press with all the rest of the woodden vessells	i li

WSRO P3/H/330

Christopher Harte of Inglesham, 7 November 1641

Total wealth £92 0s 0d

Money in his house	£4 0s 0d
Ten old books	5s 0d

In the milke house

Foure brasse kettles, two brasse potts, one brasse skillett, two brasse pannes, one brasse skimmer	£2 0s 0d
Three drinke barrells, two cowles, fyve kives, a mashinge vate, one churne	13s 4d
A cheese presse, a saltinge trough, one paile, two bucketts, bowles, dishes, trenchers and other lumber	15s 0d
Ten cheeses	£6 0s 0d
One bushell, three shovells, three pronges	4s 0d
Corne in the barne	£6 0s 0d
Two fatt hogges	£2 10s 0d
Hay in the backside	£6 0s 0d
Two younge yearlinge calves	£2 0s 0d
Foure sheepe	£2 0s 0d
Six milch Kine att fyve markes a peece	£20 0s 0d
Poultrie	6s 8d
Soyle [dung] in the backside	2s 6d
Due uppon specialties [bonds]	£20 0s 0d
Wearing apparel	£3 0s 0d
Money in the house	£4 0s 0d

Value

WSRO P2/H/607

Thomas Harris of Orcheston St George, gent. 10 July 1661

Total wealth £840 7s 6½d

Two hundred thirty and one wether sheep at 9 li per score	£103 19s 0d
	[Recte £103 10s 0d]
One hundred seventy and fower chilver sheep att six pounds thirteene shillings and fower pence per score	£158 0s 0d
Lambs one hundred and eleven att 4 li 10s per score	£24 19s 6d
	[Recte £11 9s 6d]
Five milch cowes	£15 0s 0d
Three bullocks	£4 10s 0d
Seven piggs	£8 8s 0d
Seven horses and harnesse	£40 0s 0d
Two waggons	£10 0s 0d
Three Carts	£7 0s 0d
Three ploughs	£1 10s 0d
Six harrowes	£1 4s 0d
One Rowler	£1 0s 0d
Hay	£3 0s 0d
Wool – twenty seven weight of thirtys and twelve pounds att eleven pence per pound	£37 13s 6d
Old tarry fleeces [stained with tar]	10s 0d
Lambs wool about one hundred and ten pounds	£3 13s 4d
Loakes about one hundred and twenty pounds	£1 10s 0d
Three rick stavells	£4 0s 0d
Ten quarters of wheat or therabout	£21 0s 0d
Five quarters of Barley or therabout	£6 0s 0d
One hundred ninty and five acres of Corne upon the ground att one pound eight shillings per acre	£273 0s 0d
One Chattell lease during the lives of William Coles and John Coles late of Orcheston, which were vallew at fower pounds per annum above the rent	[blank]
Cocks and hens and turkeys	£1 10s 0d
One screene, one fann, one bushell, one keaver [barrel]	£1 3s 0d
Sixteene old sacks and one new sake	£1 5s 0d
Three old troughs	3s 0d
Five dozen and fower hurdels in the fold with foldstakes	12s 0d
For long meddow in Potterne parish	£15 0s 0d
Bees – seven stocks and swarmes	£2 6s 0d
Due in money	£96 17s 11d
His apparrell and money in his purse	£15 0s 0d
Money in the house	£17 1s 4½d

WSRO P2/L/325

William Lawes, yeoman, Broade Chalke, 13 November 1672

Total wealth

	Value
20 li of old Hoppes	10s od
1 furnace, 1 pumpe, 4 covells, 3 payles	£2 10s od
One cheese presse, 6 stone troughs with other lumber goods	£1 os od
1 waggon, 1 carte, 1 potte carte	£7 10s od
One horse harnesse and ropes	£3 10s od
3 ladders	6s od
In cheese	£1 os od
8 dozens of hurdles and 1 grindestone	£1 os od
The poultry	6s 8d
6 stockes of bees	12s od
In hay	£20 os od
2 plowes, 5 harrowes, 1 seedlip with other plow tackling	£1 3s od
Apples and peares	5s od
In wooll	£18 os od
173 sheepe	£47 10s od
10 kine, 1 bull, 2 calves	£18 os od
6 bushells Malte	12s od
25 quarters of wheate in barne and rick	£20 os od
5 acres of pease and some fatches	£5 os od
40 quarters of barly in barne	£26 10s od
Wheate and fatches upon ground	£40 os od
2 reek stavills	£2 os od
8 sackes, 1 winnowing sheete	8s od
Debts oweing to him	£14 os od
Desparate debtes	£3 10s od
One pitch pan	2s od
One Fan	2s od
One willy[basket] and 2 seines [sieves for corn]	2s od
The time in one meadow untill Lady day next	£1 os od

WSRO P3/N/118

Thomas Norton of Liddiard Millicent, yeoman, 1 September 1679

Total wealth £458 10s 6d

Eight Hundred of Cheese	vii li xvs

	Value
In the Milke House	
Five Coules, two kives, keivers, two churnes four buckets, one paile, one dussen of cheese vats, one lanterne, butter skeals [scales] and other lumber	iii li viiis vid

Abrod in the grounds

In Shaw meads four bease [beasts]	xvi li
17 Milch cows	lv li
7 oxen at Binall	xxxxv li
8 shipe	v li
A ricke of hay at Henley	xiiii li
Fatting Cowes 8	xxxv li
A ricke of hay at Horsey ground	xxiiii li
5 runts	xxiis
4 beasse at Stone	xiii li
4 plow oxen	xxiiii li
A ricke of hay at Houldings	v li
Corne in the barne and backside	xxxxxxx li
2 ricks of hay in the backside	xvii li
In the backside one waine, one pot, plow, harrowes and that belonging to it	v li
6 pigs in the backside	xiii li
Poultry in the backside	iii li
In the stable to horsis, bridels and sadels, with a rug belonging to it	x li
One moult mill with other lumber	xs

WSRO P3/E/128

William Eyre of Neston in the parish of Corsham Esqr.
14 February 1683

Total wealth £493 16s 3d

Corne

1 Oate rick	£2 0s 0d
1 Barley rick	£8 0s 0d
1 wheat rick	£20 0s 0d
Barley in the barne	£20 0s 0d
Threshing in the Flowre [threshing floor] of oates	10s 0d
Wheat in the barne	£1 8s 0d

Cattle and Sheep

8 cowes	£22 0s 0d

	Value
Five yearlings	£4 0s 0d
2 little steeres and 1 heifer	£4 0s 0d
1 yoke of oxen and 2 yokes of working bullocks	£24 0s 0d
40 ewes and lambs	£12 0s 0d
60 dry sheep	£19 0s 0d
38 hoggs	£7 12s 0d
Hay in severall ricks and stacks	£44 0s 0d

Utensils of Husbandry

1 waggon, 1 waine, 2 sullows, 2 draggs, 3 harrows, 1 Roler, 3 dung potts, 4 yokes, 6 bowes, 5 hames, a paire of old Thills [shafts] old wheeles and sullowes and other small broken peeces	£22 0s 0d
Store piggs in the backside and one sow	£6 0s 0d

In the stable

His own Riding mare	£10 0s 0d
2 small mares	£8 0s 0d
4 Iron Traces, 2 hemp traces, a waggon line, a shooing line, 3 binding cords, a seed lipe, 4 old sacks, 3 paire of hames, 2 whitches and other lumber	£2 0s 0d
An old chariot and harness for 2 horses, one old coach holding	£6 0s 0d
One more mare	£5 0s 0d
Two Sadles, 2 paire of holsters, 2 bridles, 1 old pillion and cloth, a maile pillion and other lumber in the saddle room	£2 0s 0d

In the Corne Loft

One old great chest and one granary and 2 old Feather Tubbs	10s 0d

In the Cheese Loft

1 hundred and a halfe and 12 pounds of soward [soured] milke cheese at 20s	£1 12s 6d
Two Hundred and Fifteen pounds of halfe soward cheese at 16s	£1 14s 0d
4 hundred of scimmed cheese at 10s	£2 0s 0d

Corne in the Feilds

12 Acres of wheat in Shearings	£8 0s 0d
25 acres in lower parke and 7 acres in the penning	£21 6s 8d

Things in the barne

1 skreen, 1 fan and stocks, 2 old corn tubbs and sacks	1s 0d

	Value
In the rick barton	
The Rick Stavells and stone	£5 0s 0d
At the barn door	
Poultry of all sorts	10s 0d

WSRO P2/R/378

John Rawlings of Dinton, yeoman, 3 October 1683

Total wealth £226 1s 0d

In the Cheese Loft	
One bed, two bedsteads and two coffers, Three hundred of cheese and other Goods which comes to	£3 10s 0d
The Apple Loft	
Wooll and other Goods which amounts to	15s 0d
In the Brew House	
One furnace, one silt, one Mashing vate, seven trundles, three Coules, one cheese presse, three pailes, one butter churne which amounts to	£6 0s 0d
At the west end Thirty weathers	£13 15s 0d
Twenty Chilver sheep	£7 0s 0d
The Reeck of Hay which is in the Field	£3 0s 0d
At the East end flock Twenty and Four Ewes	£8 8s 0d
Twenty and Four Hoggs	£6 0s 0d
The Fan and Mill in the East end Barne and Lumber Goods	£1 0s 0d
The Old Dungpot, the Apples and Old Straw	£2 0s 0d
The Corne uppon his Estate	£47 8s 0d
Three Horses	£6 0s 0d
Seaven Cowes	£21 0s 0d
The Hay at home	£11 0s 0d
The pigges	£6 0s 0d
Four Ayes [eythes], one Dragg	£1 10s 0d
One Waggon, one Dungepott	£9 0s 0d
One Sullow and other Lumber Goods	£2 0s 0d
A Mill and Fan and other Lumber Goods	£1 0s 0d
Harness, woodropes and other goods	£2 0s 0d
The Apples	12s 0d

	Value
The Sacks	12s 0d
Due from Wm Browning Being desparate debt	£9 2s 8d

WSRO P2/H/967

Robert Hurle of Kingston Deverell, 25 September 1696

Total wealth £841 12s 8d

Four hundred of chees	£3 0s 0d
Eighteen bushells of old Barley	£1 13s 0d
In the Buttery 9 Barrells and 3 horses	£1 12s 0d
Three long Zifters, 1 Trendle, 9 pailes, one Butter Churn, one powdering tub	£1 4s 0d
In the same Buttery 2 Tubs, 8 cheses vates, 2 Virkines and other Lumber	6s 0d
In the same Room one Table Board and Frame, 3 Joynt Stooles, 1 forme , 2 Brass pans, 3 milk pailes and other Earthern wear	£1 5s 0d
The Wooll in the hous with the Beame Waites and Scales	£1 0s 0d
One Peas Rick	£4 0s 0d
One Rick of Oates	£10 0s 0d
One Wheat Rick	£10 0s 0d
Two Rick Stavells	£2 0s 0d
The Wheat in the Barne	£40 0s 0d
The Barley in the Barne and feild	£100 0s 0d
Oates and Pease in the Barne	£1 0s 0d
Two Waggons, 4 Shullows, 3 Ayes [eythes] and other plow Tacklen	£15 0s 0d
Two Waggon Lines and 3 Wood Strapes	12s 0d
Eight Picks, 6 Rakes, 1 Fork and 1 Ladder	8s 0d
The Reck [Rack] in the Stale [Stall]	3s 0d
One Roler, draughts, sheep reeks [racks] and beast Recks	£1 10s 0d
The dust [chaff] in the dust coop	10s 0d
Five Horses and Harness	£15 0s 0d
The boardes about the dust coop, the tallet, the little reck, 8 mangers, picks and shovells, 4 hand barrows and 1 Willon [basket]	15s 0d
One van [fan] and half Bushell seaves and mill, 150 sacks and shovell	£1 10s 0d
Five and twenty pigs, great and smalle	£8 0s 0d
Three acres of vatches and a half	£2 0s 0d
One gley [under ripe] Rick at Bitley, 3 load of hey in the hous ther, 6 other hey ricks at severall places	£100 0s 0d
Two yoke of Working Oxen with ther Harness	£20 0s 0d
Four Steeres	£10 0s 0d
Two Barren Heifers	£4 0s 0d
Nine Milch Cows	£22 0s 0d
Five Calves	£3 0s 0d
A hundred of fat Sheep	£102 0s 0d

	Value
Three Hundred and 10 Ewes	£108 0s 0d
Two Hundred and 40 Hogs	£88 0s 0d
Three Hundred and Sixty Wheathers in both flocks	£147 10s 0d
Four Quarters and half of Wheat Sown in the ground	£9 0s 0d
12 dozen of Hurdles old and new	£1 0s 0d
Things omitted and things forgott	£1 0s 0d

LIVESTOCK AND CROPS AT BLUNSDON ST ANDREW 1728

Although most of the farms in north Wiltshire continued to be small and family-run, mainly devoted to the production of cheese and the raising of beef cattle and pigs; a few were much larger, and along the Corallian ridge included considerable arable land. The following probate inventory from the early 18th century provides a good example of the quality and variety of crops being grown by a prosperous farmer from Blunsdon St Andrew. Clearly, he was farming a large area extending from Grundwell farm (now called Groundwell) to Hide (Hyde). His crops included wheat, barley, oats, vetches and pease, and he possessed two cwt. of clover seed. The inventory was made in December, so his wheat was already sown, whereas the spring-sown crops of barley and oats were in his barn. His livestock included no less than 43 dairy cows, 16 'weanlings' or young calves and 18 heifers, and he had 40 cwt. (i.e. two tons) of cheese in store. His prosperity and life-style is evident both from his remarkable wealth (£1369 17s 8d) and from the contents of his house which included £47 in cash, a 'Limbeck' or still for producing spirits, a spinnet and books worth £8. Unusually, his inventory also includes his stocks of bees which at £3 must have been numerous.

WSRO P1/A/289

An Inventory of all the Goods and Chattles of John Ayres of Blunsdon St Andrew in the County of Wilts, yeoman, deceased 10 December 1728

	£	s	d
For Wearing apparel and household goods	160	2	6
In ready money and book debts	47	0	0
For 1 Limbeck		5	0
For a Cyder press and trough	1	0	0
For a Lane [lathe] and tools	4	0	0
For 2 Bird Cages		10	0
For 8 flitches of Bacon	10	0	0
For a Spinnet	5	5	0
For 30 tod of wool [1 tod = 28 lbs]	21	0	0
For Books	8	0	0
For Lumber Goods		13	0
For Wheat Sowed at Grundwell	39	5	4
For Ditto sowed at Blunsdon	39	12	7

	£	s	d
For Corn in the Straw Viz.			
45 quarters Barly at Hide	69	0	0
47 quarters of Barly at Blunsdon	70	0	0
53 quarters of Wheat	127	4	0
15 quarters of Oats	15	0	0
Vetches and Pease	1	2	6
For Cattle Viz. 16 Weanlings	26	0	0
13 2 year old Heyfers and Bulls	34	2	6
5 3 year old Heyfers	22	0	0
43 Dayry Cows	193	10	0
1 Bull stag	3	0	0
144 Sheep	83	5	9
13 Horses	93	8	6
2 Colts	9	0	0
9 Store pigs and 2 fat hogs	12	0	0
For Implements of Husbandry	64	16	0
For 2 cwt. Of Clover Seeds	2	5	0
For 15 tun of Hay at Hide			
For 145 tun of Hay at Blunsdon and Grundwell	145	0	0
For Bees	3	0	0
Total	1369	17	8

TWO LARGE CHALKLAND FARMS AT DOWNTON 1709 & 1724

The following descriptions of New Court Farm and Standlynch Farm provide good evidence of the large scale and character of much of the farming on the chalkland. Both farms are situated in the wide valley of the Avon at Downton; both had well-built houses, barns and farm buildings, and extensive water meadows. The fertility of the arable was maintained by the large sheep flocks which fed on the extensive downland grazing. Dairy cows were kept on the lower pastures and meadow land. Like many other farms in the district, the value of these two had been greatly improved during the second half of the 17th century by new buildings, extension of arable land on the downland, and, above all, by the creation of water meadows providing early grass and abundant hay crops. This important development is described in detail in a separate section of this volume.

NEW COURT FARM

The freehold of this farm had been granted by the Crown to Sir Thomas Gorges of Longford Castle in 1592. In 1651 his son, Sir Edward Gorges, sold the farm to Joseph Ashe, who was created a baronet in 1660, and who acquired a lease of the whole of the manor of Downton from the bishopric of Winchester in 1662. During the 1680s Sir Joseph Ashe rebuilt the farm house at New Court on a large scale and provided a 9-bay aisled barn and other buildings. In 1689 the farm consisted of 76 acres of watered meadow, 127 acres of lowland pasture, 346 acres of arable land, and 610 acres of sheep down on the west side of the valley. During the 18th century the farm was said to have a flock of 1,600 sheep and a herd of 50 dairy cows (VCH Wilts., XI, 1980, 73-5). The following survey of 1709 provides a full account of the farm, the map referred to has not been found.

WSRO 490/788 *[*Note that A = acres, R = roods, L = lugs (perches)]*

A Particular of Newcourt Farme by Measure besides Hedges and Ditches [and?]of Pasture: as by the Map

	*A	R	L
The Dwelling Howse, Backsides and yards, orchards And gardens etc. and the drove up to 3 Gates	8	0	0
The ground called Pikes is	25	0	32
Oate Close	14	0	12
Hors Leas	8	2	0

Broad Close	22	0	20
Naggs Leas and Marsh	2	3	25
Barly Close	11	3	25
Calfes Plott	1	0	20
Cole craft	3	2	10
The grownd called Norr	29	3	0
	129	0	25
Of Watered Meadow			
The Five Acres is	6	11	17
Eleaven Acres is	11	3	9
Three Acres	2	3	34
Seaven Acres	7	0	34
Eighteen Acres	19	1	39
North Mead	1	3	19
Goose Mead and Katherine Meadows are	31	1	0
	84	3	32
Arrable Lands	42	3	38
Thirty Acres	34	0	0
Great Leyclose	17	1	20
Little Leyclose	4	3	28
Eighteen Acres	19	2	0
Way Furlong	30	3	0
40 Acres under Conybancks	42	0	0
Nine Borrow	36	2	32
Berry Pikes	40	1	9
Great Sheep Craft	4	2	37
Little Sheep Craft	3	0	21
Uper part of Fourscore acres	45	0	18
Lower Four Score acres	39	1	0
	360	3	3
The Sheep Downe	610	0	0

	£	s	d
The pasture being in the whole 127 acres and 25 lugs out of which deduct for Howse and Barnes Backsides and the Drove up to 3 gates and also for ditches and fences 11 acres and 25 lugs Remaines then of pasture 106 Acres whereof 53 Acres of it is very good pasture at £1 2s 6d per acre is	60	0	0
The other pasture is Peekes and the ground called Norr which is intended to be broaken up and sowne 3 years and to lay it downe 3 years and sowne with grass seed will then be worth at least 15s 0d per acre it being 53 acres	39	10	0

	£	s	d
In the whole of meadow near 81 Acres out of which to abate for Newcourt Maine Carriage and also to Maine Carriage for Green South Mead and Spouth Leas and for the fences 7 Acres			
Remaines the 74 Acres of meadow at £1 17s 6d per acre one with the other	138	15	0
In the whole of Arrable as by the mapp 360 Acres and 3 yards out of which to abate 14 Acres and 3 yards for ditches and hedges			
Remaines then of plowed lands 346 Acres att 11s 0d per acre yearly 3 fifth parts of it to be sowne 3 years, the other two 5th parts of it to lay downe 2 years together and sowne up with grass seed well worth 11s per acre one with the other	190	5	0
And about 50 Acres of the best downe to be Inclosed will be worth 10s 0d per acre yearly and made arrable with the rest	25	0	0
Remaines of Sheep Downe 560 Acres at 2s 6d per acre	70	0	0
	523	0	0

The yearly rent now paid for it is £460 0s 0d
The Church and Poor Rates with 34 rents of the Maine Trunk in Charleton grownd per annum one year with another, all which is paid by the Tennant £50 0s 0d

STANDLYNCH FARM

The lease of Standlynch Farm was purchased by the Bockland or Buckland family in 1572, and successive generations continued to hold it and to serve as one of two MPs for Downton until Maurice Bockland died in 1710. His nephew Philip Bockland held the farm until his death in 1724. The farm was sold in 1726. The following survey of the farm was made soon after Philip Bockland's death.

*In 1733 the landscape at Standlynch was transformed by the building of a mansion on the high ground above the Avon Valley and the laying out of a landscaped park. In 1814 this mansion, together with Standlynch farm and the surrounding estate, was purchased by the Crown and given to the heirs of Lord Nelson. The mansion was re-named Trafalgar House. The present Standlynch Farm is some way east of the farm which is described in the following survey. [*VCH Wilts., *XI, 1980, 70-1. This names the family as 'Buckland' although many contemporary sources and the monuments in Downton church and Standlynch chapel use the form 'Bockland'.].*

This Survey gives an excellent view of a large, prosperous, chalkland farm, based on the traditional 'sheep and corn' husbandry. Other sources show that as well as over 500 acres of arable, there were 116 acres of water meadow providing early feed for the large sheep flock and hay for the dairy cows. The three miles of the river Avon provided valuable fishing, and the estate yielded timber, coppice wood and peat for firing. The elaborate work necessary to create water meadows is described elsewhere in this volume. The changes made to the water courses meant that the mill had to be rebuilt in 1696 with a new weir and mill leat. At the same time an 'eel house' was built near the mill which would have provided a useful income from eels caught during their annual migration down the stream. The estate also included several smaller tenements let at copyhold tenure by the Downton manorial custom of 'Borough English', whereby the right of inheritance went to the youngest son (D.A. Crowley, 'The Manor Court of Downton in the Eighteenth Century', WANHM, *74-5, 1981, 146-60).*

WSRO 490/1068

A Particular of the Mannor or reputed Mannor [of] Standlinch and the Farm of Standlinch in the County of Wilts, Two Miles from Downton and four Miles from Salisbury, both Burrough Towns and about Seaventy Miles from London, being lately the estate of Phillip Bockland Esquire Deceased [1724]

	£	s	d
A large Good Old House called Standlinch Scituate upon the River Avon with all convenient Outhouses, Stabling for 24 Horses, Coach House and Dovehouse and Gardens well planted with fruit Trees with a fair Avenue leading to the House, Two large Fishponds well Stocked with fish, with a Wilderness of Coppice wood containing three Acres scituate near the House, Cut out into beautifull walks, the Plat Ground of the House, Gardens and Offices except the Wilderness let to the Earl of Salisbury for Seaven years last past at Sixty pounds per annum	1000	0	0
Standlinch Farm (the Lands lying altogether) Consisting of 734 Acres and upwards of Arable, Meadow well watered and pasture now let for 7 years, one year to come next Michaelmas, for £400 per annum the Farm being Extra Parochial and Tyth free at Thirty years purchased	12000	0	0
Coppice Ground called Batts Croft and a Hedge Row on the Farm Containing 61 Acres valued at £10 per acre at 25 years purchase	762	10	0
Two Closes called Curtis's grounds let for £4 per annum at Thirty years purchase	120	0	0
Standlinch Mill and Eele Fishery well Customed now let for Twenty one years to a good Tenant with a Meadow Ground and Garden containing 3 acres at Twenty five years purchase	1100	0	0
The Royalty and fishery of the River Avon extending 3 Miles with an Island, well planted with Willows in the said River worth £20 per annum at 25 year purchase	500	0	0
The Right and Claim from Standlinch of feeding cattle and of cutting Peat and Turf for all of Common Fireing in the New Forrest near adjoining worth £10 per annum at 20 Years purchase	200	0	0
A Chief Rent paid by Sir James Ash, Barronet, for Draining of his			

	£	s	d
Meadows Seaven pounds per annum at Thirty years purchase	210	0	0
Timber of all sorts on Standlinch Farm plantations and Coppice ground valued at	1492	18	0
Charlton farm, the greatest part Freehold and part Copyhold of Inheritance in nature of Borough English Hold of the Mannor of Downton at a small fyne certaine and let for 12 years (of which 9 years are to come) at £100 per annum with a reservation to increase the rent in case the Common Down be soon inclosed which may advance the Estate £50 per annum at Thirty years purchase, the Lands consisting of Arable Meadow and Pasture	3000	0	0
A large well built Tenement in Charleton aforesaid with a Garden And Orchard, worth £5 per annum at 25 years purchase	125	0	0
Timber at Charlton aforesaid valued at	112	17	0
Eight Acres of Coppice wood now fit to cut being part of Batts Croft aforesaid worth £8 per Acre	64	0	0
Thirty two Acres of Ditto at £5 per Acre	160	0	0
Tenn Acres of Ditto at £2 per Acre	20	0	0
	20867	5	0
To be Deducted in respect of a Rent of 33 5s 0d per annum Payable out of part of Charlton farm to [blank] Edsall who at the time of the purchase being an infant could not Convey his Interest therein, at 30 years purchase	105	0	0
	20762	0	0

Note: There is likewise a handsome Chappell at Standlinch seperate from the house a donative not Subject to any Episcopall Visitation, and the said Estate at Standlinch lyes not Intermixed with any other Estate as may be seen by a correct mapp of it at Mr Gales Chambers in New Inn, London

EXTRACTS FROM THE TITHE BOOK OF MINETY 1663-1676

This book was kept by Richard Browne, the vicar of Minety 1663-82. He depended for his income on the tithes paid by farmers, and in that low-lying parish most of the tithes were levied on cattle and sheep. The vicar's attempts to keep track of the stock on the farms in his parish, illustrate the difficulties he faced. Cattle and sheep were constantly being brought into the Minety pastures for short periods for fattening before being sold locally or driven on to distant markets. In addition, Minety farmers accepted sheep flocks from bleaker downland pastures for over-wintering. The complexity and confusion of this situation made the task of obtaining tithes from reluctant farmers almost impossible. Questions arose over calves and lambs born in the parish from livestock only briefly kept there or whose owners lived elsewhere. Some stock evidently belonged to dealers and drovers. Likewise there were problems over the tithe on wool from sheep flocks feeding on Minety Common for short periods. It is evident that the vicar must have spent much time counting the livestock on the parish common pastures and the various farms, and that he tried hard to insist on his rightful dues. It is noticeable that the entries refer almost entirely to tithes on livestock, including poultry and eggs, and to wool, cheese and apples, with little mention of arable crops. As well as an account of payment for tithes in both kind and money, the notebook also includes entries showing rent for the glebe and a list of parishioners paying their Easter offerings to the vicar.

The vicar's own holdings in his parish are listed in the glebe terriers compiled during the 17th century, but not all of these give information about the method of collecting tithes. The complex customary arrangement (known as a 'modus') for levying tithes on livestock, particularly on beasts brought into the parish for short periods, is listed in great detail in the glebe terrier of Highworth in c1671. A more succinct account is provided by the glebe terrier for Maiden Bradley in 1681:

> *'For a cow white (milk) 2d. For a thorough cow 1½d. For a heifer 1d. For a calf sold the tenth penny. For 5 calves, half of one. For 7 calves, one to the parson to the party (i.e. owner) 1½d, paid by the parson. For a calf killed, the best shoulder. For a calf weaned ½d. For a garden 1d. For a colt 1d. For the cattle of strangers that are depastured in the liberty the tenth penny that is given for the herbage.' (S. Hobbs, ed.,* Wiltshire Glebe Terriers 1588-1827, *Wiltshire Record Society, 56, 2003, 49-51, 197-8. 301-2).*

The sort of problems the vicar of Minety encountered in keeping an account of livestock in his parish and in levying the appropriate tithe can be seen in entries throughout his book. In 1665, for example, he noted that there were '75 sheep brought in at St Peter's tide (29 June) of Richard Jefferies of Braydon and put on Minety Common'. Later in the same year he noted 'Malmesburie faire day (11 November) John Frankham had 6 fat beasts to sell at the faire, never told it to me'. In 1666-7 there are numerous references to sheep and cows being taken in for over-wintering by Minety farmers. For example '70 sheep of John Willis came in about Candlemas (2 February) and stayed on our common till sheretime and then drove on againe. Willis and his son bought in 100 sheep at Martin's faire (Malmesbury Fair 11 November)'. In 1671 he noted that Philip Norton had 14 cows, 8 calves, 54 sheep and 20 lambs, a further 50 'wintered sheep' and '4 beasts bought in at Lammas (1 August) out of Shropshire and sold at Christmas'.

The extract given here is the section of the Tithe Book for 1663-4. The vicar's book gives a good indication of the sort of farming practised across most of the parishes in north Wiltshire during the seventeenth century. The large expanses of ill-drained rough grazing, much of it part of the former royal forests, provided adequate though scarcely abundant winter keep, but it was ill suited to arable farming. Clearly several farmers were reluctant to pay the tithes they owed; others evidently found it difficult to raise the sums demanded and instead gave the vicar a variety of goods, including cheese, corn, eggs, meat, apples, firewood and poultry. Many payments were made considerably in arrears, and the vicar's entries in his book were obviously made at different times hastily noted as the vicar walked over his parish and some are difficult to understand. The assessment, payment and collection of tithe was subject to ecclesiastical law, and an entry for 1 November 1664 indicates that a dispute with William Hawkins over tithe was being tried before the bishop's court. The vicar depended for his livelihood on tithes and could not allow himself to be defrauded, but proper insistence on his dues could hardly have made him popular in his parish. In 1664 he noted that the tithes had brought him £49 6s 11d. The entries list the livestock or goods on which the tithe was payable; the sums of money in the right-hand columns are the tithes which the vicar calculated were due to him. As well as illustrating the movement of livestock through the parish, the Tithe Book provides a remarkable list of local markets and fairs. These included Castle Combe, Cirencester, Malmesbury, Sherston, Marlborough, Tetbury and Devizes. A similar Tithe Book for Grittleton covers the years 1675 to 1702. (WSRO 1620/12).

WSRO 1190/17, folios 10-18v

		£	s	d
Tithe Book of Minety 1663-1676 kept by the vicar, Richard Browne				
Entries for 1664				
	Ed Grimes			
	The fall of a colt			3
	William Green			
	6 lambes			
	20 sheepe			
	14 calves			
	William Grove			
25 May	2 beasts sold		2	0
	2 calves fallen before Lady Day		2	0
	2 calves sold to Wm Dodswell		2	0
			6	0
	John Dodswell			
Painter Plecke – Mr Giles Poole		8	10	0
	Received of John Dodswell for Painters Plecke		10	0
	Received for John Dodswell's owne living in carrying of wood and coal	1	1	8
	Mrs Webb 1663			
April 10	11 cows she kept			
	2 cows sold to John Hawkins not calved			
	9 calves she paid for		9	0
	3 cowes of 14 were fatted			
	Baroe [farm] was her living at £65 per annum			
	Richard Greene			
He took his tithes at 25s 0d				
Paid Aprill 28				
	in wheat		10	0
	in monie		5	0
	a bushell of wheate		4	7
	1 hundred of cheese		4	8
	in monie		1	0
		1	5	3
June 10				
	Received of R Greene in full for his tithes till Lamas next, apples excepted	1	5	0

		£	s	d
	Philip Wilkins			
	3 lambs fallen of R Burts Creeklad			
	10 sheep wintered of R. Burts Creeklad			
	5 calves fallen of his own		5	0
	2 lambs of his owne			6
	Cattle taken in			
	one heyfer			2
	4 cowes		1	0
	1 fat sheepe sold			
	7lb of wool share			
			6	8
	John Browne			
May 19 1664				
	He then paid by composition for all tithes except Apples till the following Lamas after the date of these presents		7	0
	Mr Westmarsh			
May 24 1664				
	10 calves fatten		10	0
	22 sheepe rented Rich. Jordan, 15 lambs of the wintered sheepe, 1 lamb of his own		5	0
	5 sheepe shere 1lb tithe wool			8
	9 cowes		2	3
	1 heifer			2
			18	1
	Thomas Masklin			
	38 sheepe sold about Easter, fatt sheepe in theire wool			
	Lambs none			
	8 calves			
	2 colts			
	His ground rented at £53 per annum			
	9 cowes			
	1 heifer			
	108 sheepe bought Holyroode [14 September] time and shere midsomer eve			
9 May				
	5lb wool tithe			
	2 heifers fatted that had no calves			
	38 sheepe		3	2
	8 calves		8	0
	2 colts		1	0
	10 cowes		2	6

		£	s	d
	2 heifers fatted		2	0
	7 calves x 9s 0d			
	108 sheepe x 9s 0d			
	Phillip Greene			
	2 lambs			
	Phillip had a oxe fatting about Christmas			
	6 sheepe			
	3 weaned			
	1 heifer calfe sold			6
	8 piggs farowed at Christmas		1	0
	4 cowes sold barren			8
	13 cowes – a goose to be had besides			
	5 calves weaned the last year which are to be accounted in this yeares accounts			
27 May 1664				
	It was then agreed that Philipe Greene compounded for his tithes till Lamas next after the date of these presents for twentie shillings, one halfe to be paid next midsumer the other at the next Lamas following			
September 7				
	Received then for Phill. Greene tithes due at Lamas last past	1	0	0
	Willm Rundle			
	2 calves sold and 3 weaned		5	0
	14 sheepe shere 26lb wooll, in tithe wooll 2lb & halfe -?		2	0
	32 sheepe bought in & shere within 3 weekes or a month these sheepe were accounted in 65			
	6 cowes		1	6
	2 heifers of Wm Rundles			4
	4 cowes of his daughter Mary		1	0
	3 calves weaned		3	0
	1 calf sold		1	0
	3 beasts on Mr Kings ground		5	0
	Mr Allis of Poole			
November 15 '66				
	Received then of Mr Tho. Allis for his tithes of the Lammas Meade	1	0	0

		£	s	d
	Phillipe Timbrill			
November 19				
	5 lambs in all		1	3
	3lb wooll due to me		2	3
	12 calves		12	0
	1 colt			6
	22 cowes		5	6
		1	1	6
	15 sheepe shere			
	1 Pig tith			
	1 goose			
	7 turkies			
	3 cowes turned off last yeare			
	3 heifers fatted			
	Will Doighton			
May 31				
	He hath agreed for all his tithes from the date of these presents to Lamas next ensuing for the sume of thirty shillings			
June 28				
	Received then of Wm Doighton for his dues ending at Lammas next after the date of these presents	1	10	0
	Nathaniell Norton			
July 9				
	Cowes none			
	3 hoggs shere 6lb of wooll in all			
	1 score of couples bought and sold			
	Cow sold to John Weeks			
	Thorough milch heifer sold			
	John Hinton			
May 31				
	4 sheepe wintered at home			
	30 sheepe came last Lady Day from Gordon			
	4 lambs, 4 calves, 4 cowes. Aug 18 He told me that he had 3 or 4 beasts that were fat at St John Bridge Faire			
	2 thorow milch [cows in full milk]			
July 16				
	Received then from John Hinton tithes due at Lamas next after the date of these		16	0

		£	s	d
May 31	John Hinton took then his owne tithes for 16s 0d a yeare, the yeare to end at Lamas next after the date of these presents, and at apple time I have reffered it to his curtesie			
	Tho. Wake			
June 29 1663	Received then of Thomas Wake for the tithe of his Russells [? Russet apples] at 8d per pound for £9 per annum the sum of 6s 0d due at Lammas next after the date of these presents			
June 29	Received		6	0
	John Keene			
June 2 1664	He hath compounded for his tithes for this present yeare for £2 10s 0d his yere is up at Lamas ensuing the date of these presents			
August 3	Received of John Keene for Lammas dues	2	10	0
	George Barret			
August 4 1664	1 draught of fleices 20lb			
	2 draught of fleices 20lb			
	3 draught of fleices 20lb			
	4 draught of fleices 20lb			
	5 draught of fleices 20lb			
	6 draught of fleices 20lb			
	30 d. fleices 7lb			
	6 score & 7lb			
	3 fleices left unshere			
	58 sheepe shere at qtr tithes			
	54 sheepe brought in & shere June 9			
	Lambes – none			
	7 calves since he came		7	0
	13 cowes		3	3
	7 Heyfers		1	2
	3 grazing beasts		3	0
	Tith wool 3lb halfe		2	7
	2 colts unpaid			

		£	s	d
	12 sheep fatted sold to Webb unpaid			
			17	0

Mr Southbe

		£	s	d
November 26	Received then for his tithes	2	0	0

Widdowe Lookes

		£	s	d
April 6 1664	Received then of Goody Lookes for a yeres tithes due at Lady Day last before the date of these presents		2	8

Will. Warner

		£	s	d
June 10 1664	Powells Ground mowed	4	0	0
	Grove Close of the Feoffees—?	5	10	0
	Of Mr Merit a ground Hawkes	6	0	0
	His owne part in Hawkes	3	0	0
	Rec Robarts ground Ruddokes	6	0	0

He hath taken the above grounds at 8d per pound. He hath paid for Stockwells ground being Mr Merits Hawkes & his owne Hawkes 3d till Lamas next & after that at Lamas he is to pay for it 8s od for the yere as Stakewell did. For yeres viz. Powell's ground, Grove Close & Ruddokes being £15 10s od which at 8d per pound comes to 10s 4d.

		£	s	d
June 13	Received of Wm Warner		13	4
	Weaver milkes 5 cowes here			
	He paid his Rent for Fleshwerk June 29	1	13	4

John Hall

		£	s	d
June 14 1664	15 calves		15	0
	8 lambes		2	0
	20 sheepe shere 47lb		3	8
	19 cowes		4	9
	3 cowes fatted		3	0
	Mr Hayfers	60	0	0

		£	s	d
	Wid. Mapon	8	0	0
	Purleiues	8	0	0
	A goose, a turkie, Apples	[blank]		
		1	3	5

Wm Webb

		£	s	d
June 15				
	4 calves		4	0
	9 sheepe shere 20lb 2lb tithe		1	6
	2 lambs	[blank]		
	4 cowes		1	0

John Hawkins

		£	s	d
June 10 1664				
	3 lambs drove last yere, 26 lambs fell this yere		7	0
	5 sheepe of last yeres whole tithe			
	60 sheep bought at Collingburne			
	14 calves fallen		14	0
	5 piggs			
	The weight of 5 sheepe and 60 sheepe 5 score And 5lbs		7	10
	Of those 2 calves that was to fall one died and one was paid for		1	0
	26 cowes		6	6
	3 heifers			6
	14 cowes & calves bought in			
	2 calves of Mrs Webb yet to reckon for and 5 piggs that were drove not reckoned			
	All the rest made even for	1	16	0

John Pitman

1664

8 lambes
40 couples sold, 1 score hogs bred, June 24
5 calves
8 lambes
13 cowes
20 sheepe sold
19 pounds & half of wooll
16 geese
1 colt

Received May 25 1665 of John Pitman by composition for his tithes of the yere 1664 ending at Lamas in the yere 64 the sume 20s 0d.

		£	s	d
	Giles Pitman			
June 14 1664				
	18 cowes brought in May the 9th			
	[the following section faded and illegible]			
	8 sheepe shere 15lb & half of wooll			
	40 sheep sold 24 June			
	15 lambs			
	8 cows			
	3 heifers			
	1 cow & calfe sold			
	1 calfe since Lady Day			
	18lb & halfe quarter in all of tithe wooll			
December 10				
	Received of him for his whole yeres tithes the sume of fortie shillings his yere ending at Lady Day next after the date of these presents		40	0
	Robert Taylour Jun.			
June 24 1664				
	20 calves			
	20 cowes	1	0	0
	9 sheepe shere		5	0
	1 lambe	[blank]		
	9 piggs			3
	1 colt		2	6
	Robert Taylor Jun sold 3 fat heyfers & one fat bull about Christmas to Carpenter a butcher			6
November 15				
	Received then of Robert Taylour Jun by way of composition for this last yere ending at Lamas last before the date of these presents the sume of	1	16	0
	Wm Baydon			
September 1				
	Received then for his yeres tithes due at Lamas before the date of these presents the sume of seventeene shillings & sixepence		17	6
	John Frankham			
September 1				
	Received of him for tithes due at Lamas last before the date of these presents the full sume of eighteene shillings		18	0

		£	s	d
	[Entry obliterated]			
	John Johnson			
August 1	Received then xs for all his dues ending this present day		xs	
	6 calves			
	6 cowes			
	23lb of wooll in all			
	12 sheepe shere			
	Lucian Browne			
August 2 1664	Received toward his tithes the yere		1	0
Aprill 1	Received then of Lucian Browne the remaining part For this yeres tithes		xs	
	Also he was then satisfied for some thornes that I bought of him and also satisfied for his part of 5 acres			
	Mr Lavender			
August 10	Lambes none			
	Sheepe none			
	9 calves		9	0
	9 cowes & heifers		2	3
	1 colt			6
			11	9
	Zacharie Davis			
	Received then for his tithes		6	6
	Wm Tollin			
August 16 1664	Lambes none			
	5 sheep & 6lb wool in all			6
	8 calves		8	0
	8 cowes		2	0
	9 geese			10
	1 colt			6
			11	10
	Apples & peares 2 bushell			

	£	s	d
Ed Jefferie			
Lambes & sheepe none			
9 calves at Cooles			
15 cowes 6 of [his] owne 9 cowes at Cooles and to pay for the calves			
Beasts turned off			
2 calves -? Paid for			
4 Jefferies not to pay for			
Lamas due for 15 cows at grounds			
15 calves at Lady Day 65			
Lamas dues this yere 64			
John Webb says he did not pay Mr Henwood Lamas dues 65			
Francis Gibbs			
Beasts & steeres fattened …….			

[*Note: Rest of the above and the following page has been torn off*]

	£	s	d
John Wilkins			
September 17 1664			
10 calves		10	0
10 cowes		2	6
No lambes			
No sheepe			
Apples			
		12	6
Wm Tyler			
October 4			
Received then for his tithes due at Lamas last before the date of these presents		11	0
Robert Taylour's Son			
October 28			
I had of him			
Halfe a hundred of cheese		10	0
A Hundred & halfe of faggots		10	0
Fat cattle			

[*Rest of page missing*]

		£	s	d
	Thomas Lewin			
November 3 1664				
	Received then of him by John Hinton		20	0
May 5				
	Received then of Tho Lewin of Remainder of his tithes		9	8
	Widdow An Hayward			
	The lower end of the 30 acres mowed £7 0s 0d At 8d in the pound		4	8
	Wm Hawkins			
1663				
	1 part of Mintie wood			
	All the wood to W^m^ for 1664		4	2
	1 part of Moore acres		12	6
	Timbrells ground tithe for 2 yere		[Blank]	
			5	4
	An Heyward rents £7 per Annum part of the 30 Acres	1	2	0

November 1 1664

It was then agreed by John Hawkins that on condition the suit about his brother Wm Hawkins and the vicar's dues, that John Hawkins will satisffie £1 2s 0d as tithes due to the vicar & all warrantable charges shall appear to be due in the Bishop's court.

		s	d
	Mr Walter Pleydell		
	7 ewes Giles Pitman bought for the 12 of the old stock lost [word illegible] 10 ewes & lambes bought by Giles Pitman about July 9. One of them lost		
	18 lambes		
	3 lambes to be tithes		
	6 lambes out of the 7 to be	1	6
	Eggs 2d		2
	Offerings & garden 3d		3
	3lb tithe wooll due	2	3
	16s sold in apples	1	6
	7 or 8 bushells left	1	4
		6	10

		£	s	d
	4 cowes Mr Nic. Pleydell had 2 weeks in picked hain			
	Common ground Wm Tillin by Samburne 50s per annum			
	John Winkworth of Broad Summerford			
	Long Dole rented of Wm Tollin by Swill Bridge			
	Received of Mr Walter Pleydell Nov 15 the sume of		6	0
	John Mason			
December 4				
	He paid for his tithes this yere due at Lamas before the date of these presents	1	10	0
	Braydon hurst not paid for			
	For the Hurst paid May 15 1665		13	4
	John Young of Ashton			
November 15 66				
	Received then of John Young of his tithes due in this yere for Mary Bush's living		5	0
	John Webb			
February 10 1664				
	17 calves		11	0
	14 beasts		3	6
	No lambes or sheepe			
	3 beasts turned off			
	For all his beasts fatted last yeare and this present yere he paid me		4	0
	6 geese toward tithe for another yeare			
	These reckons made even for Lamas past			
	Wm Taylour of Chelworth			
February 10 1664				
	He rented of his father Rob. Taylour some 2 grounds mowed Stewards meade & cowe leaze at £x per annum. For which at 8d in the pound he paid the day above written as due at Lady Day following		6	8
	Ed. Carter			
March 23				
	Received by Wm Warner the sume of £1 9s 0d which Edward Carter paid to him for his			

		£	s	d
	tithes due to me at Lady Day next after the date of these presents	1	9	0
	Wm Coole			
	Received for all his tithes due at Lamas in this present yeare		6	0
	Andrew Parker			
February 12 1664	He paid to my wife towards his tithes which were due the Lamas before	1	6	6
	Mr Humphry Pleidell			
Jan 1	£4 at 8d in pound		2	8
	2 kine		2	5
			5	4
	Robert Masklin			
Aprill 19 66	Then he came & paid for this years tithes which was due at Lammas in the yeare 64 the same which he paid in the yere before		14	0
	Wm Taylour of Minty			
May 7 66	2 cowes			6
	2 heifers			4
	2 calves		2	0
	These dues were from Lady Day when we reckoned to Lamas following		2	10
	Offerings			8
	1 Heyfer to calve 66		3	6
	Tho Masklin			
February ult. 1664	[blank]			

		£	s	d
	Tho Rowland			
Aug 3 1664				
	Received then for his tithes in 64 ending at Lady Day last before the date of these presents the sum of		40	0
	Mr Nicholas Pleydell			
	For all his tithes at 8d in the pound	2	6	8
	Phillip Norton			
	8 calves		8	0
	2 lambes in all			6
	Sheep shere 29lb wooll in all	[Blank]		
	11 cowes		2	9
	2 heifers			4
	3 beasts turned of		3	0
	4lb wool		3	0
			17	7
	Tho Browne			
	8 calves, 1 calf killed I had a shoulder		7	0
	5lb of wooll in all			5
	3 sheepe no lambs			
	8 cowes		2	0
			9	8

1664

	£	s	d
I made of my tithes this present yeare 64 £49 6s 11d	48	9	2

ENCLOSURES IN NORTH AND WEST WILTSHIRE

Most of the chalk area of Wiltshire remained unenclosed during the 17th century, and commonfield farming, controlled by manorial courts, continued. In the dairy-farming, cattle-raising regions of north and west Wiltshire, however, there had already been considerable enclosure during the sixteenth century and enclosure by agreement made further progress during the seventeenth century. [VCH, IV, 1959, 44-6].

John Aubrey provides a vivid account of change in the appearance of the countryside of north-west Wiltshire during his lifetime:

> *The country was then (c1550) a lovely camponia as that about Sherston and Cotswold. Very few enclosures unless near houses. My grandfather Lyte did remember when all between the Cromhalls and Castle Combe was so, when Eston.Yatton and Combe did intercommon together. In my remembrance much hath been enclosed and every Year more and more is taken in. [J. Aubrey,* Miscellanies on Several Curious Subjects, *E. Curll, ed. London, 1714, pp31-2]*

For the small, family-run dairy farms, with little or no arable, enclosed fields were much more convenient for keeping livestock. Manorial control was weak, and John Aubrey commented upon the sturdy individualism and religious nonconformity of the dairy farmers and part-time cloth workers in north and west Wiltshire. [J. Aubrey, Wiltshire Topographical Collections, *ed., J.E. Jackson, Devizes, 1862, 9;* Natural History of Wiltshire, *1969 edn., i]. The improvement of grassland by enclosure, under-draining and the exclusion of livestock from neighbouring manors was in the interests of tenants as well as landlords. It is an indication of the educational standard of the majority of those involved in these agreements that of the seven freeholders and thirty copyholders who agreed to the enclosure at Brinkworth, only Tobias Crisp 'freeholder & parson', two other freeholders and thirteen copyholders could sign their names. At Charlton only five of the twenty-four tenants could sign; and at Hankerton only four tenants signed, while twelve others put their marks to the agreement. Three of the extracts are from the estates of Thomas, earl of Berkshire, who lived in the Elizabethan mansion Charlton Park. He was the younger son of Thomas Howard, earl of Suffolk and was created earl of Berkshire in 1626 [VCH* Wilts, *XIV, 1991, 41] The fourth agreement is for land at Hannington, lying in the Thames valley in the north-east corner of Wiltshire. Here the lord of the manor was Richard Swayne of Blandford Forum,Dorset, who was a lawyer of the Middle Temple.*

He was acting on behalf of his nephew, Sir Thomas Freke, eldest son of Robert Freke of Iwerne Courtney, Dorset. Sir Thomas Freke also owned the freehold of Pisworth farm which he had purchased in 1606 from Sir George Snygge, Recorder of Bristol. [C.B. Fry, Hannington, *1935, 25-8]. Together these agreements illustrate the important part landlords played in urging and encouraging their tenants to adopt improvements. Brinkworth, Charlton and Hankerton had been part of the royal forest of Braydon, which was disafforested in 1630. This provoked fierce rioting in 1631 by farmers who had previously fed their cattle in the forest and who objected strongly to the loss of their common rights. The riots were suppressed, but it was against this background that the enclosure agreements were made. [E. Kerridge, 'Revolts in Wiltshire Against Charles I',* WANHM, *57, 1958-60, 64-74].*

ENCLOSURE AT BROMHAM 1618

This is an example of the sort of small-scale agreement among tenants, supported by the lord and major leaseholders, whereby much of the land in north and west Wiltshire was enclosed during the 17th century.

WSRO 122/1

From Survey Book of Bromham, Stanley, Rowdon, Chittoe belonging to Sir Henry Baynton

25 September 16 James I [1618]

Whereas the Lord of this mannor and the Freeholders, Copyholders, customary tenants and conventionary tenants of the same mannor who have divers small parcells of Lande in divers common fields and other places of this mannor, as namely in Clinge hill, the Westfield, the Middlefield, the Pillory field, the Hooke, the Yard, Bossey, Broadmeade, and Clayes, which small parcells of Lande are laid together in equall proportion by the generall consent and agreement of all the parties aforesaid, to the intent that as well as the said Lord, as every of the said Tennantes may enjoy from henceforth the plotts of grounde allotted unto him in severaltye according to their former estates formerlye granted unto them.

BRINKWORTH ENCLOSURE AGREEMENT 15 SEPTEMBER 1631

Piecemeal enclosures had been made at Brinkworth during the previous century. At the disafforestation of the royal forest of Braydon in 1630, some 1,000 acres were reserved to the earl of Berkshire. The following agreement relates to the re-distribution and enclosure of some 250 acres allocated to the tenants in lieu of their former rights in the forest. [V.C.H. Wilts, IV, 1959, 403-6; XIV, 1991, 20]

WSRO 88/9/1

15 September 1631

Att a Court then and there holden yt was & ys consented unto and agreed betweene the right honorable Thomas, Earle of Barkshire lord of the said Mannor, and the freeholders and tenants of the said Mannor whose names are subscribed that the lord shall & may att his pleasure take in and inclose the wastes, woodes & pastures within the said Mannor and improve & convert the same to his owne use and benefitt leaving forth for commons for the tennants within the said Mannor the Marsh called Brinkworth Marshe, yet so nevertheless that there shalbe gappes & shards left in the bound and Inclosure betwixt the said Marsh and the rest of the purlieus and wastes for the tenants cattle to goe forth of the said Marshe into the rest of the wastes adjoininge untyll such tyme as all such forrayners & neighbours who pretend right of common in the said Marshe shalbe barred owsted & excluded of entercommoning in the said Marshe. And further his Lordship doth agree to assigne & allott 50 acres forth of the wastes to be inclosed for commons for such cottagers as are tenants of the sayd Mannor. In Wyttnes of which agreement wee truly subscribed [our] names. And yt is further agreed that Sir George [*—?Sir George Ivie], knight, and Mr Plat the steward of the said Mannor shall uppon viewe [*—] a fitt & convenyent way for drift of cattle and otherwyse [*—] hill, to the said Brinkworth Marshe, And the sayd [*—] and tenants are to mound the said Marshe att their chardges And the cottagers are to mound the sayd 50 acres at their chardges.

[**hole in document at this point*]

Signed by the Earl of Berkshire + Tobias Crisp 'freeholder and parson' + 6 other freeholders + 30 tenants

CHARLTON ENCLOSURE AGREEMENT 17 SEPTEMBER 1631

*Charlton's part of the former forest of Braydon was described in 1631 as overgrown with bracken and bramble. The earl of Berkshire reserved most of it for his own use, and the following agreement relates to 400 acres allocated to the 24 tenants in lieu of their former grazing rights in the forest, and 50 acres provided for cottagers. [*V.C.H. Wilts, *XIV, 1991, 45]*

WSRO 88/9/1

Charlton 17 September 1631

Att a court then and there holden yt is agreed betweene the right honorable Thomas, Earle of Berkshire, Lord of the Manor, and the freeholders and tenants of the said manor whose names are subscribed that the Lord may take in and inclose the wastes and purlieus of the said mannor and improve and convert the same to his Lordshipp's benefitt leaving forth for commons for the tenants fowre hundred acres in such place of the said wastes as lyeth most necessary and fitt for those tenants, and that uppon the Inclosures there shalbe gapps and shards in the bounds betwixt the sayd fowre hundred acres to bee left for the tenants commons and the rest of the wastes and purlieus for the tenants cattle to goe forth of those fower hundred acres into the rest of the wastes adjoininge untyll such tyme as all such forrayners and neighbours who pretend right of common in those fower hundred acres shalbe excluded of and from entercommoninge in those fower hundred acres. And further his Lordshipp ys pleased to assigne and allott 50 acres more part of his Lordshipp's wastes for commons for the cottagers of the said manor.

Subscribed by the Earl + Vicar+ 24 tenants
Only five of the tenants could sign their names.

AN ENCLOSURE DISPUTE AT GARSDON 1632

Sir Lawrence Washington, Registrar of the Court of Chancery, purchased the manor of Garsdon in 1631. Soon afterwards he was involved in the following dispute with the Earl of Berkshire over rights within the former Forest of Braydon. This case before the Court of Chancery shows the effect which 'disafforestation' had upon residents in the former royal forests. It provides evidence of the uncontrolled, poor-quality grazing available within the forests, only limited by occasional 'drifts' or drives when the owners of livestock could be identified. Energetic landowners, like the Earl of Berkshire, who was keen to improve the value of his estate and the standard of farming among his tenants, took full advantage of the change in the status of the forests. Such landowners were unlikely to be restrained by their tenants, but at Garsdon the Earl was confronted by a new lord of the manor, Sir Lawrence Washington, who had purchased the property in 1631. Moreover, Sir Lawrence was a highly-qualified lawyer, well aware of his legal rights, and in this instance the Earl was obliged 'for quietness sake' to compromise and come to an agreement with his neighbour.

PRO C2/Chas I W3/17
(Transcript in *WN & Q*, VII, 1911-13, 452-4)

TO THE RT. HON. THOS. LORD COVENTRY, LORD KEEPER OF THE GREAT SEALE OF ENGLAND, 21 JUNE 1632.

Your orator Sir Lawrence Washington, Knight, Register of this honourable Court and lord of the manor of Garsdon, county Wilts; Richard Woodroffe, Clerk, Rector of Garsdon; Anthony Hungerford, gent.; Bartholmew Hawkes; John Hurlebat; William Mudge; John Millard; Simon Otteridge; Nicholas Munden; Thomas Hayward; Ferdinando Gingell; Katherine Cobb, widow; Robert Downe also Buckland; John Griffin; Hugh Strongford; Nicholas Pantinge; David Gray; Thomas Gingell; Henry Garlicke and Richard Woodroffe, copyholders and leaseholders of said manor, complain that they used to enjoy common of pasture for all manner of beasts levant and courant in the wastes, woodgrounds, marrishes [marshes] and purlieus within the severall manors and parishes of Brinkworth, Brokenboro and Charlton, and by all the time within the memory of man had right to drive cattle into these wastes, etc., to fodder etc., at all times of the year without disturbance, except that the lords of the said manors time out of mind caused certaine drifts [roundup of livestock] to be made of all beasts feeding there and did drive them to their several pounds and impound the owners, who if they had a right of common there could take them out free of charge and drive them back again, but otherwise being strangers had to pay a fine to take their cattle out of the pound ... your orator can prove that time out of mind the tenants of Garsdon manor and parson of the glebe in Garsdon did take their cattle out of the pound without payment ... nevertheless now of late, about the Feast of St Michael th'archangel, last past, the Rt. Hon. Thomas, Earle of Berkshire, now lord of the manors of Brinkworth, Brokenboro and Charlton, being misinformed by some ill-disposed persons as to the rights of the lord, tenants and rector of Garsdon manor, or pretending that they are now extinct by some pretended unitie of possession heretofore in the said manors, together with the manor of Garsdon upon the dissolution of the Abbie, hath caused the said Hon. Earle to enclose the severall wastes, etc., so that your orators are entirely debarred from putting their cattle in ... for your orators Bartholomew Hawkes and John Hurlebat have put in cattle which twice have been impounded to their great inconvenience, and threats have been made that if necessary they will be impounded twenty times ... your orator prayeth that the Hon. Earle may be called upon to discover by what right he has made these enclosures and interrupted the said rights of common seeing that he took the said manors charged with the said commons and they were enjoyed by your orators when the said Hon. Earle came into possession of them.

Answer to the Complaint from Thomas, Earl of Berkshire 3 December 1632.

The said manor of Garsdon and this defendant's manors of Brinkworth, Brokenboro and Charlton were parcell of the possessions of the late dissolved monasterie of Malmesbury, each having their own wastes, etc., and known by their several bounds, all adjoininge his Majestie's late forest of Bradon. The lords of the above manors and also of several others, having wastes adjoining the forest of Bradon, used and claymed for themselves and their tenants commons in said forest before the same was disafforested about two years since; at which time these several lords were barred from their commons in the said forest upon His Majestie's enclosure of his soil by decree of the Hon. Court of the Exchequer. It is true that during such usage of commons in the forests, the several wastes of the manors being purlieus of the forests were by the several lords of the manors used for commons. Sir Laurance Washington and the other complainants did formerly common their beasts in the wastes, etc., mentioned in the Bill and also those of other lords of manors adjoining the forest, but your defendant doth not think this was of right, but only for convenience in their use of commons in the forest of Bradon according to forest laws. During this confusion of commoning your defendant thinketh the commoninge was little worth and often beasts having no right there got in. It is true that your defendant hath caused his wastes, woods, etc., to be enclosed to make some improvement thereof, which he hopeth is lawful, the cause moving him is that the forest of Braydon being disafforested by His Majesty and his soil therein enclosed, and also other lords having enclosed their wastes adjoining the forest, the said complainants would have made a prey of this defendant's wastes otherwise. It is true that your defendant did from time to time order drifts to be made over these wastes, but this was not to distinguish who had right of commons there, but rather to find the cattle of strangers who had no right of common in the forest of Braydon. Your defendant is informed that any right of commons of the lord of Garsdon manor over wastes of the other said manors is extinct by unity of possession according to the Rules of Law. It is true that by his orders the cattle of those placed on his wastes have been impounded. He denieth that he took the said manors charged with these commons, also if the plaintiffs have any right of commons remaining, yet their right is to have equal rights in wastes of other manors adjoining the forest, as well as his, which amount not to a third part of the wastes contributing to such their pretended right of commons. Notwithstanding, for the good of the countrie and for quietness sake, your defendant will allow a third part of such wastes in said manors on behalfe of the tenants of the Manor of Garsdon, together with the tenants of other manors adjoining as have been demanded.

HANKERTON ENCLOSURE AGREEMENT 26 SEPTEMBER 1634

*The largest part of the purlieus of the former forest land at Hankerton was taken by the earl of Berkshire. The following agreement allots 120 acres as a common for the tenants and exchanges rights elsewhere in the parish. There is no evidence that the earl built a house for an overseer of the common which was part of the agreement [*V.C.H. Wilts, *XIV, 1991, 99].*

WSRO 88/9/1

> An agreement Indented made the six & twentith day of September 1634. Betweene the Right Honorable Thomas Earle of Berks Knight of the most noble order of the Garter of the one partie, And the tenants freeholders copieholders & leasehoulders of the mannor of Hankerton of the other partie, as followeth:

In primis the Earle doth promise undertake & agree to quiett & setle the Incomons & Moores of Hankerton unto the said Tenants Freeholders Copiehoulders Leaseholders of the said Mannor, and of all others shalbe debarred from having any comon of pasture or other interest in the same Incomons & Moores. And the said Earle is to Rayle or hedge the same out unto them accordingly, and so to keepe it from tyme to tyme from the Mannor of Clottey [Cloatley] and the tenants thereof. And also the said Earle is to settle to the said Tenants Freehoulders Copieholders & Leaseholders all the inclosed peece of pasture grownd now lately inclosed, lying adjoyning unto Seelies Coppice coneyning by estimation Six schore acres more or lesse, to continue to the Tenants aforesaid for the tyme being and to come for ever. And the same shalbe enjoyed tyth-free against the Parson and Vicar of Charleton.

Item in consideration thereof, the said Tenants Freehoulders Copieholders & Leaseholders doe hereby give way and their consents unto the said Earle that he shall inclose & keepe in severall All those two grownds called Inmeade & Millanes, to hould unto him and his heires in severall for ever. The Tenant of the Farme late Brownes abating out of his Common in the Incommons, and in the said new inclosed grownd for two yeard [yard] lands, and to common for two yeards only.

Item it is agreed that William Beale and William Gagg shall not common in the Moores & Incommons for their respective Leases of Moorden and the Downes, but shall common for the same in the said late inclosed peece of grownd togeather with the rest of the said Tenants.

Item the said Earle is to allowe the said Tenants fewell in some convenient place neare adjoyning to mainteine & keepe the hedges in and about the said late inclosed peece of grownde from tyme to tyme upon request. As also the tymber for the repayreing of the gates & postes as often as need shall require, and tymber for plankes & postes to make the waies at the gates. And also tymber to build a litle house for one to dwell in to see to the grownds & Cattell there. And the said house being built, to continue & be from tyme to tyme & for ever, at the disposing of the said Tenants, Freehoulders, Copyholders & Leaseholders to some poore man to and for the purpose aforesaid.

Item the said Earle is to give his consent unto the said Tenants to have a fallowe field every yeare according to their — ⋆. And that they may devide & parte the fields either by enclosing of the meade or otherwise. And also make a mounde next the way towards Charletons field for the fencing and saving of the Lottmead, land & headens.

Item the said Tenants Freehoulders, Copieholders & Leaseholders doe hereby release & quitt their Interest of Common in all —⋆[the] residue of the wastes & Purlewes of the late Forest of Bradon. And doe agree that the owners and Lords of the same may enclose and enjoye the said residue in severalty unto their own proper Use & Uses & behoofes to them & their heires for ever at their wills & pleasure without any lett or denyall of them the said Tenants Freeholders Copyholders or Leasehoulders or any of them.

In witnes whereof the said Earle to one parte of these presents, And the said Tenants, Freehoulders, Copiehoulders & Leasehoulders to the other parte of these presents Interchangably have sett their hands, the day & yeare first above written.

[⋆ *Hole in manuscript.*]

There follow the signatures of John Bradshawe, Parson of Crudwell, William Beale Vicar of Hankerton and four other tenants together with the marks of 12 others.

HANNINGTON ENCLOSURE AGREEMENT 16 MAY 1632

This agreement provides a good description of the unimproved state of the common lands, overgrown and ill-drained, with unrestricted access and severe over-grazing. At Hannington, as in many other places, much care was taken in the enclosure agreement to extinguish annual tithe payments. The Hannington tithes were shared between the Rector, the Vicar, and John Arden who had acquired the right to the portion of tithes formerly paid to the abbess of Wherwell in Hampshire. In this agreement complex arrangements were also made for roads, paths, water courses and bridges.

WSRO 1033/42 [Note: This is an 18th-century copy of the original]

> **Articles** indented made the sixteenth day of May in Anno Domini one thousand six hundred thirty and two and in the eighth yeare of the reign of our Sovereign Lord Charles by the Grace of God King of England Scotland France and Ireland Defender of the faith etc **Betweene** Richard Swayne Esquire Lord of the Manor of Hannington in the County of Wilts And also owner of the Rectory and impropriate parsonage of Hannington aforesaid consisting as well of Glebe Lands as some special Tythes Being patron likewise of the Advowson of the Vicarage of Hannington aforesaid and John Stubbes Clerk the present vicar and incumbent of the said vicarage consisting also of Glebe lands and some special Tythes and Sir Thomas Freke Knight owner of a Farm within the said Manor called Pisworth and of another freehold within the said manor called Mr Parkers yeard lands And of another freehold within the said manor called Bupies half yeard lands and of other freehold called Mr George his freehold. And of a portion of Tythes heretofore arising within the said manor called Horazell[?] Tithes whereof one Master John Arden was lately propriate. And one Thomas Sandye owner of an other freehold containing two yeard lands in Hannington aforesaid and William Batson Gent., John Batson, Jeoffery Pinnell, Humphry Yorke, William his Sonne and Mary Yorke his Daughter, Thomas Sandry the elder, Thomas Sandry the younger, Walter Weston, Robert Marshe, William Ballone, William Plomer, John Plomer his Son, Thomas Plomer and John his Brother, Humphry Boulton, Richard Marshe, Thomas Beckett, John Jenkins, John Sanders, Robert Boulton, Walter Boulton, Thomas Shermore, Mary Edwards, William Berryman, John Yorke and William his Son, William Harper and Thomas his Brother, Edwards Sanders, Agnes Berryman and Elizabeth Willier widowes, Customary and Copyhold Tenants of the said manor of Hannington touching the Exchange and Inclosures of the said manor.

Whereas heretofore all the greatest part of the demesne lands of the said Manor and of the several freehold lands within the said Manor and of the Glebe Lands belonging to the said Parsonage and Vicarage within the said Manor and of the Customary and Copyhold lands within the said Manor and of some parcels of

Land within the said Manor of ancient time allowed and accordingly continued and employed for the repaircons of the Bridge being two akers four perch and three quarters leading over the Thames called Hannington Bridge, and of the Church of Hannington aforesaid being three akers which were called Bridge lands and Church akers and the several Commons of pasture for Sheep and other Cattle within the said Manor did lye open uninclosed and dispersed promiscuousley in small quillets and parcels as Acres half acres Rods and the like in and about the Common arable fields meadows and feedings within the said Manor. And the said Common fields feedings and meadows lying in a deep watery part of the Country where subject oftentimes to overflowing with water and thereby to rott and hungerbane such Sheep and Cattle as were put to feed theron and by reason of such moistness and rottenness of the Soile the said fields lands and meadows were most commonly so stocked and trodden down with the Cattle thereon going that all the Grass was spoyled and the profits of the said fields meadows and feedings were lost and destroyed besides many trespasses and troubles did commonly arise and grow thereby amongst the land occupiers there and owners of the said Cattle feeding there. And many Suits and Actions were thereupon commenced and prosecuted to the great disquiet and hindrance of all the Owners of any lands or of any Cattle there as well of the Lord of the said Manor as of the Vicar, freeholders. copyholders and all others any way interested in any lands or profits within the said Manor. Of all which several inconveniences and discomodities and of divers other as far forth prejudicial as those recited All and every the said parties to these presents together also with the said John Arden heretofor taking due consideration and regard and finding by experience of other the neighbour places and Parishes where late inclosures and Exchanges have been made that the very like inconveniences and discomodities were repaired and amended by exchanges and inclosures and great stoore of wood and fuel planted and raised where was little or none before and whereof there was great want and need within the said Manor of Hannington and in the whole Country thereabouts. All and every the Parties to these presents and also the said John Arden being moved thereunto for the reasons and causes aforesaid did with one Consent about nine years now last past conclude and agree to have exchanges and inclosure of the said Manor and each Parties interest to be severed and divided and so to be held and enjoyed according to their several Estates and proportions. And to the end that after such inclosures and exchanges made the Owners and Occupiers of the said inclosed Grounds might freely for their best avail use the said grounds and take the profits thereof discharged of tythes. And nevertheless the said Vicar of Hannington and his Successors and the severall propriates of Tythes both of the said Parsonage of Hannington and of the said Portion of Tithes in Hannington, should by way of real Composition and recompense have and enjoy several parts and portions of land in leu of their Tythes so to be discharged and more behooful for them than were the said Tythes in kind. All and every the parties to these presents and also the said John Arden who was the propriate of the said portion tithes Did then also with one full consent conclude and agree that the tenth acre of all such lands so to be inclosed as did formerly pay Tithes either to the Parson or Vicar or to the said Arden should be left forth of the said several inclosures in lieu of the Tithes of and for the said land so to be severally inclosed by all such of the land occupiers within the said Manor as were willing to lay forth such of their lands to be discharged of Tythes. And that all such lands so to be left out of the said Inclosure in lieu of the Tythes of the said Inclosures should be and remain accordingly to the said Vicar and his Successors and to the said several propriates of the said Parsonage and Portion of Tithes their heirs and assigns respectively according to their several former Claims and rights were to the special kinds of Tythes that might have arisen or grown within the said Inclosures and that the said several inclosures thereupon should be for ever after held and enjoyed accordingly without payment of any the said Tythes in kind. The like course having been long since taken and now continued for the Common Meades within the said Manor and for the demesnes of the said farm called Pisworth farm for which of long time heretofore no Tythe have been paid in kind but the Parson and Vicar and propriates of the said Portion of Tythes enjoyed certain Lands in the said Meadows in lieu thereof. And all and every the said Parties to these presents together also with the said John Arden did with one consent conclude and agree that Abraham Allen, Richard Trender, and John Hunt being Measurers and Surveyors of intergrity and ability and indifferently elected and chosen by all the said parties to these presents and by the said John Arden should allott divide and proportion forth each parties portion of Lands and the said Lands in lieu of Tythes and perfect and accomplish the said exchanges and inclosures and each party to be bound by such their several Allotment according to the said recited Agreement. In performance whereof they the said Abraham Allen, Richard Trender and John Hunt upon greater Advisement and mature deliberation did afterwards in or about the year of our Lord God one thousand six hundred and nineteen exactly and equally and to the general Contentment of all Parties to these presents and of the said John Arden and of all others whomsoever in any sort interested in any the lands or Tythes within the said Manor effect and finish the said several portions divisions and allotments for the said inclosures and exchanges. And their Allotments then and thereupon made were with one full consent agreed to be most equal and just insomuch that all the said parties to these presents and all others in any way interested as aforesaid Did to their great Costs and charges forwith thereupon make fences, hedges, ditches and bounds according to the said Exchanges and inclosures divided proportioned and allotted as aforesaid. And the said lands and Grounds according to that allotment have ever since been held and enjoyed in Severalty according to the said Agreement and Allotment.

There follows a detailed list of occupiers and the various lands which had been allotted to them. The agreement was signed by the Lord, the Vicar and 33 tenants. The signing was immediately followed by a manorial court at which the tenants surrendered all their lands to the steward, Thomas Stretton and received new grants as allocated by the surveyors. [*C.B. Fry,* Hannington, *1935, 28-31*].

SECURING AGREEMENT FOR ENCLOSURE PROPOSALS

As pointed out in the Introduction, it was difficult for smaller farmers to oppose the will of their landlord or to stand out against a majority of their fellow tenants. Even if an enclosure and restrictions on rights of access to commons were against their best interests, few could resist the pressure to conform. The following letter written in 1619 by Sir Anthony Hungerford of Stock, near Bedwyn to two of his tenants at Rowde, shows the sort of pressure that could be exerted. Sir Anthony was writing on behalf of his son, Edward Hungerford, a minor, to whom the manor of Rowde would revert on the death of the Earl and Countess of Rutland.

From J. Aubrey, *Topographical Collections*, ed., J.E. Jackson, 1862, 311.

LETTER CONCERNING THE ENCLOSURE OF COMMON FIELD AT ROWDE, 1619

To Robert Flower and John Lewes, These, at Rowde.

Whereas there hath bin a generall agreement by your selves and all the Tennants Free-houlders of the Mannor of Rowde, as likewise the Parsonn there, for the Inclosing of your Common Field. Whereunto my Lord of Rutland by his Steward and Mr Pewe his Officer, and my Selfe in the behalf of my Sonne, have given our assent, Since which time as well yourselves as the rest of the Inhabitants there whome this concerneth, have submitted your selves to the judgement of fower personnes equally named to see that everie wean [one] in this partition might respectivelie have what of right pertaines unto him, whoe beinge nowe willinge to doe theire best endeavour to this purpose, It is said that you two onlie, contrarie to your former assents, doe now intend to interrupt this worke, the which if you shall persever to doe I presume you wil be enforced to make good your former agreemente, with your Charge and trouble. I doe therefore wishe you for the avoydinge of bothe, quicklie to joyne with your Neighboures in this Worke, the rather for that I conceave you shall reape benifitt by this Inclosure as well as others. And soe I recommend you to God. From Stocke this xxth of Januarie 1619

Yours loveinge Friend
Anth. Hungerford

PETITION TO PARLIAMENT FROM THE MAYOR AND FREE TENANTS OF WOOTTON BASSETT. UNDATED BUT *c.*1639-40

The petition complained about the way in which the Great Park of Vastern or Fastern containing 2,000 acres in which the burgesses of Wootton Bassett had enjoyed free common rights had been enclosed by Sir Francis Englefield during the 16th century. The enclosure had left only 100 acres as common, Sir Francis Englefield died in 1587, leaving the lordship of Wootton Bassett to his nephew, also Sir Francis Englefield. The Mayor's Petition also complained that Sir Francis

II (died 1631) and his son Sir Francis III (d 1656), had obtained possession of the town's Charter and they were further restricting the rights of the burgesses. In particular they attempted to gain control of the remaining common from the burgesses, 'and did vex them with so many suits in Law'. Moreover, it was stated that the Englefields had seized the common for their own use.

Printed in *Topographer & Genealogist*, III, 1856. 22–5

. . . by putting in of divers sorts of Cattell, insomuch that at the length, when his servants did put in Cowes by force into the said Common, many times and present upon the putting of them in, the Lord in his mercy did send thunder and lightning from heaven, whch did make the Cattell of the said Sir Francis Englefield to run so violent out of the said ground, that at one time one of the Beasts were killed therewith; and it was so often, that people that were not there in presence to see it, when it did thunder would say that Sir Francis Englefield's men were putting in their Cattell into the Lawnd, and so it was; and as soone as those Cattell were gone forth, it would presently be very clame and faire, and the Cattell of the Towne would never stir but follow their feeding as at other times, and never offer to move out of the way but follow their feeding; and this did continue so long, he being too powerfull for them, that the said Free Tenants were not able to wage Law any longer, for one John Rosier, one of the free Tenants, was thereby enforced to sell all his Land (to the value of 500l). with following the suits in Law, and many others were thereby impoverished, and were thereby enforced to yeeld up their right and take a Lease of their said Common of the said Sir Francis Englefield his heires and his trustees now detaineth from them . . .

And as for our Common we doe verily believe, that no corporation in England so much is wronged as we are, for we are put out of all the Common that ever we had, and hath not so much as one foot of Common left unto us, nor never shall have any, we are thereby grown so in poverty, unless it please God to move the hearts of this Honorable House to commiserate our cause; and to enact something for us, that we may enjoy our Right againe.

> And we your Orators shall be ever bound to pray for your healths and prosperity in the Lord.

Signed by the Mayor, Jeffery Skeat and 22 others

Divers hands more we might have had, but that many of them doth rent Bargaines of the Lord of the Manner, and they are fearfull that they shall be put forth of their Bargaines, and than they shall not tell how to live, otherwise they would have set to their hands.

There is no evidence that Parliament ever considered this petition

ENCLOSURE DISPUTE AT SWINDON 1657

Another example of pressure being put upon tenants to agree to enclosure comes from the manor of Eastcott which occupied the western part of Swindon parish, between the roads leading to Wootton Bassett and Cricklade. This was mostly low-lying clay land best suited to pasture farming. The dispute over enclosure in 1657 provides information about the difficulties and inefficiency of the previous arrangement whereby much of the pasture land was shared between the tenants.

It is noteworthy that this agreement, like many others of the period before enclosure by Act of Parliament became the usual method, was registered by the expensive process of a Decree of the Court of Chancery. Initially, all the tenants were led to agree by the arguments concerning the waste and inefficiency of the old system of land-holding. When those with smaller holdings were faced with the realization that their allocation of plots of indifferent land of only a few acres, fit only for grass, was nowhere near as useful as the previous access to common grazing, they changed their minds. This is the background to the following document. Their attempt to withdraw from the agreement however, was too late. Confronted by the authority and power of the Court of Chancery they were forced to capitulate.

As in much of north Wiltshire manorial government was weak and ineffective, and during the 1640s the manor of Eastcott had been sold by Edward Martin, lord of the manor, to 34 small freeholders. Their holdings were, however, still dispersed and they shared the common pasture. After the sale the land-holding pattern was as follows:

Edward Martin's son, Gabriel, held	*81 acres*
2 others had holdings of over	*50 acres*
4 holdings were between	*40 and 50 acres*
4 holdings were between	*20 and 40 acres*
3 holdings were between	*10 and 20 acres*
8 holdings were between	*5 and 10 acres*
8 holdings were between	*1 and 5 acres*

Faced with the difficulties caused by the dispersal of the holdings and the problems of common pasture, the largest land-holder, Gabriel Martin, persuaded the other farmers to agree to a new allotment of lands within the manor, so that compact farms could be created, the difficulties of common pasture avoided, and arable land could be converted to the more suitable pasture. A surveyor and independent adjudicators were appointed and the appropriate amount of land was allocated to each farmer. At this point some of the farmers, faced with the need to fence and drain their new lands, had second thoughts and denied that they had ever agreed to enclosure. Gabriel Martin then exhibited a Bill of Complaint in the Court of Chancery, and those complaining about the enclosure withdrew their opposition. This long Bill of Complaint provides a good example of pressure from a large farmer upon his neighbours, who had much smaller acreages. It also contains much additional information about the reasons for enclosure and the methods used. The document is very long, with much legal jargon and repetition. It is too long to warrant quoting in full, but the following extracts provide the main details. The complete text can be found in William Morris, Swindon Fifty Years Ago, 1885, 507–23.

Complaint by Gabriel Martin to the Court of Chancery 23 September 1657

Oliver Cromwell, Lord Protector, to 35 named persons reminding them that they had agreed to enclosure because of the inconvenience of the previous system

And having by long experience found that the said Grounds and Premises being part Tillable, part Meadow and part pasture Ground had for a long time past remained much impoverished and Decayed by reason of the Unaptness of the Tillable grounds aforesaid for Corne and Grain which were more apt for grass and hay and by reason of the great Disorders which had a long time continued and been amongst them in keeping Cattle in their Commons there whereby the said Commons were much oppressed both by themselves and strangers and by reason the said grounds and commonable places within the said Manour were very subject to infect Sheep with the Rott and Watercore, which said Disorders and Inconveniences could not heretofore be reformed by the reason of the Disagreement and Wilfulness of some of the Inhabitants and Occupiers of land there and by reason of the diversities of Tenures and Estates and the said Grounds and premises so lying open and dispersed and the said Complainant and Defendants were disabled without excessive Charge and trouble to improve or meliorate the same which might be done with much ease and less charges if every person's land should be laid together by itself inclosed kept in Severalty and freed from Intercommoning one with another.

The defendants were: William York, Gent., Thomas Vilett, John Vilett, Edmund Goddard, Richard Vilett, Gent., William Gallimore, clerk, vicar of Swindon, John Walklett, Roger Ewen, John Holloway, William Dyer, John Law, William Harris, William Fairthorne, Robert Morse, Thomas Stitchell, Elizabeth Fluce, widow, Edward Thrush, William Stitchell, John Randolph, Gent., William Martyn, Miles Farmer, Thomas Quarles, William Barnard, John Foster, Thomas Wilde, Thomas Edney, Moses Bayly, Robert Tuckey, Charles York, Gent., John Fluce, William Avenell, John Ruddle, Richard Austin and Katherine Heath, widow. All the parties involved had accordingly agreed that 668 acres should be inclosed and allotted between the various landholders.

It was thereby further agreed and Assented unto that a Surveyor or Measurer should be had at the proportionable Costs and Charges of the said Complainant and persons before named for the Surveying and measuring of the said Lands and grounds in the said Manour and Tything and every particular Man's land so lying and being dispersedly within the said Manour and Commonable places thereof and for the Just and true dividing, severing, allotting, and Setting forth unto each person his respective Estate to be had and accepted of upon the said inclosure and for the deciding and final ending of all differences that might happen to arise concerning the same it was thereby further agreed assented unto that Indifferent men (that is to say) William Sadler, Esqr., Alexander Cleve, Gent., Giles Allsworth, Gent., Thomas White, Gent., Richard Morse, Gent., Richard Butler, Gent., and William Morse, Yeoman, or any four of them should direct the said Inclosure and allot and set forth to each man his Estate upon the same in such places as should be most convenient and fitting and according to the quantity and quality of each person's respective Interest and Estate in the premises and should from time to time decide and end all differences about the same. And it was thereby Further agreed and assented unto that the decree of this Court should be Obtained at the proportionable charges of all parties for the ratification and Corroboration of each persons Several Estate in the premises so to be Sett forth and appointed.——One John Whiting being a Common Surveyor or Measurer of Land and one of honest Reputation and very well learned and knowing in the Art of Surveying, was chosen and desired by the said Complainant and the other persons before name to measure and Survey every particular Man's Land so lying and being dispersedly within the said Manour and in the open Commonable places thereof and to give a perfect discovery and exact Estimate of the certain and direct quantity, proportion, and number of Acres of every and particular person's land in writing.

The lands were then duly surveyed and allotted to the 30 persons involved. Each person's land was to be enclosed by ditches, fences or mounds, orders were made for roads and access ways, about springs and water courses, and for redemption of tithes.

Also that each person aforenamed who had dunged or manured his land lying dispersedly in the Fields and Commonable places aforesaid with the Sheepfold since the twenty-fifth day of March 1654 and had since that time received no profit thereby either by Sowing the same with grain or feeding or cutting the same That each person should have and receive 6s 8d an acre in respect thereof of such to whom the said land so dunged and manured was allotted and appointed by the said Inclosure.

The complainant, Gabriel Martin, stated that all the persons involved had agreed to the enclosure and to accept the allocation of land which had been determined by the assessor and carefully marked out by the surveyor. He also pointed out that many of the owners had already begun to enclose (ditch and mound) their respective plots of land.

But the said Defendants and persons before named or some of them finding that the Complainant had disbursed and laid out much money about the Surveying, ditching, and mounding in his said several pieces and plotts of land and taking some frivelouse and careless displeasure against the said Inclosure had lately pretended and given out in speeches that they did never assent or agree to Inclose or take in severally the said lands grounds, commonable places, and premises and seemed to deny to accept of their several pieces and plotts of land so severally directed, appointed, and allotted to and for them as aforesaid——

And to the end all the said particular agreements and each Man's particular Allotment as aforesaid might be accepted and confirmed by the Decree of this Court. The said Complainant prayed the Aid and assistance of this Honourable Court and that the process of Subpener might be awarded against the said Defendants.

The petition of the complainant, Gabriel Martin, was granted by the Court, and the defendants were summoned to appear before it. Faced with all the majesty of the Court of Chancery, the defendants all agreed that they had given their assent to the proposed enclosure, and had undertaken to accept the plots allocated by the assessor after the survey by John Whiting 'Common Surveyor and one of honest reputation and very well learned and knowing in the Art of Surveying (as they believe)'.

And that they, the said Defendants, were and would be ready to make and execute such Legal Assurance and Conveyance for the perfecting, Establishing, and lawful Settling of the said lands and Inclosure according to every Man's particular division and allotment as should be reasonably required and as this Court should appoint and direct and did submit and were well content That the said several agreements and Inclosure in the said Bill of Complaint sett forth be ratifyed and confirmed by the Decree of the Court.

The defendants were ordered by the Court to observe their previous agreements, that they 'do observe, fulfil, and perform according to the Tenor, true Intent and meaning thereof and hereof Fail not at your peril'.

Dated at Westminster 23 September 1657.

ENCLOSURES IN SOUTH AND EAST WILTSHIRE

AN ENCLOSURE AGREEMENT FOR NUNTON 1720

WSRO 893/15 pp10-12

Court Book of the manor of Downton [Sir James Ashe, Baronet, lord of the manor] held 1 & 2 April 1720

Item, presentant in huiusce anglicanis verbis sequent. vizt

> Item we present an Agreement of certain Articles Indented bearing date the Eighth day of February 1719 and made between Jasper Bampton & John Bampton his son, William Batt, Franklin Newham, Thomas Wheeler, James Wheeler and Joseph Philips being owners and co-proprietors of certaine Lands and sheep leaze on the three common fields and downes of Nunton within this Manor, purporting an agreement between the said parties for takeing in and inclosing the said common fields and downes together with several parties, which said agreement is hereunto annexed and may more fully and at large appeare.
>
> Articles of Agreement Indented had made concluded and fully agreed upon this Eighth day of February Anno Domini 1719, Between Jasper Bampton, John Bampton his son, William Batt, Franklin Newham, Thomas Wheeler, James Wheeler and Joseph Philips being owners and proprietors of certaine Copyhold lands and sheep leaze in the three common fields and downes of Nunton within the manor of Downton in the County of Wilts as followes (vizt)

Inprimis, it is agreed by and between all the said parties that the said three common fields and also the downes containing in the whole seven hundred acres of land (be the same more or less) shalbe divided in order to be inclosed on or before the first day of March next, which division so to be made as to the downes shalbe set forth by measure according to every man's sheep leaze on the downes and fields aforesaid.

Item, it is agreed that every one of the parties aforesaid who now is owner of any ground or lands in all or any of the said three fields shall have the same quantity of land by measure and that it shalbe laid out in large pieces of

Twenty acres or thereabouts, when the quantity of any man's land will allow of the same having respect to the goodness of every man's land as now it lyes and that the lands of the said Thomas Wheeler shalbe but in two pieces in the three fields.

Item, it is agreed that the parties herein to be named shall appoint and allott the same lands aforesaid, and also shall allott to the several owners aforesaid so much lands on th'aforesaid downes as shall of right belong to them to be measured and divided by equal portions in large pieces according to their honesty and descretion and according to their several numbers of sheep leaze on the said downes.

Item, its agreed that when the said fields and downes are so allotted and appointed for the several owners it shalbe lawful for every one of them to enclose his share and proportion of lands as soon as he shal think meet and untill such enclosure the fields and downes to remaine in common as now they are untill Michaelmas next, notwithstanding it shalbe lawful for every owner of lands in the three common fields and downes aforesaid, when it is so divided and marked out to come with teames,ploughs, servants and workmen of any sort to plough, burn beak and sow any of th'aforesaid lands as shall belong to them and also to grubb the furze thereon growing and to carry away the same.

Item, it is agreed that the wheat and barley field notwithstanding such division and allotment shall continue to the several owners with the corn thereon now sown and to be sown until they have severally harvested the same.

Item, its agreed that it shall and may be lawful (when the division is made in the Barley field aforesaid) for every owner of the new allotment to sow such grass seed as he shall think meet among the corn of the now owners of the several lands aforesaid.

Item, it is agreed that every one having dead hedge on the common fields may have and take them to his own use so soon as the next harvest is over.

Item, its agreed by all the said parties that th'aforesaid William Batt (in consideration of the sum of £100 by him to them to be severally paid at Michaelmas next proportioned to their several number of sheep leaze on the downes and commonable places) shall have and take to his own use all trees and bushes of what kind and nature soever now growing and being on the said downes and that he shall clear all the said downes of such trees and bushes by the first day of August now next ensuing the date hereof, and the said William Batt is to be abated out of the said £100 his share according to his own number of sheep leaze.

Item, its agreed that whereas one Ambrose Wheeler is owner of twenty sheep leaze on th'aforesaid downes and is now beyond the seas, he shall also have his allotment on the said downes by the rule aforesaid as also his dividend of thaforesaid £100, to which agreement th'aforesaid Thomas Wheeler (being the brother) doth promise and engage for him on the strictest manner that he can.

Item, whereas one Thomas Chubb, son of Joseph Chubb the younger deceased, [is] an infant of seven years of age or thereabouts, Its therefore agreed that he shall have his share and dividend on the fields and downes aforesaid by th'aforesaid rule in as full and ample manner as if he were of full age and personally present. It being far from the intent of any of the parties aforesaid to doe him the least wrong.

Item, its agreed that all the changes in measuring th'aforesaid lands and other small necessary changes shalbe paid by the several parties aforesaid according to the number of sheep leaze (except only the change of the three common fields as to the said Franklin Newham and Ambrose Wheeler, they having no land there).

Item, its agreed by all the said parties that in case any vexatious suits do happen to arise touching or concerning the division of the lands aforesaid, either by the said Thomas Chubb or his heirs or assignes, or by reason of any highways or droves to be made and appointed through any of the downes and fields aforesaid, that then all such charge shalbe paid and defrayed by the several owners of the lands aforesaid according to their present number of sheep leaze Except the said Franklin Newham and Ambrose Wheeler as to any such charge as to any of the said three common fields for the reason aforesaid.

Item, its agreed by all the said parties to lay out, nominate and appoint to lay out the said three Common fields and downes by the rule aforesaid Oswald West of Alderbury, Peter Rook of Friern Court and John Bampton of Lodge, Gentlemen, or any two of them and with their allotment to be made as aforesaid we do promise to stand to for ourselves and our heires for ever, without quarrelling or discontent, but on the contrary to give them thanks and due praise for their paines.

> In witness whereof we the said parties have Interchangeably set our hands and seals the day and year above written. And for the performance thereof either of the said parties doth bind himself each to the other in the penalty of £500.
>
> Signed by Jasper Bampton, John Bampton, William Butt,
> Franklin Newham, Thomas Wheeler, Joseph Philips.

Followed by a detailed list of the lands allocated to each.

ENCLOSURE OF COMMONS AT SWALLOWCLIFFE 1663

This example occurs in a suit before the Court of Chancery, brought by the lord of the manor of Swallowcliffe, Walter South, against some of his tenants. His complaint concerned an agreement to enclose 459 acres of common grazing land; this was allotted as follows: 342 acres to the lord, 85 acres to the tenants divided in proportion to their grazing rights, and 20 acres to the poor. Walter South alleged that all had agreed to these proposals and that he had already spent large sums in enclosing his allocation. Now some of the tenants were objecting, no doubt realizing that the costs of enclosing a small allotment were high and its value as grazing did not compare with their previous right of access to the whole common for their livestock. Evidently their objections were over-

ruled, and the enclosure was completed. The following extract from the long legal argument sets out the lord's case and the reasons for the enclosure.

PRO C78/1270/4

... about Fower Hundred and Fifty-Nine acres of Common Wast around [and] within the said mannor wherein the Complainant and the Freeholders, Coppyholders and leaseholders have time out of mind had Common of Pasture for all manner of Cattell according to the quantity of their lands, which lying much open were much eaten by foreignners and strangers and yeilded little benefitt to the Complainant and others, the Commoners there, for prevention thereof, a communication was had betweene the Complainant and the defendants — there, for measureinge, dividing and Incloseing of the said Common, which would not onely be a great improvement to their estates, but a benefitt to the Commonwealth by Tillage and thereuppon it was agreed that the said Common should be measured, devided, inclosed and laid out in proportion for them respectively which about the thirteenth of January last was reduced into writing under their hands.

BRADENSTOKE FARM AT EASTON 1614

This description of the buildings and land belonging to Bradenstoke or Black Farm in the parish of Easton (later known as Easton Royal) was included in a manorial survey of 1614. Half of the manor of Easton was given to the Augustinian abbey at Bradenstoke in c1150; this farm, no doubt, derives the name 'Black' from the fact that the Augustinians were known from their dress as 'Black Canons'. Other properties in Easton included Easton Druce or Drews, which was given to the Trinitarian priory at Easton in 1349, and Easton Warren. After the Dissolution all these estates passed into the hands of the Seymour family, earls of Hertford of Tottenham House. It is clear from the following description that by 1614 Bradenstoke Farm was mostly enclosed into small fields and meadows which were most suitable for cattle raising and dairy farming. This process was not complete, however, and rights in parts of the farm continued to be shared with the other manors as they had been throughout the Middle Ages. The crucial importance of the meadow land for providing hay to sustain the livestock through the winter is clear from this survey. There is also evidence of 'convertible husbandry', since 20 acres of pasture is said to be 'sometime arrable'.

*Like the other farms in the parish, the farmstead stood in the village street, and the thatched farm house and barns were no doubt similar to the 23 other farms which are listed in the Survey. The description 'old and ruinous' implies that the building was ancient and in need of repair, but not necessarily derelict. One of the two rooms in the detached kitchen building was presumably used as a dairy. [*VCH Wilts, *XVI, 1999, 141–5]*

WSRO 9/15/327

Bradenstocke Farme called the Black Farme

One Farme house old and ruinous of three roomes covered with strawe. One kitchen adjoyning to the Farme of two roomes covered with strawe wherein there is an oste [?oven], one barne of seaven roomes covered with strawe. One other barne called a haie house of two rooms. And a cutting [?lean-to shed] to laie haie and fodder in covered with strawe.	
One olde orchard and garden containing	½ acre
One close of meadowe called the Cowe close cont.	2 acres
One close of meadowe next to the orchard in the place where the pound was cont.	2 acres
The great close of meadowe lieing between the horse close and drewes cont.	4 acres
One close of meadow called horse close cont.	1½ acres
One close of meadow called the west meade cont. x acres whereof th'one half lieth to the Farme called Eston Drewes als Priory and the other half is parcell of Eston Bradenstoke the which contains	5 acres
Item one close for the moste parte used as pasture and some eared [cultivated] called Longland cont. xl acres whereof half is parcell of Eston Drewes als Priory and Eston Warrens and half is parcell of Bradenstoke the which contains	20 acres
One close of pasture and sometime arrable called Old Land somewhat barren containing lx acres whereof th'one half lieth to Eston Drewes als Priory and Eston Warrens, and the other half part to Eston Bradenstoke the which is	30 acres
A close of meadowe lieing behind the close called Drewes containing 3 acres is parcell of Eston Bradenstoke	3 acres
One close of meade called the Wire meade containing vi acres whereof th'one half lieth to Eston Drewes als Priory and to Eston Warrens and th'other half is parcell of Bradenstoke cont.	3 acres
One close of meade caled the Inemeade cont. vii acres whereof one belongeth to Eston Drewes als Priory and to Eston Warrens and th'other half is parcell of Eston Bradenstoke cont.	4 acres
One close of meadowe called the Moones cont. ii acres whereof there belongeth to Eston Drewes als Priory and Eston Warrens th'one half and to Eston Bradenstoke th'other cont.	1 acres
Of meadow in tot xxv acres di.	30½ acres

ENCLOSURE OF COMMONS AT WOOTTON RIVERS 1606-7

*The following enclosure of 284 acres of common grazing land is an example of the sort of piecemeal, informal agreement between farmers which occurred throughout much of Wiltshire throughout the 17th century, often leaving few records. Wootton Rivers had two common arable fields north and west of the village, and two large areas of common pasture known as Search and Inlands. This agreement relates to parts of these areas of common grazing which were divided between those possessing rights to pasture livestock in them. Clearly, much care was taken to ensure an equitable distribution of the land. By far the greatest share went to the leaseholders or 'farmers' of the demesne farm [William Smyth] and Weeke or Wick farm [Edward Goddard]. The parson was allocated 13 acres in respect of his glebe, and the copyholders received 13 acres for each tenement. Smallholders and cottagers were also provided with land, although this may have been less useful to them than the general right to graze livestock over the whole common. Before this agreement the copyholders and cottagers had the right to feed 727 sheep on the commons, the parson had feeding for 60, the demesne farm could feed 300 and Wick farm 120. Each tenant could feed as many cattle on the commons in summer as he could maintain on his holding during the winter. [*VCH Wilts, *XVI, 1999, 233-4]. At Wootton Rivers, as in many other places, it is likely that the common was greatly over-stocked and consequently provided poor keep for all livestock. This no doubt provided the incentive for enclosure. Evidently it was expected that the allotments of land would be enclosed and provision was made for droves or access ways, as well as for access to water for livestock.*

WSRO 9/21/44

Wootton Commons called the Search and Inlandes measured and divided the 28 of January 1606 as followeth

Imprimis Edward Goddard Esquire for his 2 yardlands of the Farme of Weeke 26 acres 1 roode and 32 perches, whereof hee hath alowed to Richard Smartte 1 acre for which hee is to give to the Farm of Weeke aforesayd one harviste day worke yearely

So there remayneth and layd oute for Mr Goddard in the Searche
25 acres 1 rood and 32 perches

William Smyth gent. For his 5 yard lands to the Farme, his parteis 66 acres and 20 perches, And alowed him for Salsberye way at 2 perches broade and 63 perches long 189 perches, And for Honyford way at 20 foote broad and 67 perches long 83 perches
67 acres 3 roods 12 perches

Whereof he hath alowed to Peter Rawlins and to Edmund Grammatt 2 acres and 2 roodes for which they are to give to the Farmer there 1 harviste day worke a peece yearely, Also he hath alowed to Ralfe Baning halfe an acre for land exchanged in the feelde 3 acres

So remayneth layd out for his parte 64 acres 3 roods and 12 perches

John Cowley, parson, for 1 yard land of Glebe 13 acres and 36 perches
Tomas Tachener, gent. For 1 yard land by copy 13 acres and 36 perches
Joane Head, widow, for 1 yard land by copy 13 acres and 36 perches
Richard Head and Thomas Workman 2 yardlands 26 acres 1 rood and 32 perches
And alowed them for Honyford way at 20 foote broad at 70 perches long 88 perches 2 roods and 8 perches
Walter Winsor for 1 yardland 13 acres and 36 perches
Anthony Wotteridge for 1 yardland 13 acres and 36 perches
John Baynton for 1 yardland 13 acres and 36 perches
William Wotteridge for 1 yardland 13 acres and 36 perches
Thomas Canning for 1 yardland 13 acres and 36 perches
Peter Rawlins for 1 Cote 3 acres 1 rood and 9 perches, and alowed him halfe an acre 5 acres 3 roods and 9 perches
Richard Batchaler for 1 Cote 3 acres 1 rood and 9 perches And alowed him more 2 acres and 2 roods 5 acres 3 roods and 9 perches
Robert Hellier for 3 Cotes and 10 perches alowed him 9 acres 3 roods and 37 perches
Ralfe Banning for 1 yardland and 1 Cote and alowed him by the Farmer halfe an acre 17 acres and 32 perches
Leonard Pyle for a Cote 6 acres 2 roods and 18 perches And alowed him halfe an acre and 20 perches for a way 7 acres and 38 perches
Richard Smartte alowed him 1 acre 2 roods and 20 perches
Edward Grammatt for 1 Cote and alowed him 2½ acres 5 acres 3 roods and 9 perches
Steven King hath also Inlands for his yardland where in he hath alowed for a drove to goe to the water for any of the parishe at all tymes and wayes to the growndes or closes there adjoyning at 20 foote broade and to be hedged out 10 acres 23 perches
Sum Total 284 acres 2 roods and 29 perches

Memorandum that it was agreed that Ralph Banninge shall maynteyne a gate at the ende of the drove next to the Brook

Item, yt is agreed that the Farmer William Smyth, gent., is to keepe one gate and maintaine the same at the end of Southfield lane and nexte the Brooke.

SHEEP FLOCK MANAGEMENT AND PROFITABILITY

Sheep flocks were vital for the sheep-corn husbandry of the chalkland region. The sheep were pastured by day on the downland, and each evening were driven down by the shepherd to be folded on the arable fields. It was the large flocks of sheep which so impressed travellers across the downs, and it was the effect of their grazing which maintained the characteristic short turf and plant-rich sward. In spite of the importance of the sheep, it is difficult to find documentary evidence for the income derived from sheep farming, or of the way in which sheep flocks were managed. It must be remembered that the prime purpose of the sheep for chalkland farmers was for maintaining the fertility of the arable land; the sale of wool, lambs and surplus stock was a secondary consideration. Moreover, the maintenance of a folding flock required a regular influx of new stock to replace sheep worn out by the demands of being driven long distances each day to be close folded on the arable land. Life for the sheep on the high downland during the winter with poor quality grazing, limited supplies of hay, and exposed to every wind that blew, as well as rain and snow, was harsh and demanding. This is obvious from the number that died. For example, at Rockbourne in 1621 the skins were sold from 48 sheep which had died. Ewes with lambs were also sold to dealers and had to be replaced. Consequently there was a busy traffic in sheep, mainly at the numerous sheep fairs which were such an important feature of the chalkland region. Evidently many of the transactions were on credit. The two accounts which follow illustrate these features of flock management as well as providing an indication of the profit arising from the flock over and above its principal value as an indispensable adjunct to arable farming. Note that a 'weight' of wool was 28 pound. 'Lokes' or locks means fragments of wool detached from the main fleece and 'Lambtow' or lambswool means the finer wool from young sheep.

The Sheep Account of Sir John Cooper of Rockbourne 1620–22

HRO Photocopy 350/1 from Original Account belonging to Lord Shaftesbury of Wimborne St Giles, Dorset

Sir John Cooper had inherited the manor of Rockbourne, just over the Wiltshire border in Hampshire from his father in 1610. In 1617 he had married Anne, daughter of Sir Anthony Ashley of

Wimborne St Giles. Their eldest son, Anthony Ashley Cooper was born in July 1621. He was to inherit the Wimborne St Giles estate from his grandfather in 1628 and was later to become the first Earl of Shaftesbury. (K.H.D. Haley, The First Earl of Shaftesbury, *1968, 7-15;* VCH Hampshire, *IV, 1911, 582-4). These accounts relate to his large demesne flock which was kept separately from that of his tenants at Rockbourne. They are incomplete and consist of hastily scribbled notes which were obviously compiled for Sir John Cooper's own use and are difficult to read. Nonetheless, they show the large number of sheep kept in the demesne flock, the rapid turnover and numerous sales, and the profit made, not counting the main purpose of the flock in maintaining the fertility of the arable land.*

A Not [Note] of the Recevinges upon the Demaines for Rockborn this yeare 1620		£	s	d
Lambes				
Item soweld unto George Peroutte	50	18	0	0
Item soweld unto Simon For the	46	9	10	0
Item soweld unto another of Guishes (?)	20	4	13	4
Item soweld unto Cornish	30 lambes	6	13	4
Item soweld unto another of Guishes (?)	V	1	0	6
Item soweld unto John Hill and an other	40 prise	10	0	0
Item soweld unto Mr Webb	40 prise	10	0	0
Item soweld unto Elizes Teripork	10	1	0	6
Item unto Dabne	VI prise		18	0
Unto Matthew Newman	31 prise	6	0	0
Item soweld at Shasbery Fayer	10 prise	1	18	6
Item soweld unto Wm Berage	10 prise	1	18	4
Item soweld unto 3 men of Dunethe (?)	66 lambes prise	11	0	0
Item unto Thomas Ellricke	46 prise	10	3	4
Item unto Thomas Hide	25 prise	4	4	0
Some is of lambes	438			
	Some is	96	19	10
Wooll				
Item soweld att Burfford Fayer 3 wayt wanting 10 li prise		4	19	0
Item sowld unto William Tocker 32 wayt of wooll att 3s 6d the wayt and on(e) li over and above		58	9	0
Item for 49 li of lamto[w]		2	9	0
Item for 10 li of woll mor			2	0
Item Rec. for 3 wayt of lockes and 26 li att vid the li is		2	17	9
	Som is	68	16	9
Wool sowld				
Item sowld as much wool as did yeald the som of		36	16	6

The 30 of June 1620

	Weight	li
The whole number of sheepe at Rockborn is		885
The fiftie hogs that came from Charforde have two weight and seven pounds of wolle	2	7
The fiftie six bought yeanes bare two weight and two pounds	2	2
The ould stocke bare 33 and 14 li	33	14
Soe the whole some of flise of woole the tith paied was	34	8
The number of flises was 734		
The lokes was	3	0
Of lambs woole	4	49

25 June 1621

The Profitt of the lambs sould now at Midsomer

Imprimis sould unto John Carpenter of Whitbury 105 lambs To be paied St Leonardes day [6 November]	30	0	0

[Partly illegible note scribbled in margin: Received of this £10 and of —£20 in part £2 10s 0d in part £5 10s 0d]

Sould unto John Young 20 lambs to be paied at Michaelmas	4	0	0
Sould unto Culbert Parker —[illegible] Henstrige 41 lambs	7	13	4
Sould unto Richard Warrine 20 lambs to be paied at Michaelmas	3	13	4
Sould unto Roger Fifoot and Thomas Cornish 30 lambs	5	3	4
Sould unto Thomas Colber 20 lambs	3	6	8
Sould to Richard Young 20 lambs	3	6	8
Sould unto the Farmer Clarke of Marteine 107 lambs to be paied at Midsomer	16	0	0
Sould to Francis Weekes of Marteine to paie St Thomas day [21 December] 48 lambs	6	17	6
Summa totalis	82	0	10

Kept in the Flocke to maintaine the stocke – 45 lambs whereof seaven be my wives soe I have but 37. Soe the whole number of lambs besides my wives either sould or kept are in all 440—6

5 July 1621

The number of the sheepe now shorne at Rockborn and their profitt this yeare

	Weight	li
The ould stocke being shoren this 6 July did beare of woole	30	17
And of Lokes	3	22

The 90 bought yeawes bare of flise woole	5	1
Of Lokes		20
So the flise woole in all the the tith paied is	35	15
Of Lokes in all	4	13
The number of flises is 722		
The 35 lambs kept into the flocke bare of lambtow		36
So the whole number of sheepe at this day with my wives and the 90 bought yeawes is 842		

	£	s	d
The fiftie yeawes I bought of Henry Mihill cost	20	0	0
The 41 yeawes bought at Blanford cost	13	0	0
Paied for 4 yeawes more which Henry Mihill bought in the December (?)	14	3	4
The charge of bringing them		1	0
So I have bought into the Flocke this yeare six score and eleven yeawes which cost	47	4	4

Besides I exchanged some with Mr Parker for ould ewes about a dozen.

1621

The Profitt of the Sheepe this yeare

There was sould out of the flocke 92 ould yeawes for	22	4	0
The 36 li of lambtow was sold for	1	16	0

A Note of the Woole Sheare at Rockbourn the 5 July 1622

The woole of the wethers bought being 115
7 weight of flise woole and one weight of lokes
The Flocke of yeawes 27 weight and a halfe of flise woole the tith paied
The lokes 3 weight and one pound
The whole some of flise woole is 34 weight and a halfe
The number of flises are 703
The whole some of lokes is 4 weight and one pound
The woole of 80 lambs is 2 weight and 3 pounds

The number of sheepe in all are	912
Whereof weare bought	115
Of Lambs	80

A Note of Lambes sould at Rockbourn this yeare 1622

Sould unto Thomas Cornish and Roger Wher—(?) 40 lambs to Pay 20 December	7	0	0
To Roger Fisooke 10 lambs to pay the same day	1	13	4

To Heystings 22 lambs to pay the same day	4	10	0
To Anthony Pouncy 24 lambs to pay the same day	3	10	0
To Ould Stone 33 lambs to pay that day	4	8	8
To John Banger 10 lambs to pay St James Day next [25 July]	1	3	0
To Cl: and Yo: 32 lambs to pay the 24 of September	5	1	0
To Farmer Weekes 32 lambs to pay the 24 of December	3	2	0
To Henry Mihell 20 lambs	3	10	0
Summa	33	18	0

Sould of Lambs that yeare	223
Kept in the Flocke	80
In all	303

1622
The whole profitt of the sheepe the last year was allowing for the 36 couples I bought in to the flocke

The 438 lambs yealded as by the particulars doth appeare	96	19	10
The woole with the lokes and lambtow was sould for	68	16	9
Received for the skins of 48 sheep that have died seethens [since?] sheare tyme last	3	0	0
Received for ... [blank 'yewes 135' written in margin] yewes Sould out of the flock at Michaelmas last where of must be allowed for the sheepes bought into the flocke	36	3	10
Received for fortie six lamb skins		11	3
Received for the wole that was sould after sheartyme		2	0
	4	3	0
Summa	205	13	8

Out of this must be deducted (?) for the fiftie six couples I bought into the flocke
So there remaineth of the profitt of the sheepe but ... [blank]

25 June 1624
The Sheepe shorne at Rockbourn

Theare weare shorne eight hundred fifty fower of myne and my wife hath 45. I have theare 24 lambs and my wife 15.
The woole 52 waight the tith paid
Lokes 6 waight 26 li
Lambswool on waight
Woll brought from Shasbury to Rockbourn

Of flise woole 60 waight 28 li

Lokes 5 waight 5 li
Lambswool 8 waight 3 li

The number of Sheepe theare is 1540

The woole from of flices -? At Rockbourn is 112 weight 28 li
Lokes 12 weight one pound
Lambswool 8 waight 3 li

Samuel Stillingfleet's Sheep Flock Account 1657-61

Samuel Stillingfleet spent his life in the service of the Earl of Salisbury at Cranborne. He became 'Clerk of the Kitchen' in 1612, then rose to the position of 'Housekeeper' in 1620, and from 1635 was under steward. He died at the end of 1661. Stillingfleet's seventh son, Edward, was christened at Cranborne in 1635, and later became famous as a distinguished bishop of Worcester. Samuel Stillingfleet leased land from the Earl of Salisbury on Cranborne Chase and at Damerham. In addition he leased the right to collect tithes from the Earl of Salisbury and his sheep flock was periodically increased by the acquisition of tithe lambs. He presided over some of the Earl's manorial courts, and was occasionally involved in the conduct of the manorial court at Downton on behalf of Sir Joseph Ashe. It was Stillingfleet who saved much of the furniture and valuables at Cranborne from the pillage of the house by the royalist army in June 1643.

Like Sir John Cooper's account, Stillingfleet evidently kept these hastily written notes for his own use. They are not systematic and include no mention of costs for land or labour to be set against income. The labour involved in shepherding, gelding, washing, shearing and marking the sheep was considerable but is ignored in these accounts. They do however, illustrate the substantial income obtained from a flock of 150 to 200 sheep, the rapid turnover of sheep and the numerous markets and fairs at which the sheep were sold, although, strangely, there is no mention of the important sheep fairs at Damerham and Weyhill. Stillingfleet's accounts survive among the vast manuscript collection of the Earls of Salisbury at Hatfield House.

Earl of Salisbury's MSS, Hatfield House, Cranborne Accounts 1611-61. Account book with initials S.S.

Particulars of my sheepe and theire value 4 November 1657

	£	s	d
10 weathers sold at 11s 0d a piece	5	10	0
4 weathers sold at 9s 6d a peice	1	18	0

40 ewes sold for	13	0	0
Remainder of my sheepe were 153, which I valued at	50	0	0
I sold 40lb of lamtoe for	1	18	0
2 weight of locks for	1	6	8
10 weight of wool for	15	0	0
The Income received by my sheepe for the yeare past	37	12	8

Since Michaelmas 1657

I bought at Blandford faire 30 weathers at 6s 8d a peice	10	0	0
I bought of Richard Woods 20 gradlings at the price of	7	5	0
Also 10 weathers	4	5	0
I bought at Shaston faire on Lady Day 10 couples at	4	10	0
I bought at Ringwood market 10 couples	4	0	0
I bought 12 hogs of John King for	3	0	0
	33	0	0
I sold to Walter Haysham 8 small ewes at 5s 0d a piece	2	0	0
One ewe to George . . .		8	0
30 old weathers sold to Henry Butler at 7s 4d a piece	11	0	0
21 sheepe to George Harding	13	0	0
37 weight of wool at 10s 0d	18	10	0
3 weight and 19lb of lokes at 5d per lb at 5 ye . . .	2	5	5
Lamtoe	1	10	0
11 old weathers at Ringwood faire at 6s 8d	3	13	4
30 ewes to Rich. Woods at 6s 2d	9	5	0
	61	11	9
The profit made by my sheepe the yeare past with 18 lambs Sold to John Weeks at 2s 6d	30	16	9

The number of my sheepe at ye same time were in all 184 – besides I have increased my flockes 31 sheepe.			
Since I have bought of John King 6 couples at 8s 0d which cost mee	2	8	0
I have bred of mine owne ewes 9 lambs	1	10	0
I have receivyed for tything lambs in Boveridge and Cranborne to the number of 30	3	15	0
I bought at Blandford Fair 30 lambs which cost me	6	0	0
	13	13	0

April 1659

	£	s	d
I sold one sheepe to George Harding		15	6
More to George Harding 6 weathers at 10s 0d	3	0	0
I sold 20 weathers at Hamdon summer faire	12	10	0
I sold 1 lamb 5s 0d and 1 ewe 6s 0d		11	0
I killed 1 ewe for my household		5	0
I sold at Wilton faire 20 wethers	10	10	0
I sold 1 weather for		8	0
I sold 15 ewes at our faire at 6s 8d	5	0	0
I kild 1 chilver hog for my household		3	4
	33	2	10

Laid out £13 13s 0d
Received £82 11s 4d

Account of my sheepe made the 11 January 1659 [1660 NS]

		£	s	d
The profit arising by my sheepe the yeare paste appears to bee		38	15	6
The number of my sheep then 183				
111 at flock		45	8	0
57 weather hogs		14	5	0
15 chilver hogs		3	0	0
185	Value	62	13	0

	£	s	d
Bought since			
16 couples at 10s 9d	8	12	0
2 couples at 9s 0d		18	0
8 couples at Ringwood at 10s 0d	4	0	0
2 couples	1	7	0
7 lambs at 2s 6d		17	6
	15	14	6
Sold at St Georges fair at Wilton –			
20 weathers at 7s 6d	7	10	0
Sold 19 weathers at 11s 0d	10	9	0
Kil'd chilver lamb 1		4	0
Sold to H. Fripp which he drove to Hindon faire, 20 weathers	12	10	0
Sold 14 weathers	7	14	0
1 ewe sold		8	0
40 ewes sold to H. Fripp	15	5	0
8 ewes more sold	2	4	0
9 weight –6lb of wool	13	16	0
lambtoe and lokes	4	0	2
	74	0	2

December 1660

The profit arising by my sheepe the yeare past abating likewise for 34 weathers which are short of numbers of the last yeares flock and for 27 hogs is yet cleere	30	0	0

The number of my sheepe is 132 (recte 122)
87 at flock
38 weather hogs
7 chilver hogs

Bought 20 couples at 9s 6d	9	10	0
Bought 6 couples at 9s 6d	3	10	6
Bought 2 weathers		18	0
Bought 1 couple and 1 weather		15	0
Tything lambs 19 at 3s 0d	2	17	0
Bought 1 hog		7	0
1 stray ewe-lamb and 40 weathers	20	15	0

June 1661

47 lambs
135 in flock sheepe
22 weathers

———

204

October 1661

In stock 194
1 dead 25 November

MANORIAL GOVERNMENT

As described in the Introduction, the manorial system remained strong throughout most of the chalkland region of Wiltshire during the 17th century, and the manorial courts continued to control many aspects of farming and rural life. Most of the manors were part of one of the great estates which dominated the south and south-east of Wiltshire, and each manor commonly included at least four kinds of tenant. There were often one or two freeholders who owned their farms, but were nevertheless required to attend the manorial court and observe common regulations over cultivation, livestock and grazing land. In most manors the lord had ceased to farm the demesne land himself or through a bailiff, and this was leased for an agreed term of years at an economic annual rent. Leaseholders were also required to attend the manorial court and abide by its regulations, especially since the demesne land was frequently dispersed among that of the other tenants. At the other end of the social scale were cottagers or those holding small tenements who were described as 'tenants at will', having little security and holding their property at the will of the lord.

Finally, by far the most common tenure was copyhold, that is tenants who held their land during the lives generally of three named persons, who held successively, having as the evidence of their title a copy of the entry in the court book or roll. Copyhold tenants paid a low or nominal annual rent, and a large fine at entry or when a new name was added. In addition, copyholders paid a heriot to the lord at death, in the form of their best beast or other possession or by money payment. The important feature of this tenure is that it was subject to the customary law of each manor, and since these customs differed, even between neighbouring manors, there was great variety in the rights of copyholders and the obligations laid upon them.

MANORIAL CUSTOMS

It was manorial custom, based on long use 'beyond the memory of man' which regulated the pattern of copyholders' lives. Custom decided the conditions of their tenure, rights of grazing, access to wood, stone or other resources, common grazing, restraints on sub-letting, the level of rents and fines, rights of inheritance and widows' estates. The variety of west-country manorial customs was summed up by a mid 16th century surveyor,

> *Their customs are not so universall as if a man have experience of the customs and services of any mannor he shall thereby have perfect knowledge of all the rest, or if he be experte of the customs of any one mannor in any one countie that he shall nede of no further enstruccions for all the residewe of the mannors within that countie.*
>
> *[B.L. Harleian MS 71, ff 45–53]*

Only gradually did leases for years replace copyholds, and the system remained as a legal form of tenure until 1926. Many farmers in the north and west of Wiltshire also held their land by copyhold tenure, but since there was much less communal farming activity the power of manorial courts was much weaker and manorial custom was less crucial.

From time to time stewards recorded manorial customs in order to preserve a record and prevent disputes. Elderly tenants were required to state under oath the way in which the manor had been governed 'time out of mind'. The custumal was then written down by the steward and signed by the tenants. All other matters concerning the governance of the manor were subject to an appeal to custom and to ancient practice in 'a time beyond which the memory of man runneth not to the contrary'. The two examples which follow, chosen from different parts of the chalkland region, provide an indication of the range of manorial custom and of its influence in controlling life within each manor. It was under these conditions that most chalkland farmers in Wiltshire held their land during the 17th century, and it was under the constraints of these customs that they conducted their farming.

Customs of Collingbourne Ducis 1574

WSRO 9/9/371

The customary of Collingbourne Ducis taken the xixth day of October Anno Regne Elizabeth, xvi, 1574 by the verdict of those whose names are underwritten at a courte then there houlden uppon theire oathes viz. Robte Herne, Martyn Orton, Robte Edington, John Passion, Willm Batt, the elder, Robte Fidler, Tho. Childe, Tho. Ansten, John Webbe, Tho. Brimsdon, Willus Blackemore, Jasper Blackemore, John Benson and Richard Sprott.

And every of them saieth, presenteth, and affirmeth uppon theire oathes that theire custome and customes of the said manor of Collingbourne Ducis is and tyme out of mynd hath byn as hereafter followeth and noe otherwise to theire knowledge, that is to saie

1 First they presenteth that they ought not by anie custome to take anie estate of Copiehoulde but onlie in full and open courte.

2 Item, they presenteth that customary hould hath byn graunted usually but for two lyves, viz. The taker and an other.

3 Item, they presenteth that if anie man doe take it unto himself and unto his wife by custome the wife (the nomination notwithstandinge) shall have but her widdoes estate.

4 Item, they presenteth that they have knowen reversions to be graunted and allowed of as unto Christopher Benson and John, his sonne, and unto Robert Herne and Thomas, his sonne.

5 Item, they presenteth that after the death of every tenante, dieinge tenante admitted the wife of every such tenante shall have her widowes estate.

6 Item, they presenteth that if anie tenante dye after Michaelmas day the executor of every such tenante shall occupie and have his customary land out that whole yere viz. unto Michaelmas then next followinge and noe longer than Michaelmas if the tenante dye but one day before or Michaelmas day it self, but if the tenante dye before Michaelmas the lord or the next taker shall at Midsomer or anie tyme after enter unto the sheepe leasue and unto the wheatland that yere to be sowen and the whole after Michaelmas.

7 Item, they presenteth that usually surrenders of Copiehoulds hath been made in open court and not otherwise.

8 Item, they presenteth that if anie customary tenante doe wilfully take downe or lett fall his tenement or anie buildings thereuppon, or doe cutt downe anie principlle timber tree or trees, or ells doe lett his customary land or anie parte thereof for anie longer terme than for one yere and one day, or ells yf anie tenante doth sell or exchange his customary Land or anie parte thereof without licence in full court graunted, That every tenante and tenants soe doinge or suffering anie the premises shall forfeyt his tenement or tenements. Butt if presentment be made by the homage that anie tenement falleth into decay for lack of reparations there shalbe first three severall paines sett and the fowerth a paine of forfeyture for not repairinge the same.

9 Item, they presenteth that if anie customary tenante be attaynted of fellony or treason he shall forfeyt unto the lord his estate.

10 Item, they presenteth that uppon the death or surrender of every tenante the best good or Cattle of every such tenante is due unto the lord for a heriot but they doe not allowe anie heriot uppon the forfeyture of anie tenement for that they thinketh the forfeyture sufficient for an advantage of the lord.

11 Item, they presenteth that the tenante to the halfe yard land shall aswell paie heriot as the tenunte of the yard landes and upwards and likewise that every tenante to a mondyes land or workeland shall paie for his heriot xiid in money.

12 Item, they presenteth that yf anie widoe take a husband or committ fornicacon she shall presentlye forfeyt her widoes estate.

13 Item, they presenteth that if anie man doth take unto himself and unto another anie customary land although the taker doe paie the whole fyne he can surrender or sell noe more but his owne estate.

14 Item, they presenteth that customary land hath usually byn lett and used successivelie and not joyntelye.

15 Item, that there is noe Common to workelandes nor Mondayes land. [*Note: The tenants of these lands were originally required to provide*

labour on the demesne, in some cases every Monday. Most of such requirements had been commuted to money payments.].

Manorial Customs of Amesbury 1604

When manorial tenants reported on their ancient customs to the steward in the manor court, they did so under oath, and accordingly took the responsibility seriously. At Amesbury Priory manor in 1604 when the homage could not agree among themselves as to their customs, they appealed to the benevolence of the lord of the manor, Sir Edward Seymour.

WSRO 283/5

12 April 1604
We presente that the Custome of our mannor is that we holde by Coppie for three lives and the widdowes estate and the widdowe is to holde her widdowes estate so longe as shee keppeth her selfe Chaste, so far as we can finde, but not beinge fully Resolved nor agreed upon our Custome because we are somewhat ignorante of yt, we differe yt unto your worshipes Judgment, hopping to be aided therein.

The Manorial Customs of Amesbury 1635

Amesbury Earles and Priorye Customes presented the Third day of September Anno Domini 1635, In the eleventh yeare of the Raigne of our soveraigne Lord Kinge Charles of England etc. By us whose names are subscribed.

WSRO 283/6

Imprimis, they did present that usually Customarye land hath beene letten for three lives and the wife of anye (life) man if he bee named to bee one to have an estate for terme of her life (aswell yf) whether shee marrye or (as yf shee marrye) not.

Item, They presented that the wife of everye Customarye Tennant shall have her widdowes estate yf her husband dyed Tennant in possession, allthough hee had anye wife before named in the Coppye.

Item, they presented That yf anye Customarye Tennant dye at anye time within the yeare before Michaelmas, the executor of the dead Tennant shall injoye the Tenement till Michaelmas following, but yf hee dyed after harvest, and hath sowen anye wheate before Michaelmas, the executor of the dead Tennant shall have the Corne sowen, paying Michaelmas rent (and yealdinge some satisfaction to the Lord of the Manor or the next taker as shalbe adjudged by the hommage) but it is intended that if the tennant dy in the harvest tyme then the lord or the next reversioner may sow all such of the arrable land as shall at the death of any such tenant be unsowen and lay to be sowen for the next wheat seed season.

Item, they presented that all Surrenders of Customarye Land within the Mannors usuallye hath beene taken within the Mannors and before some of the Tennants and not out of the Mannor whereof the tenement is parcell.

Item, They presented that usuallye Two paines to bee sett uppon everye Customarye Tennant to Repaire in Cases of Reparations, and the Third time a paine of forfeyture yf yt bee not repayred.

Item, They presented yf anye Customarye Tennant doe Cutt downe anye Timber tree (warrantable), hee Forfeyteth his estate, and yf hee Cutt downe anye other tree, Then yt is fineable to the Lord.

Item, They presented That the Customarye Land may bee lett for a yeare, And yf yt bee lett for more than one yeare or exchange without Licence, That then yt is a forfeyture of their estate.

Item. They presented That uppon the death, surrender or forfeyture of everye Tennant the (beast) best beast shalbee payed to the Lord for a herriott, and everye severall Tennant to a yard Land or uppward shall paye a Herriott as aforesaid, and likewise every Tennant of a Cossett [small tenement] shall paye for a Herriott to the Lord Four Bushells of Oates

Item, They did present That yf anye Customarye Tennant doe lett fall negligentlye any house or howsinge, the Tennant soe offendinge shall forfeyt his estate.

Item, They presented yf a widdowe beinge noe Taker, doe Marrye or Committ fornication shee shall forfeyt her estate.

Item, They presented That noe Revercors [?reversions] hath beene graunted of Customarye Land.

Item, They presented That yf there bee two or three takers of Customarye land in One Coppye of graunt, the first cann surrender but his owne estate, yf the other did paye anye parte of the Fine, But yf the purchaser did paye the whole fine, Hee may surrender the whole estate.

Item, They presented that all Coppies and grauntes of Customarye land usuallye hath beene made and graunted successivelye and not joyntlye.

Item, They presented That yf anye Customarye Tennant doth hang, Drowne, or otherwise willfullye shorten his life by such like Indirect meanes, That the wife of such a Tennant shal have her widdowes estate, as anye other woman ought to have.

Item, They presente that noe Customarye Tennant maye sue or impleade one another out of the Lord's Court without Licence except the debt or accompt bee Fortye shillinges or uppwardes.

Item, They present That noe Customarye Tennant may dwell from his Tenement above one yeare and a daye without Licence.

Item, They present that yf anye Customarye Tennant bee attainted of Fellonye or Treason, or outlawed for the same, his wife shall have her widdowes estate.

John Streete
James Ratten
Richard Harrison

John Fortune his marke
Robert Humfrey his marke
William Marchant his marke

William Bundye junior his marke
Stephen Chiles his marke
Richard Bunde
Henry Pile his marke
Anthony Trotman
Robert Rutt
John Hollowaye his marke

We approve of all that is altered above sayde

(Note: The words in round brackets have been crossed out)

MANORIAL CONTROL OF COMMON FIELD FARMING

Presentments and Orders at Heale Manorial Court 1607 and 1629

WSRO 649/1

Presentments at the Manorial Court of Sir Laurence Hyde at Heale before the steward, John Poulden, gent., 4 April 5 Jas I (1607)

The following presentments of the homage at Heale manorial court illustrate the close control which was exercised over the lives of tenants in chalkland manors. Common field farming, regulations concerning livestock, and the crucial importance of the manorial sheep flock meant that a common system of farming had to be practised and manorial courts retained their power and fulfilled important functions. Tight control was also kept on common grazing and on lodgers or 'inmates' who might become a charge upon the poor rates. Manorial discipline could be exercised through fines, and by the ultimate sanction that an offender would lose the benefit of the common sheep fold on his arable land. Important regulations were made about mere or boundary stones marking the strips of each tenant in the common arable fields, and concerning the sheep flock. Tenants were required to keep their sheep in the common flock under the care of the manorial shepherd. Each tenant was required to supply hay to sustain the sheep during the winter and hurdles for folding the flock on the arable land. These would be moved each day by the shepherd. Cows were also kept together during the day under the charge of a manorial cowherd who was paid by the tenants. Particularly interesting is the long list of duties of the shepherd apparently drawn up because of previous disputes and 'former faults and spoyles'.

Homage: Egidus [Giles] Compton
Gerard Matterface
William Dawkyns
Edward Shuter
Robert Atkins
John Selfe
Michael Dawkyns

The homage present that John Harford and Christopher Whytehorne have not appeared at this Court and are each amerced vid.

The homage doe alsoe presente that the watercourse betweene Mr Gerrard Crington's lands and Christopher Whytehorne's lands is not scoured and kepte as it ought to be and daye is given them to amende the same betweene this and Allhallowtyde nexte.

The homage doe alsoe presente John Harford for tyinge of his horses uppon the Lynchards in the Corne feildes before the Corne was rydd contrarye to an anciente order made heere in this Courte and therefore he is amerced iiis iiiid.

The homage doe also presente that George Compton is deade sythence the laste Courte, And that there was a herriott due unto the Lorde of this mannor upon his deathe, which is alreadye paied, the same beinge five marks.

The homage doe alsoe presente that Roger Dawkyns is an ynmate and liveth in the widdowe Youngs howse, and tyme is given her to rydd him therhence on this syde the feaste of St Michaell the Archangell next cominge uppon paine of loasing of vs.

The homage doe alsoe present that Henry Good, vicar of Woodford, dothe from tyme to tyme suffer his rother beasts and other Cattle and Swyne to goe and feede in the Common feildes and downes of the mannor of Heal and therefore he is Amerced vis viiid

The homage doe alsoe presente that Christopher Whythorne and Richard Boldye have Removed two ynmates, which was in the saied Christopher Whytehorne's howse accordinge to an order made in the laste Courte

The homage and Tenants of this mannor doe all Consente and agree to hange the doore of the Pounde with good strongehooks and to gett a good stronge locke and a Keye to the same betweene this and Easter daye nexte, and the locke and keye to be lefte att the hayward's howse, And yf any or either of them shall fayle in the doeinge thereof, such partye soe offendinge shall forfeite and paye unto the Lord of this mannor for the same xiid.

Yt is ordered by the Lord of this mannor that John Selfe shall have a tree in his owne grounds which he shall take towards the repayringe of his Tenement, And this shalbe donne by the assignmente of two or three of his neighbours.

Yt is alsoe ordered att this Courte by the Lord of this mannor and by the Consente of the tenants of this mannor that John Harforde, freehoulder of this mannor, shal from tyme to tyme bringe and deliver unto the common Sheapeard of this mannor for the tyme beinge the daye before the lambes goe afeilde nyne hurdles uppon paine of loazinge of iiis iiiid, And that the foulde shall skypp over the saied John Harford's lande yf he shall fayle in the doeinge thereof.

Yt is alsoe ordered that yf any of the tenants of this mannor shall presume either with Castinge of netts or with any other netts to fyshe in any of the Lord's waters, that then such partye soe offendinge shall forfeite and loaze for the same offence iiis iiiid.

Yt is also ordered att this Courte by the Lord of this mannor by the Consente of the tenants and homage that noe tenente or Commoner of this mannor att any tyme heereafter shall keepe any manner of Sheepe or lambes, teggs, hoggs, or ewes uppon or in any parte or parcell of the Common downes or feildes of the mannor, but shall keepe them in the Common fould there to be foulded, and to be kepte in the onely keepinge of the Sheapeard of the Common flocke of sheepe of this mannor accordinge to an anciente ordinaunce heeretofore made in this Courte uppon paine of vi[s] viiid for everye such offence

Touching the gate to be made att the Churche, where Gerrard Matterfaces gape is, yt is Respited till the nexte Courte, but in the meane tyme Richard Boldye did openlye in the Courte promise to make upp the same gape presentlye.

Court held on 26 September 5 James I (1607) before John Poulden gent., steward.

Homage.	Gerard Mattrevers	John Selfe
	William Dawkins	Michael Dawkyns
	Edward Shuter	Alexander Goodfellow

The homage doe presente that Robert Alkins hath not appeared att this Courte, and he is spared in respecte that yt appeareth that he ys in the Kinges majestie's businesse

The homage doe alsoe presente that John Harford hath since the last Courte suffered his pigges to goe unringed contrarie to an Anciente order made heere in this Courte and therefore he is Amerced iiis iiiid

The homage doe also presente that John Hutfeilde is an inmate and liveth in Christopher Whythorne's howse. And that Alice Cornishe the daughter of Henry Younge lately deceased, is also an inmate and liveth in Johan Younges howse, and tyme is given to the saied Johan Younge to rydd the saied Alice Cornishe therhence in this syde the feaste of St Michaell the Archangell next Cominge, and tyme is given unto the saied Christopher Whythorne to rydd the saied John Hutfeild on this syde the feaste of the Annunciation of St Mary the Virgin next coming upon paine of xs a peice.

The homage doe alsoe presente that Widdowe Burrowe hath Surcharged the Common feildes of this mannor by puttinge in three horses more in the feildes than shee oughte to doe, and by puttinge in divers hoggs into the feildes more than shee oughte to doe. And therefore shee is Amerced iiis iiiid.

The homage doe also presente that Brente Smalle doth not grinde his Corne att the Lord's myll as he oughte to doe, and time ys given him from tyme to bringe his griste to the Lord's myll to be grounde within fourteene dayes after Michaelmas daye uppon paine of iiis iiiid.

Yt is nowe ordered at this Courte that Robert Alkins is made Haywarde of this mannor for one whole yeare, but his oath is respited untill the nexte Courte.

Yt is ordered by the Lord of this mannor by the Consente of the Freehoulders and by the reste of the tenants of this mannor, that all the Tenants of this mannor shall on Symon and Judes daye nexte [28 October] stake and sett out all the bounds of the mannor of Heale, and shall stake out all the bounds of everie particular man's Lande in the feildes of Heale. And this to be donne uppon paine of Loazinge of xiid a peice of everie one that shall make defaulte herein.

Agreements concerning sheep, grazing, the shepherd, cowherd and hayward made at the manorial court of Sir Laurence Hyde at Heale 23 September 1629.

WSRO 2/4

At the Courte of the mannor aforesaid by and with the Consent of Mr Hyde and of Sir Laurence Hyde, Knight, Lord of the said mannor and of all the Tenants there then presente, it is ordered as followeth

Concerning the Sheepleaze

1 That noe Tennante keepe or Lett Couples on his Leaze unless they be bredd on his Tenemente or unless he hath speciall words and a Certaine number named in his Coppy or lease for Couples

2 That noe Tennante or occupyer of any Tenemente Lett his sheepleaze or any parte thereof, but either unto the Lord of the Mannor or unto some other Tennante unless they refuze to give the full value for the same.

3 That every Tennente duely provyde and Carry to the Fould his full number of hurdles uppon paine of Loosinge the Fould and twelve pence for every hurdle that is wanting.

4 That noe Tennante att any tyme or uppon any pretence whatsoever keepe or feede any Sheepe or lambs on the downes, feilds, commons or wasts of the Mannor aforesaid other than in the Common flocke and in the Chardge of the Sheaperd for the tyme beinge of the said Mannor uppon paine of forfaitinge of iiis iiiid for every sheepe that shalbe soe kept there Contrary to this ordinance.

5 That everie Tennante or owner of sheepe shall yearly in the monthes of July or Auguste att some appointed tyme and in some Conveniente place of the downes or feilds sende or carry eight hundred of his best hay by waight for every skore of sheepe that he intendeth to winter att the flocke. And that whosoever neglecteth or refuzeth to Carry or send his hay in such proporcion and att such season as aforesaid drawe his sheepe by themselves from the flocke and fodder a parte from them and Loose the Fould.

Concerninge the Lynchards

1 That noe Tennante or other feede, graze, keepe or depasture any horsebeaste on any lynchard whatsoever until the Corne groweinge

uppon the same be first Cutt. Sub pena 10s 0d for every horse beaste at every tyme soe offendinge

2 That noe Tennante or other Leaze or graze any horsebeast by nyght in the feilds, until the whole field be Cleane rydd of every man's Corne, sub pena 10s 0d.

3 That the Tennants feede and keepe theire horses in the Bottomes as usualy they have done hearetofore without hurte or spoyle of Corne, sub pena 10s 0d.

Concerninge the Common Feilds for beasts and piggs

1 That there be yearly Chosen by the Tennants a Cowherd to keepe together all such beasts as are kept on the Feild, which Cowherd shall have the Care of the feilde, and Charge of the whole herd, and shalbe paied by the owners ratably for the beasts by the head.

2 That noe beast or pigg be driven or fedd in the feilds, until the same be Cleane rydd of every man's Corne, sub pena 12d.

3 That noe pigg goe abroade on the Feilds or wastes unringled sub pena 12d

4 That noe pigg feede on the Feilds or wasts but from the riddance of the Feilds untill St Martin's day [11 November] followeinge yearly. And that noe Tennante or other Cause his piggs to followe the plough att fallowinge, but leave the whole unto the sheepe as theire Common sub pena iiis iiiid.

5 That noe Tennante or other feede or keepe any horsebeast, rother beast, or pigg on the peazefeild, whither sowen or rydd (other then to Leaze their horses) But that the same be whoely and onely for the flocke of sheepe sub pena 10s 0d for every horse or any other Cattle

Concerning the Sheaperd

1 That in person he diligently Attende and keepe his flocke. That he absent not himself from them, but uppon urgent and necessary Cause, and then depute the same to some suffiente body, and not to Children whether boyes or girles.

2 That he keepe the flocke from eatinge or spoylinge of any man's Corne, And in Case any spoyle be donne by the flocke through his defaulte, the parties damnifyed shall paye themselves out of his wages according as two other Tennants not interessed in the saied damage shall value the same.

3 That yf any sheepe happen to sicken att the flocke, the sheaperd shal furwith give notice thereof att the owner's howse or bringe yt home. And yf any sheepe happen to dye att the flocke or Fould, the sheaperd shall bringe the Carcase to the owner's howse, or give notice thereof presently to the owner thereof after the death of the sheepe, uppon paine of paymente for the same sheepe the full value thereof to the owner.

4 That yf any sheepe be killed with stones or doggs or otherwise through the defaulte of the Sheaperd, the Sheaperd shall pay the owner for the

same as two Tennants shall value it, otherwise to be deducted out of his wage.

5 That the Sheaperd Carefully looke to the hay Reeke provided for the Flocke, and keepe the same from spoyle and fodder thereof without waste

6 That he duely and orderly pytch his fould and penn his sheepe

7 That he forbidd all woole pykers from pickinge the hurdles especially in the spring time, And he Certify theire names unto the Lord of the mannor yf they forbeare not uppon warninge.

8 That he keepe his sheepe from the Scabb or other breakinge out as much as possibly he may, And furthwith mende and Cure them (yf any happen to be scabby).

9 That he Carefully Lay fryth [cut furze] and hayne his feilds and downes [i.e. control the grazing] for the Flocke to the best benefytt and improavemente of the same.

10 That he receive noe sheepe into the Flocke but from such as have right to keepe them there, and from them noe more than theire stinte.

11 That yf any man keepe his sheepe or Lambs on the Common or wast apart from the Flocke, or yf any piggs Digg or spoyle the same, the Sheapperd furthwith dryve the saied sheepe or piggs unto the Pounde.

12 That uppon refuzall of theise Condicions, the Sheaperd be putt out, and a newe Chosen. But uppon admittance and performannce of them heereafter, to be Contynued, all former faults and spoyles of his to be forgiven and forgotten, and be duely paide his wages accordinge unto the Custome of the saied mannor, And in Case any Tennante or other deny the paymente of his wages, or tender or offer him refuse or naughty Corne, the Sheaperd uppon Complainte to be righted by the Lord of the mannor on the party soe offendinge or faylinge payment of his wages.

The Sheaperd did in open Courte Consent to the twelve Artykles above expressed and Mr Laurence Hyde and all the homage sworen at this Courte did lykewise Consent thereunto and Subscribe their names as many of them as could wryte, and the rest did sett theire marck to the same Articles, as appeareth by the Articles.

Edward Shuter is nowe att this Courte made Hayward, and sworen to be hayward for this whole yeare nowe to come

It is nowe ordered att this Courte that the said Christopher Whythorne shall nowe this yeare bringe and deliver unto the sheaperd foure hundred of good hay as the flocke spendeth the same uppon warning thereof given unto him by the Sheaperd sub pena iiis iiiid

Yt is nowe alsoe att this Courte ordered that John Harford's Tenante and Gyles Compton's Tenante, in respect that they have not brought in theire hay to the Sheaperd as they ought to have donne by the orders of this Courte, and have otherwyse broken the ordinances of this Courte, shall from hencefurthe Loose the benefytt of havinge of the Fould to Come uppon their Lande.

And yt is alsoe ordered at this Courte that there shalbe a Cowherd att every Lady day Courte named and Chosen for the Carefull keepinge together of all such beasts as are kept in the Feildes. And the Cowherd soe Chosen shall take uppon him the exercise of his place before Lammas day [1 August] then next followinge, which Cowherd shall have the Care of the Feilds and Charge of the whole herd. And yf any of the Tenants shall refuze to pay his ratable parte to the saied Cowherd for his paines, that he shall loose the keepinge of his Cattle in the said Feilds.

Yt is nowe Lykewise ordered that Robert Alkins in regard of his insolencye to the Lord of the mannor nowe in open Courte, and for refuzinge to obey the orders of this Courte, shall not from hencefurthe have the benefytt of the flocke to Come uppon his Lande.

John Poulden, Steward

Presentments and Orders at Brigmerston and Milston Manorial Court 1608–20

Brigmerston and Milston on the Avon north of Amesbury was, like Heale, part of the possessions of the Hyde family. The regular meetings of the manorial court were presided over by the steward, John Poulden. The presentments made by the jury or homage give a good indication of the close control which was exercised over all aspects of farming within the manor. Much of the business of the court was concerned with changes of tenancies, reports of the death of tenants, orders concerning the repair of tenements and the settlement of minor disputes over boundaries or access roads. There were also regular orders issued concerning the scouring of water courses, the annual survey and inspection of bounds and stone markers in the common arable fields, the provision of hay for the sheep flock and hurdles for the fold. These presentments also provide evidence of the enclosure of part of the downland, no doubt to be converted to arable, a process which was to continue gradually to encroach on the common grazing throughout the chalkland area during the seventeenth century. Shepherds had a solitary existence, spending much time with their flock on remote downland pastures. They had a reputation for being difficult, and it is clear from these orders that there had been complaints and disputes, as there had been at Heale. The following examples show the careful regulation of communal farming and, above all, the crucial importance of the sheep flock for folding upon the arable land.

WSRO 2/1

16 September 1608

Yt is ordered by the lord of the mannor and by the homage aforesaid that everie tennant of this mannor shall ringe his pigges by St Bartholomewtyde [24 August] yearlye and shall keepe them soe untyll St Martyn's tyde [11 November] uppon paine of forfeitinge to the lord of the mannor for everie such offence xiid.

Yt is alsoe ordered by the Lord of this mannor and by the homage aforesaid that noe tennante of this mannor shall keepe more sheepe or horses or any other kinde of beasts in and uppon the Common, more than he hath Common for, uppon paine of forfeitinge for everie sheepe that is founde there dayes after Michaelmas [29 September] xiid for everie weeke, and soe for everie beaste xiid the weeke. The same to be paied to the lord of this mannor for the tyme beinge.

Yt is alsoe ordered by the lord of this mannor and by the homage aforesaid that noe Tennante of this mannor shall drawe his sheepe aprinte [for marking], but he shall putt them to flocke the same daye uppon paine of loazinge [losing] iiis iiiid for everie such offence.

Yt is likewise ordered by the lord of this mannor and by the homage aforesaid that everie tennant of this mannor shall drawe his Rammes fower weekes before Michaelmas from the flocke or sooner (yf neede require) uppon paine of forfeitinge of iiis iiiid for everie such offence.

The homage aforesaid doe alsoe presente that the foulde course oughte to beginne one season att one ende of the feilde, and the other season att the other ende of the feilde.

The homage aforesaid doe alsoe presente that after the foulde course is gonne over the feilde, the farmer [i.e. of the demesne farm] for the tyme beinge oughte to have the flocke xiiii nights, and the Tennants of the farme vii nights after.

Yt is ordered by the Lord of this mannor by the consent and agreemente of the Tennants and Freehoulders of this mannor that noe Tennants of this mannor shall keepe any Sheepe but in the Common Flocke or severall after the first daye of Maye untill Sheretyme, and then to have foure dayes or more to shere them (yf neede require) uppon paine of forfeitinge to the lord of the mannor for the tyme beinge iiis iiiid in defaulte thereof.

Yt is also ordered by the lord and Tennants of this mannor that everie Tennant of this mannor shall keepe the thirde parte of his sheepe at the lease [least] in the flocke all the winter uppon paine of iiis iiiid in defaulte thereof.

20 March 1610

Presentment: Yt is ordered by the Lord of this mannor and by the tennants, freeholders and farmer of this mannor that Leonard Maton, Roger Pincknaye, Richard Cole and John Lawes shall betweene this end and the nexte Courte view the Common Downe of this mannor to th'intent that three score and fowre acres of the Downe maye be inclosed. And that the aforesaid parties shall pricke out, stake and sett furthe for everie rother beaste [i.e. cattle] one acre for everie tennant of this mannor. And that the farmer, freehoulders and everie of the tennants of the said mannor shall have such an estate of the said land as they nowe have in theire severall Tenements.

Yt is likewyse ordered by the lord of this mannor, and by the farmer, freehoulders and tennants of this mannor that everie tennant of this mannor shall bringe after the rate of thirtye pounds of haye for everie hundred of sheepe, of good sweete merchantable haye, and to bringe the same to the accustomed place on the downe by St James daye [25 July] att the furthest uppon paine of three shillings foure pence for everie hundred. And that there shalbe two sufficiente men yearly chosen by the lord, farmer, freehoulders and tenants of this mannor for the Carefull performance of this order. And that by the consent of the lord of the mannor and of the farmer and tenants of this mannor Leonard Maton and Roger Pinckney, gent., are elected and chosen for this yeare to see the performance of this order.

8 April 1612

Att this Court it is ordered that further day shalbe given for the performance of an order made att the last Court for the viewing and removing of nuisances and encroachments uppon the River within this mannor until Lammas day next [1 August].

It is also ordered that to the end no tenant of this mannor should att any tyme keepe more sheepe uppon the Commons of this Mannor than his just stynt, Richard Cole and William Phellips att two severall tymes this yere now followinge shall att such dayes as they shall agree on for that purpose, take viewe and tale of every tenants' sheepe and the same parties shall likewise take notice of such as bring not their hurdles to the common fold and shall att the next Court make presentment of such defaults as they find. And it is ordered that every sheepe that shalbe kepte above the just stint shalbe forfeyted vid for every weeke by such tenant as is owner of the said sheepe.

27 September 1616

The homage doe alsoe presente that the Coppyhoulders and tennants of this mannor are much wronged for that Leonard Maton, the farmer of this mannor doe not fodder theire sheepe three dayes and nights accordinge to the Customes of the said mannor.

Yt is ordered at this Courte that William Phillips shalbe hayward this yeare, And that everie one of the Tennants of this mannor shall give him a pennye of a yarde lande towards his paines, and a penny for everye trespass of all manner of Cattle.

Leonard Matton and Thomas Munday [to be] Tellers of the flocke and wayers of the haye.

25 September 1617

The homage doe alsoe presente that the Common sheapards of this mannor have this summer donne the tennants of this mannor muche wronge by suffringe the flocke to goe in the Cowe Downe after the twentieth daye of Marche. And the Sheapards are enjoyned not to doe the like againe uppon paine of iiis iiiid for everye such offence donne in the forenoone, and vis viiid for everie such offence donne in the afternoone

12 April 1618

It is ordered that everye tennant of this mannor shall paye xiid to the wante [mole] catcher for everye yarde lande within this mannor. And that Mr Maton and Mr Pinckney shall collect the same. And this to be done by everye tennant of this mannor uppon paine of loazinge of xiid for everye yarde lande. But yf the wante catcher shalbe carelesse or negligente about the kyllinge of the wants he shall loose his xii[d] for everye yarde lande.

Yt is alsoe ordered by the Lord of this mannor by the consent of the tennants of this mannor that everye tennant of this mannor shall for everye yarde lande att a seasonable tyme sett one timber tree of oake, ashe and elme and one fruite tree, and shall from tyme to tyme cherish and nourishe them, And yf the said trees shal decaye then they shall supplye the same. And in defaulte thereof they shall forfeit for wante of plantinge or nourishinge everye such tree xiid a peice.

For as much as the Sheepe doe every yeare breake out of the flocke and doe much harme through the Sheapeards negligence, therefore it is ordered by the Lord of this mannor by the Consent of the tennants that unless the Sheapeards be more Carefull that they shalbe furthwith discharged of beinge Sheapeards there any longer.

13 April 1618

For asmuch as it appeareth by the Anciente Court Rolls of this mannor that the number of the hurdles for the Common flocke is 183, It is now ordered at this Court that yf any tenant of this Mannor shalbe behind one weeke with his hurdles after notice thereof given him by the Sheapherd he shal forfeyte vid in defaulte thereof. And the sheapherd uppon paine of loazinge of vid shall bring home the owlde hurdles to the tenants' howses.

Yt is also ordered by the Lord of this Mannor by the Consente of the tenants of this Mannor that the homage shall betweene this and Whitsuntyde next stake out all the Tenants' lands of this Mannor, And that they shall then viewe what wronge the Leasehoulders have done to the Coppyhoulders in the feilde, and sett out and stake out the bounds, and shall presente the wrongs att the nexte Courte and by whom the same have been soe donne.

13 September 1620

Yt is ordered by the lord of this mannor by the consent of the freehoulders and tennants that yf Richard Holmes the Sheapeard shall not heare after looke carefully to his chardge and be himselfe orderly towards all his Masters as a good servante ought to doe, that then he shall not continewe here Sheapeard any longer.

Communal Action to Protect Common Rights at Stratford Tony 1620

The following extract from the Manorial Court Book of Stratford Tony illustrates the uncertainty of boundaries on the downland, the value of the grazing which the downs provided and the importance of the Rogationtide perambulation of parish boundaries. Some manorial boundaries were marked by mounds of earth or by standing stones; others by trees or trackways. Evidently the men of Stratford Tony took decisive action when their common grazing rights were threatened.

HRO 44M69/A8/3/1

4 September 18 James [1620]

Wee present *in hic anglicanis verbis sequent vizt.* That the Inhabitants of Throope in Bishopstone have unjustly encroached uppon the soyle of the Lord of the Mannor uppon Southdowne, makinge there their bound where it ought not to be. But the said Jurors present that the Inhabitants of this towne with common consent have throwne downe the same.

Rents, Profits, Perquisites and Obligations of the Demesne Farm at Broad Chalke 1631

The following description of the demesne farm at Broad Chalke occurs as part of a manorial survey of the estates of Philip, Earl of Pembroke and Montgomery, made on 16 September 1631. The whole Survey was printed in Wiltshire Record Society, Vol. IX, 1953. Not printed in that volume was a 'Particular' giving further details of the farm which is bound in the same volume as the Survey. The Particular is undated but the handwriting is contemporary with the Survey, and the reference to Ship-Money shows that it must have been compiled during the 1630s. The reference to 'Mr Gawen' does not help with dating, since the Gawen family held land at Mount Sorrel in Broad Chalke throughout the 17th century. They also held the manor of Norrington, but were deprived because of continuing attachment to the Catholic faith, as described elsewhere in this volume. In 1631 there were 36 copyhold tenants at Broad Chalke, in addition to the single leaseholder or 'tenant by indenture' who held the demesne farm; there were a further 22 copyholders at neighbouring Bower Chalke. The copyholders held tenements ranging from a farmhouse with garden, orchard, barn and other buildings, meadow, pasture, common on the downs for more than 100 sheep, three or four cows and 40 or50 acres of arable in the common fields, to those holding only a cottage, common for a few sheep and a cow, with possibly a small acreage of arable. From c1640 until after 1680 the demesne farm of Broad Chalke was held by members of the Aubrey family, including the antiquarian, John Aubrey. John Aubrey bears witness to the fact that the demesne meadows at Broad Chalke began to be watered from c1635. Throughout his time at Broad Chalke he was plagued by financial *worries, and his claim that the downland sheep flock was the most lucrative part of the farm, and that the arable produced little more than the corn rent, probably says more about his lack of farming expertise and business acumen than the profitability of corn-growing in the chalkland valleys of south Wiltshire.[*VCHWilts, *XIII, 1987, 29-33, 37-48; R.C. Hoare,* Modern Wiltshire (Chalke), *133]*

The following Survey and Particular of the demesne farm in c1631 provides evidence of farming practice on the chalkland, the crops grown, the large numbers of sheep kept, the perquisites such as conies, pigeons and labour services from the copyholders, the profit made by the leaseholder, and the continuance of communal festivities such as the feasting on St Thomas's day [21 December]. Like church ales and other seasonal diversions, such merry-making would soon cease because of Puritan disapproval.

WSRO 2057/S5 Vol. I ff 1-2
Printed in WRS, IX, 1953 pp 11-12

Tenants by Indenture

Anthony Browne, gentleman, holds by indenture, 14 November LXIII Eliz. [**recte** XLIII Eliz. i.e. 1601], by grant of William, Earl of Pembroke, to him and Margaret his late wife under fine of £40, the capital messuage or farm of Broad Chalke, all houses, barns, etc., all arable lands, meadows, leas and pastures to the same belonging, the works of all customary tenants of the manor of Broad Chalke and Bower Chalke, and the tithes of the farm, saving 6 acres of wheat payable to the prebend of Chalke and all duties of right payable to the parsonage there by composition heretofore made; also the sheep gate, sheep pasture and feeding of sheep on the south side and upon the South Fields and South Downs of Broad Chalke; also the yearly customs and services of the tenants of the manor of Broad Chalke and Bower Chalke for the washing, shearing and carrying of the sheep there going; also the tithes of the sheep and all timber trees and underwoods growing within Chalke manor. Except wards, marriages, reliefs, fines, escheats, strays, felons' goods and royalties. To which belong a dwelling house of 15 and a barn of 11 rooms, a cowhouse of 4 and a stable of 3 rooms, a pigeon house, a cart house, a garden and orchard (1 acre), closes called Barton Acre (1 acre) and Court Close (1 acre), a ground called Horse Mead (8 acres), the penning at Howe Gore (2 acres), meadows called Cozens (4 acres), Mill Mead (1½ acres), Marsh Mead (4½), Long Mead (4½) and Berry Orchard (4½), a little penning called [blank] (2 acres); of arable in the common fields, two hundred, three score and [blank] acres, whereof in the West Field 30 acres, in the Middle Field 34 acres, in the East Field 43 acres, in the South Field called Shaccombe 70 acres, the Sheephouse Bottom piece (14 acres), Wigge Furlong (14 acres), Fox Linch piece (14 acres), Cold Harbour piece ([blank] acres), Howe Gore piece (14 Acres); common of pasture for beasts upon the Cow Downs, pasture and feeding for 800 sheep on the South Down pasture and 400 on the North Down, and 2 acres of wood yearly to be had out of the Lord's coppices in the Chase. For Anthony's life. Rent 30 qtrs. Of wheat,

30 qtrs. Of barley, 20 qtrs. Of oats, 24 geese, 24 capons and 100 pigeons. Heriot 40s. Reputed [blank] yardlands. Worth [blank].

The said Anthony holds by indenture, 14 November 43 Eliz. [1601], by grant of William, Earl of Pembroke under fine of [blank], the sheep gate and sheep pasture and feeding of sheep in the south side and in the South Fields and South Downs of Broad Chalke, the tithe wool of the sheep and the yearly custom of the tenants of Broad Chalke and Bower Chalke for washing, shearing and carrying the wool of the sheep and the custom paid by the farmers of the demesne in corn and hurdles; and the warren of conies upon the South Down, Verncitch and Rowe Gore or any part of the farm of Broad Chalke. For life. Rent £20, 10 couple of conies, 10 couple of rabbits. Heriot 20s. Worth [blank].

WSRO 2057/S5 Vol. I f i

A Particular of the Farme of Broad Chalke

Meadow	
Imprimis, of meadow one close called Barton Aker	1 Aker
Item, one orchard and garden	1 aker
Item, one other Close called Pikes	1 aker
Ashe Courte Close	1 aker
A ground called Horsmeade	8 akers
A Pennyng at Honeyvore	2 akers
A meadow called Cozens	4 akers
Mill meade	1 aker ob.
Marsh meade	4 akers ob.
Long meade	4 akers ob.
One other Penning called Nawle	2 akers
One other meade called Barry Orchard	4 akers ob.
The sum of Akers of al the meadow is	34 akers
which at 30s the Aker amounts unto	£51
Errable	
Imprimis in the Noorth side there are three Feildes	
The West Feilde	30 akers
The Middle Feild	34 akers
And the East Feild	43 akers
Item, of Errable land in the South side called Shatcomb	70 akers
The Sheephouse bottom peece	14 akers
The peece at Broadstone	14 akers
Wigg Furlong	14 akers
Fopling peece	14 akers
Cold Harbour peece	10 akers
Howgore	14 akers
The sum of Akers is	271 akers

	£	s	d
Where of sowed to Wheate 80 Akers yeerely, and to Barley and Oate 100 Akers, which at 8s the Aker amonts to	72	0	0
Imprimis Pasture of feeding for 1200 sheepe uppon the downes at 20d the sheep	100	0	0
Item, Common of Pasture for Beastes uppon the downe with the tenants beasts	2	0	0
Two Akers of Wood yearely out of his Lordships Copses in the Chase	5	0	0
Item, the Piggions house at	2	0	0
Item, for Tieth Woll of 1200 sheepe at 3d the Sheepe cometh unto	15	0	0
Item, for the Tieth of a hundred Akers of Barley and Oates at £1 10s 0d the Aker	15	0	0
Item, the Tenants of Broad Chalke and Burchalke doth Eare [cultivate] and Sow 30 Akers with theire owne seede wheate being seaven quarters and a halfe at 4s 0d the bushell cometh unto	12	0	0
Item, for Plowing and harrowing 30 akers for oats at 3s 0d the Aker	4	10	0
These Severall sums are	155	10	0

Item, the Tennants doe find 30 Reapers at Harvest for one day

Item, the Tenants doe finde 30 Plowes [carts & wagons] to carrie Corne halfe a day

Item, the Tenants doe Wash and Sheare 1000 Sheepe and mow and make a meadow of 4 Akers and a halfe called the Long Meade

Item, I pay the Parson 6 Akers of the best Wheate which he can make choice of out of 80 akers and doe reape and carrie the same home into his Barne for him, which I doe accompt to be full Tieth for my Whole Crop

	£	s	d
The yeerely value of the Meadow is			
The yeerly value of the Errable land is	45	0	0
The yeerly vlaue of the Sheepe pasture with the other profitts is	72	0	0
	155	10	0
The whole profitts of the farme cometh unto	272	10	0
The Rente issuing oute of the farme is			
Deducting the sum of £127-3s-5d foorth of £272-10s-0d the yeerly benefitt of the farme will be	127	3	5
	145	6	7

The rents issuing forth of the Farme unto his Lordship

	£	s	d
Imprimis, 30 quarters and 30 pecks of Wheate at 4s 0d the Bushell			
Item, 30 quarters and 30 pecks of Barley at 2s 6d the Bushell	49	10	0
Item, 20 quarters and 20 pecks of Oates at 20d the Bushell	30	18	9

	£	s	d
Item, paied in rent mony yeerly	13	14	8
Item, 100 Piggions, 24 Cheese, 12 cupple of capons, 10 cupple of Conies and 10 cupple of Rapetts [rabbits] (in lieu of this I pay yeerely)	20	0	0
Item, the Keepe [of] 16 sheepe in my Flock for Mr Gawen at 20d the sheepe	3	6	4
Item, a quarter of Beef devided amongst the Tenants on St Thomas's day [21 December]	1	10	8
Item, I pay two Composition Piggs of a yeere ould to the Parson	1	0	0
Item, 3 quarters of Wheate baked and delivered in bred amongst the Tenants on St Thomas's day at 4s 0d the Bushell	2	0	0
Item, one Cheese devided amoungst the Tenants St Thomas's day	4	16	0
Tem, 2 bushells of Barly made and baked in horse bread on St Thomas's day		2	0
Item, Shipping mony paid to his Majestie yeerely		5	0
	5	15	0
The sum is	132	15	5

Item, for cutting and making the Grasse in Long Meade being 4 akers and a halfe, I pay the Tenants one Ramb [ram] and eleaven Gallons of Beere to be devided amoungst them

Tieth Hay paied of all the Meadowes

Item, the 30 Reapers have for theire dayes worke theire meate and drinke

Item, the 30 Plowes [carts & wagons] which carrie my Corne have theire meate and drinke

I doe accompt these Customarie services are but equally valuable with what Custom they reseve from me in Lue [lieu] thereof

Item, from Hock day [1 August] until St Martins Tyde [11 November] I am to keepe 60 Lambs for the Parson

I am to pay 8 bushells of Wheate to the Chiefe Forester of Cranborne Chase

And I am to pay 8 bushells of Wheate and 8 bushells of Barly unto the Under Forester Which Corne hath ben demanded but hath never ben paied by me hitherunto.

Presentments of the Jury or Homage at the Manorial Court of Compton Chamberlayne 1651–1660

The following examples of the reports or complaints made by the homage at Compton Chamberlayne during the mid-17th century show the range of manorial concerns and the control exercised over many aspects of tenants' lives. During the period of the Commonwealth the legal records, including accounts of proceedings at manorial courts were written in English by the steward or his clerk instead of the usual Latin. The lord of the manor was John Penruddock Esquire, and his steward who conducted the manorial court was Stephen Bowman, gentleman. These were Leet Courts which had power to deal with petty crimes, misdemeanours and nuisances within the manor; whereas the Court Baron was a non-penal jurisdiction mainly concerned with changes in tenancy, property rights and the regulation of common-field farming.

A jury or homage of twelve tenants was chosen to report under oath on affairs within the manor. They reported the death of tenants and the heriots or death dues payable to the lord, neglect of tenements and buildings by tenants, disputes between tenants, infringements of manorial customs and regulations, and any other matters of manorial concern. The complaints about chimneys in decay are a reminder of the constant danger of fire in houses with thatched roofs and closely situated along the village street. Complaints about roads, the parish officials known as the Surveyors of the Highways and the parish stocks were properly matters for the parish at the Easter Vestry meeting, but here were evidently dealt with as part of the manorial business. Feeding sheep on the roadside verges and 'droves' or access roads to the fields, and keeping sheep outside the common flock was forbidden by manorial regulations. Likewise, casting 'soyle' or dung and rubbish in the street was a matter for manorial censure. Disputes between tenants over land, hedges, boundaries and the position of boundary stones were settled wherever possible by the mediation of appointed neighbours and by appeal to the customs of the manor and local memory. The order forbidding the cutting of furze bushes on the downs is a reminder of the perennial problem of obtaining firing on many chalkland manors where the downland has few trees or bushes to provide fuel.

An unusual feature of the presentments in 1653 is the record of a 'deodand', that is the customary right of the lord of the manor to receive any animal or article which had occasioned the death of a tenant. Manorial accounts seldom contain references to national matters, military or political, but an exception here is an entry in 1659 whereby a heriot or death duty was not levied on a tenant whose horse had been 'lost', that is probably taken by soldiers, during the Civil War.

WSRO 549/1

12 July 1651

The homage doe present — the Downe hedges to be in decaye and it is ordered that they shall be sufficiently made and repayred before St Martins Day

[11 November] next upon payne of five shillings of every one makinge default.

It is likewise ordered that the Meade hedges and the hedges about the doles be sufficiently repayred by the xxth day of this October upon payne of every one makinge default to paye five shillings.

They present that the Chymney of Maudlin Oakes house is in decaye and dangerous for the Inhabitants, it is ordered to be repayred by her before All Hallows day [1 November] next upon payne of xs.

They present that the barne of Robert Nicholas is in decaye and to be repayred before the xxvth day of March next upon payne of xls.

They present the Churchwayes are in default, and it is agreed and ordered that George Comage and Richard Case, Surveyors of the highwayes, shall cause all the said wayes and other wayes in this Mannor to be sufficiently repayred and amended before St Andrews day [30 November] next upon payne of xxs.

They present that the hedges in the feild goinge to Fovent are to be planted with quick sett before Christmas next upon payne of five shillings for every one makinge default.

It is ordered that every Inhabitant shall ringe his hoggs before the xxii th of this month and so keepe them from tyme to tyme upon payne of six pence for every hogge that shall not be ringed.

5 May 1652

They present that the hedges of the Common meadowe are in default and it is ordered that they shalbe repayred by the tenth day of this instant Maye upon payne of every one making default to forfeit vs.

John Armoney hath license graunted by the Lord and Tennantes to enlarge his Smithes shoppe ten foote more in length upon the wast.

22 October 1652

The Jury present that the pound within this Leete is in decay and it is ordered that it be repayred sufficiently before the fifteenth day of November next upon payne of iis a peece for every one that shall refuse to contribute towards repayringe thereof, and John Winterbourne appointed to doe the work.

They present that the Stocks are in decaye, and are ordered to be repayred before the tenth of November next upon payne of five shillings for every one refusinge.

They present the waye going to Katherine Foord to be in decaye, Richard Cast and Francis Millward the elder are chosen and appointed to see the said waye sufficiently repayred by the xxth of November next upon payne of ten shillings a peece for either of them neglectinge the same, and upon payne of xxs a peece for every one that hath a cart and shalbe warned to carry stones towards the repayringe of the said waye and shall refuse to doe the same and for every labourer that shalbe warned to work to mend the said wayes and shall refuse to come for forfeit xiid.

They present that Susan Noatts, widdowe, who held for her widdowhood a cottage with the appurtinances in this mannor died since the last court, whereupon there happened to the Lord ten shillings for his herriott, and that John Webb, her sonne, is the next Tennant who came into the Court and desired to be admitted Tennant and was admitted and hath don his fealty.

Item, they present that no tennant shall keepe any sheepe in the droves but such as goe with the flocke upon payne of iis iiiid for every one offendinge.

Memoramdum, that John Penruddock, Esq, Lord of this Mannor hath for the fine of xxs graunted to John Armoney th'elder, the smith's shoppe and forge att the Townsend and Fifteene foote of ground at the Southe end of the said shoppe to build upon and he is to have a lease for 99 yeares if the said John Armoney the father, John Armoney his son, and Jane Armoney his daughter, or any of them shall so longe live att the Rent of xiid a yeare.

11 April 1653

They present Richard Oake for keeping his sheepe in the droves contrary to a former order, therefore he hath forfeited iiis iiiid.

They present the ditches in the drove leading to the Common meade to be in decaye for want of scouringe and clensinge. Ordered to be scoured and clensed before the first day of May next upon payne of iiis iiiid every one making default.

24 October 1653

The Jury aforesaid doe present that all the highwayes within the precincts of the Leete and likewise the Church wayes are in decaye, and it is ordered att this Court that James Elliott and Francis Miller the younger, Surveyors of the highwayes, shall see the same sufficiently repayred and amended before Midsomer next upon payne of xxs.

They present likewise that all the Inhabitants in generall within this Mannor have made soyle in the streets and highwayes within this Mannor, And it is now ordered that no person or persons whatsoever shall hereafter make or laye any soyle in the streets or highwayes within this Mannor upon payne of ten shillings for everyone thereon.

They present that Richard Oake did resceive and take away his sheepe from the hayward in the East drove as he was drivinge them to the pound, for which he is amerced iis vjd and likewise he is presented for takinge his sheepe out of the pound after they weare impounded for which he is amerced vid.

They present that one William Keate, the sonne of Nicholas Keate of Fovent, was unfortunately killed in a pasture ground belonging to Henry Martyn and lyinge within this Mannor of Compton Chamberlen by a horse of his father's which dragged him upp and downe until he died, and that the horse is due to the Lord of this Mannor.

Memorandum, That William Oake hath with the lycince of the Lord taken his Mother's Tenement and to give her five pounds a yeare for the same, or otherwise to give her meate and drinke and cloathes att her choyse, and to paye all the taxes, and hath undertaken to paye fortie shillings for a herriott after the death of his Mother.

23 October 1654

They present that Anthony Jey being summoned to serve in the Jury for the commonwealth made default, therefore is amerced xiid. Benjamin Swane and Francis Northeast for the like xiid a peece.

It is ordered that Richard Case, James Elliott, Francis Foord and Robert Elkin shall meete together and viewe the bounds betweene Mr Bushell and John Lynwood att Chalkehill before St Andrews day [30 November] next, and to sett the bounds as neare as they [can] in the anncient place againe and likewise the difference betweene John Winterbourne and John Armoney by the said day upon payne of vs for every one making default.

It is ordered that the Tennants and Inhabitants of this Mannor shal meete together on Thursday the last of this October and to walke the perambulation about the downes between this Mannor and Broadchalke and to renewe the Ancient bounds as heretofore they have accustomed.

20 March 1655

It is ordered that Francis Foord, Robert Foord and Robert Elkin or any two of them shall meete on Easter Monday next and viewe the bounds betweene John Winterbourne and John Gasper of Fovent and to Joyne with two of the Tennants of the Mannor of Fovent and if they find the bound stone to be removed out of the place where it stood, that they shall sett the said bound stone in the ancient place where it stood before upon payne of iiis iiiid for every one making default.

Nicholas Nash is chosen hayward for this yeare and for his wages he is to have halfe a peck of wheate of the owners of every yard land, and is sworne.

They present that the bounds in the Common feilds and common meads are in decaye, ordered to be repayred by those that ought to doe the same before the first day of March next upon payne of vs for every one making default.

11 October 1659

They present the death of Robert Comedge, and a herriott due, which is forgiven, for a horse of his lost in the wars, Mr Penruddock promised to allow of this.

It is agreed by the Tennants and ordered at this Court that there shall be noe furses cutt on the downe for the next seaven yeares to come. And that whosoever breaks this order shall forfeit xxs.

Be it remembered that at this Court the tenants did disowne any right of way to the Mill through the Farme Orchard, but acknowledged it to be of meere Curtesye.

Manorial Regulation at Maiden Bradley 1674–75

Presentments of the Jury or Homage at the manorial court of Edward Seymour, Duke of Somerset

WSRO 1332/59/12

16 October 1674

We present John Hurle for not Scouering up his dich at Billy Corner being a anoyance to the Cornfield there and it is ordered he scoure it by St Andrewes day next [30 November] upon payne of xxs.

We present the ancient pound at the Almshouse to be set up as formerly it hath bin and that it ought to be don by the Lord of the Mannor.

We present that Richard Clarke ought not to suffer his sheep to feed below the Mill Way.

We present M[r] John Redish [Reddish] for Letting his Sheep goe and feed below the Mill Way Contrary to Custom amerced vis viiid.

We present M[r] James Redish of the Priory for not Scoureing up the dich going down to the Mill nere Nicholas Crosses and its ordered he Scouer up the same by St Andrewes day next upon payne of xs.

We present the Custom of the field to be three sheep to an acker for the fields that are to be fed and the sheep ar not to feed the fields untill the horses and the Roder [Rother] Cattell have had the feeding of it three weekes.

We present for Constables George Moulton Junior and Edward Rodway, William Penyful and William Simes.

We present Tithingman Philip Andrews.

We present for baily Andrew Baily and Edward Hull to sarve for him.

We present George Audrey and William Dovard for wayers of Bred.

We present Michell Rise for Hayward.

We present for Ale Taster John Cox.

We present for Seallers of Lether Robert Web and Robert Lie.

We present and order that for future there shalbe putt but a bullocke to 3 acres, and hee that hath but one or two ackers is to feed according to his proportion for a weeke or two one bullocke.

We nominate and appoynte for Sheep Tellers Philip Andrewes and William Bayley who are ordered to tell twice in the yeare at least upon payne of 5s each for makeing default.

29 Aprill 1675

We presente the death of John Moulton senior, who hold for his life a Coppiehold estate parcell of the Manner and there happened to the Land two shillings and six pence for a heriot which is payed to the Baylie and William Moulton was next taker.

We present the death of William Moulton being the next taker but died before hee was possesser of it, but whare thare be any herriot dew wee know not, but iis 6d being the herriot mencioned in the copy was since paid to the Lords Baylif and the Tenement is in the Lords hands .

We present Elizabeth Annarly, widow, for letting her howse fall in decay and order she sufficiently repayre the same by Michaelmas next upon payne xxs.

We present the Custom of the Copie holde tennantes maie tak Timber for repaireing of theire housis and for all other nessisary bootes [uses] if it be upon their tenements aquainting the Lord or his baily. And fuel and firing without aquainting the Lord or his baily.

We present at the death of every Coppiehold Tenante dying befor Quarter daie his executor or executrix shall take the profit of it till the next Quarterday.

We present that the Copessis [Coppices] that ar fild [felled] ar aftar the expiration of seven yeares to be thrown out to the Commons.

We present our Custom is to Cut thornes and holly bushis uppon the Common reasonablie for the repaire of our fensis [fences].

We present, order and agree for the better and more profitable convenients of the tenants and publique good of this place and Inhabitants thereof that noe Tennant of this Mannor or other that have or shall have any Lands of Common for Sheepe within all or any of the Feilds belonginge to his Mannor or in a commonable wast ground called the Knowle or other wast doe or shall putt into all or any of the feilds or grounds aforesaid more than two sheepe or lambes to every one acre and soe proportionably to every greater or lesser quantity and not to put any sheepe or lamb into the said feilds or grounds or either of them untill the horses and Rother beasts have first fedd there by the space of fifteene dayes at least, and none to putt above one beast upon every two acres. And its further ordered that whosoever shall breake any parte of this above order shall forfeite and loose to the Lord of the said Mannor the sume of five pounds. And it is further ordered that two of the Tennants of this Mannor whome the Jury shall, from tyme to tyme, elect , nominate and appoynt (with the lords hayward there) shall from tyme to tyme and att all tymes as to them shall seeme meete, drive , tell and viewe the said Rother beasts and sheepe and make presentment to the Jury of such as shall be found faulty, and if any person or persons soe elected and nominated shall refuse to accept of the said office of teller or viewer of the said Rother beasts and sheepe, or shall be negligent in the due execution of theire office shall [they] forfeite and pay to the Lord of the said Mannor Tenn shillinges each makeinge defaults. And we doe elect and nominate Phillip Andrewes and William Baylie to be the tellers of the Rother beasts and sheepe for the yeare ensuinge. And we doe further order that no man shall cut any grass from the Linchis [Lynchets] or Baite [feed] any hors or Rudder beast untill all the feelds be rid [i.e. harvested] and the hayward to give notis in the Church when to put in theire Cattell. And we doe further order that no Tennante or any other parson [person] having any Land in our feeldes shall breake [i.e. plough] for Wheate untill the twentie first day of Aprill, and for breakeing for Barly untill the thirtieth of November. Any man plowing contrarie to this order shall forfeite ten shillings.

And wee doe further order that no man who is plowing for wheate shall turne out upon any land that is sown after the first of November uppon pain of two shillings and sixpence to the Lord of the Mannor.

Manorial Custom on the Arundell Estate c1660

This copy of manorial customs on the extensive estates of Lord Arundell of Wardour illustrates the long history and continuance of these ancient practices which had so much effect upon the lives of copyhold tenants. A note on the manuscript records that the customs had been copied by William Harman, 'steward of Courts', and that they were taken from a Ledger Book of Shaftesbury Abbey because the more recent records belonging to the Arundell family had been destroyed when the castle at Wardour was blown up during the Civil War. Since almost all of the Arundell estate had previously belonged to the nunnery at Shaftesbury, these ancient customs of the monastic manors were still in force and could be used to replace those lost in the war. The same situation applied to the two large Wiltshire manors, Bradford on Avon and Tisbury, which had belonged to Shaftesbury Abbey and were made part of the endowment of the newly-created cathedral at Bristol at the Dissolution in 1539. When there was a dispute between the Dean and Chapter of Bristol and the tenants of these two manors in 1721, the Chapter clerk, George Roberts, copied a list of the customs from 'an old Register' of Shaftesbury Abbey [BRO DC/E27/37]

This copy of manorial customs illustrates both the complexity of copyhold tenure and the long continuance of the manorial customs by which it was regulated. The importance of widows' estate is also evident, since a beneficial custom over this could deprive a landlord of a new fine on a tenement for many years.

In the following list of customs fictitious characters such as 'John Attstyle and Elizabeth his wife' and 'John Attstyle and Alice his wife' and others are used to illustrate the various rights and obligations of tenants holding their land by copy of court roll i.e. copyholders. References to 'the Lady' and 'the Ladies' throughout the document refer to the abbess and nuns of Shaftesbury, most of whom came from aristocratic or well-connected gentry families.

The abbreviated formal Latin used to illustrate the various entries in the Court Rolls has been translated and is in italics.

WSRO 2667/15/3

Shaston
The Customes belonginge to and concerninge the dissolved Monastery of Shaston in the county of Dorsett throughout the whole Barony

1 Imprimis, yf a man take a houlde [holding or tenement] to himselfe and his wife (as in this case) *To this court came John Attstyle and gave to the Lady a fine of £4 for entry and rights to have one messuage and virgate of land with its appurtenances to hold to himself and Elizabeth his wife to the end of both lives and one other life in succession.*

And yf the said Elizabeth happen to survyve her husband John Attstyle, yet shall she have noe better estate than Widdowhood (viz.) Whilst she liveth sole and chast. And yf her husband survyve her, and marry againe none of his next wives shall have widdowes estate because his first wife was named in the Copie.

2 Item, yf a man take a Bargaine to himselfe and also his wife joyntly (As this) *To this Court came John Attstyle and Alice his wife and gave to the Lady a fine of £5 for rights and entry to and in one Messuage and one virgate of land and its appurtenances, to hold the same for term of their lives* and yf this Alice doth survyve her said husband, and fortune to marry againe, yet she shall houlde her Bargaine duringe her life, for that she is a purchaser.

3 Item, yf two persons take a Bargaine Joyntly (as this) *To this Court came John Attstyle and John Attnoke And gave to the Lady for a fine £3 for rights and possession to and in one virgate of land and the appurtenances for the term of their lives while each or other shall live, successively* The first takers wife shall have noe widdowes estate except he doe survyve the purchaser joyned with him. For whosoever of the two Joyned purchasers doe survyve the other, his wife shall have widdowes estate.

4 Item, yf a man take a Bargaine *in being* (as in this case) *To this Court came John Attstyle and gave to the Lady for a Fine £10 for possession and rights to one Messuage and one virgate of land with its appurtences To hold to him and Thomas his son for them of their lives* The said Thomas his sonne must needs have it, yf he survyve his Father, because his Father, John Attstyle, died seised of the Bargaine.

5 Item, yf a man buy the Reversion of a Bargaine (as this) *To this Court came John Attstyle and gave to the Lady for a Fine £4 for the Reversion of one Message and one virgate of land and its appurtenances now in the tenure of John Dale to hold to him and Thomas his brother, for term of their lives* And yf it fortune that this John Attstyle die before this Reversion doe fall unto him, soe that he die not seised thereof, Then the grant made to the said Thomas being in the course (*Tenend*) or sequel of the Copie is nowe void and frustrate, for that the purchaser died not seised.

6 Item, every man that is named in the course or sequel of the Copie, (although he be Tennant) and die seised of the bargaine having a wife,

yet his wife shall have noe widdowes estate because he is noe purchaser.

7 Item, yf a man buy a Bargaine (as this) *To this Court came John Attstyle and gave to the Lady for a Fine £4 for possession and rights to one Messuage and one virgate of land with the appurtenances, to hold to himself and John his son for term of their lives in succession*, The same John Attstyle may sell and alienate his Bargaine when he list with the consent of the Ladie, and come to the Ladies Court and Surrender upp his estate, And by that Surrender he maketh the estate of John his son to be clerely void and of noe effect. Note that he may doe [this] in any Coppie that he hath in Reversion, whosoever be in the course or sequel of the same Coppie soe that he be not a Joyned purchaser with him.

8 Item, yf any two buy a Bargaine Joyntly together, either in reversion or possession (as This) *To this Court came John Attstyle and John Attnoke and gave to the Lady for a Fine £6 for the Reversion of one Messuage and one virgate of land and the appurtenances to have to them for term of their lives* And yf the said John Attstyle doe sell his estate to another person and make surrender thereof, yet he may not make the estate of John Attnoke void or frustrate, for it shall stande in force straightwaye uppon the Surrender for that he is Joyned purchaser with him.

9 Item, yf two persons take a Bargaine Joyntly in Reversion (as this) *To this Court came John Attstyle and Robert his son And gave to the Lady as a Fine £10 for the Reversion of one Messuage and one virgate of land with its appurtenances now in the tenure of John Roe; to hold in succession for the lives of John Attstyle and Robert, his son, and Thomas son of the aforesaid John.* Yf the first purchaser die before he be in possession of the said Bargaine yet shall the second purchaser enjoy it when it doth fall. But yf both the purchasers die before either of them be in possession Then shall the saide Thomas that cometh in the course or sequel of the copie loose his title thereof alsoe.

10 Item, yf any customary Tennant lett forth any parcell of his grounde of his customary houlde, Then the Reversioners to have it before any others payinge reasonably for it because being in possibility of the houlde he will use it better than a stranger.

11 Item, yf any man take a Bargaine to himselfe and Thomas his sonne, not naminge his wife (as this) *To this Court came John Attstyle and gave to the Lady for a fine £10 for possession and rights to one Messuage and one virgate of land with its appurtenances* Yf the said John Attstyle marry six wives, yet the last wife shall have widdowes estate for that he nameth noe wife in the copie.

12 Item, every Tennant that dieth seised of any yard lands, halfe yard lands, or farthing of lands, shall after his death pay for a herriott his best quicke Cattle.

13 Also every widdow after her death shall paye the like herriott

14 Likewise, yf any widdow claymeinge widdowes estate doe marrie without the Ladies licence, or live incontinent or unchast, and soe

founde by the homage, she doth uppon the fact forfeite her estate and shall after such forfeiture pay a herriott in manner as aforesaid.

15 Alsoe yf any Tennante lett fall his howse or suffer his howses to be in greate decaye, And uppon Commandment and paines sett by the Steward and homage will not amend it, Then the said Tennante doth forfeit his estate of such Tenement as he shall houlde of the Ladie and shall pay a herriott in manner as aforesaid.

16 Alsoe yf any Tennante die between Michaelmas and Lady Daye in Lent, Then his Executors to occupie the Tenement until after our Lady Daye payinge all Rents and duties, and also shall enjoy such wheate as is sowne, And yf he die after our Lady Daye, then to occupie the Tenement until Michaelmas payeing and doeinge as aforesaid. Nevertheless, the next Claymer thereunto shall at Midsomer take the hay, the vallow and the sheep leaze.

17 Also every Tennante of Custome shall att his first entry receive [?recite] a corporall oath to be true Tennante and beare true faith to the Lady to paye all rents and doe all Customes, Suites and Services belonging to his tenure and to yeeld with the homage and to be instified [?] by the Ladies Court.

18 Item, yf any Tennante doe dwell from his Coppiehoulde soe that there be a dwellinge howse uppon the same without licence expressed in his grante, Then he to be putt in payne of xxs-xls-cs or more, And yf he uppon those paines will not be resient then to have a paine of forfeiture by the Judgement of the Steward and homage.

19 Item, noe Customary Tennante shall be retained or serve any other than the Lady, unlesse he have a Copie of Licence, then havinge a licence his undertenant must in all things supply his place.

20 Item, yf any Tennante by verdictt of the homage be founde that he hath not sufficient goods and chattells to answeare the Ladys rent and reparations, then the Lady or her Officers may require pledges of the said homage [?*recte* tenant] And yf the Tennant cannot finde pledges, then it shall be lawfull for the Lady to seise the Government [?Tenement] into her owne hands.

21 Alsoe any offences or trespasse done amongst the Tennants ought to be determined in the Ladies Court.

22 Item, yf any Tennante make spoyle or wast or cutt downe any timber tree without licence of the Ladies Officers, then he to forfeit his estate yf the homage finde itt.

23 Alsoe it hath bin used and accustomed that the Lady and her Officers have made grants of any Coppiehoulde or Customarie Tenements out of the Court, either at Shaston or elswhere att their pleasure. And alsoe may take the Surrender out of the Court att any place, soe that there be three or foure Tennants presente to witnes.

24 Item, yf any two persons holdinge or claymeinge any Coppiehoulde by vertue of one grante or Copies, the one beinge admitted and in possession accordinge to the Customs, and the other in the sequell of the Copie enjoyned in takinge, yet the Ladie or her Officers may grant the Reversion of them both to any other person or persons as they will.

25 Alsoe the Custome is that the Lady or her Officers maye grant any Coppiehoulde for term of one life, two lives, three lives, or foure lives, either in possession or Reversion.

26 Item, the Custome is that any woeman maye take the Reversion of her husband's or any other person, And alsoe to take any houlde in possession.

27 Alsoe every Tennante must uppon reasonable warninge sen [?come] to the Court twice by the yeare and oftener yf the causes soe require. And alsoe must doe all their Customed workes, unless they be dispensed withall. And to paye their rent foure times in the year yf they be demanded.

28 Other Customes there be used which continuance of time doe establish and be not heere written.

Theise are Coppied out of the Lygyer bookes then in the Evidence howse att Wardour Castle which was lost in the warres.
Being in Number 28
By William Hurman, Steward of Courts from the Leiger Booke.

Neglect of Manorial Governance at Mere 1617

The following condemnation of the situation which had been allowed to develop in the Duchy of Cornwall manor of Mere comes from a Survey conducted by the royal surveyor, John Norden, in 1617. It illustrates the importance of an efficient manorial steward who could insure that the landlord's rights were not abused by the tenants. Mere had been notoriously badly governed by Sir Carew Raleigh, brother of Sir Walter Raleigh. An inquiry held into his conduct as steward in 1600 found that he had been guilty of many irregularities and that he had granted numerous copyhold estates at low fines in return for payments to himself, and that he had also kept a considerable part of the fines and rents which were paid. [PRO E 178/2457]. Norden lists the 58 copyholders at Mere and describes the results of years of loose manorial control as follows:

PRO LR 2/207 ff22v-23

Such is the fruite of tolleration of abuses as time hath nowe wroughte in this Mannor a general immunitie and meerly usurped freedome from anie kinde of forfeiture namelie the letting downe and to suffer his Highnesses tenements to decaie, to fell timber trees, to lett and sett their tenements soe manie yeares under coulour of one yeare and then a second, third etc. pretendinge the same all but for one yeare if it continewe 20 yeares. The ploughinge up of meadowes, denieinge the Prince's rente and the like. They hold noe forfeiture intollerable tollerations whence arise grose inconveniences fitt to be reformed.

Infringement of Manorial Custom at Downton 1682

The importance which tenants attached to their manorial custom and their watchfulness in opposing breaches of custom by lords or stewards is evident from an anonymous diary of proceedings at Downton manorial court 1679-93. There is no clear indication of the author, but from internal evidence the most likely person appears to be George Legg, a prominent copyhold tenant in Downton. The diary was evidently kept by someone closely involved in parochial and manorial affairs in Downton, and is full of references to manorial customs. It is constantly critical of the steward, John Snow, who is said to be concerned only about his own interests and those of his employers, the Ashe family. The following description of proceedings on 20 April 1682 shows the way in which John Snow is portrayed as attempting to encroach on manorial custom.

WSRO 490/916

20 April 1682
I was warned by Quinton the Hayward to appear at the Wooll Pack in Endless Street in Sarum to be a witness with the rest of the Homage and Mr John Snow, Steward unto Sir Joseph Ashe, Lord of the mannor of Downton court, to admit George Ivie, Tennant to the estate in Weeke [Wick] that fell unto him on the death of his Mother. This said George is very ill which was the cause that this was donn at his brother Hugh Ivie's house where he laies very il. And we of the Homage must be at the next Court day as is kept at Downton Ash to testify upon our Oathes at Court that the rod and paper that did mention what he holds their was given by the said Steward in the said George Ivie's hands with these words 'I doe admit you Tennant unto your estate according to the contents of the said paper and Custom of the mannor'. I find that this is against our Custom to admit any to be Tennant out of the Lordship. Therefore the said Steward is very much to blame to doe this for his private Interest. And alsoe to pick up such an Homage that most of them was ignorant of the Customs in this case. For I find by antient men Maurice Dyer, John Saunders, John Gauntlett, John Barson etc. that we cannot answer to doe it. But this said Mr Snow will allwaies bee fiddling in something for his private gaine and incroaching to break our Customs as much as it lieth in him to doe, and in these things to make a bennefit by it unto himselfe, not careing soe he have his ends in the least whatsoever that it doe prove a prejudice unto us as our customs. He cares not the wrong he does in this kind.

George Ivie's death was presented at Court on 8 April 1684.

The 'rod' mentioned here was a feature of the formal ceremony of admission to a tenancy on many manors. The incoming tenant grasped a rod or staff while swearing fealty to the lord of the manor. The correct procedure in such circumstances was regarded as of great importance in conferring legal validity to the admission.

BURN-BAKING AND CONVERSION OF PASTURE TO ARABLE AROUND MALMESBURY

The area of north-west Wiltshire around Malmesbury close to the border with Gloucestershire is part of the Cotswold fringe. Much of the district consisted of light, well-drained land which supported a sheep and corn husbandry similar to the farming of the chalklands. The increasing profitability of cereal crops brought the same pressure for increased arable as on the chalk downs; this was achieved by burn-baking or 'denshiring', a technique which involved stripping the turf, drying and burning it, as described in the Introduction. Most of the evidence for this practice comes from occasional, incidental references. An early eighteenth-century lease of part of the former royal stud at Cole Park included a close of newly-converted arable called Burnt Ground. A three-year rotation of crops was specified, and clover was to be sown every third year. (WSRO 161/31/21; VCH Wilts., *XIV, 1991, 144). At Westport, part of Malmesbury Common, evidence of burn-baking emerges in 1690 from the long-running and complex dispute over the management of the land. Under the terms of the Borough Charter nine townsmen were granted 21-year leases of closes on the Common. They spent considerable sums in converting the land to arable, and when the leases were revoked under the terms of another Charter in 1690, they claimed compensation for the money they had spent on improvements. Their complaint made in 1688-9 was as follows:*

> *Petition of John Wayte, William Robins, Edmund Sansome, Edward Browne, Robert Younge, Richard Knee, Thomas Arnold, Richard Collins and John Rogers, of the borough of Malmesbury, in the County of Wilts. Petitioners for valuable considerations paid in money, and in pursuance of a Decree in Chancery, purchased in 1685 of the Corporation of Malmesbury 13 closes, belonging to the borough, for the term of 21 years at a rent of £30 per annum; and have been at great charges in improving the said closes by burning and baking some of them. Petitioners are informed that the Bill for restoring corporations provides that all leases made since the surrender of the respective charters shall be good, unless the bodies politic and corporate shall satisfy such monies as were paid for fines and laid out in improvement. A Proviso was offered in the Commons on report, and ordered to be engrossed, for destroying of leases made by the borough of Malmesbury (only), which will be a great loss to Petitioners, who did not hear of it till it had passed the Commons. Pray to be heard against the Proviso.*

In 1714 the Borough Court ruled that any close could be ploughed and sown if it had first been burn-baked. There was to be a rotation of three crops, followed by clover. (Historical Manuscripts Commission, 24, House of Lords MSS, 12th Report Appendix Part VI, *1889, 482–3;* VCH Wilts, *XIV, 1991, 236. Mr Donald Box has kindly supplied information on Malmesbury Borough Records).*

A more detailed example comes from Corston within the ancient parish of Malmesbury. In this district much enclosure and conversion to arable was carried out during the seventeenth century. The defence of burn-baking at Corston reveals the difficulty of maintaining the fertility of arable land which was remote from the farmstead and where a sheep-fold was not available. It also illustrates the importance attached to memory, historical tradition and the custom of each manor. The extracts show that 'convertible husbandry' or the alternating of pasture and arable on the same ground was already well established. Pasture land was ploughed and cropped with corn for a few years, before reverting to grass. This integration of pasture and arable, sometimes known as 'up-and-down' farming, was an important early feature of the changes which were later to be regarded as an agricultural revolution

WSRO 490/775.

Corston

The following extract is part of a dispute in 1729 between the lord of the manor of Corston, Sir Edward des Bouverie, and one of his tenants, John Sparrow, but it refers to much earlier events and to previous lords of the manor. The long response of John Sparrow to his landlord's complaint is evidently the work of a lawyer. Likewise, Sir Edward des Bouverie employed Thomas Beach of Woolley as his legal adviser. Beach in turn had contacted a London barrister for advice. The dispute, which is typical of many contemporary suits at law over lands, tenure and manorial rights, illustrates how legal costs could frequently outstrip the value of the issues involved. It also shows the crucial importance of manorial custom. In a complaint which does not survive, Sparrow had evidently been accused of burn-baking and ploughing pasture land called Layes in Corston without the permission of the landlord and contrary to accepted husbandry practice. In his long answer to the landlord's allegation dated 30 June 1729, John Sparrow stated that copyhold tenure of a messuage and two yardlands and a cottage at Corston had been granted to his father and mother, William Sparrow and Johanna Sparrow at the manorial court on 28 September 1641. Even earlier it had been held by his grandfather. On 21 April 1682, in return for a fine of £105, the tenancy was transferred to William Sparrow, his son, John Sparrow the defendant in this case, and his daughter Elizabeth 'for their Lives and the longer liver of them, successively at the will of the Lord according to the Custome of the said mannor by Copy of Court Roll'.

His defence continued:

This Defendant doth admit that a Close called the Layes Ground which is about 25 acres is parcell of this Defendant's Copyhold Estate and Confesseth that he hath caused the same to be plowed up and pared in order to have such parings burnt if he should think fit, but hath not yet burnt them but hopes he shall be at liberty so to do in order to prepare the same Close for crops of Corn, it not being convenient or practicable for this Defendant otherwise to manure the same for that the said Close lyes near two miles distant from this Defendants house where his Stock of Cattle is kept by which Dung, Soil and Manure for his land is raised. And this Defendant saith that he doth not admit that the said Layes Ground (being the same mentioned in the said Bill of Complaint save that it differs in Quantity) is antient pasture and that this Defendant ought to be restrained or enjoyned from using the same in such manner as this Defendant shall think proper, the same at this time having in it Self evidence (besides or evidences) that it hath been ordinarily plowed, it lying in Ridges and Furrowes. And moreover this Defendant saith that he, this Defendant, believes that the same Ground had been plowed and used in Tillage in the time of this Defendant's Father's Father before the year 1640, and doubts not to prove that the same ground hath been plowed and used in Tillage in this Defendant's Father's time since the said year 1640. And this Defendant further saith that Sir Giles Hungerford and his Wife and the Lord Lexington respectively in their respective times and turns have been owners of the said mannor as this Defendant believes, and takes upon him to prove that the Closes or Grounds called the Layes Grounds within the said mannor have been plowed and converted to Tillage during their times without restriction or question concerning such plowing. And this Defendant did not expect that the Complainant, who is now Lord of the said Mannor, would have attempted to have hindered this Defendant in so using in Tillage the said ground. And this Defendant saith that within the said Manor of Corston is a large Tract of Land called Layes lying in Ridges and Furrows which carry in themselves Evidence that the same have been plowed and arrable and that the same tract of land hath been inclos'd and made into Closes or Inclosures which now retain and are known by the name of Lay grounds. And that in the said Mannor are several owners (parcell of the same Mannor) who hold such their lands for life or lives by Copy of Court Rolls, of whom this Defendant is one. And that every such Copyholder hath a Close or Closes (parcell of the same Tract of land) Called a Lay ground or Lay grounds which is or are parcell of his Copyhold Tenement and particularly Margaret Coller, widow, Jane Gale, widow, Rebecca Giles, widow, William Gale, Richard Showring and Walter Stephens are such Copyholders. Severally and every of them hath such said Layes Ground parcell of her, his or their said Copyhold Tenements. And that every of the same Copyholders memorially from time to time to this time used to plow, Till and Sow the said Layes ground without contradiction or Interruption and this Defendant believes that they have a right to do so. And this Defendant doth admit that the said Complainant is Lord of the said Manor of Corston and that within the said Manor are and time out of mind hath been Several Lands and Tenements which have been demised and demisable for one, two or three Lives by Copy of Court Roll, to Hold at the Will of the Lord according to the Custom of the said Manor. And the Defendant saith that such is and are his this

Defendants Messuage, two yard lands, Cottage and Layes Ground above mentioned. And this Defendant holds the same of the Complainant for his life and the life of Elizabeth, wife of Nicholas Ponting, who is this Defendant's sister, under the yearly rent of Four and twenty shillings and eight pence and two Herriots when they shall happen and all other Burthens, Works, Customs and Services therefore formerly due and of right accustomed. And this Defendant holds the same at the Will of the Complainant the Lord thereof according to the Custome of the same Manor. In which Mannor this Defendant insists and takes upon him to prove that for all time within the memory of Man, the said Layes Grounds and particularly the said Layes Ground of this Defendant hath been some time plowed and at other times laid down to Grasse or fallowed as to the Owner or Owners of them respectively seemed proper. And this Defendant humbly prays that he this Defendant may not be restrained or Enjoyned from plowing his Layes ground aforesaid, which at the time when this Defendant last began to plow the same this Defendant humbly conceives was not worth above four shillings an acre by the year to be let and set to a Tenant and will be of better value in Tillage in all times to come and no way detrimental to the Complainant's Fee and Inheritance thereof and therein, and this Defendant Confesses that one Mr Beach and Mr Dowden, Agents (or as this Defendant believes) of the Complainant did forbid this Defendant to plow the same Land and this Defendant said to them or one of them that he would proceed therein, then and yet being of opinion that it is Lawful for him so to Do, and this Defendant denyes all manner of unlawful Combination and Confederacy Whatsoever Charg'd against him by this Bill without that any other matter or thing in the Complainant's said Bill of complaint contained material or effectual for him this Defendant to make Answer unto, being herein and hereby well and Sufficiently Answer'd. unto,...'

John Sparrow requests that the complaint be dismissed and his costs reimbursed.

A copy of a letter dated 5 July 1729 is attached to this document. It is addressed to 'Thomas Beach Esq, at Woolley neare Bradfoird, Wilts' from Will. Huns of New Inn, one of the Inns of Court in London. Beach was evidently the legal adviser to Sir Edward des Bouverie and had referred the matter to a barrister for his opinion. Hun's response was that John Sparrow's interpretation of the manorial law and custom was the correct one and that he had proved his point. 'I believe we shall hardly maintain the Injunction against the answer, wherein he swears positively to the plowing of it antiently: but if the Defendant moves to dissolve the Jurisdiction we must defend it as well as we can'.

MANORIAL STEWARDS

The following extracts are from the accounts and correspondence of two manorial stewards, John Bennett, who was steward on the estates of Lord Arundell of Wardour from 1663 to 1676, and John Snow, steward to Sir Joseph Ashe at Downton 1662-1698. These examples, together with other sections in this volume, illustrate the multiplicity of functions which manorial stewards fulfilled and their importance in estate management.

Reliable, trustworthy stewards were essential for the efficient management of large estates. Large sums of money passed through their hands; they were often involved in negotiations with neighbouring landowners; and they had to tread a delicate path in protecting their employer's interests whilst maintaining good relations with the tenants. They also kept the landowner informed about local events and opinions, they preserved the landowner's property and interests from encroachments, from the depredations of poachers, wood-stealers and illegal settlers, and light-fingered servants.

The work of stewards was particularly important in Wiltshire where many of the major landowners were non-resident. Important decisions over tenants, rents, fines, manorial courts, farming methods, woodland, and the demesne farms were left completely to the stewards. In the absence of the lord, stewards were left in charge of house and gardens, defending their master's interests through law suits, preserving the goodwill of neighbouring landowners, conducting manorial courts and ensuring that tenants observed manorial customs and regulations. Sending money to non-resident landowners was fraught with difficulty. John Bennett and John Snow frequently took the money collected in rents to London themselves, using an armed servant as a protection against highway robbers. Money was also entrusted to tradesmen and merchants who were visiting London, or was sent by the regular carriers, although they charged large sums to cover insurance. During the 1680s Thomas Allen, who was steward at Longleat, sent money to London concealed in hampers containing game, butter and foodstuffs.

Many stewards were gentlemen and possessed property of their own. Sir Walter Raleigh's elder brother, Carew Raleigh (died 1626), was the steward of various Duchy of Cornwall manors in Wiltshire and Dorset, including Mere. Henry Sherfield, a prominent Salisbury lawyer, was steward for the Earl of Salisbury's estates on Cranborne Chase, and owned land at Winterbourne Earls. William Thynne, a kinsman of Sir James Thynne, was steward on the Longleat estate during the 1660s. (J.H. Bettey, 'The Eyes and Ears of the Lord: Seventeenth-Century Manorial Stewards in South Wiltshire', WANHM, *96, 2003, 19-25).*

WSRO 750/1

The Accounts & Notebook of John Bennett, steward to Henry, 3rd Lord Arundell of Wardour 1663–1676

John Bennett (1625–77) was a member of a gentry family that had for long been settled in south Wiltshire. He was the third son of Thomas Bennett of Pythouse, and had a remarkably varied career as soldier, member of parliament, office-holder and royal commissioner in Wiltshire and Dorset, as well as steward and man of business for the Catholic landowner Henry, 3rd Lord Arundell of Wardour. At the age of 18 in 1643 John Bennett enlisted in the royalist army and served in the cavalry regiment raised by Giles Strangways, who was a leading landowner in Dorset and Somerset. In 1645 he was involved with the Clubmen who were strongly supported in Wiltshire and Dorset. They claimed to be neutral in the Civil War, but were concerned to protect their property from the damage caused by both sides. John Bennett and his father, Thomas, were both arrested at Shaftesbury in 1645 by the parliamentary force led by Sir Thomas Fairfax, and were fined for delinquency. Soon afterwards John Bennett married Frances, daughter of Robert Toope of Shaftesbury and moved to Hook Court in Semley. Later, in a draft will dated 1663 he described himself as 'of Motcombe'. Following the Restoration in 1660 he was successful in obtaining several offices from the Crown in Wiltshire, Dorset and Somerset, and in 1667 he was elected as member of parliament for the borough of Shaftesbury, probably through the influence of Sir Anthony Ashley Cooper (later Lord Shaftesbury of Wimborne St Giles). He continued to represent Shaftesbury until his death in 1677, and was succeeded as MP for the borough by his son, Thomas. His account or note book reveals much about his life and manifold duties on the widespread Wardour estates. His regular, major task was conducting the manorial courts and collecting rents and fines throughout the Arundell properties. These included Ansty, Tisbury, Donhead, Semley, Swallowcliffe and other properties in the vale of Wardour, Fontmell and Melbury in Dorset, South Petherton in Somerset, Broad Clyst and Poundstock in Devon and numerous other small properties. Bennett's hastily-scribbled and abbreviated notes record the rents he collected, the tenancies he granted, the fines he charged for new copyholds, and his expenses in holding the various manorial courts and in taking or sending money to Lord Arundell in London. His duties also involved much travelling and extensive financial business on behalf of his employer. The notes reveal that he was paid £50 a year by Lord Arundell, but that he also possessed a considerable personal fortune. He had property at Motcombe where he lived and enjoyed an income from money lending on a large scale. Many pages of his notebook are taken up with long lists of those to whom he had lent money at 6% per annum. Loans were made to people across the west country from Bristol to the south coast and several members of the Arundell family including Lord Arundell himself were also indebted to him. For example, a list of 'Moneyes due to mee by bonds' dated 30 August 1665 has eleven persons owing sums ranging from £25 to £1,000 'lent to my Lord Arundell'. Another list of 30 March 1666 has 44 names with a total of £3,378 on loan. The rate for all these loans appears to be 6%.

In spite of his position as steward to a leading Catholic and royalist family, Bennett appears to have been staunchly Protestant himself. He called his daughters by the Puritan names of Patience and Repentance, although one of his sons was named Arundell in honour of his employer, and another was named Ashley as a compliment to his parliamentary patron. His notebook contains a copy of his will dated 18 November 1663. He left the bulk of his property to his wife, including his lands and property at Motcombe, and thereafter to his sons, daughters and to his brother. An undated codicil added a legacy to 'such child as my wife had within her at the making of the sayd will'. The child proved to be a boy who was named Robert, but who did not survive. The notebook reveals the remarkable variety of services which John Bennett rendered the Arundell family. He sent beef, pigs, butter and fruit to Lord Arundell in London. He paid keepers to take gifts of deer and swans to local gentry. Gardeners were paid for planting fruit trees at Wardour and Ansty in 1668. Lord Shaftesbury's coachman at Wimborne St Giles was given 2s 6d 'for showing my Lord Arundell the way to Lulworth Castle'. He also paid a farmer 5s 0d when one of his sheep was killed by Lord Arundell's dog. On 29 May 1670, 'Oak Apple Day' when the Restoration of Charles II was commemorated, the celebrations involved many expenses. The bowling green keeper at Shaftesbury was given 2s 0d; the keepers and 'the servants of the house' were rewarded, the 'Hare finder' was paid 5s 0d 'when you killed a brace of hares' and a further 1s 0d 'for playing the Knave'. In 1675 the steward spent £1 16s 8d for black cloth to hang around the chancel at Tisbury when Lady Arundell was buried, and on black cloth for the minister who conducted the service. Bennett's accounts show that the estate woodland at Hook and Castle Ditches was carefully managed and the parkland at Wardour was maintained. Wardour castle had been ruined during the Civil War, but Lord Arundell occasionally used the nearby farmhouse as a residence. (WSRO 413/507-9. Mr Robert Moody has kindly supplied much information about John Bennett's career; a detailed account can be found in his John Benett of Pyt House, *2003, 90-102.*

	£	s	d
17 November 1663			
Rents received from the various manors	2166	10	0
There is due from mee to the Lord Arundell on the foot of my accompt for one yeare ending at Michaelmas 1662	666	11	3
Received since for mannor rents	293	1	2
For Herriotts	32	16	8
For Rent Graine	223	19	6
For Fines	375	6	8
From John Willson [Farmer at Anstey]	546	0	0
For the rent of Funtmill [Fontmell] Mills	29	4	0
	2166	19	3
More received and due to his Majestie the Lord Sandwich as I conceave when my accompt is made up as it now stands	1600	0	0

	£	s	d
I doe owe two hundred and odd pounds for the Free (?) present butt doe hope to have some favor having lost much out of that money and chardged my Selfe with a good some nott returned by the Commissioners.			
Soe by this accompt now debtor	3766	19	3
17 November 1663			
Returned to Mr Joyce since my last account with him dated 30 March 1663 at which time he was debtor	92	2	9½
By James Berriman of Bruton	50	0	0
By Mr Whitaker	300	0	0
By John Beaton of Ivelchester [Ilchester]	90	0	0
By George Hilborne of Ivelchester	185	0	0
By Mr Gale of Tawnton	50	0	0
By Mr John Hake two bills one is paid & the other to be sent him	50	0	0
By Mr Gallington of Wells	50	0	0
By my sister Baron	100	0	0
	1067	2	9½
Paid for Mr Joyce to severall persons by his orders as appeareth by particulars	1744	19	6
	2812	2	3
Of this paid by my order to Mr Topp of Stockton	100	0	0
For Mr Hyde	18	0	0
For Mr Davis	73	14	0
For a bed per account	9	0	0
	200	14	0
The rest is paid to my Lord Arundell and must bee allowed to mee or is in his hands with 40 20s pieces of breeches money * £34 10s 4d returned to him from Bruton.			
By severall persons in October 1663	835	0	0
Returned by Mr Whitaker upon Mr Lutterell	200	1	0
All which doth make	3847	2	3
Soe due to mee more than the Chardges which sum with my 40 peeces of Gold for the Breeches	80	3	0

*'breeches money': possibly manorial fines paid by tenants for making 'breaches' or temporary enclosures in the common fields

	£	s	d
money will allmost sattisfie £200 or thereabouts disbursed by my directions.			
Disbursements to bee allowed out of the years profitts ending Michaelmas '63 are as followeth			
For expenses in Keeping Courts in Dorsett and Wiltsheire at Lady Day & Michaelmas	1	12	6
For expenses in Somersettsheire at Lady Day & Michaelmas being there above a fortnight in both seasons	3	2	6
For Messengers to warne Courts for Lady Day and Michaelmas for the whole yeare		18	6
For Letters by the post for one yeare	2	8	6
To the post boy and woman that bring my letters		8	6
Paid William Morgan for assisting to kill the Buck at Tollard for my Lord Chancellor		10	0
Paid Mr Plotts keeper Doe when he brought the venison to Sarum and Messenger that brought the Carpes at the Bell	1	5	0
Paid Mr Yeatman's Bill for the Recovery of Poundstock and for his assistance in examining sortinge wrightings at severall times	8	3	4
Paid Mr Danes at severall times for his advice cuncerning the ___?Rents	2	0	0
Paid Mr Brents man for the Lease of the Howse	1	10	0
Paid Mr Willson and was delivered [to] Mr Browne which he hath chardges himself with	4	0	0
Paid the Crowne rents due from Bridsor and Hazledon at Michaelmas '63	2	0	0
Paid for the Fees & Aquittances		2	0
Paid a yeares rent to his Maister for Funtmell [Fontmell] & Melbury due at Michaelmas '63	11	11	9½
27 May 1663			
Moneyes disburst for the Right Honarable the Lord Arundell to bee accounted for in the yeare '63			
Paid for my Lord Arundell's use to severall persons as appears by his Lordshipp's receept dated 19 December 1663	1700	0	0
1 February '63			
Paid Mr Hall by Mr Joyce	300	0	0
24 May '63			
Paid Mr Hall by my man	100	0	0
Paid my Lord in Gold	110	0	0
Paid my Lord by a bill in Lumber Street	33	0	0
Paid my Lord by Mr Groome in money & by bond	260	0	0

	£	s	d
Paid Mr Henery Arundell his halfe yeare's annuity due in February '63	300	0	0
Paid Mr Vaughan for his yeares annuity [crossed out]			
Paid Sir Robert Henley	240	0	0
Paid Mrs Harman's Interest for £700 for one yeare ending in January '63	42	0	0
Paid Mr James Mayo the husband of Ann Ellis deceased in full of a bond due from your Lordshipp's father	25	0	0
Paid in the Exchequer Office as appears by bill	15	17	6
Paid then to Mr Scowen	25	0	0
For Couch Higher [coach hire] for my selfe and man twice to London for my lodging & expenses in London, Shaston & else where for one yeare to be chardged on your account at £25 which is not a Moyety of my disburstments	25	0	0
For the return of £3000 to London	15	0	0
For my Sallary for one yeare	50	0	0
Paid Thomas Farim of Hampnett for a cottage since sold for £80 as appears by the book	50	0	0
To the Chardges by your Honors directions when I made my last account	100	0	0

	£	s	d
Moneyes paid for the Lord Arundell nott accompted			0
on the 29 July '64 and to bee accounted out of the proffitts due for one yeare ending Michaelmas '64			0
Due to John Bennett on the foot of his accompt ending at Michaelmas '63	128	6	0½
Paid Mr Messenger for my Lord by Mr Joyce as appears by receipt	300	0	0
Paid Mr Henery Arundell by my man	100	0	0
Paid by bill in the Exchequer Office	16	3	0
For money paid my Lord at Winton [Winchester]	10	0	0
Paid my Lord Pawlett due for a defect in the Survey of Sale	26	0	0
Paid Mr Plott's keeper and Mr Morgan when you were at Warder September	3	0	0
Paid for letters and Messengers whilst at Warder		3	6
Paid since to Mr Henery Arundell at two___? due in July '64	200	0	0
Paid since to my Lord	500	0	0
Paid Mr ___?of Sarum for wine & Fish whilst you were at Warder in September '64	4	10	0
Paid Mrs Hurman for Interest of £700 due in July '64	21	0	0
Paid William Clement the Gardner for trees carridge & Charges, his paines & a Gardener to helpe sett them as appears by bill	23	10	0

Disburstments to bee accompted for the Yeare 1664

	£	s	d
For expenses in Keeping Corts at Lady Day in Dorsett and Wilts	1	15	6
For expenses at the Corts in Sumersett	1	5	0
For Horse and Messenger to Carry back a Horse borrowed there		9	0
Messengers for the Corts		9	6
For the post letters, [post] woman and post boy for one yeare	2	17	6
For expenses and Coach hyer to and from London for Lodging and expenses there in July '64 , to be chardged to your Lordshipp when I make my accompts	5	0	0
For expenses in Keeping Corts in Dorsett and Wilts at Michaelmas		13	0
For my expenses in Keeping Corts in Sumersett at Michaelmas	1	3	6
For Messengers to warne the Corts		9	6
Paid and spent at Sarum in 3 dayes and nights at the Sessions and for entertaining of fower wittneses at the Inn	1	16	0
Paid two wittnesses for neglect of their worke and paines		13	6
Paid for the Inditement, warrants and fees to severall persons		11	6
Paid the Gardener for comeing to Warder when your Lordshipp was there		2	6
August the 30th '65			
Payd for a horse for my Lord Ashley	25	0	0
Payd for beef, veale and tounges [tongues]	4	4	6
Payd for 20 dozen of butter	5	0	0
Payd for piggs and a Messenger	1	2	0
August the 30th '65			
Paid for the Lord Arundell	953	16	7½
Received from him at the time	534	1	6½
Soe then due to the accountant	419	15	1
Lent to severall persons by Note	340	0	0
Due from Mr Joyce	296	2	3
In David's hands	419	12	5
	1475	10	6
Received more from Collengridge	50	0	0
Soe in trueth due to mee butt	1425	10	6

	£	s	d
Moneyes disburst by John Bennett and not accounted on the 16th June '65			
At which there was due to the accountant from the Lord Arundell	403	16	7½
Paid Mr Henery Arundell by Mr Joyce	300	0	0
Paid Mr Bourne for my Lady by Mr Joyce	200	0	0
Paid Mr Secretary Morice for the defect in the Survey of Clist [Broad Clist]	40	0	0
August the 30th '65			
Paid the Lord Arundell by Mr Joyce	300	0	0
Paid Mr Hen. Arundell in February '65	300	0	0
Paid Mrs Hurman for her Annuitty for a yeare	42	0	0
Paid Mr Polewheale in part of his annuity	6	0	0
Paid for the Lord Arundell by Mr Joyce	300	0	0
Paid by Mr Joyce more	400	0	0

Expenses and disburstments to bee accounted to the Lord Arundell for the yeare 1665

	£	s	d
For my Expenses for my selfe, man and two horses when I made my account to London and thence to Somerton in June '65, being out 3 weekes	7	10	0
Paid my man David Fetham for engroseing a Mortgage wrighting two Large paper bookes and severall wrightings for the Lord's	2	10	0
For Messengers to Petherton and else where to warn Corts at Lady Day '65		9	0
For Expenses in Keeping Corts in the west at Lady Day '65, being forth about a weeke	1	12	6
For expenses in Dorset and Wilts Keeping Corts at Lady Day '65		16	0
Paid at the New Inn for the 3 nights (/) expenses of Petherton in 3 dayes		12	0
Paid the Lord Ashlye's servant when the Swans were sent to Warder		10	0
Paid for a pound of tabacco at Oxford		12	0
Paid Sir Phillip Warwick at Oxon	10	0	0
Paid his man there	1	0	0
Paid for my horses at Oxon and the rode [road] being out – (?) 5 weekes	4	15	0
Paid for my Lodgeing there	2	0	0
Paid for my other expense being forth 5 weekes	3	7	6
For Messengers for the Corts at Michaelmas '65		6	6
For Expenses in Keeping Corts in Somersett at Michaelmas being out a weeke	1	15	6
For the like in Dorset and Wilts		13	0

	£	s	d
Paid the Procter at Sarum to gett of Kellawayes prosecution in the Bishop's Cort for the tith of Highwood and –(?) spent then a bout the business at Two severall times	1	0	0
Given Mr Freke's Groome that brought the Mare to Motcomb	3	0	0
Paid for the fees to Sir Robert Long and the rest of the officers in the Exchequer for the taking (?) of £500	13	10	0
Paid Mr Sherwin at the time for his assistance	1	0	0
Paid for 80 fruit trees, most of them sett at Ansty	2	13	6
Paid Mr Yeatman for drawing the Mortgage of Poundstock and Lodeswell	2	0	0
Paid for letters to the post and Messengers and to the woman carryer for letters for one yeare	2	17	0
For my expenses this yeare in your affaires at Shaston, Sarum and Hyndon and else where on severall occasions	10	0	0
For my owne Sallary	50	0	0
Paid for a –(?) into Oxfordsheire and the like against Geo Moor	1	17	0
For the interest of £500 for 6 months	15	0	0
For the interest of £500 for one year	30	0	0
For poundage of £500	25	0	0
For my owne Sallary	50	0	0

Moneyes oweing mee which I have taken on mee in the account for the yeare '65

James Bower	15	0	0
John Axe	1	10	0
For warren rent	1	4	6½
In John Blandford's hands	20	19	7

Expenses and disburstments to bee accounted in the yeare '66

For Expenses in Dorsett and Wilts at Lady Day '66 in Keeping Corts		15	6
For the like in Somersettsheire being out a weeke	1	16	0
For Messengers to warne the Corts		8	6
For sending the Gray Mare to Lord Pawlets to be horst		4	0
For her Keeping and to the Groome		blank	

As well as receipts and disbursements for Lord Arundell, John Bennett's account book contains many pages of lists, calculations and notes concerning the remarkable amounts of money he had lent at interest. It is impossible to make sense of all these calculations, and he must have had some additional system for keeping track of the multitude of his loans. He was obviously wealthy, and was certainly not dependant upon the £50 a year plus expenses which he received as steward to Lord Arundell. His reputation as a money-lender extended from Bristol to the south coast, and his clients included many of his own relatives, as well as Lord Arundell to whom he lent £1,000 in 1665. All were charged at 6%. The following is an example of a list of loans from 1663. The lists are very roughly written and difficult to read. They do not appear to be at all systematically compiled, but presumably they were sufficient to enable John Bennett to keep track of his many loans and to ensure that he received his interest of 6% per annum.

	£	s	d
From Mr John Topp	50	0	0
From the Sword bearer of Bristoll	12	0	0
From my Cosne John Halles	15	0	0
In Oliver's hand nowe due to mee which John Halles had	1	4	0
From Roger Gurd to mee	5	0	0
From my brother Keelt paid to Crouch	11	0	0
From William Gray of Hook on his old account	7	0	7
More for rent due at Michaelmas last £3 for Crims Meade, paid 10s, butt he must bee allowed for Carridge of wood and other disburstments.			
From William Gray of Legatts £5 4s 6d areares [arrears]	5	4	6
more for halfe a yeare at Michaelmas last From Farmer Blandford	5	7	4
From John Lush of Winscomb (I have paid it for him)	5	10	0
	126	5	10
From the sword bearer of Bristoll	11	0	0
		Paid	
From Mr Walker I will have butt £18 10s 0d in regard of his paines	18	10	0
From Mr Fuller of Wrenton			
Mr Vaughan have mortgaged	10	10	0
From Mr Small at least	10	0	0
November the 17th '63	509	0	0

It appears I have due to more upon bonds, bills, mortgages and other waies as followeth

Paid from Mr Hyde £800 the interest paid at Lady day last
From Mr Bampfeild £160 the interest paid due about December last
From James Perry £50 and 4 yeares interest due at Ladyday last
Mr Rootes and Mr.. . . (blank)

£ s d

Robert Toop £250 and £150 to my . . . (?) lately lent
Mr Hancok £20 (noe interest on the bond I doe owe him £4 on his bill)
Abraham Mathew £250 all interest paid at Michaelmas '63
John Jukes £20 all interest 6 year [be]hind if not more
Bruckle the Butch[er] £40 noe interest paid
Mr Cale of Bristoll £505 to bee paid at Lady Day next
In reddy money the £600 in the Iron Chest
Mr Stanter £70 noe interest paid, I have lent Mr Stanter £21 more

Total £233 of that £200 is Nan Bennett's owne money

Due to mee from my Sister Baron on account as appears £340
Due to mee on my br[other] Anthonyes accompt besides £700 due to severall persons on that accompt at the least £188 7s 6d
Mr George Hussey doe owe mee by a Note £100, £20 of it is my own and £80 George Stiles
Mr Christopher Phillupes doe owe mee £100 for which he sent the wrightings of his Howse, out of this I must pay Alice Biffen £56 and Mr Yeatman £23 [and] odd money
Due upon this note to mee £569 butt my brother Mathew is out of purse for some interest to Bushell's children

Some other moneyes due to mee on the 18th November '63

	£	s	d
Paid for my Lord to Mr Hurman	21	0	0
My Cosne Factor	5	13	8
Mr Osgood by bill	18	0	0
conseive much of the last two notes is disburst for mee	blank		
Mr Cottington's bill	50	0	0
A bill of disburstments for my Lord in '63 and my Sallary due	blank		

Goodman Hallock doe owe mee as appears by his notes £6 7s 0d and I doe owe him for Hay and horse leaze neer £1 11s 0d. What else is oweing my wife must pay

	£	s	d
Soe by this account due to mee with the money lent by David this 18th November 1663	7	3	4

THE ACCOUNTS OF JOHN SNOW, STEWARD ON THE MANOR OF DOWNTON 1662-1698

The Ashe family were leading west-country clothiers. Sir Joseph Ashe (1618-86) was the son of James Ashe, a clothier from Batcombe, Somerset, who appears later in this volume as a purchaser of woad for his dyeing business. Joseph Ashe was educated in London and established himself as a merchant, becoming a member of the Drapers' Company and the East India Company. He lived at Twickenham (Middlesex) and was created a baronet by Charles II in 1660. From 1651 he began to purchase land, first at Wawne and Sherburn in Yorkshire, and later New Court Farm in Downton. In 1662 he obtained a lease of the whole manor of Downton from the bishopric of Winchester. This gave him control of the Avon valley from Alderbury to the Hampshire border, the large farms at Witherington, Charlton, Standlynch, as well as New Court, and the higher land south-east of Downton itself, including Loosehanger Park. After his death in 1686, these properties were managed by his widow, Lady Mary Ashe, until their son, Sir James Ashe, came of age in 1698. Sir Joseph Ashe represented the borough of Downton in Parliament from 1662-1681.

Because of his numerous business and political concerns, Sir Joseph Ashe seldom came to Downton and the management of the estate was entrusted to his steward, John Snow. He came from Winterbourne Stoke where he owned a house, and he may therefore have acquired his knowledge of estate management from involvement with the lands of the Hungerford family there. He came to Downton with his wife and family when Sir Joseph Ashe acquired the estate in 1662, and was formally appointed steward in 1665. He was described as 'yeoman', and from his correspondence he does not seem to have been well-educated, although his accounts were carefully kept and his financial calculations were accurate. He proved to be an excellent, reliable steward, performing many services, personal and political, for the Ashe family, and advising other landowners on the management of their estates. He remained at Downton as steward until his death in 1698, and was succeeded by his son, Leonard Snow, who became steward for Sir James Ashe. (WSRO 490/1151-3; B.D. Henning, ed., House of Commons 1660-90, *History of Parliament Trust, 1983, 556-7)*

The Appointment of John Snow as Manorial Steward

The following document records the formal appointment of John Snow as steward of the manor of Downton by Sir Joseph Ashe in September 1665, after what was apparently a probationary period. This document gives a summary of the many duties a steward was expected to perform on behalf of the landlord. In fact John Snow proved to be so energetic and successful that he was given many more tasks by his employer. He maintained good relations with the voters of Downton and managed the parliamentary elections so successfully that his employer was able to remain as member of Parliament for Downton from 1662-1681. He supplied foodstuffs and livestock to the household at Twickenham, engaged servants from Downton for the Ashe family, and when Sir Joseph Ashe established a free school at Downton, it was John Snow who made the arrangements. The accounts printed below illustrate some of the ways in which Snow exploited the resources of the Downton estate on behalf of his employers. They also show his numerous visits to Yorkshire to advise on the management of the estates there. Above all, John Snow was largely responsible for developing the remarkable system of water meadows all along the valley of the Avon through the manor of Downton. This achievement is considered in the section on Water Meadows in this volume.

WSRO 490/1190

Sir Joseph Ashe, Barronett, Grant to John Snow to bee his Steward of the Mannor of Downton, September the 8th 1665.

To all Christian People to whome theise presents shall come, I Sir Joseph Aish of Twittenham in the County of Middlesex, Barronett, send greeting. Know yee that I Considering the diligent and faithful Care of my servant John Snow of Loosehanger Parke in the parish of Downton in the County of Wilts, Have given and graunted And by these presents doe give and graunt unto the said John Snow the Office of Steward and Stewardshipp of all that my Mannor and Burrough of Downton in the County of Wilts with all fees, profitts, allowances and advantages to the said Office belonging. And I doe by theise presents make, ordaine and constitute him, the said John Snow, Chief Steward of the Mannor and Burrough aforesaid, To have, hold, use and exercise the same Office of Steward and the said Stewardship, together with all fees, profitts, allowances and advantages to the same belonging, by himselfe or by suffucient deputy or deputies from henceforth during my will and pleasure. And for and during that time and terme that he the said John Snow shall continue my Steward of the said Mannor and Burrough, I have also ordeyned [. . .]* [*hole in document*] And by these presents doe make, constitute and appoynt him, the said John Snow, Collector and Receiver of all and singular the Rents, Fines, Amerciaments, Herriotts and Estreates which shalbe come due and payable unto me by Vertue and Authority of the Courts to be by him holden within the said Mannor and Burrough as also for all and singular other my Rents which now are or hereafter shall be due and payable unto me from all the Tennants and Farmers, excepte from such Tennants which shall holde any farmes, lands or tenements at worke rente, within the said Mannor and Burrough. Provided alwaies that if the said John Snow shall not within one and twentie daies next after Notice in writeing by me, my Executors or advisors to him given, make and render a true accompt and reckoning to me, my Executors and advisors or assignes of all and every the said Rents Fines,

Amerciaments, Herryotts and Estreates and also well and truly pay or cause to be paid unto me, my executors, advisors or assignes All and every such sume or sumes of money as shall uppon the same account be found to be due and by him collected or received, That then and from thence my deed or instrument shalbe voyd and of none effect. And I doe alsoe by theise authorize the said John Snow to be my keeper and preserver of all the Royalties and game within the Mannor aforesaid which are graunted to me in and by my Lease of the same Mannor and noe other, and I depute any person or persons under him to take care thereof and to use all lawfull meanes to apprehend and punish all such persons as shall without my license with Ginnes, Netts, Bowes, Guns or doggs come uppon any parte of the said Mannor to destroy, hunt or disturbe the Game contrary to his Majesties lawes in that behalfe enacted and provided.

In witnesse whereof I have hereunto sett my hand and seale. Given the Eight and Twentieth day of September in the Seaventeenth yeare of the Raigne of our Soveraigne Lord Charles the Second by the grace of God King of England, Scotland, France and Ireland, Defender of the Faith etc. Anno Domini 1665

Joseph Ashe

Sealed and delivered in the presence of

Edward Martyn, William Higforde

Extract from John Snow's Accounts for 1686

When Sir Joseph Ashe died in 1686, the Downton estate was managed by his widow, Lady Mary Ashe, until their son James came of age. At first Lady Mary was assisted by her son-in-law, William Windham, of Felbrigg, Norfolk. John Snow's accounts for 1686 were returned to William Windham, but in subsequent years he sent them directly to Lady Mary herself, who took an active interest in the running of the estate.

WSRO 490/842 folio 12

A Book of Accounts of Disbursements made for Lady Ash relict of Sir Joseph Ash by John Snow, returned to William Wyndham Esq of Norfolk 1686

	£	s	d
[July 1690 Payments for the two men from Downton to muster for 28 days at 7s 0d per day	*9*	*16*	*0*
Expenses for providing them with uniforms, carbines, powder, shot. Total cost	*25*	*19*	*10*
Received of Will Coles Esq his quarters part	*6*	*10*	*0*
Remaining for Lady Mary Ash	*19*	*9*	*10]*

	£	s	d
Paid Mr Thomas Harris as appears by his bill for 1000 of raw thongs and carriage of them to London & a bagg for to Mr John Wheeler		15	0
Disbursed at Wayhill Fayre September 27, 28, 29 in goeinge and comeinge & at the Fayre on the hill & at Andover for my selfe & hors		8	6
27 September			
Pd John Doore of Stabridge [Stalbridge] in the county of Dorsett for 20 Ewes att 6s 6d a peece which hee warranted sound att £6 10s 0d			
Bought of him 14 Ewes att 5s 0d each £3 10s 0d			
They are all prented with an L D in the side of each of them	10	0	0
29 September			
Paid John Sammon of Market Lavington for 40 weather sheep prented with a J & B & floure of deluce over head at 7s 0d a peece of which John Parry is to have one half of them by lot when equally devided	7	0	0
Pd Richard Frise of the parrish of Brunly in north Wiltshire for 104lb of cheese being 10 cheeses att 25s per hundred	1	6	4
Then bought of Richard Maggs of the parrish of Blaidon in Sumersett for 400 cwt of ordinary cheese att 15s per hundred beinge 45 cheeses	3	0	0
Pd for portrage of the said 504lb of cheese to Andover & delivered it to Mr Roger Bird, Andover carrier, to carry it to the George in Hownslow att 3s per hundred for Lady Ash		15	0
Pd for 4 sackes to put it in at 2s 8d a piece			
Pd for wax to seale up the sackes 3d		10	11
	43	6	9
September the 27th 1690			
Pd Mr Henry Miles of Madington for 10 ewe sheep at Wayhill for Mr John Robinson of Ham in Middlesex att 8s a peece £4 which the said Mr Robinson promised to pay the Lady Mary Ash on returne	4	0	0
October the 23rd			
Paid the Bishop's officers at Winchester for the rent of Newcourt for the halfe yeare ending at Michaelmas 1690			
In money £20 0s 0d			
In acquittances for taxes £5 0s 0d	25	0	0
Paid Mr Dingley for the Acquittance 1s 0d & Mr Dallin, Auditor, for *Quietus est* 2s 4d		3	4
Then I am Allowed in part of my Sallery or wages for one halfe yeare ending at Michaelmas 1690	10	0	0

	£	s	d
Paid Morris Buckland Esq by Accompt as it Appears by his Aquittence for penninge his hatches & wire [weir] gaps to Newcourt Meads for one halfe yeare ending att Michaelmas 1690	2	10	0
Pd him for his fisherman's Shuttinge downe his hatches and wire gaps for halfe a yeare the same time		15	0
December 1690			
Allowed Farmer Michell that he paid Joseph Humby & George Cumpton collectors for the 3rd and 4th payment to the pound tax assessed on Newcourt	38	6	6

[Paid taxes for other properties as follows:

Withington Farm	*£13 2s 6d*
Burclear Coppice	*6s 0d*
Bottenham	*6s 0d*
House & garden	*5s 3d*
House & garden 'in the burrough'	*7s 6d*
Church Rate & Tything Man's rate	*1s 0d]*

	£	s	d
February 7th			
Allowed Farmer Michell for his 5 load of firewood & one Tunn of Timber for one whole yeare endinge att Michaelmas 1690	3	10	0
Allowed him that he paid Ralph Haitter Tythingman towards repayreinge 3 County Bridges		6	6
	99	2	7
February the 10th 1690			
Pd to Mr Christopher Gardner £50 which is to be repaid in London by Mr Edward Gerrard at 14 days sight unto Mr Atwell & Courtnay for the use of the Lady Mary Ash and for returninge of it	50	5	0
Pd at severall times for the postage of letters of the Lady Mary Ashe's & John Wheeler's from 22nd of April to the 10th of February 1690 in all 21 letters att 2d a peece		3	6
Pd to Mr George Friend the sume of two hundred and fifty pounds which is to be paid upon returne in London at 20 days sight by Mr Richard Minefie for the use of the Lady Ash unto Mr Will Attwell and Mr Courtnay	250	0	0
Paid them for the returninge of the same	1	5	0
Paid at severall times for Acts of Parliament		11	8
	302	5	2

WSRO 490/842 folio 15

An accompt of more disbursted for the Lady Mary Ash than was in the accompt I made with her Ladyshipp att Twittenham February 25th 1690 and also what have been disbursted since that time for Taxes and other things and moneys returned

	£	s	d
Spent for my selfe and hors rideinge to Twittenham when the Lady Mary Ash was pleased to send for mee by her letter of February 11th. Spent in the whole rideinge up February 17 and 18 days		7	8
Feb 19			
Spent for my carryinge to London by water and for my lodginge two nights and for beere and breakfast in morninge and for my dinners att London & in beere and by water to Twittenham		6	5
The 26th & 27th days spent in my journey for my selfe & hors comeinge home		7	3
Aprill the 22nd 1691			
Paid the Bishop of Winton's officers at Winchester for the rent of Newcourt Farme for one halfe yeare endinge att Lady Day 1691 In money £20 0s 0d And by Aquittances for Taxes £5 0s 0d	25	0	0
Pd Mr Dingley For the Acquittance		1	0
I am allowed in part of my Sallery or wages one halfe yeare ending Lady Day 1691	10	0	0
For Mr Merrade's diett & Lodginge & for hay & oats for his Hors from June the 4th to the 20th being 2 weekes & 2 days at 10s 0d per week. Both was paid by the Lady Ashe's orders of July the 26th '91 on Mr John Pavy's account	1	3	0
Paid Tho Clarke of Odstocke for sheepe hee bought of him at Burfitt fayre	39	0	0
Pd Farmer Biggs of Rockbourne on Pavy's accompt for sheepe he bought of him at Burfitt	33	0	0
Pd by the Lady Mary Ashe's order of August the 26 on John Pavy's Accompt by his order September the first at Wilton fayre	[blank]		
Pd to James Warricke of Whichbery for 31 weather sheep att 7s 0d a peece	10	17	0
Pd Tristram Biggs for 60 weather sheep	22	10	0
Pd Henry White of Coome for 20 weather sheep	7	10	0
September the first paid him in money		3	0

	£	s	d
September the 29th at Wayhill fayre pd by Thomas Clarke and John Eastman on John Pavy's accompt	17	0	0
Pd by the Lady Ilchester's order of August the 26th 1691 on Mr John Robinson's accompt at Wilton fayre September the first			
Pd Mr Timothy Weare of Pentridge in the county of Dorsett for 50 weather sheep att 7s 6d each	18	12	0
Pd Stephen Thayne for 20 sheep	6	0	0
Pd Mr Robinson in money att Wilton		7	6
Pd more on Mr Robinson's accompt att Wayhill fayre September the 29th 1691 by Thomas Clarke & John Eastman	25	0	0
Pd Morris Bockland Esq for the peninge of his hatches and wiar gaps to pen water to Newcourt meads for one whole yeare endinge at Michaelmas 1691	5	0	0
Then paid him for his Shuttinge downe his Hatches & his wiar gaps by his fisherman for one whole yeare endinge then	1	10	0
	223	15	4

The Improved Value of Sir Joseph Ashe's Estate at Downton 1682

The two following documents were presumably compiled by Sir Joseph Ashes's steward, John Snow. Their purpose is not clear, and there is nothing to show to whom the second document is addressed and it is not dated. Nonetheless, they are of interest in providing further details of the Downton estate and showing by how much the rental value had been increased. They could be part of John Snow's riposte to the criticism he received from Sir Joseph over the cost of improvements on the estate, especially the large expense in creating the water meadows.

WSRO 490/788

The Yearly Value of Sir Joseph Ashe's Estate in Downton December the 29th 1682

	With the Improvement			But Naturally		
	£	s	d	£	s	d
In William Michall's hands the yearly value						
With the Improvement is	520	0	0			
But the yearly value as it was naturally is but				420	0	0
A part of New Court farme is in the possession of Rich. Mowland and Will Thorne and others, the yearly value with the Improvement	148	0	0			
But the value as it was naturally but				64	15	0

	With the Improvement			But Naturally		
	£	s	d	£	s	d
A part of Looshanger Parke in the possession of John Snow in value yearly	7	0	0	7	0	0
One parcell of wood grownd in possession of Morris Thomas in old parke, that he now payeth yearly	4	7	6	1	5	0
The yearly value as it is naturally						
In the Burrough of Downton in the possession of Merricke Giles and others the yearly value	5	0	0	5	0	0
There is a halfe yard Land att Bottenham at racke rent yearly [rent representing the full annual value of the holding]	10	0	0			
But the yearly value as it was Naturally is				8	0	0
In East Downton the Copyhold Land in Looshanger Parke	4	0	0	4	0	0
Witherington Farme in the possession of Henry Haitter in value yearly with the Improvement	180	0	0			
As it was naturally but				140	0	0
In the possession of Morris Thomas wood grownd Layinge to Withington in value yearly	4	7	6			
In value naturall butt				1	5	0
	882	15	0	651	5	0
There is yearly paid out of it to the Bishop Winton out of Newcourt farme £50 and out of Withington farme and the rest £12 all maketh	62	0	0	62	0	0
	820	15	0	589	5	0
Proffits of the Mannor	12	3	0	12	3	0
	832	18	0	601	8	0

The Rents of the Mannor yearly is	98	17	2
Out of which is paid to the Bishop of Winton	86	13	4
	12	3	10

Another valuation of Sir Joseph Ashe's Estate at Downton

The origin and purpose of this document is unclear. It may date from 1686 when Sir Joseph died and could have been addressed to his executors. It provides some additional information about the properties and the increase in their value

WSRO 490/787

Sirs to whome it may conserne

This is the yearly value of all Sir Joseph Ashe Barronett Estate and Estates in the Mannor and Burrough of Downton in the County of Wiltes as it was lett before it was Improved at a great cost and since Improved at that valueable cost as also the names and S^r names [surnames] of the occupiers thereof that have it now in hand and the rent they now give for it.

				Natural Value		
	£	s	d	£	s	d
A part of Newcourt Farme in the hands of Mr William Michall, by the Improveinge of 74 Acres of meadow grownd with other advantages and allowences to him in the said farme make it at the rent of £520	520	0	0			
But the yearly value that was naturally without it is butt				420	0	0
Another part of Newcourt Farme in Mr John Rennolds, Rich. Mowland and Will. Thomas hands and severall others called Green South meade and South-leas containinge 74 Acres formerly pasture and in value now with the Improvement att two pounds the Acre £148	148	0	0			
But the yearly value was naturally before Improved but				74	0	0
Another part of Newcourt farme in the possession of John Snow Being a part of Looshanger Parke over the ditch in the south side thereof in value yearly	8	0	0	8	0	0
Another part in the possession of Morris Thomas layinge in old parke about 8 Acres now let at £4-7-6 yearly	4	7	6			
But the yearly value as it is naturally but				2	10	0
	684	0	0	508	10	0
To Informe you that there is yearly paid out of all this particulars For Newcourt farme to the Lord Bishop of Winton	50	0	0	50	0	0
	634	0	0	458	10	0
Two messages [messuages] and other lands in the Burrough of Downton in the hands of Merricke Giles and others the yearly value is in all but	5	0	0	5	0	0
Copyhold Lands in the Tything of Bottenham at a rack rent now by the yeare the pasture and meadow £10	10	0	0			
But before Improvement at a valluable cost				7	0	0
	649	0	0	470	10	0
The Farme of Withington in the possession of Mr Henry Haitter as by the Improvement of 54						

	£	s	d	Natural Value £	s	d
Acres of meadow and with other advantages and allowences to him on the said farme make it now at the yearly rent	180	0	0			
but Naturally without the Improvement is but				120	0	0
One other part of Withington Farme layinge in old Parke about 8 Acres in the possession of Morris Thomas let at £4-7-6,	4	7	6			
but naturally worth but £2-10-0 per annum				2	10	0
	184	7	6	122	10	0
To Informe you that there is yearly paid to the Bishop of Winton for Withington farme £12 [?recte £9] by the yeare	9	0	0	9	0	0
	175	7	6	113	10	0
All the rents Issuinge out of the frehold and copyhold Estates in all the Tythings and liberties of the Mannor and Burrough of Downton with Charleton Knighthamhold and all the yearly proffits of the same liberties in all the said mannor is but				108	17	2
To informe you that there is yearly paid out of all Severall rents and proffitts collected for all the whole mannor and burrough of Downton paid to the Bishop of Winton yearly				91	13	4
				17	3	10
Newcourt at racke rent per annum	684	0	0			
Naturally but				508	10	0
A house and Garden in burrow [borough]	5	0	0	5	0	0
Halfe a yard land at Bottenham	10	0	0	7	0	0
Withington farme	184	0	0	122	0	0
Proffitt of the Mannor	108	0	0	108	0	0
	991	0	0	750	10	0
Payeth the Bishop yearly	150	0	0	150	0	0
	841	0	0	600	10	0

MARKETS AND FAIRS

During the 17th century 23 towns in Wiltshire had weekly markets, and 43 fairs were held within the county. Some of the latter were of ancient origin, like the fairs at Yarnbury, Tan Hill (St Anne's Hill), near All Cannings and Wilton. They occupied an important place in the economic life of the county, and some of the documents in this volume illustrate the number of markets and fairs through which livestock and crops were sold. They were also used by farmers and labourers alike for the purchase of provisions, clothing and other necessities, as well as being important social events. In spite of their importance, however, few records survive concerning the business conducted or about the buyers and sellers involved, and there are only occasional references to how far people travelled to popular markets or the most frequented fairs. Farm produce from Wiltshire was also sold at markets outside the county such as Cirencester, Tetbury, Faringdon and Shaftesbury, and at regionally-important fairs such as Magdalen Hill outside Winchester, Weyhill near Andover and Woodbury Hill near Bere Regis.

The best frequented markets such as Warminster, Hindon, Devizes, Shaftesbury, Marlborough and Swindon, tended to expand at the expense of their smaller neighbours. Road improvement and better navigation on the Thames increased the direct trade with Oxford, Reading, London, Bristol and Southampton. Early in the 18th century Daniel Defoe lamented the retreat of some traders from the open market in favour of private deals and sales by 'sample', thereby avoiding the tolls payable in open markets. He wrote

> *'The farmer, who has perhaps twenty load of wheat in his barn, rubs out only a few handfuls of it with his hand, and puts it into a little money-bag, and with this sample, as 'tis called, in his pocket, away he goes to market.*
>
> *When he comes thither, he stands with his little bag in his hand at the particular place where such business is done, and thither the factors or buyers come also; the factor looks on the sample, asks his price, bids, and then buys; and that not a sack or a load, but the whole quantity; and away they go together to the next Inn, to adjust the bargain, the manner of delivery, the payment etc. Thus the whole barn, or stack, or mow of corn, is sold at once; and not only so, but 'tis odds but the factor deals with him ever after, by coming to his house, and so the farmer troubles the market no more'.*
>
> *[D. Defoe,* The Complete English Tradesman, *4th edn, 2 vols, London, 1738, II, 266]*

A complaint to local justices concerning the abuse of local markets by dealers in sheep is included later in this section. Wiltshire justices received many complaints, especially from the cloth-working towns of west Wiltshire, about shortages of corn and provisions because of the activities of merchants in buying up supplies in order to transport them to Bristol and Bath or for carriage to London.

The effect of the development of private marketing in Wiltshire can be seen, for example, in 1661 when the county justices recorded that the 'dearth and scarcity' of corn was causing distress to the poor, who could not obtain bread. The reasons given were private sales of corn to dealers and maltsters. Faced with this situation, the justices ordered that farmers were to 'bringe forthe their corne to be sold in open faires and markets and shall not sell the same by Sample or otherwise in Inns or private houses'. The order was published in every market town in the county. [WSRO Quarter Sessions Rolls 2 Christmas 1661]

At Devizes in 1699 the Common Council received complaints that 'divers quantities and parcels of flesh, cheese, wool and woollen yarne – have not of late been carried to and weighed att the several and respective Common Beames – to the prejudice and loss of the said Mayor and Burgesses of the said Borough and theire tennants of the said faires and markets'. It was this retreat from the regulations and exactions of the open market which was a major cause of decline in so many markets long before the coming of the railways.

List of Sales at Castle Combe Fair 1663-4

In accordance with 16th-century legislation, it was obligatory to keep a record of sellers and buyers of cattle, sheep and horses at fairs, although it is likely that not all transactions were recorded. This list occurs on the final pages of the proceedings of the manorial court of Castle Combe. The volume covers the years from 1416 until the court held on 9 October 1651. At that time the lord of the manor, John Scrope, was a minor, and the heading records that William Forster, esquire, and Helena his wife, were his guardians. The steward was Anthony Rowles, gent. It is not clear who later used the volume to record sales at the fair. The accounts provide interesting confirmation of John Aubrey's statement that 'the most celebrated faire in North Wiltshire for sheep is at Castle Combe, on St George's Day [23 April], wither sheep-masters doe come as far as from Northamptonshire'. Aubrey stated that his information came from John Scrope. [J. Aubrey, Natural History of Wiltshire, *1969 edn., 114]*

The Scrope family had held the manor of Castle Combe since the Middle Ages. In 1651 John Scrope was 8 years old. His father, also John Scrope, had died in 1645 while serving in the royalist army, leaving his wife, Helena, with a two-year old son. She was the eldest daughter of Sir Theobald Gorges of Ashby, Wiltshire. She later married as her second husband, William Forster, who acted as guardian for John Scrope. [G. Poulett Scrope, History of Castle Combe, *1852, 309-10]*

Some of the pages listing sales have copies of the words, names or lines written in a different hand, and a few draft lines of poetry (e.g. 'Death cropt this rose bush, and the roses were/Snatch'd up to heaven and made a garland there,).

Also seven lines in answer to the question 'Into how many Regions is the aire divided?'.

Many of the sheep sold at the fair were warranted by the vendor to be free from diseases such as coath and liverfluke. The modern forms of some places mentioned have been added in square brackets, but it has not been possible to identify all the place names.

British Library Add. MS. 28, 211, folios 177-181
From Courts & Rentals of Castle Combe and Oxendon 1416-1664

A faire holden in Castle Combe the 23rd day of Aprill in the fifteenth yeare of the raigne of our sovereigne Lord Charles the Second, of England, Scotland, France and Ireland King defender of the faith Anno Domini 1663

Anthony Woodward of Codrington sold unto Walter Alexander of Abry [?Avebury] forty couples price twenty one pound with warr.[warranty].

William Charnbury of Bitten [Bitton] sold unto Daniell Scate of Overton in the countie of –[blank] forty couples price sixteene pound and ten shillings.

Richard White of Old Sodbury sold unto Roger Scote of Christian Malford one heifer and calfe price four pounds 8 shillings and six pence.

John Frankcum of Dynton [Doynton] in the countie of Glouc. Sold unto John Stanmours of Sagned [? Seagry] six shipe six shillings four pence a peece with warr. from this for the Space of eight weeks.

Nathaniell Haines of the parrish of Bitten [Bitton] sold unto William Husdy of Littleton ten couples price four pound and three shillings with warr.

Edward Bridgman of Cossum [Corsham] sold unto William Gingell of Malmsbury 3 heifers price eight pounds fifteene shillings.

John Ricketts of Netleton sold unto Robert Mashman of Sha — in the parrish of Milsham [Shaw in Melksham] one dry heifer price Two pounds and one Shillings.

Samuell Workman of Stanton sold unto Robert Powell of West Kynton [West Kington] nineteene Sheepe price Seaven Shillings a peece and Two over plus with warr.

John Nicholls of Nettleton sold unto John Fleetwood of Chippingham [Chippenham] one heifer price eleaven nobles.

Robert Wallis of Hullavington sold unto Edward Fleetwood of Chippingham one cow and calfe price three pounds thirteene shillings with warr.

Anthony Jakwaies of Cossen [Corsham] sold unto Thomas Sellman of Colleren [Colerne] Ten Weather Sheepe price three pounds 18 shillings with warr.

Edward Bristow of Grittleton sold unto Ezekiell Wallis of Senthenford thirteene weather Sheepe price seaven shillings six pence a peece with warr.

Andrew Blewett of Sison [Siston] sold unto Robert Tucke of Hell Marten [Hilmarton] one bull price Two pound Seaventeene shillings six pence.

John Webb of Road Stoke [?Rodney Stoke] sold unto Robert Tucke of Hell Marten [Hilmarton] one yoke of heifers price five pounds Eleaven shillings.

John Longman of Swains Wicke sold unto Robert Tucke of Hell Marten [Hilmarton] one heifer price three pounds ten shillings.

Folio 178

A Faire holden in Castle Comb the Three and Twentieth Day of April in the Sixteenth yeare of the Raigne of our Soveraigne Lord Charles the Second of England Scotland France and Ireland King, defender of the faith etc Anno Domini 1664

Obediah Cheltnam of Ditcherige [Ditteridge] sold unto George Lewes in the parish of Breinble [?Bremhill] one Cowe and Calfe price is – £5 5s 0d.

Thomas Cottle of Wallcutt [Walcot] sold unto Andrew Salter of Chippingham one Cowe and Calfe price £3 18s 6d.

Elizabeth Coates of Marshfield sold unto Thomas Badham of Peausem [Pewsham] Forest one Blacke Cowe and Calfe price £4 9s 0d.

William Smith of Beathwicke [Bathwick] sold unto Nathaniell Norton of Mynte [Minety] in the countie of Glouc. nine couples and one barren ewe price 8s 8d a peece with warr.

Daniell Bullocke of Hullavington sold unto John Lewes of the parish of Brimble [Bremhill] one black Lyned heifer price £4 6s 8d.

William Croome of Bitton sold unto Henry Pollett of Chippenham in the county of Wiltes one heifer and calfe price £2 15s 0d.

Edward Watts of Aldrington [Alderton] sold unto Simon Blicke of Cockellberry in the parish of Chippenham one heifer and calfe £3 10s 0d.

John Britteine of North Stocke [North Stoke] in the countie of Somersett sold unto John Harris of Sperttle [Spirthill] in the parish of Brimble [Bremhill] in the countie of Wiltes one browne Cowe and Calfe price £4 11s 8d.

John Sloud of Frampton Cotterrell in the Countie of Glouc. sold unto John Harris of Sperttle in the countie of Wiltes one blacke Tayyle Cowe and calfe £4 8s 0d.

Alice Barne of West Kynton [West Kington] sold unto John Lewes of the parish of Brimble [?Bremhill] one black Lyned [cow] price £3 17s 0d.

John Millsham of Longly Berrell [Langley Burrell] neere Chippenham sold unto Hugh Dodemeade of Raddly [?Rudloe] in the parish of Box eighteene sheepe price 10s 0d a peece Two shillings being abated with warrending to be sound.

William Woadham of North Wrexall [North Wraxall] sold unto Sammuell Pitt of Brokenburrough Eleaven Couples price Seaven Shillings and Six pence a Couple warrenting them to be sound.

Thomas Sargent of Horton sold unto John Peirce of Cossume [Corsham] one black heifer price eleaven Nobles and one shillinge.

John Hottkins of the parish of Hawksbury sold unto Lawrence Duck of the parish of Cossume [Corsham] 5 sheepe and 4 lambs price Seaven shillings a peece warrenting them to be sound.

Henry Cheapeman of Millsume [Melksham] parish sold unto Thomas Hathway of Stanton Quentin one Score of Ewes and Lambs price £7 14s 6d warrenting them to be sound.

Nichollas Skinscotte of Acton Turfield [Acton Turville] sold unto Phillipp Cambridge of Yeate [Yate] Two Cowes and Calfes price £8 0s 0d.

Joseph Gwin of Miles Kynton [Kington St Michael] sold unto Phillipp Cambridge of Yeate [Yate] one blacke bull cropt in the nere ear price £1 17s 6d.

William Woodward of West Littleton sold unto Richard West of Cossume [Corsham] six couples price Seaven shillings six pence a peece warrenting them to be sound at this present time.

John Coave of Tedbury [Tetbury] sold unto Robert Charles of Atford [?Atworth] Two heifers price is £4 5s 0d.

Sarah Edwards of Collerin [Colerne] sold unto Adham Clerke of Malmsbury one reed heifer and one reed stere price is £6 0s 0d And two Black yrlings besides £2 0s 0d.

Thomas Russell of Tormarton sold unto Thomas Sellman of the parish of Cullerin [Colerne] one score of Sheepe price £5 17s 6d warr. sound at the present.

John Thorner of Acton sold unto William Wastfield of Cossume [Corsham] 9 Chilver hoggs and one weather hogg price Seaven groates a peece and six pence over warrant them to be sound.

John Reede of Beach sold unto Richard Hammons of Greetnam [Grittenham] in the parish of Brinkworth three score sheepe price £25 12s 0d warrant them to be sound at the present.

William Turtell of Broad Somerford sold unto Richard Hamons of Greetnam in the parish of Brinkworth Seaventeene dry Sheepe price nine [shillings] a peece wanting four shillings warrant them to bee sound.

Charles Kyte of Swinford sold unto John Osburne of Yeaten [Yatton Keynell] Ten hoggs price 50s 0d warrant sound.

Thomas Beaser of Hynton sold unto John Pullen of Dracutt [Draycot Cerne] one heifer and calfe price £3 0s 0d bateing Two Shillings.

George Roadman of Kingswood in the county of Wiltes sold unto Jonathan Blinkoe of Dracutt [Draycot Cerne] one heifer and calfe price £3 5s 0d.

Edward Bridgman of the parish of Bitton in the countie of Glouc. sold unto William Jeffrey of Box Two Bullocks price is £12 7s 6d.

Hugh Henning of Surrendell sold unto Joseph Gwin of the parish of Miles Kynton [Kington St Michael] four earlings all cropt in the farr ear price £4 9s 6d.

Susane Ceele of Marshfield sold unto William Bayden of Myntee [Minety] in the countie of Glouc. one Cow and Calfe price three pounds fifteene shillings warrant thim to be sound.

Jeremy Isaac of Tormarton sold unto John Thomas of Worken [?Worton] in the parish of Poteren [Potterne] in the countie of Wiltes one Cow and Calfe price £3 1s 0d.

Henry Persons of Little Badmenton sold unto William Sanders of Chewton Kainsome [Chewton Keynsham] in the countie of Somersett four score and two sheepe price 7s 3d a peece.

George Fry of Lacock parish sold unto Isaac Tyler of Derham [Dyrham] in the county of Glouc. one score of weather hoggs price £7 15s 0d warrant them to be sound.

John Burnett of Beach sold unto Richard Hallier of Hell Marton [Hilmarton] in the county of Wiltes Two heifers and calfes price £6 19s od.

Jeremy Goodhind of Safford [?Saltford] in the county of Somersett sold unto Richard Hallier of Hell Marten [Hilmarton] Two black heifers and calves price is Six Pounds five shillings.

Ezekiell Hollis of Slattenford [?Slaughterford] sold unto Richard Hollier of Hell Marten one Cow and calfe price is £4 14s od warrent him to be sound.

Thomas West of the parish of Box sold unto Samuell Billett of the parish of Cossume [Corsham] nine sheepe and six lambs price is £3 14s od warrant them to be sound at the present.

Edward Brant of the parish of Chippenham sold unto John Davis of Nettleton Ten Sheepe price 7s 9d a peece warrant them to be sound.

John Brewer of Ford in the parish of Wraxell [Wraxall] sold unto Adham Clerke of Malmsbury one brone Heifer price £2 4s od.

Sarah Hottkins of Old Sodbury sold unto William Humpfries of Aldeington [Alderton] one black Cow and calfe with a slitt in the farr eare price £4 os od.

Richard Hottkins of Yeate [Yate] in the countie of Glouc. sold unto John Daniell [of] Cossume [Corsham] two earlings price £3 1s od.

Henry Cannings of Beath Easton [Batheaston] sold unto John Alding of Cossume [Corsham] nine ewes and lambs price nine shillings a peece one shilling being abated of the price warrant them to bee sound.

Walter Smith of Cullerin [Colerne] sold unto Robert Willett of Aldenton [Addington] in the countie of Buckinghamesheire Twenty couples price £11 5s od.

Thomas Beme of Derham sold unto John Bates of Brenson [Braunston] in the county of Northampton 15 sheepe and 5 lambs price £5.

Walter Hazzellwood of Langredge [Langridge] in Somersettsheire sold unto John Bates of Brenson in the county of Northampton Three score couples price £30 os od.

John Gale of Chippingham sold unto John Bates aforesaid 20 hoggs price £9 13s 4d.

George Clerke of Swainswick in the countie of Somersett sold unto John Benson of Nether Shudborough [?Shugborough, Staffs.] in the county of Warwicke forty couples price £22 12s 6d.

John Hathaway of the parish of Wick and Abson sold unto John Stanmore of Sagred [?Seagry] one score of weather hoggs price £5 16s 8d warrenting them to be sound.

John Frey of Miles Kynton [Kington St Michael] sold unto Joseph Tomson of Hankerton in the county of Wiltes one black heifer and calfe price £3 11s od.

Giles Maynard of Charle Comb [Charlcombe] sold unto Joseph Tomson of Hankerton aforesaid in the county of Wiltes one black heifer and calfe price £4 10s od.

Furdinando Frapell of Stone Easton in the county of Somersett sold unto John Hand of Cullerin [Colerne] 30 weather hoggs price is £10 11s od warrent them sound at this present.

Richard Little of Cossume [Corsham] sold unto Joseph Tomson abovesaid one black cow with a Starr in the forehead Three pounds nine shillings.

Edward Scudmore of Frampton Cotterell in the county of Glouc. sold unto Daniell Pitt of Brokenborrough one -alla [yellow?] sparked cow price is 51s 0d warrent him sound at this present time.

John Lester of Hannam [Hanham] sold unto Thomas Morton of Stanton Quinton one score of couples price is £9 warrent them to be sound.

William Howbin of North Stock [North Stoke] sold unto Daniell Pitt of Brokenburrough one heifer and calfe price £2 1s 0d.

William Higgs of Horton in the countie of Glouc.sold unto Thomas Croome of South Wraxell [South Wraxall] one heifer and calfe price is £3 17s 0d warrent to be sound at the present.

Mary Smith of the parish of Cullerin [Colerne] sold unto Joseph Tomson of Hankerton one blacke Cow price is £4 8s 0d.

William Beaker liveing at Myntee [Minety] in the parish of Cossume [Corsham] sold unto Obediah Cheltenham of Ditcherige [Ditteridge] one blacke heifer cropt in the neere and slitt in farr ear price £2 4s 0d.

Thomas Hayward of Luckington sold unto Thomas Sellman of Cullerne [Colerne] Ten weather hoggs price is 7s 4d a peece warrent them to be sound for the present.

John Aubrey's List of Wiltshire Markets & Fairs 1684-5

Bodleian Library, Oxford, MS. Aubrey 2 (John Aubrey's MS of the *Natural History of Wiltshire*), ff. 147v-8, quoted in J. Thirsk & J.P. Cooper, eds., *Seventeenth-Century Economic Documents,* OUP, 1972.

Fairs

To adjust these two following chapters, I should consult with our farmers, graziers, and butchers; but not having that opportunity (here in London), I will set down concerning them what occurs to my memory, and touch only at the principal ones.

The most celebrated fair in Wiltshire for sheep is at Castle Combe on St George's Day (23 April) whither sheepmasters do come as far as from Northamptonshire. Here is a good cross and Market house; and heretofore was a staple of wool as John Scrope, lord of this manor, affirms to me. The market here is now very inconsiderable.

At Wilton is a very noted fair for sheep on St George's Day also; and another on St Giles, *sc.* September the first. Graziers etc. from Buckinghamshire come hither to buy sheep.

At Chilmark is a good fair for sheep on St Margaret's Day, *sc.* 20 July.

Bulford (near Salisbury) a fair on Lammas Day [1 August]. 'Tis an eminent fair for wool and sheep. The eve is for wool and cheese.

At the city of New Sarum is a very great fair for cloth at Twelftyde [6 January] called Twelfe market.

In the parish of All Cannings is St Anne's Hill (vulgarly called Tann Hill) where every year on St Anne's Day (26 of July) is kept a great fair within an old camp called Oldbury. The chief commodities are sheep, oxen, and fineries. This fair would be more considerable but that Bristow [Bristol] fair happens at the same time.

At Devizes several fairs but the greatest is the green (new) cheese at Michaelmas [29 September]. It continues about a week.

Wilton was the head town of the county till Bishop Bingham built the bridge at Harnham, *anno*—which turned away the old Roman way . . . and brought the trade to new Sarum, where it hath ever since continued.

Weyhill Fair is in Hants, adjoining Wiltshire. It is an extraordinary great one and lasts —. Here is a mean old church where St Thomas Becket was sometime a priest, and they say did some miracle. After his canonization hitherto were made frequent pilgrimages at this time of year (which is his —). The concourse of people was so great that hucksters brought walnuts and other fruits and accommodation (here are not above half a dozen houses); and this was the occasion and rise of this famous fair which (I believe) is held only by prescription [i.e. without a charter].

Magdalen Hill Fair, near Winchester, is also a great fair. They send cheese thither from Gloucestershire and from north Wiltshire.

A Survey of the Markets and Fairs of Highworth 1725

WSRO 1033/269

The weekly market and the two fairs held each year at Highworth are an example of similar institutions to be found throughout Wiltshire. They played a crucial part in the trade in livestock, corn and dairy products, but generally only isolated or incidental references to their importance survive. Highworth fairs were held each year on the feast of St Peter ad Vincula (1 August) and the feast of St Michael the Archangel (29 September). Ownership of the markets and fairs was evidently considered to be a profitable investment. In 1672 it had belonged to a lawyer, William Blomer of Hatherop, Gloucestershire, who sold the rights to his brother John Blomer of Hatherop for £700. John Blomer then sold 'the profits, customs and tolls' of the markets and fairs to Sir John Webb and Dame Mary Webb of Canford, Dorset, and in 1686 they sold the rights to Thomas Freke of Hannington for £800. At the time of the Survey the markets and fairs belonged to William Freke. In c1680 John Aubrey wrote that the market at Highworth had declined because of the plague and the effect of the Civil War, and it had been overtaken in importance by the market at Swindon.

> *At Highworth was the greatest market, on Wednesday, for fatt cattle in our county, which was furnished by the rich vale; and the Oxford butchers furnished themselves here. In the late civill warres it being made a garrison for the King, the graziers, to avoid the rudeness of the souldiers, quitted that market, and*

> *went to Swindon, four miles distant, where the market on Munday continues still, which before was a petty, inconsiderable one. Also, the plague was at Highworth before the late warres, which was very prejudiciall to the market there; by reason whereof all the countrey sent their cattle to Swindon market, as they did before to Highworth'. [J. Aubrey,* Natural History of Wiltshire, *1969 edn., 115]*

This Survey of 1725 is of interest in showing the scattered disposition of livestock and dairy products within the market, the way in which tolls were levied, and the number of inns and taverns which provided refreshment for those coming to the market. It also lists the tenements which enjoyed the lucrative right of erecting standings or stalls along their frontages on market days and during the annual fairs. The 'cribbs' were mangers where the livestock could be fed.

A Survey of the Profitts of the Marketts and Faires and of the Wast Grounds of Highworth in the County of Wilts and of severall Tenements thereon belonging to William Freke Esqr Taken in the Yeare 1725.

Imprimis, The Bailywick of Highworth consisting of the profitts of the Markett and Fairs arising by one penny for pitching and one penny for showing goods in any parts of Highworth, Eastrope and Westrope and for Standing and Cribbs according as can be agreed on. The Toll of Graine is the Brass Dish used for that purpose (containing about one pint) out of each Four Bushells and so in proportion. The Toll of Cattle (if sold) Four pence per Score for Sheep, the like sum of Four pence, for each horse, for a Cow beast two pence, and for a pigg one penny. And also all the slatted Butchers shambles (except one in possession of Henry Marsh and another in possession of William Weston). All which Bailywick is now rented by Daniel Adams who also received the Quitt rents of the Tenements hereafter mentioned and pays the yearly rent of **£30 0s 0d**

Item, The Markett House of Highworth with the Roomes over it and the Profitts of the weights there, being one penny for each draught not exceeding One hundred weight. And if Cheese be pitched and not weighed the like is to be paid for Pitching. This rented by Ditto att **£18 0s 0d**.

Item, One Shop under the Markett House rented by Mr Shorter att the rent of **15s 0d**.

The Extent of Ground whereon the said Marketts and Fairs are kept.

The Sheep Marketts are kept along the Sheep street from the house of John Smith being the Signe of the Royal Oake to the lower part of the Butcher Rowe along the South side of the Street and from the Church Yard Gates att the End of the said Street to Mr North's Barn, where Cribbs may be erected by Mr Freke for that purpose, but the Inhabitants sett up Cribbs on the North side of the said Street against their respective houses for their owne Benefit.

The Beast Marketts are kept in the Broad Street next to the house of William Brind called The Crowne Inn. And from thence along by the Bear Inn and the Parsonage and also from the Crowne to the Swan Inn and in all the

Street thereabouts and none but Mr Freke have liberty to sett up Standings in the said Broad Street and the Markett Place so farr as the house called or knowne by the name or Signe of the Sun (other than and except that William Davis Esqr and [blank] Coleman Widow may each of them erect and sett up one Standing opposite to the new Dwelling house of her the said [blank] Coleman and that John Boothe may erect and sett up one Standing opposite to the new Dwelling house of the said William Davis as the same have usually been erected and sett up). And from the said house called the Sun up the High Street Westwards the Inhabitants may sett up Standings against their respective houses and Mr Freke is entitled to one penny only from each person showing goods there.

Att Fairs Mr Freke may keep Cattle in all the Streets and places in manner as att Marketts and also along the Streets and Roads and on all the Greensward and waste Grounds at the South end of Highworth aforesaid and may erect Cribbs and other Conveniencys for that purpose, (Except only that the Inhabitants on the East side the Street att the South End of the said Towne may erect and sett up Cribbs close up to and against their respective houses on the East side the said Street for their own benefitt) and Mr Freke may erect standings att Fairs in and about all the said Streets and Markett place and no other person or persons have or hath liberty to sett up any Standings there in any other manner than they may do on Markett days as is hereinbefore mentioned.

The Tenements on the Wast Grounds etc.

	Yearly Quit Rent
Imprimis, One tenement att the South end of Highworth between the Roads leading from there towards Swindon and Hannington being now in possession of Mary Streat and called The Blue Boys containing in length four and thirty feet with the outhouse att the end thereof containing in length eight feet	1 0
Item, One other tenement adjoining and being on the South part of the former now in possession of John Moss consisting of two rooms below and containing six and twenty feet in length with an outhouse containing eighteen feet with a garden containing eighty and nine feet in Circumference wherein grows an Elm and five small Ashes	1 0
Item, One other Tenement adjoining and being on the South part of the last mentioned Tenement being now in possession of William Crooke containing Two Rooms below and in length six and twenty feet with an outhouse containing in length thirteene feet	1 0
Item, One other Tenement containing one Room and one Buttery below and adjoining to and being on the East side of the last mentioned Messuage and now in possession of Mary Crooke being twenty feet in length and having one Elme and an Ashe growing before the House	1 0

Yearly Quit Rent

Item, Some ruinous outbuildings att the South end of the said house containing twenty feet in length and claimed by the said Mary Crooke as belonging to the Tenement in her possession — o o

Item, One Tenement adjoining to and being on the East side of the said Tenement in possession of Mary Crooke and containing twenty feet in Breadth and having two Elmes and a Sycamore growing before it and now in possession of Philip Gale — I o

Item, One Stable in possession of Thomas Perin lying on the East part Of the said Tenement in possession of the said Phillip Gale containing in Length ten feet — o o

Memorandum the said Thomas Perin says Mr Thomas Freke deceased gave him leave to build the said Stable and also that he purchased the fee of the house adjoining of him and pays no Quitt Rent

Item, One Tenement att the East end of the Row att the Townsend — I o
of Highworth aforesaid now in possession of John Watkins containing In length fifteen feet and in breadth twelve feet and an half — I o

Item, One other Tenement in possession of Mary Giles in length thirteen feet and an halfe with a hovel att the South end being five feet in length and situate att the South End of the said Row and adjoining to and being on the East part of the said Tenement in possession of the said John Watkins — I o

Item, One Tenement in possession of Christopher Leader adjoining to and being on the North part of the said Tenement in possession of the said Mary Giles and consisting of Two Roomes below and containing fifteen feet and an halfe in length and having the Street both sides — I o

Item, One Tenement on the North part of the last mentioned Tenement consisting of two Roomes below containing in length seventeene feet and now in possession of Barnaby Gibbs having the Street on both sides — I o

Item, One Tenement adjoining to and being on the North part of the last mentioned Tenement containing in length seventeene feet and now uninhabited and much out of repaire — I o

Item. One Tenement adjoining to and being on the North part of the said uninhabited Tenement consisting of one room below and containing one and twenty feet and an halfe in length and claimed by Francis Moss for the remainder of a term of 60 years granted by Lease — o o

Item, One Tenement on the North part of the last mentioned Tenement containing nineteene feet in length in possession of Margarett Edwards who claims the same by Lease — [o o]

Item, One Tenement in possession of John Lay adjoining to and being on the North part of the last mentioned Tenement containing in length forty feet and consisting of Three Roomes below, and one other Tenement on the West part of the last mentioned Tenement consisting of one Roome below and now in possession of Thomas Moss, which two last mentioned Tenements were formerly but one and are claimed to be held by Lease 0 6

WATER MEADOWS

The development and rapid spread of water meadows was the most important agricultural advance in Wiltshire during the 16th century. From the introduction of a complete scheme for carefully-regulated watering of the meadows at Wylye in 1632, the advantages of early grass and abundant hay soon led to similar projects elsewhere. The main features and the usefulness of water meadows are described in the Introduction. By the end of the 17th century they had already become an established feature of farming over much of the chalkland area of Wiltshire, Hampshire and Dorset.

This section will concentrate mainly upon the remarkable large-scale scheme for creating a series of water meadows along more than three miles of the river Avon, south of Salisbury starting in 1665. The following documents illustrate the complexity and costs of the undertaking. Hatches had to be built in the fast-flowing river, new channels or 'carriages' had to be excavated for the water, and hatches, weirs and subsidiary channels had to be installed to divert the water across the meadows. The surface of each meadow had to be ridged so that the water overflowed evenly into the drains, covering the whole meadow in a thin sheet of moving water. The whole operation had to be carefully supervised by a 'waterman' or 'drowner'. The result was a much earlier growth of grass than would have occurred naturally, and a more dependable crop of hay during the summer. The following documents also illustrate a further difficulty in establishing water meadows. Agreements had to be secured with other landowners, millers, fishermen and others who had rights or interests in the water. Yet another complication on the river south of Salisbury was the protracted scheme for creating a canal or 'navigation' linking Salisbury with the coast at Christchurch. The promoters of this project also needed a major share of the water, and a waterway uninterrupted by bridges, weirs and hatches.

In view of the difficulties, complexity and costs of the plan to create water meadows along the Avon from Alderbury to Downton it is a wonder that it was successfully completed. The credit is due to two men, Sir Joseph Ashe and John Snow. Sir Joseph Ashe lived in Twickenham in Middlesex, but in 1662 he leased the large manor of Downton from the bishop of Winchester. He also became one of the members of Parliament for the borough of Downton. When Sir Joseph Ashe died in 1686, the estate was for a time managed by his widow, Lady Mary Ashe, before it passed to their son, Sir James Ashe, who held it until his death in 1734. John Snow, yeoman, lived at Loosehanger Park in the parish of Downton, and acted as steward to the Ashe family for the Downton estate. He was succeeded as steward in 1698 by his son, Leonard Snow. Extracts from John

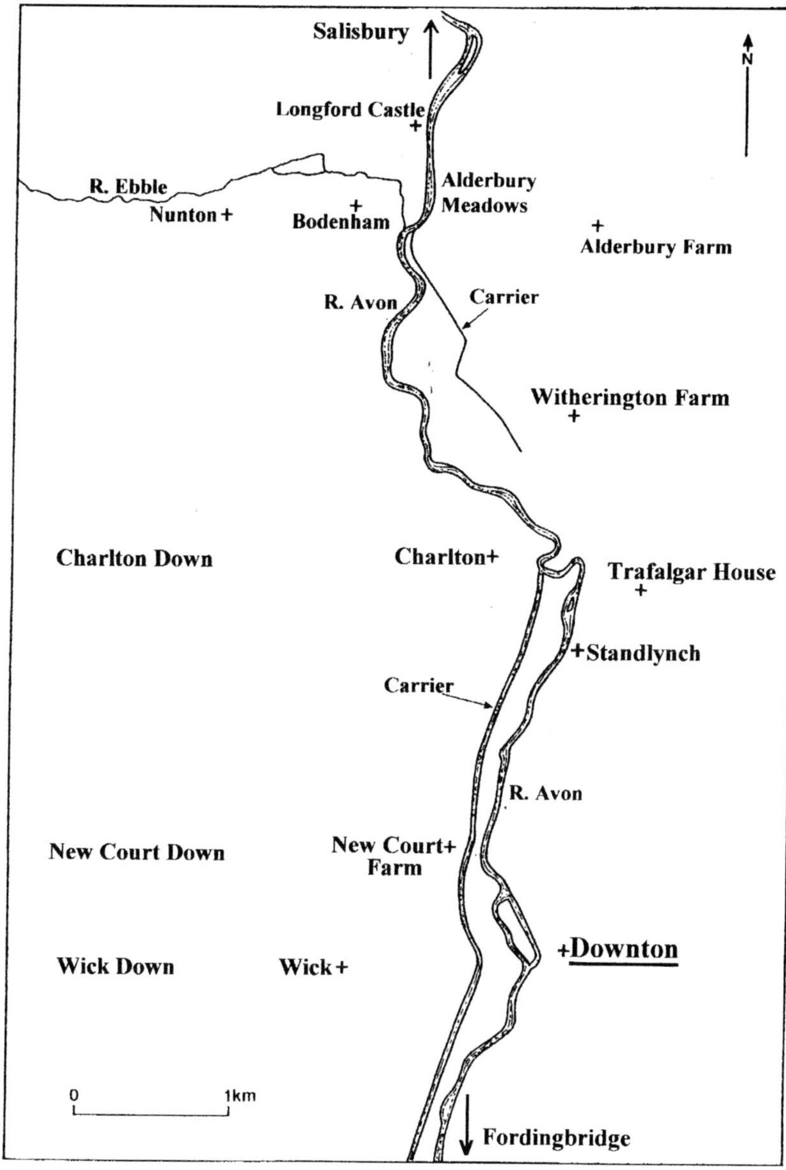

The River Avon between Salisbury and Downton

Snow's account book are reproduced earlier in the volume, and further detail about Snow and his employer will also be found in the Introduction.

*The Downton estate leased by Sir Joseph Ashe included several farms, including Witherington, Newcourt, Standlynch, Charlton, and Loosehanger Park. A particular of Newcourt Farm in 1682 shows that there was a farmhouse which had been rebuilt at the expense of Sir Joseph Ashe in 1680, a large, aisled barn of nine bays, 127 acres of enclosed pasture, 74 acres of watered meadow, 360 acres of arable and 610 acres of sheep down. The yearly rent was £460 [490/787; 788]. The lease of Downton was highly profitable for the Ashe family. An account of 1682 shows a rental income of £830 a year, while the annual rent paid to the bishop was £150. The Downton lease therefore brought Sir Joseph an annual profit of £600. Sir Joseph Ashe took a close interest in the Downton estate. He also took seriously his position as member of Parliament, obtaining the grant of two annual fairs and establishing a free school in the borough. [*VCH Wilts.*, XI, 1980, 41]. Since he resided in Twickenham, his hastily-scribbled and barely-legible letters to John Snow, as well as the steward's replies, provide evidence for the administration of the estate and the progress of the water meadow project. In the absence of the landlord, it was John Snow who was responsible for pressing ahead with all the complex negotiations and the major work required. Sir Joseph Ashe evidently supported the scheme, but in his letters he complained constantly about the expense and interfered at every stage. It is clear that John Snow was an enthusiastic supporter of the benefits of water meadows. The scheme eventually cost a good deal in excess of the original estimate of £2000, and John Snow had to endure a barrage of criticism from his employer. Eventually in a remarkable agreement of 1674 John Snow responded by undertaking to rent the water meadows himself if a tenant could not be found to pay the rent demanded. This proved not to be necessary. In addition, John Snow endured many complaints about flooded roads and damage to the river banks. In 1674 he was obliged to obtain signatures from local residents certifying that he had not made the roads impassable and that the banks of the river had not been damaged by his excavations. [490/911; 490/912].*

The project began in 1665 and involved the excavation of two major new channels or 'carriages' 24 feet wide, from Alderbury all the way to Downton and beyond. From these channels subsidiary trenches had to be dug to carry water to all the suitable meadows along the valley. Apart from the main channels, the work involved was prodigious. At Witherington Farm 54 acres of water meadow were created, and at Newcourt Farm, farther down the valley, 74 acres of water meadow were made. Other meadows were laid out at Bodenham, Alderbury, Charlton and Standlynch. Eventually more than 250 acres of water meadow were created.

The construction of the main carriages involved securing the agreement of other landowners and tenants through whose property the new channels were dug. The costs of building stone hatches in the fast-flowing Avon were inevitably heavy. The banks had to be strengthened to prevent flooding, bridges for carts, cattle and pedestrians had to be built, and compensation paid for the loss of fishing and grazing rights. During the years 1665-1680 John Snow was involved in securing more than 40 complex agreements, including lengthy legal negotiations with neighbouring landowners, such as Lord Coleraine, Sir John Webb and Thomas Jervoise. Tenants whose grazing rights were temporarily restricted by the hauling of stone and timber or the excavation of earth had to be compensated as, for example, in 1685 the 'Earbidgers of Alderbury' that is, herbagers or those with grazing rights on the common meads. In spite of the costs and of Sir Joseph Ashe's complaints, the scheme was evidently a success and was copied on a smaller scale on neighbouring estates, for example, on the river Ebble at Nunton and Odstock and on the Avon at Britford.

Once the water meadows were established, careful arrangements had to be made to ensure that all users had a fair share of the water. This can be illustrated by an agreement of 1685 between Sir Joseph Ashe and Walter Bockland Esq (sometimes spelt Buckland) who leased Standlynch and also represented Downton in Parliament. This specified the periods during which the hatches on the main channels could be closed to divert the water to Witherington meadows. The periods were as follows:

30 November to 30 December
11 January to 9 February
24 February to 12 March
25 March to 12 April
30 April to 19 May
12 July to 22 July
19 August to 28 August

Every other year the periods of closing and opening the hatches were to alternate. Whenever the water was not required, it was to be made available to others. In any case the water drained back into the stream after it had flowed over the meadow, but much of the nutrient which it contained would be deposited in the first meadow. The advantages of water meadows, as well as the expense and complexity of their creation are illustrated in the documents which follow. [J.H. Bettey, 'The Development of Water Meadows on the Salisbury Avon 1665-90', Agricultural History Review, *Vol. 51, Part II, 2003, pp 27-36].*

List of Documents

Letter from Sir Joseph Ashe to John Snow 16 April 1665

This letter dates from the beginning of the project to create water meadows on the Downton estate, and at this stage Sir Joseph Ashe was evidently enthusiastic about it. As well as discussing other manorial affairs, he urges John Snow to proceed with the scheme for watering as quickly as possible and to use every expedient to secure the essential agreement of the tenants at Charlton for the main channel of water to pass through their land. Later, he became alarmed at the cost of the project, and was much less encouraging. The letter was evidently scribbled in haste.

WSRO 490/909

London 16 April 1665

John Snow

I perceave by Mr Barnabye you have put my Mare under another Farryer. Let me know when I may expect him home and what is to be done to him

The articles I have retturned signed and sealed to Mr Barnabye. I have added 2 clauses in favour of those people. Pray get your willingst people to seale first and soe goe on as fast as you can, that we may put our afaires afoot. I have not yet met Mr Dove, soe soone as that is don you shal goe about that alsoe. I long to heare that you are at the Lodge setled [settled] that I may depend on your Care there.

If you find any rub [opposition] with the Charleton people, sweeten it by making their grounds rich and that I wil oblige them one way or other to their enrichment. Be sure to keepe off a rupture and if you see cause Invyte the persons there to a dynner and be merry with them. Delay noe tyme but keepe the scent hott. Take money of some of my tenants to pay for such horses you shal buy at Amsbury faire and put our afaires soe as you may give me a good account of them. Know of Mr Barnabye if the moneys ordered to him by Browne be in his hands or retturnd [returned]. Let me know what the Bayly [bailiff] sayth and what Mr Buckland doth for the widow put [two words illegible].

I am your loving friend

Joseph Ashe

Summary of Agreements for Creating the Main Channels or Carriages 1665-90

WSRO 490/891

A Particular of Agreements and Leases relating to the Watercourses, Dreins etc. in Downton

26 September 1665

An Agreement under the hand and Seal of John Proud touching a Cutt in Alderbury Mead

26 September 1665

Richard Helliar's Agreement with Sir Joseph Ashe concerning a Main Carriage through the Grounds of the said Helliar in Alderbury Meadow

28 September 1665

An Agreement Between Sir William Turner and Sir Joseph Ashe touching a Trench to be Cutt through Alderbury Mead

13 August 1666

Indenture between Giles Eyres Esq. of the one parte and Sir Joseph Ashe of the other part Purporting a Leas for 99 years to the said Sir Joseph Ashe of 13 Acres and ½ of Meadow in Alderbury Common Mead with power to make Trenchers, Watercourses etc. at 8s 0d per Annum rent Executed by Giles Eyres.

13 August 1666

Indenture Between Joan Board, Widow, of the one parte and Sir Joseph Ashe of the other part purporting a Lease for 99 years if the said Joan should so long live unto the said Sir Joseph Ashe of 105 [?] in Alderbury Mead and of the Main Carriage for water in the said Meadow Ground at 14s 3d per annum rent –Executed by Joan Board.

13 August 1666

Indenture between John Froud, husbandman, of the one part and Sir Joseph Ashe of the other part Purporting a Lease to Sir Joseph Ashe of 6 Lugg of Ground for 99 years if the said Froud should so long live at 1s 6d per Annum rent. Two parts of this Lease. The Counter part executed by Sir Joseph Ashe, the other part not executed.

13 August 1666

Indenture between Richard Helliar, yeoman, of the one part and Sir Joseph Ashe of the other part, Purporting a Lease to the said Sir Joseph Ashe of 80 Luggs of Ground Cutt for making a Main Carriage etc. in Alderbury Mead and the Main Carriage or Trench therein and of other Luggs in Alderbury

Mead. To hold for 99 years of the said Richard Helliar should so long live at the rent of 6s 9d per Annum. Two parts of this Deed, but Neither of them Executed

30 August

Indenture between John Sadler, Gent., of the one part and Sir Joseph Ashe of the other part Purporting a Lease of 103 Luggs at the upper End of Alderbury Mead and the Main Carriage or Trench therein and of other Luggs in Alderbury Mead. To Hold the said Luggs then in the Tenures of the Widow Curtis and William Curtis after the expiration of the Estates of the said Widow Curtis and William Curtis for the term of 1000 years, and to Hold the other Luggs therein mentioned for the like Term of 1000 years from Michaelmas then last part at the Severall rent of 33 0s 7½d payable as therein mentioned – Executed by the said John Sadler.

26 September 1665 & 9 October 1665

Two Agreements on Paper tacked to the above Indenture touching the Leasing of Severall Luggs to Sir Joseph Ashe. The one from Margaret Curtis dated 26 September 1665. The other from John Sadler dated 9 October 1665.

Without Date

An Agreement between Nicholas Elliott and Sir Joseph Ashe touching a term of 500 years in certain Luggs in Budhall Mead – Executed by Nicholas Elliott.

7 October 1666

Agreement between Sir Joseph Ashe and Walter Bockland Esq. touching a Carriage out of the River Avon for drowning some Grounds belonging to New Court Farm. Executed by Walter Bockland.

1 October 1669

Indenture between Sir Joseph Ashe of the one part and Henry Noyse, yeoman, of the other part, Whereby the said Sir Joseph Ashe, In consideration of the yearly rent of 6s 0d and for other considerations. Enfeoffs the said Henry Noyse and his Heirs of a Close of Meadow Ground containing about 2 acres called the Summer Leaze, situate in Charleton. Counterpart executed by Henry Noyse

20 September 1665

Articles of Agreement between Sir Joseph Ashe and Henry Noyse concerning a Carriage of Water for the Drowning his Meadows – Executed by Henry Noyse.

1 October 1666

Indenture Between Sir Joseph Ashe of the one part and Henry Noyse of the other part Purporting a Lease from Sir Joseph Ashe to the said Henry Noyse of 30 Luggs part of 40 Luggs in Charlton late in the possession of Margarett Curtis and then in the Tenure of the said Sir Joseph, To Hold for Term of 990 years at the yearly rent of 1s 0d – Executed by Henry Noyse.

13 October 1669

Agreement Indented Between Sir Joseph Ashe of the one part and Henry Noyse of the other part concerning some Carriages for Water to be Cutt by the said Noyse and a Footway in Summer Leese Close – Executed by the said William [Henry?] Noyse

25 March 1673

Counterpart of a Lease from Giles Eyre to Sir Joseph Ashe for Severall Luggs of Land used in Green Main Carriage and whereon the School House is Built for the Term of 1000 years at £3 16s 6d per annum rent – Executed by Sir Joseph Ashe

20 November 1685

Indenture Tripartite between Sir Joseph Ashe of the 1st part, Maurice Bockland Esq. of the 2nd part, and Edward Clarke and Thomas Stringer Esq. of the 3rd part, Purporting (inferal) a Leese from the said Edward Clarke and Thomas Stringer of 10 Luggs unto the said Sir Joseph Ashe and Maurice Bockland for the term of 99 years, if the [blank] persons therein or as any of them should so long live, at £1 12s 6d per annum rent. – Executed by Maurice Bockland, Edward Clarke and Thomas Stringer.

6th & 7th June 1688

Indenture of Lease and Release Between James Ivie, clerk, of the one part, and Dame Mary Ashe of the other part, Whereby the said James Ivie in consideration of £20, Grants, and conveys unto the said Dame Mary Ashe and her heirs, 17 Luggs of Ground part of a Watercourse with the Banks thereto adjoyning in a Ground called Rhodes. Executed by the said James Ivie and a Receipt Indorsed for the consideration money.

19 September 1690

Indenture Between Thomas Reading, clerk, of the one part, and Dame Mary Ashe, widow, and Maurice Bockland Esq. of the other part, Purporting a Lease of 72 Luggs Main Carriage or Trench unto the said Dame Mary Ashe and Maurice Bockland from the Feast of St John the Baptist [24 June] then last past for the term of 99 years if the said Thomas Reading should so long live at the yearly rent of 18s 1d. – Executed by the said Thomas Reading.

Making the Channels or Main Carriages for the Water from Alderbury to Downton 1666

The following list made in April 1666 provides details of the first stage in creating main carriages for the water so that it could be diverted by hatches to water various meadows in turn. Those through whose land the channels were dug were compensated for the loss of their land by Sir Joseph. The reason for two columns recording the amount of land taken is not clear. A 'lug' or perch measures 16½ feet; a 'ham' is a meadow.

WSRO 490/903

An account of the ground measured by the Severall persons hereafter named in Aprill 1666, which ground being then Cutt and covered in Alderbury Common mead for a maine Carrig for Conveyeing the watter in to certin meadows belonginge to Withinge and Stanlinch as followeth:

	Lugs	Lugs
Imprimis, Jane Sadler, now Esq. Bucklands		103
Mr Matthew Webber		14
A part of the old Mill Streem the east side next the ham belonging to Withing farme only	32	
John Snow in the east corner of the ham	4	
A ditch 6 foot broad on the west side the old mill Streem belonging to the said ham	12	
Mr Barnett, the vicar of Alderbury part in the caraidg and part on the north west corner of the 4 acres		12
A part of the old mill Streem below the South east corner of the ham belonging to Standlinch on the west side and to Withington on the East side	70	
Giles Eyre Esq. The west end of his upper picked Acre		18
Mr Barentt aforesaid his upper picked acre		16
Giles Eyre aforesaid his other picked acre		20
A part of the old mill Streem the East side belonging to Withington and the west to Standlinch	5	
Mr Barnett aforesaid the east end of his 4 acres		44
Mr Eyre aforesaid the east end of his 4 acres		44
Richard Garlick a part of his ground		38
Mr William Turners		50
A part of the said mill Streem the east side belonging to Withington and the west to Standlinch	5	
John Frowds next Ex meade		6
Mis[tress] Beards now Mr Rofs [?Ross]		57
The said Mis Beard in width	28	
And in her acre in the said Common mead shee hath a part Of the old mill Streem or Swath allowed therefore		20
Richard Hilliers the East part of his Acre		27
The said Richard Hillier hath granted by Sir Joseph Ashe, Barronett, in Lew of 10 lugs more of his acres, a part of the old mill Streem or swath		10
The summe totall of the ground to be paid for att £3 a lug When the deductions are taken out, Remains 323 lugs, That is 2 Acres and 3 lugg	156	479

The names of the persons that measured the ground a fore said in Aprill 1666, and their helpers

	s	d
Thomas Smith for Two days work	3	0
William Alloway two days work	2	8
Robert Godwin two days work	2	8
Joliffe Hill the elder, two days	2	4
John Fanstone one day	1	3

Robert Lincoln and Walter to help show the Bounds two days
In the Behalf of Alderbury men concerned in the saide mead:
Henry Hunt, two days
Leonard Pilgrim and Thomas Gold
for showing the bounds two days

Letter to John Snow from Sir Joseph Ashe 5 February 1671

This communication is typical of many others which survive from Sir Joseph Ashe to John Snow, his steward at Downton. It illustrates the close interest Sir Joseph took in all aspects of the management of the estate at Downton. He was concerned about the continuing work on the water meadows, and on securing the necessary agreement from his tenants, Brewer and Michell, as well as about negotiations on fishing rights along the river. Evidently the newly-established water meadows were already producing good crops of hay, so that John Snow could sell fodder to neighbouring farmers. Sir Joseph encouraged the planting of new crops such sainfoin, and the improvement of farms on the estate, but was always cautious about the possible costs. He obviously wished to discourage settlement on the waste at Downton, a problem which is described in the section 'The Labouring Poor' in this volume, and he encouraged John Snow to make an example of John Moore by demolishing his illegally-erected cottage.

Other parts of the letter refer to the parliamentary representation of Downton. As one of the MPs for the borough, Sir Joseph Ashe was interested in acquiring the houses whose occupants possessed the right to vote for him and for his fellow MPs, Sir Giles Eyres of Alderbury who represented Downton from 1661-1670, and Maurice Bockland of Standlynch, who was MP for Downton from 1678-1699.

WSRO 490/910

Letter from Sir Joseph Ashe

5 February 1671

John Snow

I have received your long letter, wherewith you have a letter from the Bishop to David Stockman, to cease the sute [suit], but you must tell Mr Radleigh that the legal chardges disburst herein, I did agree Mr Radleigh should pay, for without that the Bishop would not Pay it downe. This I am sure is the cheapest for all sides and therefore the best, but you must know Stockman knowes not this, for then the bishop sayes he mought make his payments the greater. I suppose this will put some charg to his frowardness and by degrees I shel lower his sayles. I have told Mr Eyres and Coles as much as I have written you.

If Browne Jnr pretences are nothing but the Interest of the money, that I have in a manner remitted therby to encouradge the payment, I feare Best layes hold of it, if not, what I could gett is my owne, and Browne Jnr this terme you shal have my order to agree it aswel as you can——? With him. I would have you find out some person at Salisbury that goes by Browne Jnr and give that person a letter, that he delivers him your Copyes and soe you will have them ?

I am glad you have handled Newman pretty well, spare him not, that he may see his folly. You take the best way with Moor to bring an ejectment, make him an example, pursue it close, and downe with his Cottadge that the Justices may see they may show their teeth, but cannot byte. We shal then bring the rest to duty.

As to Mr Buckland, I would know his lodging and I wil speake with him and setle al things between us, but for his fishing, I question whether he hath any tytle at all for in the 6th yeare of Edward the 6th by a Survey taken of the Manor, the whole fishing was demised by Copye of Court for the terme of lives vizt:

To John Mapal at	6s 8d
To Roger Eastman at	16s 8d
To Richard Abarrowe	6s 8d

Now how those copyes comes to be freeholds being neither in the power of Bishop or Lesser [Leasor] to doe it, is worth Enquiry wherin Cantloe can give you some insight if followed, and the best way as things now are is to take his fishing of him. In case we can lett it at about the rate we pay and then we can rayle the River and let his Weir goe downe when he please.

I shal not goe into the North til Aprill and til then you shal not come up, soe wil have tyme to finish the Accounts and settle things til Michaelmas. I shal enquire about this Sir John Shaw you speake off who is not my acquaintance, but I know how to make him my friend. I wil see to gett him to doe us alright therein. I approve of sowing the St Foine seed in the ground you mention, but let the fences be wel kept up, or the sheep wil come in and destroy it.

This hard weather I hope wil bring you Customers for our Fodder, which now begins to be understood with you wel enough.

I am of opinion it is a good thing to Improve Brewer's farme but you must have a respect to the chardge and when you have fully computed that, let me have it and I shal resolve it. The lying low of those grounds and grovelly [i.e. well-drained gravel sub-soil] may make as beneficial to Brewer that feeds them as Katherine Mead is to Michell and I thinke your removinge Jollyffs house as you propose is the Cheapest and best way and perchance may gett some timber of your [?] for it. Give me therfore an account of your agreement about the watering and your chardge and you shal goe about your house next month and finish it before you goe into the North.

Touching Mr Elliott's houses, they are not at al significant to the election as long as Mr Eyres and I agree, and you may be sure they wil put a high price on them, but if I had a list of the values and what they demand for them after Mr Elliott's life, and the price like me I wil buy them, and therfore looke into it and let me know [word obliterated].

I shal acquaint Sir Francis Chaplin of what you write, and they wil be at a chardge to gett Cantloe to doe them right. You wil doe wel to make use of this occation to doe your owne busynes alsoe.

I am your loving friend,

Joseph Ashe

London 5 February 1671

John Snow's Explanation of the Costs of Making the Water Meadows 1672

The following incomplete fragment if a note by John Snow survives in a small and much-repaired volume recording expenses on channels, hatches and bridges and payments made to numerous labourers. Most of these expenses are dated 1717, but a few are in John Snow's hand and are dated 1672. John Snow evidently needed to defend himself from the allegations made by his employer, Sir Joseph Ashe. This brief statement illustrates the difficulties he faced with such a large untried project and the problem of accurate surveying to ensure an even flow of water and adequate drainage.

WSRO 490/896

Fragment of a Note written by John Snow in 1672

Memorandum: the reasons why the Expence of the before mentioned works came to near duble the expences at first proposed was that when I came on the place and found that none of the meads would drawe into the river above the fishing wyar which caused me to get out the workes otherwise than at first proposed and made a drayne all up the meads to drawe them below the said wyar which caused 5 or 6 Trunckes more to be made than designed which Trunkes and all the hatches and stops proved very chargable by reason the Ground was so boggy where they was put in and all the meads so soft that no teems [teams of horses or oxen] could com near the places with anything and the fetching gravill so far and the materialls was very expensive and likewise the makeing the west maine carriage and west maine drayne under the trees and among the mores [roots] not at first designed to be made there which is much the better and the wheeling the clay so far to strengthen the maine carriage banks and raise boggey places in the meads and the sinkinge of all the knoules [?holes] by reason the earth was wanted to raise the falls which will now be the best ground [rest of the document does not survive].

Other parts of the notebook contain details of payments made to numerous labourers for digging sections of channels or for other work on the meadows. Most of those expenses are dated 12 October 1717.

The Purchase of Land for the Main Carriage 1673

WSRO 490/903

George Fulford his acquittance for the money for his ground

6 May 1673

I George Fulford doe hereby acknowledge that the day and yeare above written I have received of Mr John Snow in the behalfe of Sir Joseph Ashe, Baronet, the full sum of Twenty Five Pounds and Fifteen Shillings in full satisfaction of a bargaine and sale for parte of my Meads in Weeke [Wick]. I say received by me.

George Fulford

In the presence of
Thomas Smith
John Fanstone
William Alloway

Agreement of John Snow with Sir Joseph Ashe concerning the Water Meadows 25 November 1674

WSRO 490/904

Whereas Sir Joseph Ashe of Twittenham in the County of Middlesex, Baronet, since that I, John Snow of Loosehanger, came into his service hath by my hands and by my advise layd out great somes of money importinge above Two thousand pounds upon drowning his Meadowes in the parish of Downton that belong to New Court, Wythington and those meadowes in the possession of John Brewer, which hitherto have not rendered him any proffitt. And whereas I have suggested to the said Sir Joseph Ash that the aforesaid meadowes contayning in all about 200 acres have had their improvement suitable to the moneys desbursed, I John Snow, doe therefore undertake to make out that the 70 acres as are drowned belonging to New Court farme, which before they were watered were not worth to be rented at more than eighty pounds per annum. are now worth One hundred and eighty pounds per annum, and the 50 acres at Withington which before this Wateringe were not worth above twenty pounds per annum are now well worth one hundred pounds per annum and all chardges —(?) great and small tymber excepted to be borne by the tenants. And the 74 acres belonging to Brewers farme were not worth above £74 per annum and are now worth one hundred forty eight pound per annum the tenants bearing the chardges as aforesaid, I doe hereby undertake to procure tenants for this farme of Brewers at the rate of £148 per annum as aforesaid, or otherwise I John Snow wilbe Tenant to it my selfe for the terme of fower yeares and after the terme encrease the rent as the same shall deserve, which I presume may be about £40 per annum more. And in case Sir Joseph shal thinke fitt to separate the meadowes from New Court farme, I will undertake to find tenants for those 70 acres at one hundred and eighty pounds per annum or be tenant to them my selfe, and in lyke manner for Wythington Meadowes at one hundred pounds per annum and all on the conditions aforesaid to commence after the expiration of the present leases for the terme of three yeares.

In witness whereof the parties to these presents have interchandgably put their hands this 25th day of November 1674

Joseph Ashe
John Snow

An Acknowledgement to certify the Judge of the Sessions that the water cours through the Burrough of Downton is not stoped but is pasable for carts and carridges in 1674

WSRO 490/912

To all Christian people to whom theis presents shall come, we whose names are hereunto subscribed at the request of John Snowe of Loosehanger in the parish of Downton, yeoman, doe hereby Certify that whereas Sir Joseph Ash, Baronet, was presented by the Hundred Jury at the last Quarter Sessions holden the twelveth day of January 1674 for stopping the watercourse running through the Burrough of Downton to the nuisance and damage of his Majesties subjects passing the highways through the Burrough aforesaid: We whose names are hereunto subscribed upon examination of severall of the inhabitants of the Burrough aforesaid and other knowing men, As also upon our owne viewe, do finde that the Watercourse and Horsebridge and Footbridge is very sufficient and is not at all prejudiciall or any publique nuisance or damage to his Majesties subjects in passing or repassing through or over the same To the best of our information or knowledge or viewe thereof taken by us present two and twentieth day of February Anno Dom. 1674. In Witness whereof we have hereto subscribed our names.

Inhabitants of Bottenham and Nunton

4

Inhabitants of Britford

5

Inhabitants of the Burrough of Downton, East Downton & Week

13

Support for John Snow and the Water Meadow Project 1674

WSRO 490/911

To all Christian people to whome theis presents shall come and shall or may concerne, Wee whose names are hereunto subscribed at the request of John Snowe of Loosehanger in the parish of Downton in the county of Wiltes, yeoman, doe hereby Certifye That whereas at the Assizes holden at the Citty of New Sarum for the said County of Wiltes on the eighth day of August now last past the said John Snowe was presented by the grand Jury for throwinge in of stones and Rubbish into the river of Avon within the liberty of Charleton within the said parish of Downton, Wee whose names are hereunto subscribed upon our examininge severall of the inhabitants of Charleton aforesaid, and by the viewe and Judgement of severall Judicious and able men, and by our owne viewe, wee finde That the earth and gravell throwne in on the south side of the said river, against the ground of the said John Snowe and of one James Barrowe in Charleton aforesaid, is for preservinge the same grounds from wearinge and wastinge away by the river aforesaid and is not any publique nuisance or damage to his Majesties subjects or to the said river to the best of our information or knowledge or viewe thereof taken by us this present twoe and twentieth day of February Anno Dom. 1674. In witness whereof wee have hereunto subscribed our names given the same day and yeare.

G. Ralegh	Thomas Claude	Charles Barnes
Robert Chaundler	Henry Barnes	William Michell
George Noyes	John Moody	John Leery

The Benefits of Water Meadows 1676

Two contemporary copies of this petition survive among the records of the Ashe family estate records of Downton. It is dated 1676, but there is no indication of its authorship or specific purpose. It does, however, reveal clearly the advantages to be derived from water meadows, the enthusiasm of the author and the possible problems which he foresees in obtaining an equitable share of the benefits. An interesting feature of this document is that whereas in most places water meadows were chiefly valued for providing early grass for the sheep flocks, at Downton the emphasis is on the production of butter and cheese and on fattening beef cattle. This reflects the easy access from Downton to markets in Salisbury and Southampton, and the growing demand for butter, cheese and beef.

WSRO 490/890

Argument to shew what greate profitt may redound to the owners of Land upon a free ymprovement, by drowninge wateringe or drayninge as followeth (vizt):

Imprimis, By soe doeinge there will be a greater increase in hay
Item, There will be greate increase of cattle

Item, Thereby will be a greater increase of Corne

Firste, That there wilbe a greater increase of Hay by wateringe of Meadowes is knowne by common experience

2. Hay beinge plenty men may keepe the more Cattle whereby theyre ground may be much bettered and ymproved.

3. Theyre ground being thus bettered and ymproved there wilbe a greater increase of Corne and the after Grasse of their grounds thus ymproved wilbe of greate benefitt for the feedinge of Cattle both to fatt and alsoe for butter and cheese.

Theis thinges considered wee desire that there may be a free ymprovement by drowninge or drayneinge of Meadowes in all such places where it may be done withoute prejudice to other men.

Objection 1. But what yf there be any Mill either above or belowe that may be hindered by it.

Answer Wee desire that soe much of the Water may be ymployed on the ground as may not hinder the Miller from makeinge use of his Mill to grinde, the Miller not lettinge the Water goe idle through his Hatches which may be ymployed for the benefitt of his neighbours. And yf he that ymployeth the Water on his ground shall any way hinder the Miller he shall make satisfacion accordinge to the wronge done and have free liberty to use the Water provided that the wateringe of the ground doth not soe much hinder the Miller, but that he may grinde to serve his occasion.

Objection 2. What yf the stoppinge of the Water doth rayse it over another man's grounds to his hindrance

Answer Wee desire that the person soe stoppinge the Water may have liberty to goe into the ground soe overflowed and rayse a Bancke to secure the same ground (yf it cannot be done in his owne). And cut a drawer to take away the dead Water allowinge satisfacion for the ground soe used.

Objection 3. Yf the Water doth fall of upon another man's ground to his hindrance

Answer Wee desire that all ditches and by lakes may be scoured accordinge to the Lawe and where it may be conveniente that all crooks and windings of the Water be tooke of and sett straite for the better passage of the Water. And yf there be noe Lawe ditch to receave the Water nor the Water cannot be drawne away upon the ymployer's ground let him have liberty to make a drawer in another man's and lett the Owner of that ground have satisfacion accordinge to his damage.

Wee desire that leave be granted to lay tunnels under or make carriages over any Law ditch or streame or river or any other place where neede shall require for the drawinge away or bringinge in of the Water allowinge satisfacion to every man accordinge to his hindrance. And firther that all stoppages that are made upon rivers by encroachment or by settinge of trees or by any other way either in rivers lawe ditches or by lakes may be removed and that the rivers and Statute ditches be kepte scoured and cleansed to prevent all anoyances and that there be a liberty graunted for the settinge upp of Wiers for the drowninge of the Meadowes. And yf the Wires fall oute to be betweene twoe mens grounds let there be liberty graunted to fasten them on each side makeinge satisfacion if any man be injured thereby.

Objection 4. If any man have ground where he cannot bringe in the Water but through another man's ground.

Answer Wee desire that there may be liberty graunted to make currents or carriages for the bringe in of the Water through that ground which lyeth betweene the streame or river and the ground to be drowned and let satisfacion be given accordinge to the worth of that ground that shalbe diged up or covered with Bancks for the bringinge in of the Water. And because the Owner of any ground may dye or by some other meanes the ground may become another mans, all [who] shall possesse the ground in tyme to come shall take such satisfacion as was at firste adjudged to be accordinge to the damage, unless by longe continuance the damage shall become greater, and then the satisfacion shalbe given accordingly, and the Millers alsoe shall take such satisfacion as was att firste adjudged excepte as aforesaid.

Objection 5. If the Water shall offend any high way.

Answer Wee desire that the way may be made sufficiente by them to whom it doth belonge, and yf afterwards the way be prejudiced by reason of drowninge, those that have share in the drowninge shall equally pay theyre parte towards the repayreinge of the way soe farre as the way shalbe prejudiced by them. And for encouragement to them that have but a short tyme in any ground that is to be drowned, as but one life or a widdowhood, yf his tyme be expired within five pounds chardges for the same, than let he or they that shall possesse the ground after his terme is expired shall pay Twenty shillings every yeare for five yeares to the executors or administrators of him or her that was at the firste chardges and soe proporcionable upon expendinge a greater sume. And where severall men shall have ground lye one before the other upon any streame or river which hath not water enough to drowne all att once, then lett the Water be ymployed upon each man's ground by course soe many dayes one as the other accordinge to theyre proporcion of ground, and as for those that have the head grounds it shalbe att theyre owne chardge to sett up stopps for the use of the theyre owne ground and for conveyinge of the Water to theyre neighbours. Further wee desire for the encouragement of Tenants that they may have liberty to sett Tymber upon theyre liveinge for the makeinge of hatches, stoppes, trunks and bridges for the use of drowninge because all such thinges are immoveables. And that where there are Statute Ramholes upon any river or streame they may be made into a hatch according to the Statute, and hatches sett on each side to prevente greate floods. And that noe man may have power to sue another for any offence done by drowninge, but that it may be decided by a Jury of men and twoe or more such men as have skill and judgement in drowneinge to be chosen by the parties att variance, which jury and Arteficers haveinge viewed the place and given theyre Verdict concerninge the wronge, it being approved of and conformed by some justices of the peace, all differences may be ended.

And as for those grounds which some do mowe and others doe feede, yf the major parte doe agree that it may be drowned, wee desire that it may be done, and soe likewise for the inclosinge of Commons for drowninge. And lastly that all covenants and agreements be drawne and kepte in the court rolls or parish registers.

And whereas all rivers and streames doe wholy belonge unto the Kinges Majestie, our requeste and humble desire is that there may be liberty graunted for the settinge upp wires and hatches where there may be profitt made by drowninge, floatinge or leavyinge of any grounds which wilbe a greate benefitt unto the Comon Wealth. And there may be a yearly revenewe payd unto his Majestie proportionally by the Acre [*document decayed*] every man shall have alloted. And that wee may be ympowered to acquaint you further on such thinges for drowneinge as may be beneficiall to the Comen Wealth.

A Water Meadow Agreement 1676

WSRO 490/894

Articles and Covenants of Agreement Indented, had, made, Concluded and agreed upon the Five and twentieth day of Aprill in the Eight and twentieth year of the Reigne of our Sovereigne Lord Charles the Second by the Grace of God King of England, Scotland, France and Ireland, Defender of the Faith etc.. Betweene the Right Honorable Henry Lord Coleraine of the one parte and Elizabeth Clarke of Nunton in the County of Wilts., widdow, and Edward Frowde of the Citty of New Sarum in the County of Wilts., Maltster, of the other parte, as followeth, vizt.:

Imprimis, The said Henry Lord Coleraine in Consideration of the summe of Twenty Shillings of Current English money unto him by the said Elizabeth Clarke and Edward Frowde well and truly before the sealeing and delivery of these presents in hand paid, and in Consideration of the Rent and Covenants hereafter in these presents mentioned on the parte and behalf of the said Elizabeth Clarke and Edward Frowde their heirs and assignes to be paid and performed, Hath Given and Granted and by these presents doth Give and Grant unto the said Elizabeth Clarke and Edward Frowde and to their severall and respective heires and assignes for ever the use and benefit of the Water out of the water course or streame above the Paper Mill in Nunton aforesaid, to be drawn and conveyed by one great Trench or Main Carriage from the said Water Course or stream by the South end of the said Paper Mill and on the North side of severall houses, down the street of Nunton aforesaid unto the Grounds of the said

Elizabeth Clarke called the Long Close and Pinhouses Mead and unto the Grounds of the said Edward Frowde called West Mead, Mill Mead and Saunders Mead, and also the Grounds of the said Edward Frowde above the said Paper Mill called by the name of Mill Mead. Which said great Trench or Main Carriage is to be made and mainteyned at the proper costs and charges of the said Elizabeth Clarke and Edward Frowde their heires and assignes which shalbe owners of the said Grounds

Item, The said Elizabeth Clarke and Edward Frowde in Consideration of the Grant aforesaid and of the Covenants and Agreements hereafter in these presents mentioned on the parte of and behalf of the said Henry Lord Coleraine, his heires and assignes which shalbecome owners of the Grounds aforesaid, doe Covenant, Promise and Grant to and with the said Henry Lord Coleraine. his heires and assignes by these presents, That the said Elizabeth Clarke and Edward Frowde and their heires or assignes shall and will yearly and every year from henceforth for ever well and truly pay or cause to be paid unto the said Henry Lord Coleraine and his heires and assignes that shalbe owners of the said Water Course or Mill Streame the Rent or summe of three pounds of current English money at the Feasts of the Nativity of St John the Baptist{ 24 June] and the Birth of our Lord God [25 December] or within twenty dayes next after the said feast dayes by even and equall portions.

Item, The said Henry Lord Coleraine for himself and his heires doth Covenant, Promise and Grant to and with the said Elizabeth Clarke and Edward Frowde and either of them, their and either of the respective heires and assignes by these presents, That they the said Elizabeth Clarke and Edward Frowde, their heires and assignes duly paying the Rent and performing the Covenants in these presents mentioned on their parte and behalf to be paid and performed. Shall and may from time to time by their servants or agents take to their owne use the Water of the said Mill Streame and have liberty to pen and Shutt downe all those hatches belonging to the Mill aforesaid dureing all and every the time and times hereafter in these presents limitted for them to have the benefit of the said Mill Streame for Watering and ymproveing their said Grounds, without doing any wilful hurt or prejudice.

Item, It is Covenanted and Agreed by and between the said parties to these presents that the Water of the said Mill Streame shalbe taken and made use of by the said Henry Lord Coleraine and his heires and assignes for ymproveing his Meadow Grounds called the Mill Meads, as by the said Elizabeth Clarke and Edward Frowde and their heires and assignes for ymproveing their said Grounds. And the same use or benefit of the Water to be taken by Turn or stem as followeth, that is to say the said Henry Lord Coleraine and his heires and assignes to have the turn or stem for first use of the said Water one year, and the said Elizabeth Clarke and Edward Frowde and their heires and assignes to have the turn or stem the next year, and so from year to year to be continued *alterius vicibus*.

Item, It is Covenanted and agreed that the first turn or stem for making use of the said Water by the said parties to these presents and their respective heires and assignes shalbe yearly when Sir John Webb's Meads (vizt: Kingmill Meads and the Marsh at Odstock and Mr Bampton's Meads called Kings Mill Meads and Home Mead at Nunton shalbe watered or drowned, so as they be drowned before the second day of February. But if they shall not be watered or drowned before that time in any year, then the said party to these presents and the heires and assignes of the said party who as aforesaid is to have the turn or stem for first use of the said Water, shall and may begin his turn or stem on the second day of February and every turn or stem to be taken by any party to continue Fourteen Dayes and Nights together. And then the stem or turne for the other party ymmediately to begin or succeed.

Item, It is further Covenanted and Agreed by and between the said parties to these presents that either of the said parties and their heires may make use of the said Water in any turn or stem when the other party as aforesaid might or ought to use it (in case the party whose turn it is be not ready or prepared to make use of it) on till the said party shalbe ready and no longer. And the same not to be reckoned any parte of the turn or stem of the party so making use of it.

Item, The said Henry Lord Coleraine for himself and his heires doth Covenant, promise and Grant to and with the said Elizabeth Clarke and Edward Frowde and their respective heires by these presents That he, the said Henry, Lord Coleraine and his heires shall and will from time to time for ever hereafter keep and maintaine the hatch belonging to the Mill Wheel of the said Paper Mill and the Fender hatch and Landfasts thereto adjoyneing and the Bancks of Earth and the Flood hatch on the North-west of the Mill Pond and the Landfasts these adjoyneing to the said hatches in good repair so as for want thereof the ymproveing of the said Meadow Grounds shall not be obstructed or hindered.

In witness whereof the said parties to these Articles have interchangeably set their hands and seals even the day and year first above written Anno Domini 1675

Witnesses: James Gordlen
William Lawrence
John Snow

Letter from Sir Joseph Ashe to John Snow, 22 March 1677

WSRO 490/909

I have your tedious letter of the 15th, and I thinke this Cursed Wateringe hath given me 10 tymes the trouble that all the other concernes of my life hath done, and am never free. But you layd out my money on hopes people would be kind, who prove –[?] that ought to have been bettered managed.

I presume you will now follow Chatle till you get your money into your hands. Pray thanke Cossen Wyndham for his kindness and take some tyme to discourse the River. I have spoken with Mr Goldston, who adviseth me to goe to Dr Davenant that gave your Land to the Vicar and he wil right us and make Foot be honest. Doe you therefore ryde over to Gillingam with this letter and heare what he says. If he will send for Foot, desire to carry your letter, it is lykely he wil make him doe no right, if not know if he will write me an answer. You wil send it. Pray tell Mr Buckland I have but my old rent by your wateringe. He getts £100 per annum by his Watring and he ought to concerne himselfe aswel as I doe, especially being on the place. In case these people wil not set up the rayles and gates, then goe on with your prosecution. There must be noe stop now, and therefore doe it vigorously.——

London 22 March 1677

Joseph Ashe

Letter from Sir Joseph Ashe to John Snow 15 April 1678

WSRO 490/909

John Snow London 15 April 1678

I have receaved your Letter of the 8th April, and when you will consider the perpetual troubles and constant laying out of money, and noe coming in, you need not wonder I am sicke of those designes. And let other men fal into my circumstances they wilbe as weary as my selfe. But those that enjoy a proffitt and quiett may be ever contented, and when that tyme comes, soe will I. You have settled the matter with Dr Davenant very wel. Therefore, choose 2 persons to joyne with his men and let them adjudge it, but you must let Mr Buckland name one of the two. I doe thinke Mr Buckland may nourish the prankes played about the Rayles and burning the gates. That is natural enough, but surely you have more sense than to thinke he wil put out both his eyes to put out one of myne. He makes £100 per annum proffitt by his wateringe but I make none out of myne. Such whymseys that you enterteyne doe but delay tyme and if you speake with Mr Buckland 'tis better to declare fact than otherwise and then you know what to trust to and though you doe not thinke fitt to doe somwhat that we may prevent at our pleasure the watering there, as wel as he hath in his power to prevent us on New Court syde, we shal repent it too late. Perchance we may doe it with Mr Done as wel as with Turnne which pray consider off. The letter from John Ash doth me some satisfaction to that point. I would have you hold Mr John Wyndham in your discourse and direct things as much as you can. I have spoken with my Lord Clarendon and he tells me that Salisbury men have noe power to assign their grant to any others and hath entered a Caveat to that purpose.

When you see it convenient ye may come up to Mr Draper, but for my coming down I know not when it wilbe, for I must first goe to Norfolke to bring home my Wyfe. Pray thank Mr Michel for his gammon, You may send it to Hounslow as you used to doe and when I know your tyme shal send for it.

You must write me the age of the man you have for me and what is the wages he expects and then I'll send you my answer. Several of the Ewes you bought were rotten and are dead. This was an ill parcell. I shall mynd Mr Martyn of your Court Rolls that tyme be not lost. I like well the £80 you made of the trees.

I am, Your

Joseph Ashe.

Costs of Establishing and Maintaining the Water Meadows

The following accounts for work done on one section of the Downton water meadows in 1685 are part of a much larger series. They show the work involved and the heavy expense of making and repairing the channels, drains, hatches and bridges. The accounts also illustrate the careful way in which John Snow organised the complex operations, and provided Sir Joseph Ashe with a detailed record of expenditure. No doubt this was required by Sir Joseph who was constantly worried by the costs of work on the water meadows. Maurice Bockland who leased Standlynch Farm, and Henry Haitter who leased Witherington farm, would both benefit from the work being done, and no charge is recorded for the use of their 'plows', that is teams of horses or oxen. By 1685 some of the original hatches needed repair or renewal, work was required on the main carriage, and some bridges had to be rebuilt. The accounts show the extent of the work involved, the large quantities of stone and timber piles required to provide foundations in the soft ground by the river bed. They also had to withstand the force of a river liable to violent floods. Some of the tasks were evidently undertaken at piecework by partnerships of men coming from a distance and lodging nearby; other work was done by locals paid by the day ('daymen'). Much of the work was paid for by the 'lugg' which was normally reckoned as 16½ feet. In these accounts, as in the other surviving documents, the efficiency and organising ability of John Snow in supervising the complex work is impressive.

WSRO 1946/Box 12 (5)

An Accompt of more disburst by and between Sir Joseph Ash Barronett and Morris Buckland Esq. in makeinge and settinge up a cart bridge over the maine or great drayne made for Witherington and Standlynch meadows, And also about settinge up or building the Freestone hatches at head of the maine carriage made for wateringe the Aforesaid meadows, and also for and towards the new makinge and settinge up the other two cases of hatches Standinge Athwart the great maine carriage in broad mead at Withington farme. Don since May the 15th 1685

First, the Accompt what is disburst about the said bridg over the the great maine drayne

	£	s	d
Squire Bucklands plow for the carridge of two loads of the freestone used in the Landfast one tunn and ½ to a load being 3 tunns att 6s od per tunn is		18	0
Henry Haitter for carridge of one load being one tunn and one halfe att 6s od for Tunn		9	0
John Clos for carridg of two loads being 2 tunns		12	0
Edward Magwick for carridg to two Loads beinge 3 tunns att 6s od per tunn		18	0
George Noyes for carridg of 3 loads with his plow beinge 4 Tunns ½ att 6s od per tunn	1	7	0

	£	s	d
Henry Haitter's plow for carridg of one load of Sand and one load of Chalke	0	0	0
Squire Buckland's plow for carridge of two loads of chalke from Standlinch Hill	0	0	0
Squire Buckland's plow for carridge of one halfe of two tunns and 27 foot of timber bought of Morris Thomas	0	0	0
Henry Haitter's plow for carridge of the other halfe of the said Timber att	0	0	0
Morris Thomas for the said timber bought of him at Moore Farme cops being two tunns one halfe and 7 feet beinge in 12 eeces att 16s per Tunn used about the said bridg	2	2	10
Squire Buckland's plow for the carridge of 3 quarters and 5 bushels of lime from Joseph Stokes Brick Kill att	0	0	0
Joseph Stokes for the said 3 quarters and 5 bushels of lime att 4s 0d per quarter		14	6
Squire Bucklands plow brought 1400 of brickes that they had at home that was Stokes brickes att 10s 0d per Thousand		14	6
Squire Buckland for carridg of them at 4d the hundred		4	8
Paid John Lawrence for all the freestone used in the land fast on the west side beinge 60 feet att 3½d per foot		17	6
Paid him for the peece in the middle beinge 62 feet of parpen wall at 7d per foot	1	16	2
Paid him for the Landfast on the east side beinge 70 feet att 3½d per foot	1	0	5
	11	14	1

Paid severall labourers for makeinge of bays and pounding of water and digginge out the foundations for the said bridg and other worke don about it June the 11, 12, 13, 15, 16, 17, 18, 19, 20, 22, 23

	s	d
James Noyes for helpinge about it 8 days at 18d per day and for one quarter of a day	12	4
Henry Plasket for helpinge 6 days	9	0
Paid Rich. Bennett for 7½ days att 18d per day	11	3
Paid John Grey for 7 days att 12d per day	7	0
Paid Nicholas Taylor for diginge Chalke and for helpinge about it for himselfe and his sone Nicholas both of them 5 days and one ½	5	6
Paid Robert Best for helpinge 3 days one ½	3	6
The masoninge worke don in fittinge and settinge the freestone at the same time. Paid John Lawrence for 6 days att 2s 6d per day		
Paid William Mould for 5 days att 2s 6d per day	15	0
Paid Siffy Fry for helpinge lay the bricke worke on the peere and land fasts one day and 3 quarters att 18d pr day	12	6
Paid him for his son William Fry's servinge of the massons in the time above said 8 days	2	0
	4	0

	£	s	d
John Snow for settinge out the foundation for the said bridg and or directinge of the workmen about it for 4 days and ½ att 3s 4d per day		14	10
Paid James Noyes and Rich. Bennett for their Squareinge of the remainder of the Timber bought at Hale and the timber bought of Morris Thomas being 5 tunns att 18d per Tunn hewinge		7	6
Richard Longyears for his goinge to Moore Farme cops to measure the timber bout [bought] of Morris Thomas		1	0
Paid James Noyes and Rich. Bennett for sawing of the gird for the said bridg and slittinge of Timber peeces and two Stockes for hatch plankes all beinge 740 feet at 3s 0d per Tunn	1	1	0
Paid John Eastman, Thomas Hatcher and Rich. Mowland for all the carpentry worke don about it for 2 days a peece att 16d per day a peece		8	0
Paid Thomas Eastman for 2 days		1	0
Valentine Edsell for 2½ pounds of nayles used about it att 5d a pound		1	0
For takeinge up the bays and coveringe of the bridg with gravell July the 1 and 2		3	0
Paid Rich. Bennett for one day		1	6
	7	1	5

Hatches across the River Avon

With a large volume of water, variable flow and regular winter floods, strong hatches with deep foundations were essential on the Avon. The following specification shows the work necessary to provide hatches which could be used to divert part of the river along the main channel to water the meadows, but which could be raised at other periods or in times of flood. To resist the force of the river, the structure was to be strongly built of stone, with secure foundations in the bed of the river. Other accounts refer to the stone coming from the quarry at Fovant. There were to be eight apertures or 'eyes' for the water to pass through, each with a timber hatch which could be raised or lowered to divert part of the current into the meadows. Between each aperture there was to be a strong stone wall which is referred to as a 'parpin'. This specification lists the amount of good-quality ashlar stone required.

WSRO 490/903

The Dementions of a Case of Hatches at the South End of 18 Acres, March the 26th 1691.

The Dementions of a Case of Hatches to be built with stone ware the south end of 18 acres next the River Avon for the wateringe of Green Southmead and South Lees. The said hatches in breadth in

the cleare as it appears by the first paper sent to the Quarriars, but 20 foot 4 inches, divided into 8 eyes of 2 foot 6 inches one half inch in each eye, but since the Quarriars hath been directed, if the stone will hold it, to make them 22 foot in the cleare divided into 8 eyes of 2 foot 9 inches in each eye in the cleare, with 7 parpin walls, 4 of them to be 14 inches parpin and the two of them 15 inches parpin and one of them 18 inches parpin, and in higth all of them 8 foot below the rabbitt [rebate] and 15 inches above the rabbitt, in all 9 foot 3 inches, and not to hatch backe behind but to hold to be 9 foot 3 inches long each Stop or a little better, all contayninge of parpin 83 foot in each parpin in the whole	581 feet
The head Stones 2 foot long each, higth 14 inches contayns	30 ft 4 ins
The bed with the Stone zill at head of one foot deep 8 foot 6 inches in length, the backer stones of the said bed to be about 18 inches broad at tayle and 15 inches deep to serve instead of a timber zill next the false bed of 29 foot in length by the first directions athwart and as much as the stones will hold to make the eyes wider not to exceed 2 foot 9 inches in each eye which will be 30 foot and 8 inches in the cleare and 6 inches allowance under every parpin wall and the two side walls contayneth in the whole bed with the zills of the whole breadth under parpins and all	236 feet
The pound pannill in length upwards 5 foot and in breadth next the upper zill by the first directions 29 foot but by the last directions if the stone will hold it 30 foot 8 inches and to spread one foot wider on each side at foot of the pound pannill contayneinge in the whole	165 feet
The side walls in length from the head zill backwards of Ashlar 8 foot 6 inches each end and 4 foot 6 inches in higth	76 feet
The side walls for the whings [wings] above the uper zill forwards, the south side wall 10 foot long at Bottom and so to hatch backe to two foot long a top the north side wall in length upwards 6 foot at bottom and two foot atop and in higth about 6 foot contayninge	60 foot
A wall to be made on the false bed on each side with burrs 6 foot 6 inches in length each and in higth 4 foot	52 feet
The two head Stones on the side walls	4 ft 8 ins
	1205 ft 0 ins
[*Written on the back*]	
The false bed in length downwards 5 foot and in breadth next the backer zill stones 29 foot, but by the last directions if it will hold 30 foot 8 inches and to spread 6 inches wider on each side, contayninge in the whole	157 ft 0 ins
	1362 feet

Hatches, Channels and Bridges for the Water Meadows

The complex arrangements for diverting part of the river Avon and distributing the water evenly over the surface of various meadows in turn are clear from the following document which lists all the equipment. It was compiled in 1691 following a particularly fierce flood. The 'Hand' was a set of hatches in the river, and a 'burnell' or 'bunnell' was a conduit for the water. The 'Navigation bridge' was one of a series of bridges designed to allow barges to be drawn along the stream, as part of the proposed canal or navigation which it was hoped would provide a link between Salisbury and the sea. The list illustrates how expensive it was to equip and maintain a water meadow, ensuring a sufficient flow of water and adequate drainage.

WSRO 490/892

An account of the Hand in the River Avon at the head of the main Carriage in Charlton grounds for Newcourt farme, and the severall cases of Hatches, trunks, burnells, stops and bridges belonging thereunto standing in and upon the main carriage and other carriages in the meadows belonging to the said Newcourt farme for watering the said farme meadows.

The Hand in the River Avon wants repairing

The Navigation bridge wants rayles on both ends otherwise in good repair

The head case of Hatches of 11 eyes standing in Charlton grounds which are thrown down by the flood and in Mr Buckland's fisherman, are now building with stone behind them for James Barrow to goe into his lower mead in winter time

Three water gates between James Barrow and Henry Noys the younger to be repaired with stone this summer

A trunk under the main carriage near the Lane towards Charlton grounds lying in the upper Side Road mead ditch for draining severall grounds in Charlton

In indifferent repair

A case of small hatches of –[blank] eyes at the upper parte of Reper road

In indifferent repair

A bridge and 3 water gates to goe over into Charlton Lane over the main carriage

To be forwith repaired

A case of hatches at the upper end of the lowe part of Road mead

To be repaired with the old wood £7

Two Stops to be made with stone in the East Bank of the main carriage in the upper part of the lower part of the upper Road mead

Nine severall stops made with stone in 1686 in the Est banke of the main carriage in the lower part of the lower Road mead

A Trunke under the main carriage at the lower part of the upper Road mead between ten acres and the lower part of the upper Road mead for the draining of Charlton grounds

A hatch and a Bunnell out of the 10 Acres main carriage

Much out of repair

Two cases of Hatches built with stone in 1686 in Ten acres mead one of 5 eyes on the East side and the other of 4 eyes on the west side

A small trunk under the main carriage belonging to the 4 eye hatch

A great case of Hatches athwart the main carriage with a house over it built in 1686 with stone

In good repaire

A bunnel timber hatch of stone and bricck on the west side

A case of hatches new built standing at the upper end of 18 Acres athwart the main carriage

In indifferent repair

A case of timber hatches standing at the head of the main carriage for drowning of 18 Acres

Very much out of repair

A Bunnel to draw out the dead water out of the head of 18 Acres carriage

To be repaired with old timber

Two pair of timber sluces athwart the main carriage towards the lower end of 18 Acres

In good repair

A brick bridge for a Cart in the old ditch between 18 Acres and Worth, lately built

In good repair

A foot wooden bridge across the main carriage by the Cart way that goes over from Worth into 18 Acres

In indifferent repair

A brick, stone and timber bridge in the top, built in 1686 over part of the main drain in 18 Acres

A case of Hatches of 3 eyes built with stone in 1686 for drawing out the dead water of 18 Acres and shutting it down to help drown Great Catherine mead
In good repair

A pair of water gates at the lower end of Worth, must be made 3 gates
Much out of repair

A small case of hatches in the East side of the main carriage for Worth mead

A bridge over a main drain and a case of hatches under for 18 Acres, which case serves to drown the little Worth mead

A foot Bridge across the main carriage that serves little Worth mead and Hampworth mead

A stop hatch to drown part of little Worth mead

A case of hatches across the main carriage for drowning great Katherine mead

A bridge behind those hatches for a mill, market and church way and a way into great Katherine mead for cattle in the winter time

A bridge over against Newcourt farme gate over the main carriage in great Katherine mead belonging to Green South mead and South Leays

A case of hatches standing near those last mentioned in the head of the main carriage for drowning of Great Katherine mead

Three stop hatches that stand upon the East side of the main carriage of Katherine mead for drowning of Goose mead

A pair of sluces across the main carriage of Katherine mead for drowning the highest part of Katherine Mead
Out of repaire

An Archt bunnell under the Cawsey [causeway] with stone and brick
In good repair

Two trunkes of brick in great Katherine mead and Goose mead to be made over 2 drains in the East side of the main carriage for Carts and cattle to pass over

Ten archt bunnells and stop trunkes under the Cawsey in Goose mead and great Katherine mead

A great case of hatches and house over them for drowninge of little Katherine mead standing on the ground called Walton on the west and little Katherine mean on the East

These are designed to be removed

A Trunk or bridge and case of Hatches under them for letting out the dead water from little and great Katherine meads

This is designed to be removed.

A List of Hatches, Water Gates and Bridges for Watering Witherington and Standlynch Farms compiled in 1691

This is part of a much longer list of the hatches and other equipment for watering all the meadows on the Downton estate in 1691. The details given illustrate the complexity of the system, the various landowners involved, and the fact that constant repairs were needed to keep it in good working order. It lists the numerous bridges which had been constructed to give access to various parts of the meadows, including the bridge across the main carriageway 'for the use of the Navigators' [bargemen], on the canal which it was hoped would extend from Salisbury to the coast. A note on repairs which had been made to the hatches and bridges was evidently added later in 1691, but is in the same handwriting.

WSRO 490/893

An account of all the cases of Hatches, Stop Hatches, Bunnell Hatches, Trunkes, Water Gates, Cart and Foot Bridges standing in and upon the several main Carriage bankes and draynes belonging to Witherington Farme only and to be repaired and maintained at the charge of the owner thereof

A case of hatches of 8 Eayes lately built of stone and timber at the head of the main Carriage for the Moor and a Brick wall upon the north side thereof next Alderbury ground about a lugg in length and several perches of railes set all along next Alderbury ground and out of Witherington Moor

In good repair

Seaven bunnell hatches in the south east bank of the main Carriage

In good repair

1 bunnell drawing hatch for draining part of the dead water out of the main Carriage

In good repair

15 Bunnell stop hatches in the bank on the east side of the main Carriage

In good repair

1 other Bunnell drawing hatch for draining the dead water out of the next part of the main Carriage

In good repair

3 stop bunnells more in the same main Carriage Bank

In indifferent repair

1 Case of Hatches of 4 Eyes at the head of the small main Carriage Eastwards out of the great Main Carriage in the Moor

Much out of repair
These are repaired with stone 1691

6 Stop hatches in the same main Carriage bank in the South East side in the 8 Acres being part of the Moor

Much out of repair

1 Case of Hatches of 5 Eyes a thwart the main Carriage South East part of the Moor that water the 5 Acres

Much out of repair
These are repaired in 1691

2 Stop hatches in the south side of 8 Acres part of the Moor

In bad repair
Repaired

1 Stone and brick trunk bridge between the Moor and 5 Acres

In good repair

Eight stop hatches being small ones in the lower part of the Moor over the bridge called 5 Acres

Out of repair

A footbridge over the main drayn for part of Alderbury mead and part of the Moor between 5 Acres and 8 Acres

In indifferent repair

A cart bridge between dry Leaze and 8 Acres part of the Moor

In good repair

Two water gates at the lower end of the Moor next the back side between dry Leaze and the 5 Acres

In indifferent repair

A Bridge, the under work stone and brick, the top timber, over the main drain by the stables of Witherington farme

In good repair

A great case of hatches of 7 eyes on the East side of the main Carriage for Broad Mead at the Head of the Main Carriage for dry Leaze and Orchard Mead

Much out of repair and to be made good this yeare
Repaired in the yeare 1691

Two stop hatches on the North side for part of the upper part of the Moor

Out of repair

One small bunnell hatch on the East side of the main Carriage belonging to Broad Mead

Out of repair
Repaired in 1691

This detailed Survey continues all along the Main Carriage . As part of the same Survey the following list gives details of another section of the system for watering Witherington and Standlynch.

June 10th 1691
An account then taken of all the cases of hatches, bridges and Trunks standing in and upon the Main Carriage for Watering of the severall grounds belonging to Witherington Farme and Standlinch Farme which are from time to time repaired at the joynt charge of my Lady Mary Ashe and Morris Buckland Esq.

The Hand upon the main River Avon against my Lord Colraine's Mead belonging to Longford House, and Mr Stringer's meadow late Mr Doves called Eighteen Acres

Wants stone and timber to repair

The bridge across the head of the main Carriage in 18 Acres which was set up for the use of the Navigators

Some posts and rayles wanting at each end, the rest in good repair

A case of hatches of 10 Eyes with a house over them built with stone standing near the head of the main Carriage between Witherington and Standlinch. The land fasts behinde the hatches are supported with timber piles

In good repair

A bridge for Carts and cattle athwart the main Carriage. The land fasts and parpins stone, the rest with timber in Alderbury Meed

In good repair

A wooden Trunk athwart the main Carriage and under the great Carriage and bank near the corner of Axe Mead for drayning part of Alderbury

Common Mead in the old mill stream belonging to Witherington and Standlinch

In very bad repair

A stone hatch to drayn the main Carriage at all times when the Meadows are not drowned into Witherington and Charlton ditch

In good repair

Three water gates between the Common mead at Alderbury and the upper end of Witherington Moor to preserve the cattle from comeing out of the Common Mead of Alderbury into the Moor and out of the Moor into Alderbury Mead

These are down and must be rebuilt

A case of hatches of 6 Eyes, the land fasts stone, the rest timber athwart the main Carriage near the Knowl in Broad Mead well supported in the land fasts behind with timber piles

In indifferent repair

A cart bridge on Mr Buckland's main Drayn in Standlinch ground a little below the Mill ham of Witherington, the under wake stone and brick, the upper part timber

In indifferent repair

Hatches standing in by and upon the main Carriage in Alderbury Mead upon Sir Giles Eyres land which is in Lease to Sir Joseph Ashe for 80 years not yet Expired to be repaired and maintained wholly at the charge of Morris Buckland Esqr

A Case of hatches a thwart the Main Carriage in Alderbury Mead in Sir Giles Eyres land for the penning of the water to Axe Mead

A case of hatches of stone and timber at the head of the main Carriage for Axe Mead in Sir Giles Eyres land

A case of Hatches of 3 Eyes on the west side of the main Carriage in Broad Mead

And a small main Carriage about 8 or 9 lugg in length cut through my Lady Ashe's ground and a bridge standing over that part of the ditch belonging to Witherington and Charlton land for drowneing a ground late Robert Newman's deceased, afterwards Sir Stephen Fox's and now Morris Buckland Esqr.

To be continued during the will and pleasure of My Lady Ashe

An Accompt of more disbursted as aforesaid about settinge up the case of Freestone hatches at head of the maine carridg made for Withington and Standlinch meadows

Paid severall men for pullinge downe the hatch howse and the old hatches and settinge of him up Againe to put lime and other materialls in and for hewinge of piles and for driveinge of them to make bays and a bridg over the river in to the mill ham to use about the said hatches and for diginge out of the land fast of the old hatches and for pulinge of them up and for Showleinge [shovelling] up the water gravell in the river at Bottenham [Bodenham] bridg to use about the new hatches and severall other sorts of worke don . . .

	£	s	d
[Long list of payments to workmen and 13s 4d paid to John Snow for 4 days directing the work]			
Total	11	6	8½
Squire Bucklands plow for carridge of two dozen of hurdles to make bays, and bows and lops from Looshanger to make piles for the bays and bridg over the river 1 load		blank	
Paid William Bussle for the two dozen of hurdles att 2s 6d per dozen		5	0
For 14 Stickes to make great piles that came out of the Frenches that was my owne att 7d a peece		8	2
For 15 Stickes more of Sir Joseph Ashes Timber that was bows and lops at Looshanger for to make piles for the bridg at 5d a peece		6	3
Squire Bucklands plow and Henry Haitters plow for fetchinge 71 Stickes –(?) bows at Moore farme cops [copse] that was bought of Morris Thomas being one load a peece		blank	
Morris Thomas for the said 71 small stickes to make great piles at 4d a peece	1	3	8
Paid Morris Wordly for Elmeinge of the Straw and thatchinge of the hatch house to hold lime and other materialls in		4	4
Barneby Rumsey for one Thousand of last nayles to last the said house		2	0
Robert Oakeford for amendinge of the canvis bay			4
James Rodes for one basket to carry lime and one flasket to carry chalke		2	0
[Paid] him for one renseeve [sieve] to dress the water gravell att			6
Morris Giles for two cords at		1	0
Paid Charles Shellow for a Bissom [broom]			1
Paid for greese for the truckles			4
July the 27 1685 was received of Joseph Stokes 10 quarters of Chalke lime att 4s 0d per Quarter	2	0	0
Squire Bucklands plow for carridg of the said lime to use about the said hatches at		blank	

	£	s	d
July the 31st and August the 5th was delivered by Lawrence Holdbrooke 24 hors load of Mels Lime in 24 sackes all of them beinge 9 quarters att 10s 0d per quarter delivered in place	4	10	0
Paid Thomas Best for diginge of 18 Loads of Chalke used to back the freestone for fillinge at 6d per load		9	0
Squire Bucklands plow for carridg of 9 loads of chalke		blank	
Henry Haitters plow for carridg of 9 loads of chalke		blank	
	9	12	10

An Accompt of all the freestone carridg used about the said head hatches and the hatches in broad mead

	£	s	d
May the 23rd, 27th, 30th and June the 3, 9, 26 and July the 4th and 9th and 15th days was carryed by Thomas Penrudockes Esqr two teems 9 loads a peece beinge in the whole 18 loads at 2 tunns a load maketh 36 Tunns att 6s 0d per Tunn	10	16	0
May the 21, 23 and June the 3rd and July the 9th and 24th days Will Nightingales plow carryed 5 loads beinge one tunn and one halfe at a load being 7 tunns and one halfe Tunn att 6s 0d per Tunn	2	5	0
Christopher Bayliff for carridg of 5 loads at the same time att one tunn and one halfe at a load maketh 7 tunns one halfe at 6s 0d per tunn	2	5	0
Stephen Fownd for carridg of 7 tunns one halfe at the same time att 6s 0d per tunn	2	5	0
Walter Luke for carridg of one load being two Tunns att 6s 0d per Tunn		12	0
John Mussell for carridg of one load being one Tunn one ½ at 6s 0d per Tunn		9	0
Walter Hibert for carridg of one load beinge one tunn and one halfe at		9	0
Joseph Parritt for carridg of 3 loads bewinge 4 Tunns one ½ att 6s 0d per Tunn	1	7	0
Rowland Alcocke for carridg of one load beinge one tunn and one halfe att		9	0
John Cox for carridg of 13 loads being 13 Tunns att 6s 0d per Tunn	13	18	0
George Noyes for carridg of 14 loads at one tunn one halfe to a load is 21 tunns att 6s 0d per Tunn	6	6	0
Farmer Haitter for 2 loads being 4 tunns	1	4	0
John Newman for carridg of 5 loads beinge 7 Tunns one halfe	2	5	0
Edward Madwicke for carridg of Tenn loads at 1 tunn and one ½ to a load is 15 Tunns	4	10	0
	39	0	0

	£	s	d
Allowed Alderbury people for damages don the Earbidgers there by carridg of freestone downe throw [through] Alderbury mead with plows drove for the landfasts of the two payre of hatches in broad mead	1	0	0
And was paid Edward Prince of Bremmer for measuringe the ground out and covered in the maine trench two days		4	0
John Sanger for one day and paid Thomas Smith for helpinge about it			6
Paid Rich. Smith and his partners for sinkeinge of 6 lugs and ¾ in length of the said maine carridg above the lower hatches in broad mead the breadth 18 feet and in depth 11 inches one ½ att 1d per foot is 17d per lug		9	6
Paid them for wheeleinge of it into the fales [?holes] in broad mead 12 lugs att 17d per lug more		9	6
Paid them for Sinkeinge of one lug below the lower hatches the breadth there 17 feet and in depth one foot 6 inches att 1d per foot is 2s 1d per lug, diginge and throwinge		2	1
Paid them for fillinge it up in to the wheelbarros againe to wheele it away ½d per foot is 12½d the lug and for wheelinge it away into the fales 24 lugs of att ¾d per foot for two Stages is 4s 1d per lug		5	1½
Paid them for wheelinge away one lug more that was throwed out by the day men		5	1½
Paid them for Sinkeinge of 6 lugs more in length below the said hatches and in breadth 17 feet and in depth one with the other one foot 2 inches att 1¼d per foot diginge, throwing it out and placeinge it 2s 1d per lug		12	6
Paid them for cuttinge downe the sides of the bankes wider one foot 3 inches upon a side on both sides is 2 feet 6 inches and in higth 3 feet att 1d per foot is 7½d per lug for 7 lugs		4	5
Paid William Musle and his partners for 4 lugs in length and in breadth 17 feet and in depth 9 inches att 1d per foot is 14d per lug diginge		4	8
Paid them for wheelinge of it to raise the banks above Squire Bucklands hatches and to ram by the sides of his hatches 18 lugs of att 1d per foot is 1s 5½d per lug		5	10
Paid them for 14 lugs more in length and in breadth 17 feet and in depth 8 inches att 1½d per foot diginge and throwinge of it out and placeinge it up in the backside is 14½d per lug		16	11
Paid them for cuttinge downe the sides of the bankes 6 inches upon a side wider which maketh on both sides to be 18 inches in breadth and in higth 3 feet it beinge in length 18 lugs att 4½d per lug		6	9
Paid them for wheelinge away 4 lugs of it 16 lugs of att 6d per lug		2	0
	4	4	5
	3	2	6

	£	s	d
	2	5	10
	3	11	1
	2	9	4
	2	11	4
	3	5	3
	23	14	3

An Accompt what was paid Severall men for and towards their quarters which laid out from whome [home] while they was about doinge the aforesaid lugworke att 1d the night a peece

Paid John Harris, Francis Harris, Will Hardin towards their quarters for 4 weekes a peece att 6d the weeke a peece	6	0
Paid George Stephens towards his quarters for 3 weekes att 6d the weeke	1	6
Paid Robert Atkins for his quarters 6 weekes	3	0
Paid Richard Alkins and John Horten 4 weekes a peece	4	0
Paid Hew Rose for 4 weekes	2	0
Paid Rich. Smith for 5 weekes	2	6
Paid Nicholas Pears 4 weekes	2	0
	[no total given]	

December the 9th was spent and paid at Alderbury Ine [Inn] for what was spent there about meetinge of the Earbidgers of Alderbury common mead at the makeinge the Agreement with them	1	4	0
Allowed them, (Alderbury Men) for damages don by plows goinge throw [through] Alderbury mead with the freestone used about broad mead hatches	1	0	0
Paid Edward Prince for his helpinge measure the ground cut and covered in the maine carridg and Accomptinge it –(?) for 2 days		4	0
John Sanger 2 days and paid Thomas Smith for helpinge about it			6
For two thousand of last nayles used about lastinge the house	3	9	0
For writinge out all the aforesaid Accompt up the workemens worke and takeinge up the Accompt 2 days		6	8
	4	8	8

A Water Meadow on the Kennet at Ramsbury 1668

Water meadows were not only established along many of the valleys in south Wiltshire during the 17th century, but the idea was also adopted in other parts of the chalklands and in the valley of the Kennet. This lease of a water meadow at Ramsbury confirms John Aubrey's statement that the technique was introduced along the Kennet during the 1640s. He stated that 'Watering of meadows about Marleborough and so to Hungerford was, I remember, about 1646'; elsewhere he described how 'The watered meadows all along from Marleborough to Hungerford, Ramesbury, and Littlecot, at the later end of Aprill are yellow with butter flowers'. [J. Aubrey, Natural History of Wiltshire, *1969 edn., 51, 104] This lease refers to the fact that the meadow at Ramsbury was being watered or 'floated' in 1642. The high rent charged for the meadow illustrates the value attached to the early grass and abundant hay which such meadows provided. The annual rent of £11 for seven acres of meadow was more than double what could be charged for an unwatered one. The value of this riverside meadow in a convenient situation to be watered is also evident from the careful details of this professionally-drawn lease or indenture. There is no mention of hatches in the river, and possibly these were not necessary, but much care is taken over rights to the water, the trenches for bringing the water, and, equally important, to drain it off again.*

WSRO 212A/27/27

Lease from Stephen and John Gillmore of Marlborough to John Stone of Ramsbury 21 December 1668

This Indenture made the one and Twentieth day of December in the Nyneteenth yeare of the Reigne of our Soveraigne Lord Charles the Second by the grace of God King of England, Scotland, Frannce and Ireland defender of the faith, Between Stephen Gillmore of Marleborough in the County of Wiltes, Tanner, and John Gillmore, sone and heire apparent of the said Stephen Gillmore th'one parte and John Stone of Ramsbury in the County aforesaid, Chandler, of th'other parte Witnesseth that the said Stephen Gillmore and John Gillmore for and in consideration of the yearely rent covenants and agreements hereafter in and by these presents reserved, mentioned and expressed Hath devised graunted and to ferme letten and by these presents doth demise graunt and to ferme lett unto the said John Stone All that meadow ground called or Knowne by the name of Upper Od Marsh situate lyeing and being in Ramsbury aforesaid conteyning by estimacon seaven acres be it more or lesse now in the tenure and possession of Edward Judd as the tenant and leassee of the said Stephen Gillmore **To Have and To Hold** the said meadow ground with all and singular the pertennces herein before demised by these presents unto the said John Stone his executors, administrators and assignes from the one and Twentieth day of December next coming for and during and untill the full end and terme of Eight yearess fully to be compleat and ended (yf the said Stephen Gillmore, Margery his wife and John Gillmore his son or any of them shall so long live) **Yeilding** and paying therefore Yearely during the said terme Eleven pounds of Lawful money of England on the feast days of St John the Baptist [24 June] and St Thomas th'appostle [21 December] by even and equall portions. And yf it shall happen the said yearely rent of Eleven pounds or any parte or parcell thereof to be behind and unpaid by the space of Tenn dayes next after either of the feast dayes for payment thereof aforesaid being lawfully demanded That then and in such case it shall and may be lawfull to and for the said Stephen Gillmore, his executors and assignes into all and singular the premises herein before demised by these presents with the appurtennces wholley to re-enter and the same to have againe re-possesse and enjoy as in his or theyr former estates anything herein And the said John Stone for himselfe doth covenant and promise to and with the said Stephen Gillmore by these presents That he the said Stephen and his assignes shall or lawfully may from and after the comencement of this demise and graunt untill the second day of March then next following have ingresse egresse and regresse into and upon thye said meadowe ground for the cutting, repaireing and amendment of the hedges and bounds thereunto belonging and apperteyning att his and theyr will and pleasure and also have take and carry away to his own use such wood and fewell as shall be left of the said hedges and bounds after the same shall be so cutt, repaired and amended by the said Stephen Gillmore, nevertheless the said John Stone, his executors and assignes shall and will from and after the said second day of March during the residue of the said terme well and sufficiently repaire, amend and keep aswell the said hedges and bounds of the said meadow ground as also the sinke made of Tymber and other materialls for drawing the water out of the said meadow into the said other meadow in and with all necessary and usefull reparacions thereunto belonging and apperteyning and att th'end of the said terme shall so leave the same yet nevertheless the said John Stone, his executors or assignes shall not cutt any of the quick setts growing parte of the said hedges or bounds without the consent of the said Stephen Gillmore. His executors or assignes thereunto first had and obteyned and also that the said John Stone, his executors or assignes shall not plow upp or convert to tillage the said meadow ground or any parte thereof nor convert it to any other use but to meadow or pasture and also shall beare, pay and discharge all ordinary parish payments and th'one halfe of other taxation ymposed or assessed for and in respect of the said Stephen Gillmore for himselfe doth covenant and promise to and with the said John Stone by these presents that he the said Stephen and his assignes shall beare, pay and discharge the moytie and one halfe of such payments as shall be ymposed or assessed to be paid out of for in respect of the said meadow ground for royall aid or such like millitary charge as shall be payable unto the king's Majestie, his heires and successors during the said terme. And further, whereas Edward Gillmore, gent., deceased being in his life tyme seized in his demesne as of fee as well of and in another meadow lyeing in Ramsbury aforesaid called also by the name of Oadmarsh and adjoyning to the River there on the North side thereof as also of such parte of the said River as is adjoyning to both the said meadowes with all liberty, privilege, advantage and commoditie which might be made or raised by reason or meanes of such parte of the said River and the water thereof by his Indenture beareing date the twentyth day of March in the seventeenth yeare of the late King Charles the first [1642] did graunt, bargaine, sell, alienate and confirm unto the said Stephen Gillmore, his heires and assignes for ever full power, licence, liberty, authority and interest to make use of such parte of the said River whereof the said Edward Gillmore was seized as aforesaid for the floating of the said meadow by these presents demised with the water thence to come and be drawen into the same meadow for the bettering and ymproving thereof and also to come in and uppon the said other meadow of the said Edward Gillmore and there either by making trenches therein or by more husbandlye and convenient wayes and meanes to draw and lett forth such water so used or to be used for floating as aforesaid out of the said other meadow last menconed [mentioned] into uppon by or through the same meadow att all tymes when need shall require. **Also** this Indenture further witnesseth that the said Stephen Gillmore for the consideration aforesaid doth demise, graunt, assigne and to ferme lett unto the said John Stone power, licence, libery and interest to make use of the said River for floating of the said meadow by these presents demised for the bettering and ymproving thereof and to come in and uppon the said other meadow and either by making trenches therein or other wayes or meanes to draw or lett out thence the water so to be used as fully and effectually as the same is graunted unto the said Stephen Gillmore in manner aforesaid **To have and to hold** the same unto him the said John Stone, his executors and assignes from the said one and twentyeth day of December next coming for and duering the said terme of Eight yeares fully to be compleat and ended. And the said John Stone doth covenant and promise to and with the said Stephen Gillmore, his heires and assignes by these presents that yf for any thing done or to be done by the said John Stone, his heires or assignes any suit or action shall be commewnced against the said Stephen Gillmore, his heires, executors or assignes in or uppon the said meadow by these presents demised for any cause or matter whatsoever, That the said John Stone, his executors or assignes shall save, defend and keepe harmeless the said Stephen Gillmore, his heires, executirs or assignes of and from such suit or action and all damages and demands concerning the same. And the said Stephen Gillmore and John Gillmore doe covenant to and with the said John Stone that the said John Stone, his heires and assignes shall or lawfully may hold and enjoy the said meadow hereby demised duering the said terme without lett or denyall of the said Stephen Gillmore and John Gillmore or any claymeing under either of them. In Witness whereof the said parties to these present Indentures Enterchangably have sett theyr hands and seales, given the day and yeare first above written.

Agreement for a Water Meadow on the River Nadder at Burcombe 1716

WSRO 2057/M23

Manorial court of Burcombe and Ugford [Earl of Pembroke lord of the manor] 25 April 1716

Presentment of the Homage

Item, wee present that whereas Matthew Pitts Esqr intends to sett up a pair of hatches att the End of Holletts Meadow in order for drowning not only his

three Meadowes within this Mannor called by the severall names of Holletts, Long Draughts and After Ham, But also for drowning severall other meadowes within the said mannor belonging to Elias Chalke, William Selwood, Thomas London and Elias Downe, tenants of the said manor, It is thereupon ordered and agreed upon by and between us, the said homage, That the said Matthew Pitts being att and paying all the Costs, Charges and Expenses in or about setting up the aforesaid hatches all and every of them, the said Elias Chalke, William Selwood, Thomas London and Elias Downe shall and will permitt and suffer the said Matthew Pitts to bring the said water (soe comeing through the said hatches to be erected as aforesaid) throw any part of that meadow groundes where workmen shall adjudge it most convenient for their work, and it is agreed that every one of them the said Elias Chalke, William Selwood, Thomas London and Elias Downe, their and every of their assignes and servants shall have priviledge to drowne their groundes or meadowes with the same water comeing throw the said hatches in due and equall time and proportion one after another as their lands severally lay. A workman or head drowner being Chosen betweene the said Mr Pitts and all other the tenants aforesaid to direct and sett out every one of the said parties their respective stems of drowning as aforesaid.
Item, wee present that every person befor named shall bear, pay and discharge all Costs and Expenses att his own Charge for making the mayne Carriages, Stopps and Works for drowning as aforesaid soe farr and upon his their ground is soe watered.

Presentment of the Homage at the Manorial Court held 21 April 1718

Item, wee doe appoint and order Ambrose Phelpes to be the person or Agent for floating our Meadowes with water and drawing it of againe as the said Ambrose Phelpes shall see proper until the next Court to be held for the said Mannor in Anno 1719

[This appointment was repeated annually until 1723 when the Court Book ends]

CAPITALIST ENTERPRISE IN WOAD-GROWING

The profitability and remarkable increase in the cultivation of woad for use in the cloth industry was discussed in the Introduction. The surviving records of the wealthy Salisbury clothier, George Bedford, his son, also George, and the prominent lawyer, Henry Sherfield, reveal many aspects of this lucrative trade in the early 17th century. The crop required a considerable investment of capital. Woad was a hungry, demanding crop which could only be grown on the same land for a few seasons. Old grassland had to be rented for short periods, primitive mills had to be constructed for processing the woad leaves, and rough sheds erected to store the woad. It was moulded into balls which gave off a strong, unpleasant smell during a period of fermentation. Growing the crop employed many people; husbandmen had to be employed to cultivate the land and sow the seeds; many people were involved in weeding the plants, harvesting the leaves, and in the processes of milling and balling and the carriage of the dye. Those employed were distinguished by the smell and by their blue colour. During the late 16th and early 17th centuries George Bedford the elder leased many acres for woad-growing along the borders of Wiltshire, Dorset and Hampshire. In 1594, for example, he leased the whole of Ashcombe Warren in the parish of Berwick St John from Bartholomew and Francis Horsey. The lease was for three years, and Bedford agreed to a down-payment of £135 and an annual rent of £6 13s 4d. He thus obtained 200 acres of which 65 acres could be cultivated for woad. The Horseys agreed to manure this land with their sheep flock. The rabbits were to be kept on the rest of the warren, and independent assessors were to certify that '500 couples of coneys' remained at the expiry of the lease. [HRO 44M69/L28/3; L44/17].

Bedford also leased land for woad in Blagdon Park on the borders of Wiltshire and Dorset, and on the downland at Martin. When he died in 1607 George Bedford left 18 tons of woad worth £400 and 'an old woade house and fower woad mylles whereof twoe are at Marten and twoe at Blagdon'. [HRO 44M69/L44/16-18] His son, George Bedford, grew woad at Canford and Sturminster Marshall in Dorset. Henry Sherfield grew large quantities of woad on his land at Winterbourne Earls and Stratford sub Castle. A valuation of his estate in 1608 includes 'woade of the last yeare and this yeare yet in my hands £800'. In 1610 he leased 120 acres on Cranborne Chase for four years from Edward and Thomas Hooper of Boveridge in order to grow woad. Sherfield's woad was processed by Henry Cabell, a dyer of Salisbury. [J.H. Bettey, 'The

Cultivation of Woad in the Salisbury Area', Textile History, *9, 1978, 122-117); J.B. Hurry,* The Woad Plant and Its Dye, *1930; J. Thirsk,* Alternative Agriculture, *1997, 79-96].*

The following Inquiry into woad-growing in Wiltshire in 1585 was made in consequence of a Proclamation by Queen Elizabeth issued from her palace at Richmond on 14 October 1585. This complained that large areas of fertile ground were being converted to the cultivation of woad, 'to the great damage of the commonweal'. The Queen feared that food production would suffer and that there would be a dearth . She therefore ordered that no new ground should be broken up for woad, and that woad should not be grown 'within four miles of any market town, or other town occupying the common trade of clothing, or of any city within this realm or within eight miles of any house of her Majesty's reserved for her access'. All those growing woad were to certify the quantity of ground and its situation. [P.L. Hughes & J.F. Larkin, eds., Tudor Royal Proclamations, *II, 1969, No 678; III, 1969, No 802].*

The restrictions on woad-growing were later relaxed, but the Queen, like many of her subjects, continued to object strongly the obnoxious smell created by the process of fermenting woad leaves to make 'woad balls'. It was feared that the stench would create infection. Addressing the House of Commons the Queen urged that 'when she cometh in progress to see you in the country, she may not be driven out of your towns by suffering it [woad] to infect the air too near them'. [J. Thirsk, Alternative Agriculture, *1997, 85-8].*

The results of the 1585 Inquiry for Wiltshire were as follows:

Woad Growers in Wiltshire in 1585

PRO E 163/14/9

Wiltes.
Certificate of the High Constables within the said Countie touching the sowinge of oade [i.e. woad] as followeth:

The name of the towne	*The owner of the ground*	*The Tenant thereof*	*The No Acres*	*thequalitie of the same*
		The Hundred of Chipenham		
Slaughterford	The Duchess of Somerset	John Webbe	v acres	Pasture i Arable ii Meadow iii
Writhwraxall	John Mallett	John Webbe	½	Pasture
Coullerne	New College in Oxford	John Webbe	iv di [½]	arable

The name of the towne	*The owner of the ground*	*The Tenant thereof*	*The No Acres*	*thequalitie of the same*
	The Queen's Majestie	John Webbe	i	arable
Collerne	New College in Oxford	Robert Freeland	xi	arable v past. vi
	Mr Butler	Tho Symson Rich Bennett	i	pasture
Langley Burrell	Humfrey Reade gent.	William Eyrris	x	arable

The Hundred of Underdiche

The tithing of Milford	The Bishop of Sarum	Henry Beeford	ix	
		Tho Marshall Robert Eayer	xxviii	arable
		John Baylif	xliii	arable

The Hundred of Elstub and Everley

Collingborn	Tho Dowse		xxv	arable xx barr [barren] v
Fifilled	Edw Payshart		xi	arable
Urchfont	The Duchess of Somerset	Robert Green	xvi	pasture
Allcannings	The Duchess of Somerset	Robt Nicholas gent	vii	pasture

Branch and Dole Hundred

	John Basted Nicholas Mussell		i	garden ground

The Hundred of Kinwardstone

Burbage	The Lord Helford	John Ball	ii	meadow

The name of the towne	*The owner of the ground*	*The Tenant thereof*	*The No Acres*	*thequalitie of the same*
		The Hundred of Hieworth, Cricklad and Staple		
Sevenhampton and Estroppe	John Waneford Esq	The same John	xxiii di	pasture of the meane sort
Lint	Edw Fettyplace Esq	John Stock gent	xiii	pasture of the best
		The Hundred of Frustfeild		
Whitparishe	Tho Whitt Esq John Hurst	John Gaunlett Tho Mychell	xx di iiii	Rough ground grubbed for the purpose
		The Hundred of Amsbury		
Orkingham	John Plain?		iiii	arrable
		The Hundred of Malmesbury		
Chatley	John Warneford Esq		xxvi	pasture
		The Hundred of Selkeley		
Alborne	Geo and Tho Waldron gents Richard Goddard		ix vi di	
Ogbourne St George	William Young Vyncent Raymon		vii iiii	
Lockeridge	Edw Passior		iii	meadow
Wynterborn	Tho Browne		iii	
		The Hundred of Whorwellesdon		
Edington	Lord Marquess of Winchester	Peter Hayward	xiiii	meadow of the middle sort
Southwick	William Trencher Esq		i di	pasture

The name of the towne	*The owner of the ground*	*The Tenant thereof*	*The No Acres*	*thequalitie of the same*
Coulston	John Lambegke		viii	iiii arable iiii pasture

The Hundred of Dunworth

Westhache	Tho Bennett gent	Tho Bennett Tho Roose Henry Payne	xii	Meadow and pasture
Easthache	William Thresher Michall Grey	Tho Bennett Tho Roose Henry Payne	ii di	Meadow and pasture

The Hundred of Westbury

Westbury	The Queen's Majestie Tho Saunders Tho Webb gent	John Edwards Jone Phipp Tho Whatam	xv acres I roode	xiii pasture ii acres i roode arable

The Citie of New Sarum

New Sarum	Peter Hayward Robert Boston and others		ii	in garden ground and other plotts of ground

1585

Sum totall of the said severall kinds of ground employed to oade within the said County of Wiltshire this yere

cccxli acres I roode viz.

Meadow	xxvi acres
Pasture	iiii ^{xx} xiii acres iii qu [?quillets i.e. small plots]
Arrable	lxiii acres iii qu
Bared ground	xxix acres di
Rough ground	xx acres di
Good ground	xxiiii acres ii qu
Garden ground	iii acres

[Similar figures for woad grown in various counties including Wiltshire can be found in B.L. Lansdowne MSS 54(24) ff 124–125v; 57(28) f 132].

The following additional references to woad-growers in Wiltshire in 1585 are taken from a collection of declarations made by growers stating the acreage they were cultivating and certifying that the crops were not near any village or town. The declarations are in the form of letters addressed to Sir John Danvers, High Sheriff of Wiltshire, from the various growers. They are lengthy and repetitive, and the main points of each letter can be summarized as follows:

PRO E163/15/1

Certificates made to Sir John Danvers, High Sheriff of Wilts in pursuance of the Queen's Proclamation from those who have sown woade in the county: Declaring that the crops have been sown far from any town or habitation.

December 1585

Growers	*Woad Acreage*
John Ball of Burbage	1 acre in garden ground
Edward Passyon of Fyvefild	3 acres of meadow ground 6 acres in the common arable fields
George Walrond of Aldbourne & his brother [Thomas]	2 acres in the common fields 9 acres in 'a barron grounde adjoyinge to the Chace of Aldbourne not fyt for any other purpose as to be sowen with any manner of greyne because yt layeth upon the spoyle of deare and connies wherby no other profytt is to be hadd, and this beinge the firste yeare that my brother and my selfe have sowne ode'.
Henry Payne of Tysbury	xiiii acres of which iiii were meadow, the rest pasture and arable
John Warneford of Sevenhampton	xxiiii acres most pasture all lying in the parish of Highworth
William Trenchard of North Bradley	2 acres meadow pasture and garden ground
John Bayley (Bayliss) of St Martins in the City of New Sarum sowed	43 acres of former sheep pasture
John Allyn of Myldenhall	9 acres of newly broken ground
George Bedford of the City of New Sarum yeoman	1 acre in Milford and 7 acres of arable in the common fields of Milford

Growers	*Woad Acreage*
Thomas Marshall haberdasher and Robert Eyre clothier of the City of New Sarum	1 enclosed ground formerly a conniger [warren] containing 10 acres at Laverstock Another 5 acres in Laverstock of pasture Another 2 acres of sheep down in Laverstock Another 1 acre of pasture in Laverstock Another newe enclosed ground taken forth of the common feilds of Milforde near New Sarum Another 2 acres in the common fields of Milford
William Eyers of Salisbury	10 acres at Chippenham formerly arable
John Lambe	5½ acres in Cowlston part arable part pasture
Robert Boston of New Sarum	½ acre in various small plots at Laverstock
John Webbe of Slaughterford	10 acres of former pasture & arable
John Gauntlett of Whiteparish & Walter Drewe of Motson Southampton Co.	10 acres of sheep pasture in Whiteparish
William Younge of Ogbourne St George merchant	3 acres of arable and 4 acres of coney warren in Ogbourne St George
Vincent Rayman of Ogbourne St George 'merchant of the Staple of England'	4 acres of arable in Ogbourne St George

HRO 44M69/L26/2

Valuation of Henry Sherfield's estate, 18 October 1608

Credits owing to him on speciality [i.e. with contractor's bond]	£1210 19s 0d
Ready money	£ 360
Sheepe	£ 300
Wool	£ 140
Horses & tackling	£ 50
Woade	£ 500
Corne	£ 200
Leases in Blagdon parke	£ 20

Woade mylles & furniture		£ 10
Household stuff		£ 240
Kyne & Rother beasts		£ 26 6s 8d
Hogges & pigges		£ 20
Plate		£ 68
	Total	£3145 5s 8d

Another valuation on the same sheet dated 18 October 1608 also lists

'In woade of the last yeare & this yeare yet in my hands	£800
910 sheep	£173
Woade mylls	£ 10

HRO 44M69/L25/11

A Noat of the woad that was made this year 1628 of the first making

Ambrose West has had 20 hundred	£ 13 6s 8d
Mr Colborn of Lacoke had 3 hundred	£ 2 5s od
Delivered to Cabull 4 hundred for which he paid in part payment	£ 31 18s od
Delivered to Wm Singer of Bradford by Mr Roger Sherfield's appointment 4 hundred	
Sent to Newbury 3 hundred	
Sent to Andover 4 hundred	
Sent to London 10 hundred	
Delivered to Mr West 4 tunn and 12 hundred at 11s the hundred	

So that the parcell of woad in all delivered seaven tunns

44M69/L/25/12

A noat of the Second making of woad that was made this yeare 1628

Sent to mills	3 cwt
Delivered to Cabill	3 cwt
Sent to Andover	2 cwt
Delivered to Cabill	3 cwt

The account books and correspondence of the two Bedfords and Henry Sherfield include numerous references to the sale of woad to many dyers and clothiers, including customers from Salisbury, Devizes, Lavington, Lacock, Bradford, Newbury, Hungerford and Andover. In 1610, for example, James Ashe, a leading clothier from Batcombe, Somerset, ordered 12 cwt. of woad from Henry Sherfield 'or more yf yt can be spared'. The letter was endorsed by Sherfield 'I sent upon this letter 11 August 1610 by William Tucker 12 cwt of my Woade for which Mr Ayshe doth owe me after £21 the tonne'. The following bonds entered into by farmers show the initial work involved in growing woad and the way in which this was organised. The crop is variously named as 'woad', 'oad', or 'wood'.

Each of these bonds commits the various farmers to cultivate the land and sow woad on behalf of George Bedford in return for specified sums of money. Of the farmers involved, only the last, William Lammann, signed his name. The others all made their mark. The terms 'ear', 'vallowe', 'plowe', 'harrowe', 'roole', and 'dragge', all refer to different methods of ploughing, cultivating and preparing the ground for the woad or a corn crop.

Bonds for the Cultivation of Land for Woad or Grain 1596-1603

HRO 44M69/L57/2

Bond between William White of East Martin, husbandman, and George Bedford of New Sarum, clothier, for £12.

21 May 1597

Be it knownen to all men by these presents That I, William White of Easte Martyn in the Countie of Wiltes, husbandman, for and in consideration of the Some of Twelve Pounds and odd moneye of currant Englishe moneye to me before the sealing hereof in hand payed by George Bedford of the Cittie of Newe Sarum in the sayd Countie of Wiltes, Clothier, dothe assume and promise for me, myne executors and assignes To eare and sowe for oade or corne Twelve Acres of Grownde of the sayd George Bedford or his assignes in Blagdon Parke in the Countie of Dorsett for the space of three yeares from the daye of the date hereof in manner and forme following, that is to saye, this firste yeare to be eared three tymes so muche of the sayd Twelve Acres of grounde as it shalbe Thoughte good by the sayd George Bedford or his assignes to his most profit. And for thother two yeres of the said three yeares to vallowe and sowe with two earthes the sayd Twelve Acres of grounde to the best profit of the sayd George Bedford and his assignes. To the which assumuncion and promise aforesaid, I the sayd William White doe bynd me, myne executors and administrators unto the sayd George Bedford, his executors and assignes for the trewe performance thereof. In witness whereof I have hereunto sett my hande and seale, the one and twentyth daye of Maye in the nyne and thirtythe yeare of the Raigne of our Soveraigne Ladye Elizabeth the Quenes Majestie that nowe ys.

HRO 44M69/L57/3

Bond between William Sivior of Martin, husbandman, and George Bedford of New Sarum, clothier, for £6.

12 July 1597

The Condition of this Obligation is such that whereas the above bounded William Sivior nowe at the sealing hereof hath hadd and receyved of the abovenamed George Bedford the Some of Sixe pounds of Currant Englishe moneye, If therefore the sayd William Sivior, his executors or assignes, shall plowe or eare in Blagdon Parke in the Countie of Dorsett Twelve Acres of grounde there of the sayd Beorge Bedford or his assignes at such seizenable tymes as shalbe thought meete by the sayd George or his assignes, in manner and form following, that is to saye, All the hare grase grounde of the sayd twelve acres to be eared three several tymes, and the residue of the sayd twelve acres to be eared once. And the sayd twelve acres also to be edged and dragged at the tyme of sowing to the best profit of the said George or his assignes, betweene the Feast daye of Sainte Andrewe th'appostle [30 November] next ensuing the date hereof and the first Daye of Maye then next followinge. And further if the sayd William Sivior, or his assignes doe soe much worke for the sayd George Bedford or his assignes as shall come unto the Some of Fortie Shillings eyther in tillage or carridge after the rate as is gyven to his neighbours and the same worke to be done betweene the XXVth of August next ensueing the date hereof and the Feast of Pentecost then next followinge which sayd fortie shillings the sayd William Sivior hathe recyved of the said George before thensealing hereof. That then this Obligacion to be voyd and of none effect or els it to stande, remayne and be in his full force strength effect and vertue.

HRO 44M69/L57/4

Bond between William White of East Martin, husbandman and George Bedford of New Sarum, clothier, for £14.

15 March 1597

The condition of this presente obligacion is suche that if the above bounden William White, his executors, administrators and assignes or anie of them doe bringe Four carte loads of wood or woade from Blagdon Parke to the Cittie of Newe Sarum for the above named George Bedford, his executors or assignes, at or before the fifteenth daye of Maye next ensuinge the date hereof. And alsoe doe plowe, eare, sowe and edge Tenn Acres of grounde in Blagdon Parke in the Countie of Dorsett for the said George Bedforde, his executors or assignes at or before the Twentieth daye of October next ensuinge the date hereof, the sayde George Bedforde, his executors or assignes, fyndinge wheate for the sowinge thereof, That then this presente obligation to be utterly voyde, of none effecte or els to stande remaine and abide in his full power, force, effect and vertue.

HRO 44M69/L57/5

Bond between Henrie Whittyer of Boveridge, yeoman, and George Bedforde of the City of New Sarum, clothier, for £6.

24 April 1602

The condicion of this obligation is suche that if the above bounden Henrie Whittyer, his executors or assignes doe and shall at anytyme when he or they shalbe thereunto required duringe the tearme of one yeare nexte ensuinge the date hereof, in good and husbandlike order and sorte and for the best commoditie and profitt of the above named George Bedforde, till, plowe, eare and harrowe for the said George Bedforde Ten Acres of ground lyinge and beinge in Blagdon Parke in the countie of Dorset to sowe oade in, That then this obligation to be void and of none effecte or els it to stande, abide and remayne in his full power, strength and vertue.

HRO 44M69/L57/6

Bond between Edmund Sweeteaple of West Martin, husbandman, and George Bedforde of the city of New Sarum, clothier, for £6

3 July 1602

The condicion of this obligation is suche that if the above bounden Edmunde Sweeteaple, his executors and administrators or assignes doe and shall at his and theire owne proper costs and chardges at suche tyme as Bedforde, his executors or assignes at or before the three and twentieth daye of April nexte ensuinge the date hereof, till, plowe, eare, harrowe and roole in good husbandlike order and sorte and for the beste benefitt and comodie of the said George Bedforde, twentye acres of earrable lande lyinge in Blagdon Parke in the counties of Dorset and Wiltes, such as the said George Bedford or his assignes shall assigne and appoynte, That then this presente obligacon to be voide and of none effecte or els it to stande and remayne in his full strengthe and vertue.

HRO 44M69/L57/7

Bond between John Harris of West Martin, husbandman, and George Bedford of the City of New Sarum, clothier, for £10.

4 November 1602

The condicon of this obligacon is suche that if the above bounden John Harris, his executors, administrators or assignes doe and shall well sufficiently and in good husbandlike order and sorte till, plowe, eare, harrowe and sowe to and for the above named George Bedforde, his executors or assignes, Twentie ackers of lande lyinge and beinge in Blackdin Parke in the countie of Dorset whereof fower are to be sowen with oade, sixe with barlie and ten with peason, at or before the Twentieth daye of Aprill nexte ensuinge the date hereof . That then this present obligacon to be voide and of none effect or els it to stande, abide and remayne in his full power, strength and vertue.

HRO 44M69/L57/8

Bond between William White of Martin, yeoman, and George Bedford of the city of New Sarum, clothier, for £15.

9 November 1602

The condicon of this obligacon is suche that if whereas the above bounden William White hath granted and lette to thabove named George Bedforde All that parte or parcell of grounde called and knowen by the name of Old Close lyinge and beinge in Blagdon Parke in the countie of Dorset conteyninge by estimacion ten acres, be it more or lesse, To holde from the feast of St Michaell th'archangell [29 September] nexte ensuinge the date hereof for the tearme of three yeares then nexte followinge, Yf therefore he, the said George Bedforde, his executors and assignes shall and maye peaceablie and quietlie have, holde and enjoye the said parte or parcell of grounde called Old Close by and duringe all the said tearme of three yeares aforesaid without the lett or deniall of the said William White, his executors or assignes or of any other person or persons whatsoever, And also if the said William White, his executors or assignes doe and shall at his or theire owne proper costs and chardges well sufficientlie and in good husbandlike order and sorte and for the best benefitt and profitt of the said George Bedforde yearely and every yeare during the said tearme at such tymes and seasons as the said George Bedforde, his executors or assignes shall appointe grubb, eare, till, plowe, vallowe, harrowe, dragge, rowle and sowe for the said George Bedforde the saide parte or parcell of grounde called Old Close to sowe wheate, barlie, oade or other grayne he, the said George Bedforde, findinge and providinge seede to sowe the same. That then this presente obligacon to be voide and of none effecte or els yt to stande, abide and remaine in his full power, strength and vertue.

HRO 44M69/L57/9

Bond between Edmunde Streate of Tidpitt in the parish of Martin, yeoman, and George Bedford of the city of New Sarum, clothier, for £16.

17 March 1602

The condicon of this obligacon is suche that if the above bounden Edmund Streate, his executors, administrators or assignes (at his and their owne proper costs and chardges) doe and shall Betweene the Feast daye of St Andrew th'appostle [30 November] nexte ensuinge the date hereof and the three and twentieth daye of Aprill then nexte followinge well sufficientlie and in good husbandlike order and sorte and for the best benefitt and commoditie of the said George Bedforde till, plowe, eare and harrowe with one earthe for the sowinge of oade one grounde of the said George Bedford's called Rowe Coppice conteyninge by estimacon Sixteene Acres be it more or lesse, lyinge and beinge in Blagdon Parke in the countie of Dorset, That then this obligacon to be voide and of none effecte or els it to stande and remayne in his full strength and vertue.

HRO 44M69/L57/10

Bond between William Lammann of Martin, husbandman, and Jeffery Lammann, husbandman, of the same place and George Bedford of the city of New Sarum, clothier, for £15.

29 May 1603

he condicon of this obligacon is suche that if the above bounden William Lammann and Jeffery their or either of theire executors, administrators or assignes or any or either of them doe well and sufficiently and in good husbandlike sort eare, plowe, harrowe and dragge by and for the use, best profitt, benefitt and advantage of George Bedforde of the Cittie of Newe Sarum in the county of Wiltes, Clothier, his executors or assignes shall appointe the one moytye or half parte of one close of pasture grounde commonly called or knowne by the name of Smalle Thornes lyeinge and being in a place or uppon a downe called Martyn Downe in the county aforesaid nexte unto a highe waye commonly called Blandforde Way betweene the Feast daye of All Saints [1 November] next ensuinge the date hereof and the fowerteenth day of Aprill then nexte followinge to be done in manner and forme as aforesaid, and to the best profitt, benefitt and advantage of the said George Bedforde, his executors and assignes as aforesaid, That then this obligacon to be void and of none effecte or els yt to staye, abide and remayne in his full power, strength and vertue.

Sales of Woad

Woad grown by Wiltshire entrepreneurs such as George Bedford and Henry Sherfield was sold directly to clothiers and dyers rather than to the merchants involved in the long-standing trade in imported woad. The two following letters illustrate both the scale of the trade and some of the problems encountered. The writer, Roger Sherfield, was the younger brother of Henry Sherfield. Roger obviously acted on behalf of his brother, whose extensive business affairs, legal practice, money-lending and membership of the House of Commons meant that he spent much time in London. The religious tone of the letters reflects Henry Sherfield's strongly-held Puritan views. These were later to involve him in trouble when he smashed a medieval stained-glass window in St Edmund's church, Salisbury, on the grounds that because it depicted God the Father it was popish and idolatrous. Henry Sherfield was married twice, but had only one daughter of his own. The Roger referred to in the letters was a son of the writer, Roger Sherfield. He was no doubt in France and the Low Countries as a result of a project financed by Henry Sherfield, of which details are given in the Introduction. The purpose was to obtain details of the cultivation of oil-seed rape, cole and madder on the Continent, and to acquire seeds and roots for cultivation in England. This project was successfully completed by Henry Sherfield's step-son, George Bedford, who grew madder plants for dye near Appledore in Kent. Sherfield's account book reveals that he grew rape and cole on his Wiltshire lands. The precise nature of the 'danger' referred to in the second letter is not clear. There was the fear that the foul smell of fermenting woad would breed infection, but it is more likely to have been the possibility of commercial or legal threats from merchants and monopolists with vested interest in importing woad rather than any physical jeopardy. [J.H. Bettey, 'Henry Sherfield of Salisbury', Hatcher Review, *9, 1980, 19-27; W.H. Price,* The English Patents of Monopoly, *1906, 149].*

HRO 44M69/L63/5

To my Loving brother Mr Henry Sherfield in Mynsinge Lane, London. 7 August 1627

From Roger Sherfield, Wallop
Most deere and Lovinge brother in especiall I hoape that god doth continewe your health. Had I noe cause to write to you, yeat must it not be a shame to me the neglect thereoff then most apparent having some cause, although I could never nor ever did you any substantial good, yeat I have and ever will endevour the same. Yf wordlie things concerninge us shall not fadge [?], I doubt not but wee at length shall achieve the better things.

What is the true cause I knowe not, but your woade answereth not your expectacon. I caused your baylie [bailiff] to meet me at the Devizes where wee had full conference with Coborne after his having twoe – [?samples] of the oade. After the expense of many words and best eloquence, wee solde unto him five Tunne after the meane rate of xxis vid the hundred and hee to paye your man for the carriage of the same to Lavington vid for every hundred. I was willinge to have had him had all, but hee would not except hee might have had our espnatle [?] daie [i.e. long credit] for the rest. Wee intende this weeke with the best care we can use. to take and sende him one loade and soe the rest with speede convenient. I hoape there is noe dainger but I will not come neare it. Hee will shortlie paye Davydd Gayne [Henry Sherfield's servant] som xl or l li and the rest about a moneth after Michaelmas. Had I not made a true triall of a sufficient dyer of Nubery [Newbury, Berks.] which had tried it and came to my house with a seeminge willingnesse to deale for all, but by noe meanes woulde geve more than xixs the hundred, hee saide hee woulde be as good a chapman [dealer] as an other, desiringe to heare from me when I shoulde make full triall. I have wrytten to him the trueth of the proceedinge, it may be hee will come on, yf not wee might cast aboute.

Fye on this troblesome world, when we have a full broode of children and they under our wings, with a weepinge noyse offend us. Neverthelesse we flie after the Bussard [Buzzard] for theire preservation. Because it pleased you in your last letter to remember Roger, I have the rather sent you in this his letter which doth in some sort troble me and very much his mother. Yf you can afforde us better reasons for his soe longe stay, than we can apprehend praie lett us have them. And soe remembringe my hartie love to my Sister [i.e. sister-in-law]. I leave you boath to god, prayinge him to blesse, preserve and keepe

Your Lovinge brother
Wallop 7 August 1627. Roger Sherfield

HRO 44M69/L63/6

To my Lovinge brother Mr Henry Sherfield in Mynsinge Lane, London

From Roger Sherfield, Wallop
Most Lovinge brother my god I hoape hath preserved you in health. My Cosen John Wrothesley had my letter directed unto Colborne and I make noe question but it proved the xx li for Poultney. Your Baylief nor my selfe have had noe money of Colborne, nether was our bargaine to have any before hee had good proffe of the oade, hee beinge the onlie cause that we have sent none to Lavington as yeat for him, where I, accordinge to our agreement, procured a howse for the receipt of his whole some, for hee although hee was in your woade howse and sawe your woade and understood the neareness of dainger, it nothinge frited him, but it seemeth tyme and better consideracon caused him to send word that by noe meanes it should be sent untill his mynde were better resolved. God forbid I shoulde have in hand or be acquainted with sendinge of that which might be daingerous for the receiver without enlarginge my letter in clearinge doubts, I presume with god's favour it shall be noe dainger to anye. I doubt not but eare longe we shall laye in this whole bargaine att Lavington in Cranlies brothers howse with his owne consent, but in the meane space your people with other work have not bin idle, for they have caried three loades for one Mr Houghton of Nubery, twoe of them to his howse, the other to his dye howse in Hungerford, for hee hath bought all besides that Colbornes five Tunne. Hee giveth just as Colborne doth, and xiiis iiiid for every tunns carridge, but beleeve mee I shoulde never have brought him to the price had not Colborne first seized. Without doubt the most is made, money being had, but I hoaped better of it. I feare it was not well ordered in makinge, and I beleeve you would say soe yf you sawe it. You have good stoare of woade on the grounde at the Castle [i.e. Stratford sub Castle]. Davyd Gayne doth in trueth bestire him well in your affaires, and in my Judgment deserveth well. It cannot be hurtful if hee by you understand my good applause.

I may not forgett to tell you that we heare nothinge of Roger. I thanke you for your good consideracons, my wiefe hath ruminated them and well digested all and nowe resteth in good plight. You wryte that you have bin a little trobled in observinge where he dated the last letter which you nowe supposed you had sent inclosed in myne, consideringe that it was dated at Caen, and his repaire for newes from mee –[?] looke in his letter, I thinke hee speaketh not of St Mallos neither did I –[?] speake of that Towne, soe I wonder howe hee came in, I did wryte that he spent for the most of his tyme in St Loe, and for your better information hee att Caen as I thinke, received both money and letters from St Loe by the conveyance of his factor, one Mr Thomas Seale, whoe is lidger there for Mr Seale of Southampton. Mr Seale of Hampton hath latelie tolde a neighbour of myne that his Factor whoe is nowe in Garnesey [Guernsey] did wryte him a letter that Roger was removed from Caen to Paris, with an intent to visite an universitie in the Lowe Countries and soe for England. If he hath performed this and hath written as you –[?], he [?is]- worth the whistlelinge, for god I praye so blesse, preserve and keep you with yours, and I fear not but I shall have yenough of him.

Your ever Lovinge brother
Roger Sherfield

Wallop 7 [?**recte** 30] August 1627

Endorsed: 30 August 1627 from Salisbury by Tom Sherfield.
Endorsed: From my brother Roger Sherfield 30 August 1627

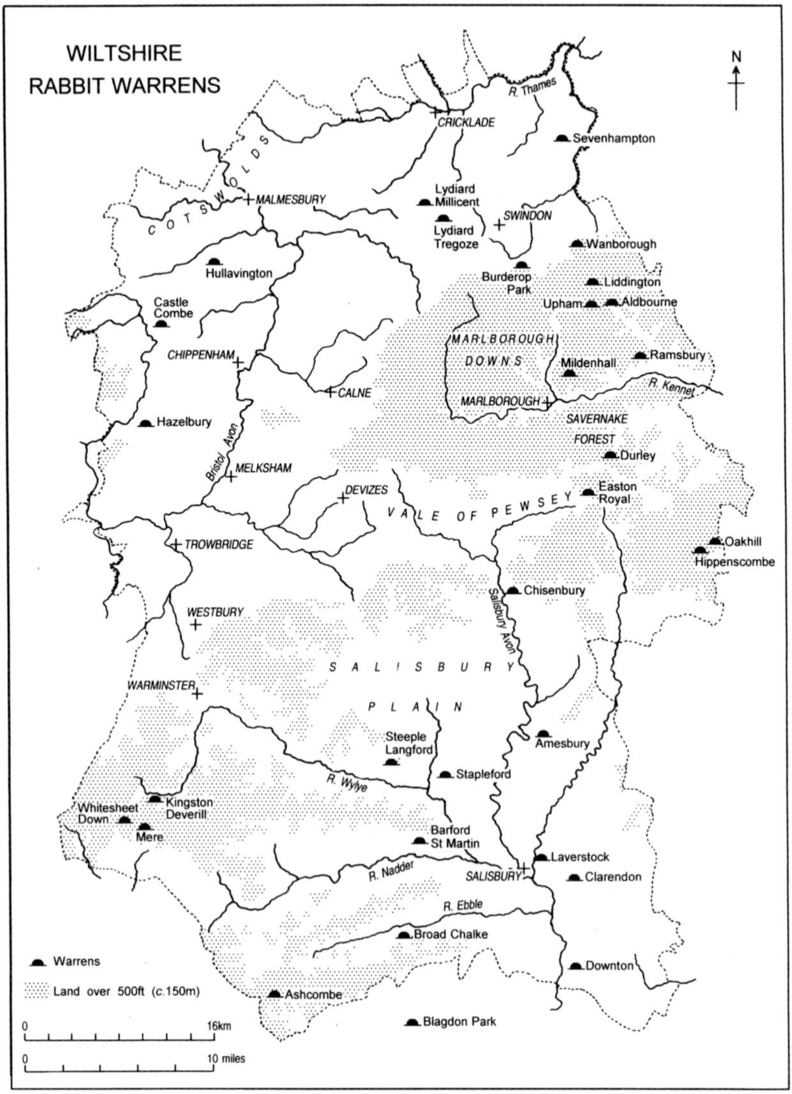

Wiltshire rabbit warrens, map produced by James and Tina Bond, and reproduced with their kind permission.

RABBIT OR CONEY WARRENS

*The number of 'Warren' or 'Warren Farm' place-names which survive all across the high chalk downland bears witness to the profitability and scale of the former trade in rabbits. An alternative name for a rabbit warren was 'conygre', which also occurs as a place-name across the chalklands. During the 17th century the adults were always referred to as 'coneys', and only the young or immature were described as 'rabbits'. At Broad Chalke in 1631, for example, the rent of the warren included 10 couple of coneys and 10 couple of rabbits. [*WRS*, IX, 1953, 11-12]. Coneys were valued for their flesh and skins, and for their fur which was used in the manufacture of hats; their capacity to breed rapidly meant that warrens provided a lucrative use for thin chalkland soils.*

*Some Wiltshire warrens had been established during the later Middle Ages. The most famous was at Aldbourne where many thousands of rabbits were produced during the 15th century. In 1434, for example, 1000 rabbits valued at £14 were supplied to the royal household, and the warren was let for £40 a year. [*VCH Wilts*, IV, 1959, 18; XII, 1983, 78-9]. Among numerous other early warrens in the county were those at Castle Combe, Lydiard Tregoze, Berwick St John, Tidcombe, Clarendon, Mildenhall and Broad Chalke. In his will of 1598, the Bristol merchant, Sir John Young, left to his wife, Joan, his mansion in Bristol and his warren at Hazelbury. From Hazelbury she was to have 'two hundrethe cupple of connies yearlie to be taken uppon the warren groundes there to her said use at such time as she shall require the same'. [PRO PROB 11/74].*

The documents which follow illustrate the large production of rabbits in the 17th century and the high rents paid for the lease of warrens, either in money or in very large numbers of rabbits. It was generally reckoned during the early 17th century that 200 coneys would produce enough progeny to bring in a profit of £20 a year, at a cost of no more than £2. This was a higher yield than could be achieved by any other livestock. [J. Thirsk, ed., Agrarian History of England & Wales 1640-1750, *V (ii), 1985, 544]. During the course of the century, however, the increasing profitability of corn crops, coupled with the problems which rabbits escaping from warrens caused to neighbours, meant that in many places the rabbits were destroyed and the land was converted to arable. The use of the former warrens at Ashcombe and elsewhere on Cranborne Chase for the cultivation of woad has been described earlier in this volume. On the exposed downland the rabbits had to be carefully managed if they were to survive the harsh winters and deep snows of the 17th century. The following documents provide evidence of the artificial burrows or 'berryes' which were provided for them, and the provision of hay, bracken and 'rowe' or coarse grass during the winter. At Amesbury in 1609, for example, a Survey of the Park noted that 'two rounde Coney berryes' had been constructed, and 14 couple of coneys had been installed in them. [WSRO 283/6 Book D 1605-9]. Without access to food, rabbits would starve during prolonged periods of frost and snow, and were, therefore, provided with branches of elder, hazel and other bushes from which they could nibble the bark. Leases often gave warreners licence to cut branches for this purpose. Much care was taken to protect the rabbits from predators such as stoats, weasels, foxes and hawks, and there are numerous references to traps, 'falls' and 'engines' for catching vermin. Warrens were also enclosed with banks and fences in an attempt, not always successful, to prevent the rabbits from straying.*

The most common variety was the familiar wild rabbit which was described by 17th century warreners as 'gray'; some black rabbits were also kept and these commanded a higher price. When Sir Charles Somerset was making a new warren on his estate in Monmouthshire in 1582 he sought gifts of rabbits from his friends, and, for example, wrote to Matthew Smyth of Long Ashton asking for 'as many doe conyes as convenyently you can spare, not prejudicing your game, the most black, yf you have any store'. [BRO AC/C26]. Rabbits were caught for sale using ferrets, nets and 'coney-dogs'. The rapid acceleration and high speed of a rabbit over short distances meant that clever and speedy dogs were required. They were normally muzzled to prevent damage to the rabbit carcasses.

Warrens were often provided with a 'lodge' where the warrener and his family lived, as well as with sheds for the storage of equipment. This enabled the warren-keeper to maintain a close watch on the rabbits, since poachers were an even greater problem than predators. Warrens on the Longleat estate were especially vulnerable to poachers from Warminster. In 1687 they attacked one warren in broad daylight, threatening violence to the warrener and his wife and breaking the windows of the lodge. There were numerous similar incidents involving the poaching of both rabbits and deer. [D.R. Hainsworth, Stewards, Lords and People, *1992, 219]. Warren keepers were frequently prosperous men, handling large and profitable transactions. Their business was far from being peripheral or the concern of the lowest section of society. Rabbits were sold in local markets, but many were also purchased by dealers for sale in London.*

Rabbits are notoriously destructive creatures, and there were many 17th century disputes over the damage they caused. The documents which follow show that rabbits destroyed woodland and coppices, and were often highly unpopular with neighbouring arable farmers whose growing crops were eaten by rabbits escaping or straying from warrens. Although there are numerous references in the following documents to fences and 'pales' around warrens, these did not provide an adequate barrier to burrowing rabbits. Before the introduction of wire-netting in the 19th century, rabbits could not totally be prevented from escaping, and it was not easy for warren keepers to live in harmony with their farming neighbours. The record of disputes and legal suits about warrens and the damage caused by rabbits provides a fruitful source of information about the subject. For example, throughout the 17th century there were recurrent complaints to the earls of Hertford from tenants at Tidcombe about the damage caused by rabbits from the large warrens at Hippenscombe and Oakhill. In 1631 and 1632 the rabbits were said to have invaded corn fields and to have destroyed large areas of woodland and coppice. In 1639 there were complaints about the large numbers of rabbits being bred in the warrens, and it was alleged that the tenants, John and Edmund Vincent, were enjoying an annual income of £320 from the sale of rabbits. Complaints continued during the century, until in 1710 it was stated that the warrens had been abandoned and the land ploughed. It was alleged, however, that because of the large number of rabbits formerly kept, all the timber trees and valuable coppice wood had been destroyed. Evidence in this case was given by Edward Lisle of Crux Easton in Hampshire, author of the influential farming treatise Observations in Husbandry. *Lisle farmed at Crux Easton during the early 18th century. He was involved in the dispute over the warrens as a trustee in the marriage of one of the litigants. [WSRO 9/17/22; 9/17/23; 9/17/34; 9/17/35; PRO E134/1658/Mich. 24]. At Mere in 1617 the surveyor, John Norden, reported 'There was a warren upon a downe called Swincombe which by the petition of the tennants was destroied and they were to paie £4 for a rente in lieue thereof'. He added 'they have discontinued the rent for some yeares past – to be recovered'. [PRO LR2/207 ff 24-24v].*

The warren at Aldbourne gave rise to even more complaints and court cases over the number of rabbits and the damage they caused. Partly this was the result of confusion over the bounds of the Chase and the limits of the warren within it. The following extracts illustrate the succession of disputes over Aldbourne warren and the remarkable number of rabbits produced there during the period 1617-25. Throughout the 1650s and 1660s there was a succession of legal suits involving the Earl of Pembroke who had leased the Chase, the freeholders and tenants of Aldbourne and the various keepers of the warren. Parts of the warren were converted to arable during the 1670s, but the North Walk remained as a warren, and John Aubrey described the rabbits from Aldbourne as 'our famous coney-warren; and the conies there are the best, sweetest, and fattest of any in England; a short, thick coney, and exceeding fatt'. By the end of the 17th century there was said to be a stock of 8000 rabbits at Aldbourne, increasing annually to 24,000. [PRO STAC 8/212/6; Calendar of State Papers, Domestic, *1660-85, 279-81; WSRO 1883-288; J. Aubrey,* Natural History of Wiltshire, *1969 edn., 59]. The difficulty of confining rabbits and the damage they caused, together with the rising profitability of corn crops, led to many warrens being converted to arable during the second half of the 17th century. For much of the century, however, the production of huge numbers of rabbits in warrens was an important aspect of Wiltshire farming.*

[J. Sheail, 'Rabbits and Agriculture in Post-Medieval England', Journal of Historical Geography, *4, 1978, 343-55; J. Bettey, 'The Production of Rabbits in Wiltshire during the Seventeenth Century',* Antiquaries Journal, *84, 2004, 380-92]*

A Lease of Mildenhall Warren 1586

WSRO 442/1 ff260v-261

Survey of Mildenhall 17th September 28th Elizabeth [1586]
Lord of the manor Sir Walter Hungerford
William Jones claymeth to holde for terme of his life of the grant of Sir Walter Hungerford, knyght, by Indenture made to John Jones, his father, deceased, and to hym the said William and Stephen Jones his brother, lykewise deceased, dated on the feast of St Michael th'archangel Anno sedo Elizabeth Regina, All that Warren Lodge, Game and Slaughter of Conyes lying in the parishe of Mildenhall called by the name of Burredge with all and singular th'appurtences to the same belonging, Paying therefore yerly of Rent foure hundred Couple of Conyes to be spent at the Mansyon house of the Lord so that he kepe house any where within Thirtye miles of Mildenhall to be fetched and carryed away at the charge of the Lord, his heire and assignes. The tenant fyndyng unto those that shall fetche them horse meate and mans meate as often as they shalbe so fetched. And if the Lord shall happen not to dwell within Thirtye miles of Mildenhall then the tenant to pay of rent x li at our Lady Daye and Michaelmas by even porcyons [portions]. The tenant by covenant shall at their owne charges when nede shal require during their severall termes repayre the said Lodge, taking sufficient house boote [right to timber for house repairs] upon the premysses by th'assignment of the Lord, his heires or assigns, Provided allwayes and the Lord doth covenant that it shalbe lawfull for the tenant at all tymes when nede shall require to take sufficient matchwood to be spent within the said Lodge. And also to pleache the frythe [brushwood, undergrowth] of the Berryes as also to cutt frythe to stragge [cover] the berryes and to make Gynnes [gins] for the destruction of vermyn. And the tenant doe covenant to kepe from hurte of the said conyes the woodds called Thickett Sound and Matham. And if it happen the said foure hundred cuople of Conyes to be behinde and not paid in forme aforesaid if the Lord happen to kepe house as aforesaid, and if not then if the said rent of x li be unpaid by a moneth after anye of the said feasts of payment. That then the Lord and his heires may reenter, the Indenture notwithstanding Attornyes to geve possession Thomas Franklin, Thomas Cooke and William Hull
Rent 400 couple of conyes or x li

[For lease of the warren in 1613 see WSRO 442/2 f.344]

A Lease of Easton Royal Warren 1608

Considerable information concerning the management of rabbit warrens is to be found in this lease. The fact that the Earl of Hertford and his steward were prepared to go to the expense of such an elaborate and complex agreement is an indication of the value and profitability of a warren. The site of this warren is still known as Congyre Farm, and is only 2½ miles from the Earl's mansion at Tottenham Park. Clearly the Earl was particularly concerned about the conduct of this warren, and reserved the right to graze his own livestock on it. The term 'coney-catcher' was used by contemporaries for rogues and those practising deception; undesirable men were evidently attracted to warren-keeping and the Earl was anxious that such persons should not be established close to his house. The terms of the lease illustrate the importance of preserving the artificial burrows or 'berryes' for the rabbits, the need to maintain the traps for predators, and, above all, the importance of confining the rabbits within the warren, so that they did not damage the crops of neighbours. It was the problems caused by escaping rabbits which made warrens unpopular, and the impossibility of keeping the rabbits confined was eventually a major reason for the decline of warrens.

This particular lease provides good evidence of the productivity of rabbits within a warren. Clearly, a breeding stock of 600 couples could be expected to produce each year sufficient progeny to bring a good income for the warreners, as well as producing 500 couples as rent. The lease reveals that in addition to the £5 per annum as money rent, the 500 couples were valued at 10d per couple making a total of £20 16s 8d, or the large sum of £25 16s 8d total rent. The warren was a profitable investment, both for the Earl and for the warreners.

WSRO 9/15/17

This Indenture made the firste day of December in the yeres of the Raigne of our most gratious Soveraigne Lorde James, by the grace of God of England, Scotland, France and Ireland, Kynge, defender of the faith etc. That is to saye of England, France and Ireland the Sixthe and of Scotland the Two and Fortithe, Between the Right Honourable Sir Edward Seymour, Knight, Baron Beauchamp and Earle of Hertford of th'one parte and Michiell Clarke th'elder of Eston in the Countie of Wiltes, yeoman, and James Whithart, husbandman, of th'other parte Witnessth that the said Erle for divers and sundrye good causes and considerations him, the said Erle, thereunto especially moving, Hath demised, betaken and to fearme letten and by these presents doth demise, betooke and to fearme lett unto the said Michaell Clarke th'elder and James Whithart and theire assigne or assignes, All that his Warren commonlye called or knowne by the name of Eston Warren standinge and beinge in and uppon one Close of pasture of the said Erles commonly called the Conygere within the parish of Eston aforesaid in the said Countye of Wiltes, conteyninge by estimation One hundethe and fiftye acres sometyme devided into severall closes and nowe beinge together all in one close. And also all that his game of Connyes within or uppon the said Warren close or grounde, together with all the increase and breed that shall or may hereafter renewe, growe or become thereof, and with free liberty of keeping, feedinge and killinge of Connyes within or uppon the said Waren close or grounde. And also all that the said Erle, his close pasture or earrable grounde beinge in Eston Priorye conteyninge by estimation Sixteene acres between the land of the said Erle being parcell of one of his Lordship's manors of Burbage in the tenure of William Baynton and Martha Pye, widowe, on the one side, and a parcell of grounde called the Breache on the west side, the lane leading betweene Burbage and Eston on the southside, and one other parte of the said Erle his land on the northe side of newlie inclosed and nowe beinge inclosed with a hedge from other partes of the said close called the Breach. To have, houlde, use, occupie and enjoye the said Warren and game of Connyes and also the said close of paasture or earrable and all other the premisses before by these presentes demised or mentioned to be demised unto the said Michaell Clarke the elder and James Whithart and theire assignes from the feast of the Annunciation of the blessed virgin Marye [25 March] last before the date of these presentes forthewards for and duringe and to the full end and terme of Twelve yeres from thence next ensuinge fully to be complete and ended if the said Michaell Clarke the elder and James Whithart, or either of them shall so longe lyve. Yeildinge and payinge yerelie for the said close of pasture or earrable grounde newlie inclosed conteyninge by estimation Sixteene acres before demised or mentioned to be demised Fyve poundes of currant Englishe money at two termes in the yere most usuall, That is to say at the feast day of the Annunciation of the blessed virgin Marye and St Michaell Th'archangell [29 September] by even and equall portions. Provided alwayes and uppon Condition that if it shall happen the said yerelie rent or any parte thereof to be behind unpaid by the space of twentye dayes next after any of the said feast dayes in which it ought to be paied, the same havinge been lawfullye demanded at the house or lodge in the said close called the Connygre and not paied, that then this presente graunt and demise and the estate before limited to cease, determyne and be utterlye voyde, and that from thenceforthe it shall and may be lawfull to and for the said Erle, his heires and assignes, and every of them into all and singular, the premises mentioned to be demised and into every parte thereof whollie to reenter, and the same to have agayne, repossesse and enjoye as in his or theire former estate, and the said Michaell Clarke the elder and James Whithart and their assignes and everye of them from thence utterlie to expell, putt on and remove anie thinge in these presentes to the contrary conteyned in anie wyse notwithstandinge. And the said Erle for himselfe, his heires, executors and assignes and for every of them, doth covenante, promise, graunte and agree to and with the said Michaell Clarke the elder, James Whithart and theire executors, administrators and assignes and everye of them, by these presentes in manner and forme followinge, That is to saie that he, the said Erle, his heires and assignes shall and will yerelie, during the said terme for the consideration aforesaid, uppon reasonable request to be made to the said Erle, his heires or assignes, or to his or theire Surveyor, woodward or other officer for such purpose from tyme to tyme to be appointed, allowe and by themselves, or some or one of theire said officers appointe unto the said Michaell Clarke the elder and James Whithart, or theire assignes sterned, [?dead] sere [withered] and dead topped tree nowe or hereafter standinge or beinge in or uppon anie of the said Erles severall woodes or groundes within Eston aforesaid, Bowdon or Savernak Forest in the said countye of Wiltes in or uppon anie of them, the fellinge and carriage whereof to be at the proper costs and chardges of the said Michaell Clark the elder and James Whithart, or of theire assignes. And also that it shall and may be lawfull to and for the said Michaell Clarke the elder and James Whithart, and theire assignes to keepe, depasture and feed from tyme to tyme duringe the said terme one horse beaste in or uppon the said warren close or ground aforesaid called the Connigere. And the said Michaell Clarke and James Whithart for themselves, and either of them, theire heires, executors, administrators and assignes doe and doth covenant and graunt joyntelie and severally, to and with the said Erle, his heires and assignes, to and with everye of them, by these presentes in manner and forme followinge, that is to say, that they the said Michaell Clarke and James Whithart, or theire assignes shall and will, for and in consideration of this demise or lease, yelde, paie or deliver unto the said Erle, his heires or assignes yerelie duringe the said terme, Fyve hundrethe Cooples of Connyes reckoninge Fyve score Cooples of Connyes for every hundrethe, the said Connyes ro be such as shalbe then at the tyme of the deliverye thereof, good, sweete and mete to be served, used and spente in the house of the said Erle, his heires or assignes, and such as shall from tyme to tyme be Bredd and kept in or uppon the said Erles warren close or grounde before demised, and the said Connyes to be delivered yerelie duringe the said terme betweene the feast of the Annunciation and the Purification of the blessed virgin St Mary [2 February] in every one yere at such of the said Erle his nowe mansion houses within the said Countye of Wiltes, as the said Erle, his heires or assignes, or any of them shall from tyme to tyme like best to chuse and appointe, and at such severall dayes and tymes between the said two feasts every yere duringe the said terme and in such quantitye, number and proportion, at every several day and tyme as shalbe required or demanded by the said Erle, his heires or assignes, or by anie of his or theire officers or servants of houshold, uppon reasonable notice or warninge thereof before given at the dwelling house or lodge situate or being in the said close of pasture commonly called the Conigere in the said parishe of Eston. And further that if they, the said Michaell Clarke and James Whithart, or their assignes shall for want of demande or request to be made by the said Erle, his heires or assignes, or by his or theire officers or housholde servants fayle or forbeare to deliver or serve in the said full and whole number of Fyve hundrethe Cooples of Connyes in anie yere duringe the said terme, then they, the said Michaell Clarke and James Whithart or either of them or theire or either of theire assignes shall content and pay or cause to be contented and paid unto the said Erle, his heires or assignes for so many Cooples of Connyes as shall so happen in the yere duringe the said terme not to be delivered served in after the rate of tenn pence for every coople the same to be paid to the said Erle, his heires or assignes in one whole and entire some in or uppon the feaste day of the Purification of the blessed virgin St Mary in every or anie yere if the said terme wherein there shalbe anie such faylinge of deliverye of the said Connyes then due or paiable at or without the said Erle's mansion house within Tottenham alias Tottnam Parke in the said Countye of Wiltes. And further that they, the said Michaell Clarke and James Whithart, or either of them or theire assignes shall and will from tyme to tyme and at all tymes duringe the said terme at theire own proper costs and chardges, in and by all and all manner of nedefull and necessary reparations, well and sufficientlie repaire, amend and keepe or cause to be well and sufficientlye repaired, amended and kepte aswell, the boundes, fences and inclosures of, within or about the said warren close or grounde and premises before demised or mentioned to be demised, as all the burrowes, banckes and berryes, flapps, trappes and falls nowe beinge within or uppon the same, or which hereafter duringe the said terme shall by the said Michaell Clarke and James Whithart or their assignes, be thereuppon newelie planted or erected and the same so well and sufficientlie repaired, amended and kepte at or in thend or other determination of the said terme shall beare and yelde upp. And also that they, the said Michaell Clarke and James Whithart and either of them, theire and either of theire assignes, shall and will at in thend or other determination of the said terme have unto the said Erle, his heires and assignes, for the store thereof, in or uppon the said warren close or grounde before demised Six hundrethe Cooples of Connyes at the leaste of like Reckoninge or take for every hundrethe as aforesaid. And further that they, the said Michaell Clarke and James Whithart and either of them and theire and either of theire assignes shall not at any tyme duringe the said terme licence, assigne or sett over theire estate or interest before by these presentes demised of, or in the said warren or game of Connyes or the said close or pasture or earrable before by these presentes demised, nor demise, lett or sett the same or any parte thereof, duringe the said terme to any person or persons whatsoever (other than the said dwelling howse or lodge with the Curtilage and gardens to the said lodge inclosed and the said close of pasture or earrable called the Breach and the pasturage and feedinge for one horsebeaste to be forementioned to William Hutchins of Eston aforesaid duringe all the terme before expressed so as the said William Hutchins, Michaell Clarke and James Whithart doe so longe lyve) without the speciall licence of the said Erle, his heires or assignes in writinge under his or theire hands and seales first had or obteyned for the same. Nor shall reteyne or keepe any person or servants under them, to walke the said warren close or grounde which shalbe misliked by the said Erle, his heires or assignes, but shall from tyme to tyme during the said terme remove and putt of such service or attendance there every such person or servants whome it shall happen the said Erle, his heires or assignes to mislike of uppon notice or warninge geven by the said Erle, his heires or assignes of such theire mislike. And further that neither the said Michaell Clarke and James Whithart nor their assigne or assignes, shall at any tyme during the said terme make, erect or mayntayne any berryes, banckes, borrowes in or uppon anie of the Commons or wast groundes adjoining unto the said warren close or grounde before demised, or in or uppon anie groundes of the tenants and inhabitants within Eston aforesaid nere, adjoining and without the boundes of the said Warren close or grounde before demised, nor shall increase the said game of Connyes to such or so great multitude as shal exceede the number of Connyes which were bred and kepte in or uppon the said warren close or grounde before demised, within Eighte yeres last past before the day of the date of these presentes, so as the tenants and inhabitants aforesaid shall or may not have just cause to exclayme or complayme that they be grevouslye tresspassed or oppressed by the said game of Connyes for the avoydinge of the offence or inconveniences aforesaid. And the said Michaell Clarke and James Whithart for themselves, and either of theire heires, executors, administrators and assignes doe and doth covenante and graunt to and with the said Erle, his heires and assignes to and with every of them by these presentes that it shall and may be lawfull to and for the said Erle, his heires and assignes to and for every of them from tyme to tyme and at all tymes duringe the said terme, to bringe, pasture, feed and keepe in or uppon the said warren close or grounde before demised, the close of pasture or earrable grounde conteyninge by estimation Sixteene acres last inclosed in the breach and devided with a newe made hedge from the residue thereof onlye excepted, such and so many sheepe called Teggs [i.e. wethers] of the said Erle, his heires or assignes as shalbe placed or kepte in or uppon anie closes or groundes of the said Erle, his heires or assignes, situat and beinge in the parishe of Eston aforesaid, in such manner and forme and for so longe tyme as to the said Erle, his heires or assignes, or to his or theire bailiffes shalbe thought good and expedient. And also that it shall and may belikewise lawfull unto the said Erle, his heires and assignes yerelie during the said terme at or after the feaste of the Annunciation of the blessed virgin St Mary to bringe in, pasture, fodder, feed and keepe in and uppon the said warren close or grounde before demised (except as before is excepted) such and so many rother beasts [cattle] and horsebeasts of the said Erle, his heires or assignes as shalbe thought convenient by the said Erle, his heires or assignes, or his and theire bailiffs to be kept foddered and fedd with fodder there untill the said Erle, his heires and assignes, or his and theire bailiffs shall like to place the said Rother beasts elsewhere in anye of theire parkes or other groundes whatsoever.

In witness whereof the parties have interchangeablie putt theire handes and seales to the same. Anno Domini 1608

Sealed and delivered in the presence of Edmund Pykes, Gregory Boys, John Barnes, Robert Fleming.

Aldbourne Warren in 1617

This description of the coney warren on Aldbourne Chase is from the Survey of the manor conducted for the Crown by John Norden in 1617. This illustrates the size of the warren, the problems caused by the rabbits and the difficulties of dealing with the situation.

PRO LR2/207 ff 100-108

Aldbourne

There is a spacious warren of Coneys in graunt by lease to the Earle of Pembroke but nowe in the use and disposition of Thomas Walronde Esquire, the rent to the Prince is said to be per annum [blank].

The number of Conyes are said to be much increased and to annoye the tennants much in theire corne and grasse and take the benefitt of a large circuit of barren lande which yett might be converted to much better and more certaine profitt but in the conversion seemeth greate difficultie.

There are certaine coppices within the Chase in name more than in nature as they have byn used. And are in graunt by lease to Mr Tho. Walrond, who is alsoe farmer of the Mannor, Steward, Bailie and Woodward, who having all absolute commaund hath all subjecte to his disposinge. Hee is an honest gent and of manie friends that are tennantes to the mannor

A dispute over a Warren at Upham on Aldbourne Chase 1618-21

PRO STAC 8 /212/6

This is a complaint to the Court of Star Chamber by Henry Marten, Esq of Aldbourne. He possessed a warren of 12 acres called Heyleaze adjacent to Aldbourne Chase, 'yet absolutely without the precincts of the Chase'. It was alleged that Thomas Walrond of Aldbourne had obtained a lease of the Chase and of rabbits there, and had combined with others including the keepers of the king's deer in the Chase, namely Thomas Spainswick, Richard Neale, Thomas Gardiner, William Cresson and William Bryan, 'being all of them able bodyes and fitt to attempt unlawful acts' to undertake 'the destruction and spoyle of your said subject's warren, and of the game of Conyes there, the same ground being stored with a good and plentifull game'. Henry Martin also complained that on 20 August 1618 Thomas Walrond with his sons and others 'took kill'd and carry'd away one hundred couples of your said subjectes Conyes and wickedlie laye ferretts dung and other noysome and hatefull things to Conyes in the holles of the burrowes within the same warren to th'end to drive awaye your said subjectes Conyes and game and make them forsake his said warren'.

On 5 May 1621 Thomas Walrond and others replied to the complaint of Henry Martin. He stated that he had a lease of Aldbourne Chase from William, Earl of Pembroke, 'stored and replenished with conyes there breedinge and increasinge'. He also claimed that Martin's pasture land was not a warren, and that his rabbits had been enticed away by Martin through the dead hedge or fence which divided the two properties. For quietness sake he had allowed Martin to take 'a couple of Conyes weekely', but Martin, his sons and his servants had

. . . made such a noyse as thereby this defendants said games of conyes in the said Chase have been frayed from theire feedings — and have been more and more disquieted whereby alsoe the poulterers of London which used to buy Conyes of this defendant have been some way disappointed as this defendant hath heard whereof the plaintiff having been enformed did not redress the same in his owne servants. —

This defendant confesseth that he did put some of the said ferrets dunge and garbage into some of the holes of the plaintiff's Cony berryes [burrows] which he had made in in the said grounds soe neer by the said dead hedge that the Conyes did worke out newe holes under the said hedge into the said Chase And this defendant further saith that sythence the plaintiff's denyinge of the said poachinge and takinge of Conyes in the plaintiff's said ground and makinge of new burrowes, some of the plaintiff's sonnes and servants have often hunted, taken and killed many Conyes in the night tyme in the said ground called Hayleaze. And when they had ended theire hunting they did then whoope and hallowe and beate the hedges and bushes with their staves and pull theire doggs by the eares of purpose to make them Crye and suffer them to hunte with open mouths [i.e. without muzzles] that with the noyse thereof they might fright, dryve away and disturbe the said Chase Conyes from their feedings and hinder the keepers from takinge of Conyes in the said Chase and did expresslye say they would soe doe to hinder this defendant and his fellowe keepers of the said walke from takinge of any Conyes in the said walke. . . .

And alsoe some of the plaintiff's sonnes and servants have used to ly in wayte in the evenings and when the said Chase Conyes were feedinge abroade towards the said plaintiff's grounds, they suddenly arose and came betweene the burrowes and the Conyes in the said Chase with Cony doggs with them and did hunte and dryve some of the said Chase Conyes into the plaintiff's said ground into the said newe burrowes which the plaintiff had purposely made to receave them And some of the plaintiff's sonnes and servants came to the plaintiff's house and fetched netts and other engins and some of the rest of them did in the meane tyme keepe them in the said holes of purpose to kill them there, And did alsoe cutt holes and meshes in the plaintiff's owne hedge of purpose to lett the said Chase Conyes into the plaintiff's said ground and into another corne field of his adjoyninge the said Chase And when the defendant and others, his fellowe keepers in the said Chase have offered to stoppe these holes and meshes for safeguard of the plaintiff's Corne from being spoyled by the said Conyes, Some of the plaintiff's sonnes or servants have forbidden them and have threatened some that yf they did stoppe them they would make some of their gutts hang about their heeles or words to that effecte. . .

There are many more similar accusations, and also references to the King's deer in the Chase 'walking and feedinge amongst the said game of Conyes'. The keepers confirmed that during their regular night-time walks through the Chase to protect the deer, they had encountered Martin's sons and servants, carrying staves and weapons, and driving the coneys from the Chase into their own warren.

The Sale of Rabbits from Wiltshire Warrens to Reading and London 1624

Details concerning the scale of the trade in rabbits from Wiltshire emerge from the depositions of witnesses in a case brought by the Crown in the Exchequer Court against John Bayley of Reading. Only the evidence of two witnesses survive, but it is clear that Bayley, who was a wholesale buyer of rabbits and other game and also had a retail shop in Reading, had been charged with illegally buying and re-selling game from royal properties, especially from Aldbourne Chase.

The first witness was Owen Rennyston, a poulterer aged 44 years, from Little Allhallows, Gratious Street, London. He deposed that he knew Bayley as 'a buyer of connyes by whole sale of many persons from theyr groundes and some mens slaughters'.

PRO E134/22 James I Michaelmas 21

Betwixte the first daye of Marche was twelve moneth and Candlemas daye [2 February] laste . . . within the time mentioned in the Interrogatories the said

Bayley did sell and cause to be delivered to this deponent or [his] Sone for him sixe thousand gray connyes or thereabouts, and of blacke connies Fyve hundred or thereabouts within the said terme and the sayd Bayley did also sell connyes besides in his owne shoppe at Readinge, and this deponent did pay for every hundred of gray connyes three pounds one shillinge and eight pence or thereabouts and for blacke connyes he payd Fyve pound the hundred delivered at Readinge.

Within the tyme mentioned in the Interrogatories this deponent had partridges from the sayd Bayley but how many he knoweth not. He doth not know whether he had any phesants or not, but this deponent sayth that George Buckingham of Gratious Streete bought as this deponent hath heard all the sayd Baylies fowle at Readinge.

Only a fragment of this deposition survives.

The Questions and Answers of William Longe, 2 June 1624

PRO E 134/22 James I Michaelmas 37

Interrogatories to be ministered to witnesses to bee produced on the parte and behalfe of the Kings Majestie against John Baylye of Readinge in the County of Berks. Defendant.

1. Imprimis doe you knowe the said John Baylye and how longe have you knowne him to be a common ingrosser and buyer and seller of Conyes.
2. Item, how many horse Loades of Conyes Black and Gray have you brought weekly from the said Bayley betwyxt St James tide [1 May St James the Less] and Michaelmas [29 September] last, likewise betwyxt Michaelmas and Candlemas [2 February] last to the Poulterers of London and what quantitie of Conyes doth a horse loade conteyne and for what price by the horseloade, by the hundred or by the thousand did the said Bayley sell the same to the Poulterers aforesaid.
3. Item, hath hee the said Bayley any warren of his owne for conyes or of whome doth he buy and ingrosse the same Conyes to your knowledge and where and to whome doth hee usually sell the same Conyes agayne. Sett downe the names and dwellinge places of those persons of whome he buyeth the said Conyes and likewise to whom he selleth the same agayne.
4. Item, is he able to deale in the ingrossinge of the aforesaid Conyes of himself or hath he any parteners in any of the aforesaid Conyes which he did ingrosse for what quantitie hath hee had any parteners and for what quantitie did he delae by himself, if you know of any parteners sett downe theire names.

Depositions of witnesses on his Majesties behalfe against John Bayleye of Reading in the County of Berks., defendant, taken before Lawrence Tanfelde

Kt., Lord Chiefe Baron of his Majesties Court of Exchequer the 2nd day of June in the yeare of the raigne of our Soveraigne Lord James by the grace of God of England, France, Scotland and Ireland King, defender of the fayth etc., the 22nd of Scotland, the 5th July 1624

William Longe of Longlane in the parishe of St Sepulchres, London, Poulterer aged thirty yeres and upwardes Sworn and examined the day aforesaid

1. To the first Interrogatory this Deponent sayeth that he doth know John Bayley and he hath knowne him twoe yeres or thereabouts and he hath knowne him almost twoe yeres to have bought and sould Connyes.
2. To the 2nd Interrogatory this deponent sayth that neyther he nor this Defendant nor any other to his knowledge have within the tymes mencioned in the Interrogatories brought any Connyes to London, but this deponent sayth that a horseload of Connyes is 300 of Connyes and a horseload of gray connyes are worth Fifty shillings and a horselode of Black Connyes are worth about £4, but how the sayd Bayly sould any Connyes to the Poulterers he knoweth not.
3. To the 3rd Interrogatory this deponent sayth that he thinketh that the sayd Bayley hath warrens of Connyes of his owne or els doth rent groundes, and this deponent sayth that about a fortnight after Bartholomew's tyde [24 August] last was twelvemoneth this deponent did begin to fetch Connyes from Maximillian Deacon and John Gilbert of Awborne [Aldbourne] Chase in the County of Wiltes and soe this deponent continued from that tyme till it was twelvetyde [6 January] after and this deponent brought twice in a week weekly sometimes one horselode and sometymes twoe horseloade and sometymes more and sometymes lesse unto the sayd Baylyes howse in Readinge, but when the defendant first bargayned with them he knoweth not, and this deponent also sayth that dureing the tyme aforesayd he did alsoe fetch some from Edward Jones a keeper nere Aburne [Aldbourne] and this deponent hath alsoe received Connyes at Aburne brought from Liddiard which he brought to the sayd Baylyes howse for him, and this deponent had some Connyes alsoe from the keeper of Sir Francis Jones warren [at Ramsbury] who then was liveinge, and the Connies that the defendant did sell to any poulterers in London were all sould to Mr Remmiston a poulterer in Gratious Streete who caused them to be fetcht from the defendant's howse in Readinge, and many Connyes the defendant sould at his owne shopp in Readinge, and more to this Interrogatory he cannot depose.
4. To the 4th Interrogatory this deponent sayth that what Connyes the defendant bought he bought for himselfe without haveinge any partener or parteners to this deponent's knowledge.

Signed: William Longe

Lease of Durley Warren 1624

Notwithstanding its excessive legal verbiage, this lease provides information about the management of a warren and the productivity of the rabbits. The fact that such a detailed lease was thought to be necessary, and the annual rental of 1,520 rabbits, is an indication of the profit which was expected from this large warren. The lease also mentions the two lodges, the fence or 'pale' surrounding the warren, the artificial burrows provided for the rabbits and the various traps used to catch predators. The rabbits were provided with food during the winter and were protected from cold and snow by bushes and bracken spread over the burrows. Provision was made for the welfare of the deer in Savernake forest, both red deer and fallow, and 800 rabbits were to be left in the warren at the conclusion of the lease. It is an indication of the reproductive capacity of the rabbits that a breeding stock of this size was considered sufficient to provide a warren-keeper with enough rabbits for his own livelihood, as well as producing the annual rental of 760 couples.

WSRO 9/22/19

This Indenture made the last day of December in the yeres of the Raigne of our Soveraigne lord James by the grace of God King of England, France and Ireland, defender of the Faith etc., the one and twentieth and of Scotland the seaven and Fortieth, Betweene the right honorable Sir William Seymour, Knight, Baron Beauchamp and Earle of Hertford of th'one parte And Thomas Cary of Wylton in the county of Wiltes, yeoman, of th'other parte, Wyttnesseth that the said Earle as well for and in consideration of a surrender under forme of lawe made unto the sayde Earle by the sayd Thomas Cary of all his estate, right, title, interest, possession, clayme and demand which he claymeth to have for terme of certaine yeres yet to come and unexpired of and in the warren commonly called or knowne by the name of the Greate Warren in the grounds of the said Earle commonly called by the severall names of Durley Heath and Haveringes Heath within the severall parishes of Greate Bedwin and Bowebache als Burbage in the sayd county of Wiltes or within eyther of them, and all that other warren commonly called or knowne by the name of the Lyttle Warren in one other of the sayde Earle's groundes inclosed with pale lyinge and beinge within the parish of Borebache als Burbage aforesayd in the sayde county of Wiltes together with two lodges thereon standing with other appurtenances thereunto belonging as by our Indenture of lease thereof made to the sayde Thomas Cary by the Right Honorable Edward, late Earle of Hertford deceased, bearing date the fyfteenth day of Aprill in the seaventh yere of the Kinges Majesties raigne that nowe is of England, France and Ireland and of Scotland the two and fortieth at lardge appeareth. As also for divers good causes and reasonable considerations, him, the sayde Earle hereunto especially moving Hath demysed betaken and to ferme letten and by these presences doth demyse, betake and to ferme let unto the sayde Thomas Cary, his executors, administrators and assignes All that the sayde warren called the Great Warren situate and beinge in the sayde Earles groundes commonly called or knowne by the severall names of Durley Heath and Havinges Heath in the severall parishes of Greate Bedwin and Borebache als Burbage in the sayd county of Wiltes or within eyther of them together with the lodge thereon standinge. As also that his game of Connyes within or upon the sayd warren or grounde together with all the increase and breede that shall or may hereafter renew, growe or come thereof with free lyberty of keeping, feedinge and kylling of Connyes within or upon the sayde warren or grounde so far and for such lardge scope and cyrcuite of grounde within the same only as hath ben heretofore used and accustomed during such tyme as one Matthew Whyte was keeper of the sayde warren or grounde to the sayde earle deceased As also all that lane conteyning by estimation two acres be yt more or lesse lyeinge betweene Tottenham parke and Durley Fyelde as also one lyttle close called or knowne by the name of Bentley close conteyning by estimation half an acre be yt more or lesse and adjoyninge to the sayde parke on the west syde thereof Together with the common of pasture or feedinge for two kyne or rother beastes and two horsebeastes to goe depasture and feede in the Forest or chase of Savernake in the sayd county of Wiltes yerely from Holyroode daye [3rd] in Maye untill St Martyns daye [11th] in November and likewise common of pasture and feedinge for twenty sheepe yerely to be kepte on the commons of Durley as far for the as the Tennantes there have heretofore used and accustomed.

To have and to holde, use, occupye and enjoye the sayd warren, lodge, game of Connyes, Lane close, commons of pasture and all other the premysses before by these presents demysed or mentioned to be demysed to the said Thomas Cary, his executors and administrators and assignes from the Feast of the Purification of the Blessed Virgin Mary [2 February] last past before the date hereof for and during and unto the full end and terme of one and twenty yeres from thence nexte ensuing and fully to be compleate and ended And the sayde Earle for himselfe, his heires, executors and assignes and for every of them doth covenant, promise, grant and agree to and with the sayde Thomas Cary, his executors, administrators and assignes and every of them by these presentes in manner and form followinge that is to say That yt shall and may be lawfull to and for the sayde Thomas Cary, his executors and assignes and every of them for the better increasing of the sayde game of Connyes from tyme to tyme and at all tymes during the sayd terme to store, furnish and replenish the sayde warren or grounde with so manye and suche number of Connyes as he or they shall thinke good so as the whole game of Connyes there to be kepte, do not at any tyme during the sayd terme growe or exceede to any greater number or proportion than may well or conveniently be kepte and mayntayned only upon so much and such places or parcells of the sayd grounde as have ben heretofore used and imployed for the keeping and feedinge of Connyes during the tyme that the sayde Matthew White was keeper of the sayde warren or game of Connyes there. And likewise that yt shall and may be lawfull to and for the sayd Thomas Cary, his executors, administrators and assignes and every of them as well for the preservation and increasing of the sayd game of Connyes as for the killing and destruction of all such vermyn as may hinder, hurte or destroy the same from tyme to tyme, and at all tymes during the said terme to make up, plant, repayre and new erect or cause to be made up, planted, repayred and newly erected such and so many bakes, berryes, borowes, flappes, traps, falles and other engines whatsoever as by the said Thomas Cary, his executors, administrators and assignes shalbe so made and devised as that they may not in any wise be hurtful to the sayde Earle, his deere within his sayde Forest or chase of Savernake, nor to his tenantes cattell there depasturinge or goinge during the sayde terme. And further that the sayde Earle, his heires and assignes shall and will at all tymes and from tyme to tyme during the sayde terme aswell for and towards the mayntenance and reparacyon of the sayde lodge before by these presents demysed, as for and towards the repayring and newe erectinge of the flappes, traps and other engines before mentioned upon reasonable request to be made to the sayde Earle, his heires and assignes or to his or their Surveyor, woodward or other officer for such purpose from tyme to tyme to be appointed, allowe or by themselves or any of them the sayde officers appoint and set forth suffycent and convenyent rough tymber nowe or hereafter standing or growinge in or upon some of the sayde Earles woods or other groundes not distant above foure myles at the most from the sayde warren or grounde before mentioned, the felling, squaring, carryinge and setting up whereof to be at the propper costes and chardges of the sayde Thomas Cary, his executors, administrators or assignes. And also that yt shall and may be lawfull to and for the sayde Thomas Cary, his executors, administrators and assignes and every of them to have and take yerely during the sayde terme at seasonable tymes in the yere ten reasonable and indifferent cartloades of fyrewood to be spent within the said lodge above demysed and not elsewhere and also six reasonable and indifferent cartloades of rowe [rough grass] and bushes for the covering and dressing of the sayde berryes within the [?] of the said Earles woods or other groundes not distant above foure myles at the most from the sayde warren or grounde before mentioned by the appointment, delivery, survey or warrant of the surveyor, woodward or other officer of the sayd Earle, his heires and assignes for that purpose from tyme to tyme to be appointed, the felling, cutting downe and carryeinge of which fyrewood, rowe and bushes to be at the only propper costes and chardges of the said Thomas Cary, his executors, administrators and assignes. And the said Thomas Cary for himself, his executors, administrators and assignes and for every of them doth covenante, promise, graunte and agree to and with the said Earle, his heires and assignes and to and with every of them by these presents that he, the said Thomas Cary, his executors, administrators and assignes shall and will for and in consyderation of this demyse or lease, yeeld, paye or deliver unto the sayde Earle, his heires or assignes yerely during the said terme Seaven hundred and three score couples of Connyes reckoning five score couples of Connyes for every huundred the sayde Connyes to be eyther such as the sayde Thomas Cary, his executors, administrators or assignes may best provyde or get in any other warrens and shallthen be at the tyme of the delivery thereof good, sweete and meete to be served, used and spent in the house of the sayd Earle, his heires and assignes or els to be such as shall from tyme to tyme be bred or kept in or upon the sayde Earles warren or grounde before mentioned and shalbe taken as well in the best as in the worst partes thereof without eyther making choice of the grounde to hunt or culling of the Connyes to be delivered yerely during the said terme yerely in manner and forme following, that is to say, every yere betweene the feast of St Mark the Evangelist [25 April] and of the Purification of the Blessed

Virgin, St Mary at such of the said Earles mansion houses within the said county of Wiltes as the sayde Earle, his heires or assignes, or any of them shall from tyme to tymes lyke best to chuse and appoint. And at such severall dayes and tymes between the sayd two feastes every yere during the sayd terme and in such quantity, number or proportion at every such severall day or tymes as shalbe requyred or demanded by the sayd Earle, his heires or assignes, or by and of his or their officers or servantes of houshold upon reasonable notice or warning thereof before geven at the lodge standing in or upon the sayd Haverings Heath within the said Greate Warren Provided allwayes that the sayd Thomas Cary, his executors, adiministrators or assignes, or any of them shall not be hereby compelled to pay, yeld, deliver or serve in more than twenty couples of Conyes at any one tyme in any one day during the sayd term and no more than Fowerscore Couple of Conyes in any one weeke during the sayd terme. And that at every tyme during the sayd terme when the sayd Thomas Cary, his executors, administrators or assignes shalbe requyred or appointed by the sayd Earle, his heires or assignes or by any of his or their officers or servants of household to yeeld, deliver or serve in Twenty Couple of Conyes in any one daye during the said terme there shalbe notice and warning thereof geven by the space of two whole dayes at the least before, at or in the sayd lodge standing in or upon the sayd Haverings Heath within the sayd Greate Warren. And further the sayd Thomas Cary for himself, his executors, administrators and assignes and for every of them doth covenant, graunt and agree to and with the sayd Earle, his heires and assignes and to and with every of them by these presentes in manner and forme following That is to say That yf the sayd Thomas Cary, his executors, administrators and assignes shall for want of demand or request to be made by the sayd Earle, his heires or assignes or by his or their officers and household servants fayle or forbeare to deliver or serve in the full and whole number of seaven hundred and threescore couple of Conyes in any yere during the sayd terme That then he, the sayd Thomas Cary, his executors, administrators or assignes or some or one of them shall content or pay or cause to be contented or payd unto the sayd Earle, his heires or assignes at one whole or entyre some in or upon the feast day of the Anncyation of the Blessed Virgin Mary in every or any yere of the sayd terme wherin there shalbe any such fayling of delivery of the sayd Conyes then due and payable at or within the sayd Earles mansion house within Tottenham als Tottnam park in the sayd county of Wyltes, And further that he, the sayd Thomas Cary, his executors, administrators or assignes and every of them shall and will from tyme to tyme and at all tymes during the sayd terme at their owne propper costes and charges (with the allowance aforesayd from the sayd Earle, his heires and assignes in all and all manner of needefull and necessary reparations well and suffycyently upholden, mayntayned, repayred, amended and kept aswell the sayd lodge as all the Burrowes, banckes and berryes, flaps, traps and falls nowe being within or upon the sayd warren or grounde before mentioned or which hereafter during the sayd term shall by the sayd Thomas Cary, his executors or assignes be thereupon newly planted or erected and the same so suffycyently upholden, mayntayned, repayred, amended and kept at or in the end or other determynation of the sayd terme shall leave and yeeld up. And also that the sayd Thomas Cary, his executors or assignes shall and will or in the end or other determynation of the sayd terme leave unto the sayd Earle, his heires or assignes for the sport thereof, in or upon the said warren or grounde before mentioned fowre hundred couple of Conyes at the least. And that neyther he, the sayd Thomas Cary, his executors or assignes, nor any of them, nor any of their assignes, nor any other parson [person] or parsons [persons] by their or any of their cosent, commandment or procurement shall kill any of the deare of the sayd Earle or his heires during the sayd terme without his or their specyall lycence or warrant for the same. And yf yt shall happen any such deare to be so kylled contrary to the true meaning of these presentes That then the sayd Thomas Cary, his executors and administrators and every of them and every of their assignes so offending shall pay unto the sayd Earle or his heires for every of his or their doe or male deare under a Soer so kylled Fyfty shillings and for every Buck or Soer Fyve pounds and for every red deare six poundes thirteen shillings and fowre pence of lawfull money of England. And that the sayd Thomas Cary, his executors or assignes shall not keepin his service in the sayd warren any such parson or parsons as the sayd Earle, his heires or assignes doe or shall will or doth at any tyme justly dislyke of and upon just cause hath justly deserved to be expelled and avoyded out of the sayd Earle his sayd warren and out of the Earle his groundes Provyded allwayes that yf yt shall happen the sayd Thomas Cary, his executors, administrators and assignes or any of them for want of demand or request to be made by the sayd Earle, his heires and assignes in forme before expressed, the full and whole number of seaven hundred and three score couple of Conyes in any yere or yere during the sayd terme whereby the sayd Thomas Cary, his executors or assignes shall come and growe indebted unto the sayd Earle, his heires, executors or assignes the some of fyve markes or more for such conyes not served, payd or delivered to the sayd Earle, his heires or assignes according as in this Indenture expressed, and that the some of fyve markes or more shall remayne behind and unpaydd by the space of Fyfty dayes next after the denand thereof made at the lodge of the sayd warren nowe standing or being in the payd Cony warren called Haverings Heath aforesayd in the hearing of the sayd Thomas Cary, of his wife or any of his children or servantes of the age of Fowerteen yeres or upwards and not payd within the sayd Fyfty dayes next after such demande or request made for the same that then and from thencefourth this lease, demyse and graunt to cause, determyne and be utterly voyde to all intents and purposes as though the same had never beene had nor made, anything herein contained to the contrary thereof in any wise notwithstanding.

In witness whereof the partyes to this have interchangeably putt their handes and seales to the same. Geven the day and yere first above wrytten Anno Domini 1624

Licence to Destroy Coneys on Durley Common 1633

This illustrates the difficulties caused to neighbours by rabbits escaping from warrens. Here the rabbits were evidently doing much damage to the common grazing land. The warren itself, covering c150 acres, continued to exist at Durley until 1703 when it was enclosed and converted to farm land. A sketch plan of c1707 shows the site divided into 13 enclosures. [WSRO 1300/360; 9/7/43. VCH Wilts., *XVI, 1999, 79-80].*

WSRO 1044/7

These are to authorize all and everie of my Tennants or theire servants within the hamblett of Durlye parcell of my mannor of Burbage Esturmyes in the Countie of Wilteses, to teake, kill and destroye all the Connyes feedinge and beinge within the prycints and bounds of the Sheepe Common belonginge to my sayde Tennants within the sayde hamblett and also to breake the soyle of the sayde Common where any burroughes of the Conneyes are, for the digginge oute and destroying of the sayde Conneyes, by all lawefull and fayer meanes. In wyttnes wheere of I have heereunto sett my hande and seale the xxiiiith daye of January in the ixth yeere of the Reigne of our Soveraigne Lord Kinge Charles, of England, Scotland, France and Ireland Kinge Anno Domini 1633

24 January 1633

Jane Beauchamp

Clarendon Park Warren 1612

The long-established and lucrative warren in the royal park at Clarendon was actually suppressed by royal command. James I was greatly addicted to hunting and concerned about the preservation of deer. He also wanted a smooth surface within the park where he could gallop without fear of 'coneyboroughes' [rabbit holes]. The account of his orders about the warren in Clarendon park comes from an enquiry made in 1612 concerning the woodland, the park pales or fences and the warren. In particular, the enquiry addressed allegations that the keepers and woodwards had illegally sold timber from the park. Depositions of witnesses were taken at Salisbury (New Sarum) on 29 December 1612. The witnesses were William Phillips of Wilton aged 42, who was Mayor of Wilton; Thomas Marshall of Downton, esquire, aged 68; James Birch of New Sarum, gent., aged 70; and John Fussell, gent., aged 50, who had been appointed by Queen Elizabeth as a 'quarter keeper' in the royal park.

PRO E178/4728

William Phillips stated
— he, this deponent, was present in Claringdon Parke aforesaid before the said game of Conies was fullie destroyed when he heerd the Kinges Majestie commande the right honorable, the now Earle of Pembroke, that the game of Conyes should be destroyed because the same by reason of the Conyboroughes was dangerous for his Majestie to ride after his dellight and sport, as alsoe would bee then better for the increase and preservation of his Majestie's' deere there. And this deponent further saith that the said Earle of Pembroke hath received

greate yearlie losse by the destroying of the said game of Conyes, but to what value he knoweth not.

John Fussell deposed
— that about eight or nyne yeares past hee, this deponent, was present in Claringdon Parke and heard the Kinges Majestie aske the right honorable, the nowe Earle of Pembroke, whether the Conyes in the Parke were distroyed or not, and alsoe heard my lorde answere that they were distroyinge and should be distroyed, and likewise heard the Kinge thereupon further commande that the same should bee done accordinglie as well for his Majestie's better likinge his delight and pleasure without danger in rideinge as alsoe for the better increase and preservation of his highnesses game there. And hee further saith that hee, this deponent, did then at the same tyme of his Majesties being at Claringdon abovesaid, likewise heare it reported that the cause wherefore his Majestie would have the same Conies distroyed was by reason of a fall which his Majestie had taken by a Conyborough in some other parke or place elsewher.

Lease of a Warren in Burderop Park, Chiseldon 1696

Warrens continued to be profitable throughout the 17th century, as is evident from the following lease. A high rent of £30 per annum was charged for a four-year term, even though grazing rights for sheep and cattle during the summer were not included and there was an obligation to maintain the pale or fence around the park. This was a large warren, and one thousand rabbits valued at £5 per hundred were to be left as a breeding stock at the end of the lease. It is noteworthy that Francis Vicars, who took this lease, came from Aldbourne which continued throughout the 17th century to be the foremost place for rabbit production in Wiltshire. As was usual, the Burderop warren included a lodge for the warrener to live in. The lease also includes references to the artificial burrows provided for the rabbits, to traps to catch vermin and to snare the rabbits, and to 'brouse', that is bracken and undergrowth used to cover the burrows to protect the rabbits and provide food for them during harsh weather in the winter months. The 'Extraordinary Taxes' which are mentioned in the lease refer to the new Land Tax which was first imposed on real estate from 1692.

WSRO 1178/50

This Indenture made the five and twentieth day of March 1696 and in the Eighth yeare of the Raigne of our Soveraigne lord William the Third by the grace of God of England, Scotland, France and Ireland King, defender of the Faith etc. Betweene Oliver Calley of Over Wroughton in the County of Wiltes Esqr of the one part, and Francis Vicars of Albourne in the County aforesaid of the other part **Witnesseth** That for and in consideration of the Rent and Covenants herein after mentioned and reserved and which on the part and behalfe of the said Francis Vicars, are to be paid and performed, and for divers other good causes and considerations him hereunto moveing, He, the said Oliver Calley, **Hath** demised, graunted and to farme letten, and by these presents doth demise, graunt and to farme lett unto the said Francis Vicars **All That** his one inclosed ground called Burdrope Parke situate, lyeing and being in the parrish of Chisledon in the said County of Wiltes with the Warren of Conies therein now being, and alsoe the Liberty of keeping, feeding and killing of Conies of and within the same ground (Except and alwayes reserved out of this demise and graunt unto the said Oliver Calley, his heires and assignes all and all manner of Trees, Woods, underwoods and hedgrows now standing, growing or being, or which at any tyme hereafter shall stand, grow or be in or upon the premisses demised or any part thereof, and alsoe the depastureing, goeing and feeding of one horsebeast and thirty dry sheepe or Eighteene couples of Ewes and Lambs every yeare of the Terme demised from Lady Day [25 March] to Lukestide [18 October] in every yeare in and upon the premisses demised) **To Have and To Hold** the said ground and Warren and all other the premisses with the appurtenances (Except before excepted) unto the said Francis Vicars, his Executors, Administrators and Assignes, from the day of the date of these presents for, by and dureing and untill the full end and terme of foure yeares from thenceforth next and Immediately ensueing and fully to be compleate and ended **Yeilding** and paying therefore the yearely rent or sume of Thirty pounds of Lawfull money of England in manner and forme following (that is to say) Twenty pounds upon the one and twentieth day of December and Ten pounds upon the four and twentieth day of March in every yeare, the first payment to begin and to be made upon the one and twentieth day of December next ensueing the day of the date of these presents. And if it shall happen the said yearely rent of Thirty pounds or any part thereof be behind and unpaid by the space of fourtteene dayes after any or either of the said dayes of payment in which it ought to be paid as aforesaid (being Lawfully demanded) that then and from thenceforth it shall and may be Lawfull and for the said Oliver Calley, his heires and assignes into all and singular the premisses or any part of thererof in the name of the whole to reenter and the same to have againe repossessed and enjoy as in his and their former estate and estates and thing in these presents conteyned to the contrary thereof in any wise notwithstanding. **And the said** Francis Vicars for him and his heires doth Covenant, promise and graunt to and with the said Oliver Calley, his heries and these presents in manner and forme following, (that is to say) that he, the said Francis Vicars, his Executors and assignes, shall and will from tyme to tyme dureing the said terme demised, beare, pay and discharge all and all manner of rates, taxes, dueties and Impropriations to the Church poore and highwayes for and in respect of the premisses. And shall and will well and sufficiently repaire and amend the Park pale and bounds of the premisses, he, the said Oliver Calley, his heires and assignes, provideing and allowing timber cutt and prepared into fitt lengths for the doeing thereof. And shall and will in like manner keepe all the houseing belonging to the premisses in good Tenantable repaire, and soe leave the same repaired at the end of the said terme of four yeares. And shall and will at the end of the said terme leave all the Burrows in the said ground demised whole, Tenantable and not mangled or decayed and all the Trapps or falls, now being or which hereafter shall be made, sett or planted in and upon the demised premisses well and sufficiently made and planted. And the said Francis Vicars, for him and his heires, doth further Covenant, promise and graunt to and with the said Oliver Calley, his heires and assignes, That he, the said Francis Vicars, his Executors and Administrators, shall and will leave upon the premisses demised One Thousand living Conies at the end of the said terme or to pay and recompense unto the said Oliver Calley, his heires and assignes, five pounds of lawfull money of England for every hundred of Conies that shall be wanting, and soe proportionably for every greater or lesser number to be viewed and estimated by two indifferent men, the one to be chosen by the said Oliver Calley, his heires and assignes, and the other by the said Francis Vicars, his executors and assignes, to be viewed and estimated and the money paid at the end of the said terme or within one month after. **And** it is agreed by and betweene the said parties that if upon such view and estimate to be made as aforesaid, it shall be judged by the said two men to be chosen as aforesaid that there shall be left on the premisses demised at the end of the said terme above the number of One Thousand living Conies, Then the said Oliver Calley shall pay unto the said Francis Vicars, his executors or assignes five pounds for every hundred of living Conies soe exceeding the number of One Thousand Conies, and soe proportionably for every greater or lesser number exceeding to be paid in manner aforesaid, or abated out of the last rent if any then remaine due. And it is further agreed that if either party shall refuse to choose one indifferent man as aforesaid then the other party to choose both. **And the said** Oliver Calley for him and his heires doth Covenant, promise and graunt to and with the said Francis Vicars, his executors and assignes, That he will pay and discharge or abate out of his rent all Extraordinary Taxes to be rated upon the premisses or on the said Francis Vicars, his executors and assignes in respect of the same, and will find and allow convenient Timber and cutt it into fitt lengths to be used in repaire of the pales and bounds of the premisses, and in hard weather will assigne and allow convenient brouse for the Conies. And that he, the said Francis Vicars, under the rents and covenants aforesaid may hold and enjoy the premisses (except before excepted) dureing the terme without his lett or deniall or any claymeing under him. **In Witness** whereof the said parties to these presents have hereunto interchangably sett their hands and sealesa the day and yeare first above written.

Sealed and delivered (the six penny stamp being on) in the presence of

John Foster
George Brind
Richard Lord

Endorsed
Francis Vicars Lese of Burderop Park made 25 March 1696 for 5 years the rent £30

Controversy over the Conversion of Hippenscombe Warren to Arable 1709

As mentioned in the Introduction to this section, the warren at Hippenscombe, on the eastern border of Wiltshire, part of the estate of the Earls of Hertford, gave rise to many complaints throughout the 17th century. Situated on thin chalk soil, a rabbit warren had been established by the early 17th century, with a lodge for the warrener. There were already complaints about the destructiveness of the rabbits in 1631, and a lease granted in 1633 obliged the tenant to destroy the rabbits. This was not done, however, and the rabbits continued to multiply; by 1657 the sale of rabbits was said to be worth £130 a year, but that much damage was being caused to both arable crops and woodland. [WSRO 9/17/35]. Further details of the warren at Hippenscombe and the neighbouring warren at Oakhill which were said to be 'between the forests of Chute and Savernake' emerge from evidence taken by an Exchequer Commission meeting at the 'Starre' in Andover. The warren was leased by Sir Alexander Tutt, and John Hull of Titcombe, yeoman, aged 69, deposed that £160 per year was made from the sale of coneys from the warren at Hippenscombe. Again, there were many complaints about the damage caused by the rabbits. The dispute arose over the tithes payable on the coneys produced at Hippenscombe. [PRO E134/1658/Mich 24].

The controversy between warreners and the other tenants at Hippenscombe continued for the rest of the century. The following evidence comes from a suit before the Court of Chancery in 1709-10. This arose from a dispute between Lord Charles Bruce, Earl of Ailesbury and the Johnson family who leased Hippenscombe, and had let the warren to an under tenant. In a complex action, Lord Bruce sued Richard Johnson and Katherine Johnson, daughter of Mary Johnson, widow, of Bowden Park, Wiltshire, for damage caused by their under tenant in ploughing up some of the land at Hippenscombe. Edward Lisle of Crux Easton, Hampshire, the agricultural writer, was involved because of his friendship with Mary Johnson. She had persuaded him to be a trustee in the marriage settlement when her daughter Katherine Johnson married David Gains, gentleman. Thus Lisle was one of those sued by Lord Bruce. The lengthy documentation produced as a result of this law suit contains much information about the management of the warren, controversy over the rabbits, the gradual conversion of the land to arable, and a brief history of the warren during the previous century. Eventually the matter was settled out of court, with the payment of £360 to Lord Bruce by Richard Johnson. The area of land involved at Hippenscombe was large, amounting in total to more than 800 acres. The controversy over the most profitable use of the land, and the gradual replacement of rabbits by arable land growing wheat and barley, is typical of what happened on most Wiltshire warrens during the 17th century. Although much of the land at Hippenscombe was hilly and unsuited to arable, it was agreed that it might be profitably used as 'sheep sleight' or grazing land for sheep which could be folded on the arable and increase the yield of corn.

The destruction caused by the rabbits is clear from the evidence in this case. By gnawing the bark of trees and nibbling the shoots of young saplings, the *rabbits destroyed valuable woodland, and prevented the re-growth of coppices of hazel which provided spars for hurdles, thatching and fences. [*VCH Wilts, *XVI, 1999, 228]*

WSRO 9/17/34

Summary of the Case concerning Hippenscombe Farm lately called Hippenscombe Warren 1709

Addressed to the Right Honorable the Lord Bruce at Henley Parke by Guilford, Surrey

The Tenant's Case for Hippenscombe 1709

9 Charles I [1633-34] William Earle of Hertford demised the same to Richard Browne Esq., by the name of Hippenscombe Farme and 11 Coppices and all the Bushy and Rough Grounds thereto belonging, for 99 yeares, determinable with 3 lives, under the yearely Rent of £10. And in that Lease a Covenant on the Lessees part to destroy the Coneys, but to preserve the Woods, or as much thereof as was then undestroyed. That during the Civill Warr the Coneys multiplyed exceedingly, and did destroy the most part of the remaining Woods.

18 November 27 Charles II [1675] The Lady Elizabeth Seymour demised the premises to George Johnson Esq., by the same or such like Description, Hence from the determination of the former Lease for 99 yeares determinable with 3 lives, under the same yearely Rent of £10.

Afterward the Farme house, Barnes and Stable being Casually burnt, and not one timber tree then being on the premises, the present Undertenant at his owne cost to the Amount of £360 rebuilt the same. And for that purpose bought timber of the Earle of Ailesbury's Woodward at Collingborne.

9 William III [1697-8] the Widow and Executrix of the said George Johnson (having purchased the remaining Estate under the former Lease granted to the said Richard Browne), did Surrender to Thomas, Earle of Ailesbury, both the former and later Lease. Whereupon the said Earle (by her Agreement) Granted the premises to Edward Lisle Esq., and Richard Johnson, by the name of Hippenscombe Farme and the Warren and Game of Coneys called Hippenscombe Warren, and all Lands, Meadows, Pastures, Woods, Coppices, Free Warren and Hereditements thereto belonging, for 99 yeares determinable with 3 lives, under the said yearely Rent of £10 and an Heriot payable on death of every principall Tenant. By which Lease the Lessee is not restrained from ploughing.

Therefore, and for that the ploughing up of land stored with Coneys is not Wast in Law where the Ground is not a Warren by Charter or Prescription; And for that the ploughing up of part of the said land called the Warren tended to a perpetuall Improvement of the Annual value of that Estate, as will Appeare on proof, the Undertenant had liberty given him on a valuable consideration to plough up 190 Acres of the said Warren during his Terme, whereof at Michaelmas 1709, 11 yeares were to come. Before such ploughing of the said 190 Acres the Rack Rent of the premises was £160 per Annum, but since the ploughing £200 per Annum hath been and will continue for 11 yeares to come the standing Rent. And for 5 yeares between Michaelmas 1701 and Michaelmas 1706 the Undertenant paid £220 per annum. And soe much per annum he offers to give for a Lease of 21 yeares to commence at the Expiration of the said 11 yeares soe that the liberty of ploughing the said 190 Acres be continued.

Otherwise but £160 per annum.

The present Undertenant for preserving the Arable in good Hart [heart] is obliged by Covenant not to plough above 400 Acres in any one yeare. And has performed that Covenant. Besides the Undertenant at his owne cost hath planted and preserved on the premises above 300 young trees of Oak and Ash; and expended £40 and upward in making Ditches for the better bounding of the severall feilds, but hath not committed any wast as suggested. The whole demised conteyns about 830 Acres, wherefrom of Arable 600 Acres, of Meadow 15, of Pasture 40, of Wood ground 15, and of other land more proper for a Sheep Sleight than a breed of Coneys 160 Acres.

To prove that the Coneys did by Degrees destroy the Coppices and suffered not grasse of any value to grow in that part called the Warren soe that the land from yeare to yeare appeared without any Sward thereon: That the Stock of Coneys there kept was from time to time sold by one Undertenant to another, and never reputed to belong to the Lord of the Fee [i.e. freehold]: That the said 190 Acres soe ploughed is a good sort of Arable, more proper to bear Corne and Graine than for any other use, and will after the end of the present Undertenant's terme be of greater profit in way of tillage than in any other way, and soe continue: And will in the Intervalls of ploughing bear better Grasse and more in quantity for Cattle than it would probably have borne before such ploughing: That the continuing of the said 190 Acres to be for ever Arable will be a perpetuall Improvement of the yearely value of that Estate: And that the preserving of the said 160 Acres (yet unploughed) for a Sheep Sleight will be an Additional Improvement: but the maintaining of Coneys thereon, the contrary, as appears by severall Affidavits herewith delivered.

That if Men of Skill in Husbandry can show better wayes or meanes for Advancing the Annuall value of that Estate the Undertenant will readily Comply thereto.

That the Undertenant will undertake to make it evident that the Officers of My Lord Bruce have been misinformed in severall matters relating to the premises, which might give occasion to the Bill lately Exhibited for restraining the further ploughing of the said 190 Acres, whereof 100 Acres ought according to the Course of good Husbandry to be ploughed in this Season. And the non-ploughing thereof will be a greate Damage to the Undertenant, without benefit to any other.

Upon the whole the Undertenant humbly Submits to the Judgement of My Lord Bruce, hoping that his Lordship will permit him to plough in this Season the said 100 Acres of the said 190.

Depositions of Witnesses concerning Hippenscombe 30 January 1709

Richard Mason of Fernham in the County of Southampton, Gent., Robert Randoll of the same place, Yeoman, Richard Collins of Chute in the County of Wilts, Yeoman, Griffith Aprichard of the same place, Yeoman, Richard Poor of Blackden in the said County of Wilts, Shepheard, and William Beale of Biddesden in the same County, Yeoman, doe severally make Oath that they doe severally well know the Farme called Hippenscombe Farme in the said County of Wilts, and alsoe the land to that Farme belonging of late yeares called the Warren.

And that these deponents have severally knowne the same viz. The said Richard Mason for near Seaventy Yeares past, the said Robert Randoll, Richard Collins and Griffith Aprichard respectively for forty yeares past and upward, the said Richard Poor for near Seaventy yeares past and the said William Beale for fifty yeares past or thereabouts. And these deponents doe severally say that they have heretofore credibly heard and believe it to be true; that all that part of the said land called the Warren which hath been ploughed up within ten yeares last past was Antiently Coppice land in which were bred a great number of Coneys; and that those Coneys by degrees destroyed the Coppice Wood there growing and the Stooles thereof and from that time forward destroyed all the Herbage where the said Coppice Wood grew, and suffered not Grasse of any value there to grow, soe that from yeare to yeare the same land appeared naked and bare without any Sward thereon. And these deponents doe alsoe severally say that they have credibly heard and believe it to be true that all the Stocke of Coneys which during the memory of man hath been kept on the said land called the Warren, hath been from time to time sold by one Undertenant to another without Interruption; and was allwayes reputed to belong to the Undertenant for the time being and not to the Lord of the Fee or to his Immediate Lessee of the said Farme. And this deponent, William Beale, saith that about one and thirty yeares now last past, he, this deponent, was present as a Witnesse when one Robert Mundy (who had been Undertenant of the said Farme and then goeing of [leaving]) sold to Benjamin Farrenden the succeeding Undertenant all the Stocke of Coneys then being on the said land called the Warren. And these deponents doe further severally say upon their Oaths that the land before mentioned to be ploughed up within two yeares last past (and which may conteyn about One Hundred and Ninety Acres) is a good sort of land for Tillage, and is and will allwayes continue to be more Apt and proper to bear Corne and Graine (convenient times of rest thereof as of other Arable lands being allowed) than for any other use whatsoever; and will after the end of the present Undertenant's terme therein turne to greater profitt in way of Tillage than in any other way: and soe continue. And will in the Intervalls of ploughing bear (in all likelyhood) better Grasse and more in quantity for Cattle (and more particularly for Sheepe) than it could probably have borne before the ploughing thereof. And upon those Grounds and reasons (which these deponents take to be Undenyable) they severally believe that the continuing of the said One Hundred and Ninety Acres to be for ever Arable, will be a perpetuall Improvement of the yearely value thereof and of the said Farme in Generall. And that the preserving of the Unploughed part of the said land called the Warren for a sheep sleight onely will be an Additional Improvement of the same Farme, but the mainteyning of Coneys on the said unploughed part the contrary.

The sayd Richard Mason, Robert Randoll, Richard Collins, Griffith Aprichard, Richard Poor and William Beale came voluntarily and were sworn the one and thirtieth day of January Anno Domini 1709 at Andover in the County of Southampton by me, Charles Imber, Master in Chancery.

Signed by
Robert Randoll, Richard Collins and Griffith Aprichard,
The marks of Richard Mason, Richard Poor and William Beale.

THE LABOURING POOR

Seventeenth-century farming depended upon a large and poorly-paid labour force which was employed intermittently throughout the year. The accounts printed in this volume show that even on large demesne farms only a few men such as the shepherd, carter, drowner and thresher were regularly employed. For tasks such as winter cultivation, drainage, hedge-laying, sheep-shearing, hay-making and above all, corn harvesting numerous casual labourers were engaged. Some of these men had small farms or were part-time craftsmen, but many depended upon day-labour for their livelihood. Inevitably, these men were unemployed for long periods each year, and they were the poorest members of the community. Nonetheless their labour was essential for a successful farming economy.

In north and west Wiltshire the small family-run dairy farms needed little casual labour, but there were many mixed farms with a proportion of arable, needing help at seed-time and harvest. In addition it was landless labourers who transformed the landscape by clearing the former royal forests and enclosing the land for agriculture. They undertook the back-breaking toil of removing the tree stumps; they drained the fields, planted and maintained the hedges, drove cattle to distant markets and their families provided the army of spinners required by the developing cloth industry. On the chalklands they were responsible for the heavy work necessary to create the water meadows. They extended cultivation on the downland and supplied the irregular labour without which the large arable farms could not function. The growth of this sector of the population during the 17th century led to major problems of poverty, homelessness, begging and crime. Unsuccessful government legislation attempting to deal with the indigent poor and the sturdy beggars continued throughout the century. Established communities feared their shiftless neighbours and were alarmed at the inexorable rise in the poor rates, while depending on the labour they supplied, although they sympathised with the plight of honest and hard-working paupers.

Little evidence survives concerning this under-class of casual labourers and their families. They generally possessed no wealth and seldom made wills or left probate inventories. They usually occur in the records only as names in the parish registers, or when appearing before the justices of the peace at Quarter Sessions accused of offences or as recipients of parochial poor relief. There are, however, numerous references in manorial surveys and elsewhere to concern over the erection of dwellings or hovels by paupers on roadside verges, waste land and manorial commons. The practice increased greatly throughout the

17th century as population grew and it became more difficult for casual labourers to find accommodation. On the claylands there were extensive commons and looser manorial supervision, so that it was easier to find sites, but there was less demand for casual labour. On much of the chalklands the vigilance of landlords, stewards and manorial courts strongly resisted intrusion on the commons, but even here illicit dwellings multiplied. In his Survey of Mere in 1617 John Norden noted that 13 cottages had been erected without licence on the manorial waste and the inhabitants were paying no rent. [PRO LR2/207 ff 24v-25]. A survey of the cottages on the extensive commons in the large manor of Steeple Ashton in 1637 listed no less than 138; many had been there for more than thirty years, and a few for even longer. Over the years they had evidently been made into fairly substantial dwellings and most included gardens, several of which measured more than half an acre. The figures for cottages in each part of the manor were as follows:

Brokers Wood	*37 cottages*	
North Bradley	*29*	
West Ashton	*32*	
Semington	*9*	
Hinton	*11*	
Steeple Ashton	*15*	*[WSRO 947/1237].*

*Lacock in 1610 was said to be 'surcharged by the multitude of inmates and those of the poorest sort to the number of sixtie persons like to lye in the Streete for want of houses'. The owner of the manor, Olive Stapilton, together with the vicar, Richard Rooke, and other parishioners petitioned the justices of the peace in Quarter Sessions for permission to erect 15 cottages on the manorial commons, and asked that those already erected without licence by 'good and honest people' should be allowed to remain. [*Historical Manuscripts Commmission, Various Collections, *I, 1901, 81-2; Cunnington 31]. At Purton in 1625 the parishioners complained that 'upwards of three score cottages' had been built and that the poverty-stricken occupants made an insupportable charge on the poor rates. [*HMC Various Collections, *I, 1901, 95].*

The figures for the dimensions of these dwellings given below show their tiny size and flimsy nature. Most were of extremely rudimentary construction, far removed from the modern meaning of 'cottage'; they can be more properly described as 'hovel', 'cabin' or 'hut'. No doubt the furnishings were as flimsy as the structure. Many were erected overnight on the erroneous, but widely-held belief, that such rapid construction somehow gave squatters' rights. An indication of the construction and rapid erection occurs in the court rolls of Alderholt just over the Hampshire border in 1625. The tenants complained to the manorial steward that a poor labourer, Richard Cooke, 'intends either this night or the next to set up a house (which he hath already framed) upon the common of Alderholt, and hath placed straw upon the common in the place he hath made choyce of to erect his house in'. The tenants objected because they claimed that the number of squatters who had already built hovels on the common was so great that the grazing land available for their livestock was severely restricted. [Hatfield House, Salisbury MSS, Cranborne General 1620-29, 9 May 1625]. An example from Downton in 1698 of a similar insubstantial dwelling, built overnight by driving posts into the ground to create a framework, is given below. The petitions from Melksham in 1628 quoted below also mention that the cottage was 'newlie erected and sett upp in the night'. In spite of manorial restrictions and the complaints of established residents, squatters' settlements grew up in many parts of Wiltshire during the 17th and 18th centuries. Although the original rudimentary dwellings have long since been replaced by substantial houses, examples of squatters' settlements established around a common can still be recognized, for example around Warminster common, and scattered about the former commons at Broughton Gifford, Steeple Ashton, Dilton Marsh, Semley, and in ironically-named settlements such as Ireland in North Bradley, Scotland in Southwick, Cuckolds Green near Worton, Little London in Heytesbury and Little Salisbury in Milton Lilbourne.

The following examples illustrate this feature of 17th-century rural life in Wiltshire.

Cottages on the Waste at Urchfont

WSRO 283/17 ff93-4

From the Manorial Survey of Urchfont 1606 & 1630

Much of this survey is in Latin and has been translated into English. The original survey was made in 1606 and was up-dated at various times up to 1630.

Cottages within the Manor and upon the waste there without licence and rent presented by the homage 24 October 4 James I 1606. Enlarged there 4 October 15 [recte 6] Charles I 1630 and now in the occupation of the persons written below viz.

1. John [Gallett crossed through] Fisher holds one cottage next to his brother William Fisher in peppercombe containing in length 13 feet and in width 8 feet, built about 30 years ago 4 James I
2. Thomas Bennet and Edrus Crewes one cottage in the upper greene containing in length 14 feet and in width 10 feet with a garden containing 2 perches built about 2 years ago 4 James I
3. Robert Willis one cottage in the upper greene containing in length 14 feet and in width 10 feet, built about 1 year 4 James I
4. Edrus Hailes one cottage in Crookmarsh in length 14 feet and in width 10 feet with a garden containing 3 perches erected about 5 years ago 4 James I and 6 perches of land in Crookmarsh adjoining the cottage
5. Thomas Byssie one cottage in Crookmarsh in length 12 feet asnd in width 10 feet erected about 18 years ago 4 James I
6. William Fisher one cottage within Peppercomb Hill containing in length 13 feet and in width 10 feet with a garden 3 perches erected about 16 years ago 4 James I

7. John Earle one cottage in Upton-velk containing in length 12 feet and in width 8 feet erected anno ult 4 James I
8. John Richards and [blank] Byssy one cottage in Upton vilk containing in length 13 feet and in width 10 feet erected anno 4 James I
9. John Elmes one cottage in Upton Vilk in length 10 feet and in width 8 feet erected about 12 years ago in Fryers Lane xpe Upton Well 4 James I
10. Robert Wootton & John Hotkins one cottage in Upton Vilks in length 14 feet and in width 10 feet erected about 10 years ago 4 James I
11. William Hobbes, Humfrey Snelgrove, John Covell and Elizabeth Chaundler one cottage containing in length 14 feet and in width 10 feet erected about 2 years ago 4 James I
12. William Penrose one cottage in Upton Velk containing in length 14 feet and in width 10 feet erected about 2 years ago 4 James I
13. Maurice Alexander one cottage at Peppercombe Lane containing [blank] erected by order of the churchwardens and [housing?] paupers ther 4 James I
14. Thomas Willsheire one cottage newly erected containing 3 perches at Fishways under Hambank 6 James I
15. Edward & John Hewlet one cottage containing 1 perch lying at Peasgaston bank erected about 5 years ago 8 James I
16. William Blanket one cottage containing 1 perch at Peasgaston lane in the street erected about 2 years ago 6 James I
17. Elizabeth Hobbes one cottage in length 12 feet and in width 12 feet in the street of Urchfont at Uptowne well erected 6 James I
18. Thomas Myles one cottage at Fiverways under Hambank containing in length 16 feet and in width 12 feet erected 8 James I
19. Maria Odie one cottage at Fiveways under Hambank containing 12 feet erected about 6 years ago 6 James I
20. Richard Heath one cottage in Crookwood <u>xpe</u> the Farme Moore containing 3 perches erected about 24 years ago 9 James I
21. William Whelpley one cottage at north end of Peasgaston lane containing one perch erected about 40 years ago e.g. James Rex I
22. Walter Balles one cottage in Wedhampton common containing in length and width 16 feet and erected 30 years ago 10 James I
23. Richard Powell one cottage there containing in length 11 feet and in width 11 feet erected about 30 years ago 10 James I
24. Thomas Carter one cottage there in length 15 feet and in width 10 feet erected about 30 years ago 10 James I
25 John Chaundler one cottage in length 10 feet and on width 10 feet erected about 30 years ago 10 James I

[*Note: numbers 22-25 are bracketed presumably because they are all on Wedhampton Common*]

26 Yardland Tithing 26 Thomas Whelpley one cottage containing 16 perches lying in Hoops Greene erected about 20 years ago
27 Anton Whelpley one cottage there and adjacent
28 Maurice Alexander one cottage in Peppercomb Bottom containing one perch and a half 2 James I

29 John Fisher one cottage in Peppercomb Lane adjoining William his brother containing in length 12 feet and in width 8 feet erected 30 years ago 4 James I

Anno Charles 15
30 Robert Harding one cottage at Fishway erected 3 years ago
31 Arnold Berry one cottage there [erected] 5 years ago by order of Sessions
32 Edith Marthew one cottage under Peasgaston Banck de antiquo
33 Edrus & John Hewlett one cottage there erected de antiquo

Great Roll, Quarter Sessions, Devizes, Trinity 1628

WSRO A1/110/1628

No 135 Petition from the Parishioners of Stapleford to the Justices

May it please you to be advertised by your humble supplicants the Parishioners of Stapleford That whereas one John Morley, a poore and aged man of our sayd parish is destitute of a dwellinge house for himself, his poore wife and children, we the sayd Parishioners, with the assent and consent of the Lord of the Manor, have allotted forth a Plotte of Grounde in a conveniente place within our parish and at our Costs and Charges have alreadie begunne in consideration of his distressed estate to erect and set down a house to the use of the sayd poore man, his wife and children.

But because to erect without Licence any Cotage without the allowance of Fower acres of Grounde thereunto is against the Lawes, we the sayd Parishioners before we would finish the Buildinge, have first petitioned Your worships intreatinge your favourable allowance thereof Which if it take its wished evente, the sayd poore man for his parte with his wife and children shalbe bound to praye for your worships. And we for our parte shalbe ready to finish the worke begunne.

Signed by the four overseers of the poor + 3 other parishioners.

No 136 Petition to the Justices of Wiltshire at Devizes from parishioners of Melksham

May it please you in all humble manner to be advertised That whereas one Elias More of the parish of Melksham in the said Countie of Wilts, husbandman, hath of his owne accord newlie erected and sett upp in the night a Cottage in some parte of the Common of the Tythinge of Benacre within the said parishe of Melksham contrarie to the Statute in that case provided, and to the greate annoyance of all the inhabitants of the same Tythinge by reason of the soyle and impost which the said More doe make, for the said Cottage soe built doth stand neare unto a watercourse, which watercourse runneth into a well which is used by the most parte of all the Inhabitants of the same Tythinge to fetche there water. And further the Children of the said More have a Loathsome decease called the White Scurfe which is infeccious. In consideration of which infeccious inconveniences that may come to the inhabitants of the same tythinge our humble desire is that the said More maye be Compelled by order of the Sessions to pull downe the said Cottage. And that by order of the Sessions that yt maye be referred to the Church Wardens and to the Overseers of the Poore of the said parish of Melksham with the consent of your petitioners hereunder written to make choyce of some fitt place within the same tythinge or parishe of Melksham to build a Cottage for the said More. And your petitioners whose names are hereunder written shall pray for your worshipps health longe to continue.

Signed by Sir John Jennings and 4 other parishioners

No 137
The first petition is followed by a second as follows:

To the Justices of the peace of Wiltshire at the Sessions to be held at Devizes

Our duties remembered, may it please yore to the Advertised: That Elias More of the parish of Melksham in the Countie of Wiltes., husbandman, being destitute of an habitation desireth by your allowance to erecte a cottage upon some of the waste placs of Beanacre within the said parish of Melksham. And we th'inhabitants of the said parish whose names are underwritten, Knowinge that he hath lived as an honnest and poore man, and hath obteyned the Consente of the Lord of the Royaltie of the same place, and pittying his Distressed estate in regard of himselfe, his wife and Five small children who are likely to perish through want of harbour, do hereby Signifie both our consents unto his disyres, and that we conceave that it wilbe a worke of greate mercy to satisfie his humble request, which we leave unto the most favourable consideration of your worthiness and wisdomes.

And so doe humbly take our leave Julie the Second 1628

Signed by the Overseers + 29 parishioners.

Order against Illegal Settlers or 'Outcomers' at Donhead in 1663

The growing burden of parish rates to support the poor is reflected in the following order made at the manorial court of Henry, Lord Arundell of Wardour, held at Donhead on 4 May 1663.

WSRO 2667/13/405

Item, present *in hic anglice verbis* whereas we have had a former order that noe Tennant within this tenement shall lett his tenement or parte of his tenement to any Outcomer without such Outcomer give good security by bond with 2 Suretyes for the discharge of the parish where such tenement lyes from al trouble and charge which may growe or come upon such parish or the Inhabitants thereof by reason of such Outcomers inhabiting there in the present or future. And whereas by reason of the discontinuance or remisse observerance of the said order this Mannor have suffered many great inconveniences, It is desired that the said order may be continued. And accordingly at this Court it is ordered that the said former order shall now be reviewed and confirmed with this further addition that yf any Tennant of this manor doe or shall transgresse this order, that he shall forfeite to the Lord of the Mannor 40s upon presentment made thereof in this Court. And if after such presentment he shall continue such undertenant until the next Court after to be held in the Mannor and presentment be againe made thereof as aforesaid, that he shall then forfeit 40s more. And soe att every Court upon presentment made of his continuance of such undertenant he shall forfeite 40s as aforesaid

The Demolition of an Illegal Squatter's Dwelling at Downton 1670–72

The exasperation of landlords and manorial stewards with illegal settlers occasionally reached such a pitch that cottages were actually demolished. The process was not easy, however, and the following account shows the difficulty of obtaining redress through the courts. The manor of Downton was leased from the bishop of Winchester by Sir Joseph Ashe who lived at Twickenham. He represented the borough of Downton in Parliament. The expenses of entertaining voters and securing their votes for the election of 1670 are contained in a volume of accounts kept by the manorial steward, John Snow. Nearly £200 was spent in lavish hospitality, meals, wine, ale and tobacco. At the back of the volume and in a different hand is a list of the costs of court proceedings against John Moore, an illegal squatter, and money spent in demolishing the cottage or hovel which he had erected for himself and his wife. The protracted process was conducted through the courts, and the expenses include inducements given to court officials, witnesses, guarding the accused and the fees to the lawyers, Giles Eyres at Warminster, and Francis Coales and Giles Eyres at Salisbury. There were also expenses for demolishing the cottage. The compiler of this account is unknown, but he was evidently not an educated man.

WSRO 1946/Box12

An Accoumpt of what was disbursted in and about the pullinge downe John Moors Cottage on the wast within the Mannor of Downton

January the 9th day 1670

Laid out for one Inditment against John Moore for the Continnuinge paid for drawinge the bill of inditment 2s 6d which is entered in sum other Accoumpt

Then paid the Bayliff that wated on the grane Jury to cum to deliver him 4d

Paid to the Carryar to deliver him into the Court which is all Ready Enttered 4d

An Accoumpt of what it Coast at Warminster Sessions

	£	s	d
July the 25th day 1671			
for my supper and Phillip Rooke		1	2
The 26th in the morninge spent in beare and bread			8
Then for dinner for Phillip Rooke and my Selfe		1	0
Then for siper for Rooke and my Selfe			10
Paid to the Clarke of the Peaces for a copy of Moorse Inditment to show the Counsell		3	4
Gave Mr Gilles Eyres for his advice and pledinge		10	0
The 27th day paid the Clarke of the Peace for drawinge one other bill of Inditment against John Moore and his wife for Continuing the cottage		2	0
Then paid the Ballif that wited one the grayn Jury to deliver the bill			4
Then paid the Carryar for the delivery to the Court			4
Then Phillip Rooke and my Selfe in the morninge and on the way cominge home		1	0
Then paid for hay for my gelden and mare for two nights and two dayes at 8d a peece		2	8
Then paid for two peckes of oats for them		1	4

January the 9th 1671

Following the hearing at Warminster John Snow was encouraged to go ahead with the action against Moore in a letter from Sir Joseph Ashe dated 5th February 1671 which is printed in the section on Water Meadows in this volume. Sir Joseph wrote 'You take the best way with Moor to bring an ejectment, make him an example, pursue it close, and downe with his Cottadge that the Justices may see they may show their teeth, but cannot byte. We shal then bring the rest to duty' [WSRO 490/910]

WSRO 1946/Box 12

An Accoumpt of what was spent in tranisinge [transacting?] the business at Salsbury Sessions against Moore and his wife

	s	d
Paid Thomas Nicholas for his time in it	1	6
Then gave Mr Gyles Eyres for his fee in it	10	0
Then paid for what Nicholas and Rooke spent in beare and fire in the morninge		6
Then paid for oure 3 dinners and for beare	2	6
Then paid for old Nicholas supper and for fire and beare at night and morninge	2	6

	£	s	d
Then paid for hay and oats for the horses		1	3
	2	3	3
Aprill the 3rd 1672			
Paid Mr Frances Coales for all his trouble and followinge the Shute against Moore howse for the full Charge of bringinge the Right of possession as it apears by his bill	2	12	9
Aprill the 30th			
Paid the under Shreve for to give his warrant of the possession To two bayllifes to give it to me in the howse	1	5	0
Then gave him one pint of sacke		1	0
Then I paid Thomas Aitkens and William Gyles to Execut to —? The goods		1	0
May the 9th day			
Paid John Eastman and Thomas Hatcher for helpinge pull downe the materialls one day a peece		2	8
Then to John Brewer for Cuminge to Carry away the materyalls		1	6
May the 9th day			
Paid Mr Swanson's Clarke for a warrant to keep the peece		1	0
May the 10th			
Paid 6 men that was Carryed in for th'oyer time in it to witness what they saw and hard [heard] them swere in it		6	0
Then spent on them in beare and Cake –John Brewer, John Eastman, Thomas Hatcher, Thomas Smith, William Low, William Gyles		3	0
	5	4	11
recte	[5	1	11]

Cottages at East Downton 1676

WSRO 490/785

This is to give notice to the gentlemen of the Jury of the Court Leet that they make a true returne of all the Cottages Erected on the wast within each severall Tythinge by him selfe and the names of all those that live in them, and the names of all those that have Taken in any plot of Grownde on the wast within all the severall Tythings distinctly by them selves where it is Taken in there may be no more Increas of that Nusence

The Cottagers of East Downton 1676

Robert Moore	William Cinnis	John Bownd
Thomas Tutt sen.	John Reeves	George Newman
Thomas Tutt jun.	Richard Brasvill	George Littlecott
Richard Chalke	Robert Sinear	Richard Bownd
Joseph Chalke	Wid. Read	John Newman
John Chalke	Wid. Wiatt	Wid. Hatchett *
Wid. Roff	Thomas Humby	Roger Read *
John Barham	Custec Collence	Wid. Wikens *
John Dible	William Luke	James Triphoke
Richard Gerrit	Simon Marshment	William Russle
Edward Madgwicke	Roger Newman	William Linly
Thomas Morgan	Henry Goolden	Robert Payne
George Gooldne	John Wyatt	Wid. Bidlecum

**these are crossed out*

Load Hill Incroachments that have no Cottages

Nicholas Wilson	Joseph Stokes	Will Merryfield
Henry Read	John Stokes	Richard Longyears
John Grey	Robert Wheatley	Robert Stoure
Richard Gilliatt	William Vine	Matthew Shutton
William Shutter	John Petty	Thomas Caulet
Richard Bampton	Thomas Martin	James Gandy
Charles Shellow	Kitt Wornell	Thomas Eastman
Thomas Umphrey	Robert Gandy sen.	Will. Rennolds
Nicholas Taylor	Richard Mowdy	Rich. Sheereinge
John Newman sen.	Roger Mowdy	Richard Nutbeame
John Newman jun.	Roger Read	William Colds Esqr
Thomas Nicholas	Wid. Wilkens	John Blake
John Early	Wid. Hatchett	Wid. Holloway
John Rose	John Meggs	John Clarke
Thomas Stotes sen.	James Rennolds	Henry Pelley
Thomas Stotes jun.		

4 Parcells of ground Taken in in Trimbury Lane

Roger Gaulet Linell Tutt

One plot of ground Taken in in Charleton.

Continuing problems with squatters at Downton 1677

Established residents and copyhold tenants also resented the influx of squatters who occupied common grazing and could impose a heavy burden on the poor rates. A list of presentments made by the Homage at the manorial court of Downton in 1677 includes the following complaint.

WSRO 490/916

Item, wee present that there are severall incroachments made on the Tennants Common and on the Lord's Waste by setting up of Cottages, and wee desire that care may be taken that noe more may be erected.

Controversy over squatters on the waste at Downton 1694

This petition and letters illustrate the scale of the problem and the strength of the controversy over the squatters' settlement on the common. The letter from John Snow also shows how indispensable manorial stewards were to the non-resident owners of manors. The Statute of 1601 (43 Elizabeth) which is referred to in the letters forbade the building of cottages unless four acres of land were attached.

WSRO 490/925

Petition to the Justices from the Churchwardens and Overseers of the Poor of Downton concerning Cottages 5 February 1694

Wee, the Church Wardens and Overseers of the parish of Downton in the County of Wilts., Doe pray his Majesties Justices of the Peace that they will consent unto the puttinge of Jane Chalke, widow, and John Marchment into the Cottages in a place called the Drove adjoyninge to Richard Chalke's on the East side and John Hevill in a cottage in Rotten Row next the highway on the South side of Christopher Collence's on the East side of Joane Reads, and Thomas Humby in a cottage on the East side of the Common, the widow Bist on the South side and William Vine on the North side, and John Mussellwhite and Shusanah Fanstone, widow, in a cottage on the East side of Woodfolds Hill att the East end of Arthur Rolphs and Richard Prince in a cottage on the south side of Kighterrat Lane west from William Saunderses, and Richard Roby in a cottage on the south east side next Will Reynoldses and Richard Nutbeam in a cottage att the west end, and on the north side of Blacke Lane etc. These beinge poore persons within our said parish, and want houses for their habitations, and these being cottages built on the wast of the said manor many years since which are att the dispose of the Church wardens and overseers of the poore accordinge to the Statuett of 43 Eliz. Which wee doe thinke are convenient habitations for them.

James Simons
Ephraim Davis Churchwardens

David Done
John Snelgar
Joseph Humby Overseers of the Poore

Wee whose names are here under written his Majesties Justices of the Peace of the County of Wilts. Aforesaid doe consent hereunto.

Witness our hands this 5th of February 1694

John Young		
Giles Eyre	Thomas Stringer	
Sam. Eyre	James Lynch	Will Hearst

I would have a stop put to this until farther Consideration
B. Winton, bishop of Winchester.

Letter from Benjamin Wyche and others to Lady Mary Ashe concerning cottages on Downton Common 14 February 1694

WSRO 490/909

Madam,
Mr Snow hath delivered declarations in ejectment to turne out a great many poor Creatures out of their small Cottages built upon Downton Common. Your Ladyship will see it is the desire of the Churchwardens and Overseers of the Poore of Downton that these poore people may continue in their cottages undisturbed. Several justices of the peace have sett their hands like wise to the paper as also the two Mr Justice Eyres and the Bishop of Winchester has set his hand to it wherein he desires a stop may be putt to the proceedings against these poore creatures. I doubt not but that this besides your own Charitable disposition will prevaile with your Ladyship to give imediatt orders to cause any farther prosecution and not to harken to the advises of Mr Snow, who is little moved with the Cryes of the poore where a little small Interest is concerned. Your Ladyship's pardon for giveinge you this trouble and I am though unknowne to you

Your Ladyship's most humble servant
14 February 1694 Ben. Wyche

Jane Chalke, widow	Thomas Humby	Rich. Hoby, a plot of ground
John Marshman	John Musslewhite	Rich. Nutbeame, a plot of ground
John Kevil	Susanah Flanstone	John Wyatt
	Richard Prince	Robert Cooper

Letter from John Snow at Downton to Lady Mary Ashe at Twickenham 16 February 1694

WSRO 490/909

Madam
Yours of the 16th instant received, I beg leave to give your Ladyship an Answer

to the several particulars therein contained. As for Mr Borland's herriots I never promised him they should be remitted and therefore I know of no reason he had to express his thanks towards me upon any such Account. I think 'tis not material for your Ladyship to take any Lease of the penninge of the Weare and the Weare Gaps from Mr Borland till Mr Duncomb's work is finished, and in the meane while to let matters continue as they are; and I do likewise think that 'tis not any way advisable for your Ladyship to take any Lease of the Water from Mr Borland for by such an Act you will acknowledge your Water to be his, whereas 'tis your Ladyship's, as being Lady of the Manor of Downton. If Mr Duncomb be desirous to take a License for digging clay and sand for making of Brick, and for digging Chalk for burning of Lime, he must come into Court and Request it, which for a small fine may be there granted him; and this hath been the Method within the Manor of Downton in such Cases.

Of your Ladyship's designs to have an Abstract of so much of the Court Rates as may be material for the prefering Your Rights and Interest within the Manor of Downton, I think there will be a necessity to have it done here (here I can provide Mr Stillingfleet's Directions and Instances). There is no occasion of Making an Abstract of the whole, and indeed that would be a Work too tedious for any one to undertake.

I will take care to send Mr Wheeler's Thoughts by the first Conveniences.

I can not as yet hear of any Tenant to succeed Farmer Michell for New Court Farm, but I shall use all the Industry I can to procure one; but if it happens that no tenant or tenants can be found for it, then there will be a necessity to put in a stock, and to have servants to manage the same.

I received the papers about the Cottagers signed by the two Justices Eyres. The person that wrote you the letter (Mr Wyche) is Clerk to Mr Samuel Eyre and your letter will find him at Sergeant's Inn in Chancery Lane. There are in the whole upon Downton wast above 100 Cottages, besides many small Enclosures which I believe have all been Erected since the Statute [of 31 Eliz. C7, 1588-9] by which Statute there is £10 Penalty for the Erection and 40s by the month for the Continuance of every such Cottage. But the Jurys of Courts will not [implement?] them, So that we may have no other way but to deliver Declarations of Ejectment, and to get writs of possession, and the Sheriff to execute them. I find that most of these Cottagers set up Titles under other people from whom they have accepted Conveyances, which I suppose they have severally done In pursuance of Advice they have received from some of our Learned.

By the Paper sent you there is some Colour for Law by the aforementioned Statute for what you designed thereby. But 'tis well known that none of these Cottagers are Impotent, for that about 10 or more of them with their own money paid fines for their Houses, and have stocks of Cattle upon the Commons, and receive no Relief of the Parish. But on the contrary live very well. Every summer enlargeth the number of Cottagers and Encroachments, so that some effectual Course might be taken, at great Expense, to stop these proceedings. If you please, Madam, you may in your letter to Mr Wyche let him know that I have been one of the best Benefactors under Sir Joseph Ashe and your Ladyship and others towards these poor Cottagers in the parish of Downton by finding

Employment for them at Home and abroad, and that you would be glad to hear from him or any other of any Interest that I have ever made to my self by reason of such Cottages erected; and that I have not obeyed the orders of Sir Joseph Ashe and you from time to time given me for the Demolishing of these Cottages and throwing open the enclosures.

The Justices of the peace ought to be put in mind that all the presentments have been made at their privy sessions of the great numbers of people that have from time to time been fit by the Statute to be put abroad to service; that yet they have taken no orders or care herein which is the present cause of the great Increase of Cottagers. I believe you would not be against the Erecting or Continuing of a certain number of Cottages that should be decreed to Continue for the habitations for poor Impotent People, if you could once Reduce or put a stop to these Cottages now in being.

I humbly conceave, Madam, 'tis absolutely necessary for you to stand upon your Right, and to get some of the present Cottages thrown down, especially such as are bought and sold by the Cottagers.

Madam, Your most faithful servant.
John Snow.

An account of such persons as were concerned about breaking the Lady's wast in the Franchicis of Downton and erecting a new cottage there 16th May 1698

WSRO 490/932

Monday 16th May 1698
An account of those that in a riotous manner broke the Lady's wast within the Franchises of Downton by digging holes in the ground to putt in posts for erecting of a Cottage on the wast, the said worke being begun the day & yeare abovesaid, and notwithstanding the workmen (whose names are hereunder) were forbidden by John Snow, servant to the Lady Ash from proceeding any further in the said worke, yett in contempt thereof they have proceeded & finished the said Cottage.

Nicholas Lawes, senior who is owner of the Cottage
Samuell Wheeler Carpenter
Walter Sheppard Apprentice to Abe Wheeler

Joseph Clarke, junior who thatched the said Cottage
George Noble who breaded the walls of the said Cottage
One other man who holpe digge the holes for erecting the Said Cottage

SELECT BIBLIOGRAPHY

ABBREVIATIONS

AHR	*Agricultural History Review*
EcHR	*Economic History Review*
JHG	*Journal of Historical Geography*
P & P	*Past & Present*
WANHM	*Wiltshire Archaeological & Natural History Magazine*
WRS	Wiltshire Record Society (formerly Wiltshire Archaeological Society Records Branch

Indispensable for any investigation of historic farming in Wiltshire are the volumes of the *Victoria County History of Wiltshire*, especially volume IV, and the parochial histories. The numerous histories of individual towns and villages within the county also contain much information. In addition, the following works are particularly useful:

Aubrey, J. *The Natural History of Wiltshire,* edited by J. Britton, 1847. Later publication edited. by K. Ponting, 1969.

Aubrey, J. *Wiltshire: The Topographical Collections*, edited by J.E. Jackson, 1862.

Bennett, (Canon). 'The Orders of Shrewton 1599', *WANHM*, 23, 1887, 33-9.

Bettey, J.H. 'The Cultivation of Woad in the Salisbury Area', *Textile History*, 9, 1978, 112-7.

Bettey, J.H. *Rural Life in Wessex 1500-1900*, 2nd edn.1987.

Bettey, J.H. *Wessex from AD1000*, 1986.

Bettey, J.H.'The Development of Water Meadows in the Southern Counties', in H. Cook & T. Williamson, eds., *Water Management in the English Landscape*, 1999, 179-95.

Bettey, J.H.'Downlands' in J. Thirsk, ed., *The English Rural Landscape*, 2000, 27-49.

Bettey, J.H. 'The Eyes and Ears of the Lord: Seventeenth –Century Manorial Stewards in South Wiltshire', *WANHM*, 96, 2003, 19-25

Bettey, J.H. 'The Development of water meadows on the Salisbury Avon 1665-90', *AHR* 51, Part ii, 2003, 27-36.

Bettey, J.H. 'The Production of Rabbits in Wiltshire during the Seventeenth Century', *Antiquaries Journal*, 84, 2004, 380-92]

Blith, W. *The English Improver Improved*, 1652.

Boswell, G. *A Treatise on Watering Meadows*, 1779.

Bowie, G. 'Watermeadows in Wessex', *AHR*, 35, 1987, 151-8.

Brentnall, H.C. 'A Document from Great Cheverell', *WANHM*, 3, 1950, 430-40.

Cobbett, W. *Rural Rides*, Everyman edn., 1912.

Cook, H. & Williamson, T. eds., *Water Management in the English Landscape*, 1999.

Cowan, M. *Floated Water Meadows in the Salisbury Area*, 1982 (South Wiltshire Industrial Archaeology Society, Monograph 9)

Cunnington, B.H. *Records of the County of Wiltshire: being extracts from the Quarter Sessions Rolls Great Rolls of the Seventeenth Century*, 1932.
Davis, T. *A General View of the Agriculture of the County of Wiltshire*, 1794; 2nd ed, 1813.
Defoe, D. *A Tour Through England and Wales*, Everyman edn., 1959.
Edwards, P. *The Horse Trade of Tudor and Stuart England*, 1988.
Fry, C.B. *Hannington: The Records of a Wiltshire Parish*, Gloucester, 1935.
Goddard, C.V. 'Customs of the Manor of Winterbourne Stoke 1574', *WANHM*, 34, 1905-6, 208-15.
Hoare, R.C. *History of Modern Wiltshire*, 6 vols., 1822-44.
Hobbs, S. *Wiltshire Glebe Terriers 1588-1827* (WRS, 56, 2003).
Hurry, J.B. *The Woad Plant and its Dye*, Oxford, 1930.
Jackson, J.E. 'Chippenham, Notes of its history', *WANHM*, 12, 1870, 259-92.
Jackson, J.E. 'On the History of Chippenham', *WANHM*, 3, 1856, 19-46.
Jackson, J.E. 'Selwood Forest', *WANHM*, 23, 1887, 268-94.
Jackson, J.E. 'Vale of Warminster', *WANHM*, 17, 1878, 282-306.
Kerridge, E. '*The Agrarian Development of Wiltshire 1540-1640*', typescript thesis Ph.D., London University, 1951.
Kerridge, E. 'The Notebook of a Wiltshire Farmer in the early seventeenth century', *WANHM*, 54, 1951-2, 416-28.
Kerridge, E. *Surveys of the Manors of Philip, Earl of Pembroke and Montgomery 1631-2* (WRS, 9, 1953).
Kerridge, E. 'The Floating of the Wiltshire Water Meadows', *WANHM*, 55, 1953, 105-18.
Kerridge, E. 'The Sheepfold in Wiltshire and the Floating of the Watermeadows', *EcHR*, 2nd Ser., 6, 1954, 282-9.
Kerridge, E. 'Revolts in Wiltshire against Charles I', *WANHM*, 57, 1958, 64-75.
Kerridge, E. 'Agriculture c1500-1793' in *VCH Wiltshire*, IV, 1959, 43-64.
Lisle, E. *Observations in Husbandry*, 1757.
Manley, F.H. 'Customs of the Manor of Purton', *WANHM*, 40, 1917-19, 110-18.
Manley, F.H. 'Parliamentary Surveys of the Crown Lands in Braden Forest (1651)', *WANHM*, 46, 1932-4, 176-84.
Moody, R. *John Benett of Pyt House*, 2003
Overton, M. *Agricultural Revolution in England*, 1996.
Pugh, R.B. *Calendar of Antrobus Deeds before 1625* (WRS, 3, 1947).
Rickard, R.L. *Progress Notes of Warden Woodward for the Wiltshire estates of New College, Oxford, 1659-75* (WRS, 13, 1957).
Scrope, G.P. *History of the Manor Ancient Barony of Castle Combe in the county of Wiltshire*, 1852.
Sheail, J. 'Rabbits and Agriculture in Post Medieval England', *JHG*, 4, 1978, 343-55.
Steele, N. 'Sir Joseph Ashe: An Advocate of Watermeadows', *Hatcher Review*, 13, 1982, 125-32.
Thirsk, J. ed., *The Agrarian History of England and Wales*, IV, (1500-1640), 1967.
Thirsk, J. ed., *The Agrarian History of England and Wales*, V, (1640-1750), 1984.
Thirsk, J. *Alternative Agriculture*, 1997.
Thirsk, J. ed., *The English Rural Landscape*, 2000.
Worlidge, J. *Systema Agriculturae*, 1669.
Young, G.M. *'Some Wiltshire cases in Star Chamber'*, *WANHM*, 50, 1942-4, 446-51.

INDEX OF PERSONS AND PLACES

Places are in Wiltshire unless otherwise stated.

INDEX OF SUBJECTS

The following subject index is inevitably selective, since subjects such as sheep, cattle, pigs, wheat, barley and other crops occur on almost every page, as do references to cultivation and harvest. The aim has been to include all major references to farming methods, new crops, livestock management, innovations, land ownership and working conditions.

WILTSHIRE RECORD SOCIETY
(AS AT MARCH 2005)

PRIVATE MEMBERS

ADAMS, MS S, 23 Rockcliffe Avenue, Bathwick, Bath BA2 6QP

ANDERSON, MR D M, 6 Keepers Mews, Munster Road, Teddington, Middlesex TW11 9NB.

APPLEGATE, MISS J M, 55 Holbrook Lane, Trowbridge BA14 0PS

BADENI, COUNTESS JUNE, Norton Manor, Norton, Malmesbury SN16 0JN

BAINBRIDGE, MS V, 45 Parklands, Trowbridge BA14 8NR

BAINES, MRS B M, 32 Tybenham Road, Merton Park, London SW19 3LA

BARNETT, MR B A, 17 Alexandra Road, Coalpit Heath, Bristol BS36 2PY

BATHE, MR G, Byeley in Densome, Woodgreen, Fordingbridge, Hants SP6 2QU

BAYLIFFE, MR B G, 3 Green Street, Brockworth, Glos GL3 4LT

BENNETT, DR N, Hawthorn House, Main Street, Norton, Lincoln LN4 2BH

BERRETT, MR A M, 10 Primrose Hill Road, London NW3 3AD

BERRY, MR C, 9 Haven Rd, Crackington Haven, Bude, Cornwall EX23 0PD

BISHOP, MRS S M, Innox Bungalow, Market Place, Colerne, Chippenham SN14 8AY

BLAKE, MR P A, 18 Rosevine Road, London SW20 8RB

BLAKE, MR T N, Glebe Farm, Tilshead, Salisbury SP3 4RZ

BOX, MR S D, 73 Silverdale Road, Earley, Reading RG6 2NF

BRAND, DR P A, 155 Kennington Road, London SE11 6SF

BRITTON, MR D J, Overbrook House, The High Road, Ashton Keynes, Swindon SN6 6NL

BROOKE-LITTLE, MR J P, Heyford House, Lower Heyford, Bicester, Oxon OX25 5NZ

BROWN, MR D A, 36 Empire Road,

Salisbury SP2 9DF
BROWN, MR G R, 6 Canbury Close, Amesbury, SalisburySP4 7QF
BRYANT, MRS D, 1 St John's Ct, Devizes SN10 1BJ
BURGESS, MR I D, 29 Brackley Avenue, Fair Oak, Eastleigh, Hants SO5 7FL
BURGESS, MR J M, Tolcarne, Wartha Mill, Porkellis, Helston, Cornwall TR13 0HX
BURNETT-BROWN, MISS J M, Lacock Abbey, Lacock, Chippenham SN15 2LG
CARR, PROF D R, Dept. of History, 140 7th Ave South, St Petersburg, Florida 33701 USA
CARRIER, MR S, 9 Highfield Road, Bradford on Avon BA15 1AS
CARTER, DR B J, JP PHD BSC FSG, 15 Walton Grange, Bath Road, Swindon SN1 4AH
CAWTHORNE, MRS N, 45 London Road, Camberley, Surrey GU15 3UG
CHALMERS, MR D, Bay House West, Bay House, Ilminster, Somerset TA19 0AT
CHANDLER, DR J H, Jupe's School, The Street, East Knoyle, Salisbury SP3 6AJ
CHARD, MR I, 35 Thingwall Park, Fishponds, Bristol BS16 2AJ
CHURCH, MR T S, Mannering House, Bethersden, Ashford, Kent TN26 3DJ
CLARK, MR A G, Highlands, 51a Brook Drive, Corsham SN13 9AX
CLARK, MRS V, 29 The Green, Marlborough SN8 1AW
COBERN, MISS A M, 4 Manton Close, Manton, Marlborough SN8 4HJ
COLCOMB, MR D M, 38 Roundway Park, Devizes SN10 2EO
COLE, MRS J A, 113 Groundwell Road, Swindon SN1 2NA
COLEMAN, MISS J, Swn-y-Coed, Abergwili, Carmarthenshire SA32 7EP
COLES, MR H, Ebony House, 23 Lords Hill, Coleford, Glos GL16 8BG
COLLINS, MR A T, 11 Lemon Grove, Whitehill, Bordon, Hants GU35 9BD
CONGLETON, LORD, West End Farm, Ebbesbourne Wake, Salisbury SP5 5JW
COOMBES-LEWIS, MR R J, 45 Oakwood Park Road, Southgate, London N14 6QP
COOPER, MR S, 12 Victory Row, Wootton Bassett, Swindon SN4 7BE
COULSTOCK, MISS P H, 15 Pennington Crescent, West Moors, Wimborne, Dorset BH22 0JH
COVEY, MR R V, Lower Hunts Mill, Wootton Bassett, Swindon SN4 7QL
COWAN, COL M, 24 Lower Street, Harnham, Salisbury SP3 8EY
CRIGHTON, MR G S, 68 Stanford Avenue, Springfield, Milton Keynes MK6 3NH
CROOK, MR P H, Bradavon, 45 The Dales, Cottingham, E Yorks HU16 5JS
CROUCH, MR J W, 25 Biddesden Lane, Ludgershall, Andover SP11 5PJ
CROWLEY, DR D A, 7 Gibbs Mews, Alfred Street, Westbury BA13 3DT
CUNNINGTON, MS J, 1177 Yonge Street, #214, Toronto, Ont. M4T 2Y4, Canada
D'ARCY, MR J N, The Old Vicarage, Edington, Westbury
DAVIES, MRS A M, 283 Longstone Road, Iver Heath, Bucks SL0 0RN
DIBBEN, MR A A, 18 Clare Road, Lewes, East Sussex BN7 1PN
DYSON, MRS L, 1 Dauntsey Ct, Duck St, West Lavington, Devizes SN10 4LR
EDE, DR M E, 12 Springfield Place, Lansdown, Bath BA1 5RA
EDWARDS, MR P C, 33 Longcroft Road, Devizes SN10 3AT
ELLIOTT, DR J, South Barn, Old Standlynch Farm, Downton, Salisbury SP5 3QR
ELRINGTON, PROF C R, 34 Lloyd Baker Street, London WC1X 9AB
FIRMAGER, MRS G M, 72b High Street, Semington, Trowbridge BA14 6JR
FLOWER-ELLIS, DR J G, Swedish Univ of Agric Sciences, PO Box 7072 S-750 07, Uppsala, Sweden 1972
FORBES, MISS K G, Bury House, Codford, Warminster
FOSTER, MR R E, The New House, St Giles Close, Gt Maplestead, Halstead, Essex CO9 2RW
FOX, MS B, 7 Crespigny Road, Hendon, London NW4 3DT
FOY, MR J D, 28 Penn Lea Road, Bath BA1 3RA
FROST, MR B C, Red Tiles, Cadley, Collingbourne Ducis, Marlborough

SN8 3EA
FULLER, MRS B, 65 New Park Street, Devizes SN10 1DR
GALE, MRS J, 169 Spit Road, Mosman, NSW 2088, Australia
GHEY, MR J G, 18 Bassett Row, Bassett, Southampton SO1 7FS
GIBBS, MRS E, Home Farm, Barrow Gurney, Bristol BS48 3RW
GODDARD, MR R E H, Sinton Meadow, Stokes Lane, Leigh Sinton, Malvern, Worcs WR13 5DY
GOODBODY, MR E A, Stockmans, Rectory Hill, Amersham, Bucks
GOSLING, REV DR J, 1 Wiley Terrace, Wilton, Salisbury SP2 0HN
GOUGH, MISS P M, 39 Whitford Road, Bromsgrove, Worcs B61 7ED
GOULD, MR L K, 263 Rosemount, Pasadena, California 91103 USA
GRIFFIN, DR C J, School of Geographical Sciences, University of Bristol, University Road, Bristol BS8 1SS
GRIFFITHS, MR T J, 29 Saxon Street, Chippenham SN15
GRUBER VON ARNI, COL E E, 11 Park Lane, Swindon SN1 5HG
GUNSTONE, MR L, 29 Dorset St, Bath BA2 3RA
HAMILTON, CAPTAIN R, 1 The Square, Cathedral Views, Crane Bridge Road, Salisbury SP2 7TW
HARDEN, MRS J O, The Croft, Tisbury Road, Fovant, Salisbury SP3 5JU
HARE, DR J N, 7 Owens Road, Winchester, Hants SO22 6RU
HARTE, DR N, St Aldhelm's Cottage, 5 Stokes Road, Corsham SN13 9AA
HATCHWELL, MR R C, Cleeve House, Rodbourne Bottom, Malmesbury SN16 0EZ
HAYWARD, MISS J E, Pleasant Cottage, Crockerton, Warminster BA12 8AJ
HEATON, MR R J, 16 St Bernard's Crescent, Harlow Road, High Wycombe HP11 1BL
HELMHOLZ, PROF R W, Law School, 1111 East 60th Street, Chicago, Illinois 60637 USA
HERRON, MRS Pamela M, 25 Anvil Crescent, Broadstone, Dorset BH18 9DY
HICKMAN, MR M R, 184 Surrenden Road, Brighton BN1 6NN
HICKS, MR I, 74 Newhurst Park, Hilperton, Trowbridge BA14 7QW
HICKS, PROF M A, King Alfred's College, Winchester SO22 4NR
HILLMAN, MR R B, 18 Carnarvon Close, Chippenham SN14 0PN
HINTON, MR A E, Glenside Cottage, Glendene Avenue, East Horsley, Surrey KT24 5AY
HOBBS, MR S, 63 West End, Westbury BA13 3JQ
HOLLEY, MR R J, 120 London Road, Calne SN11 0AH
HORNBY, MISS E, 70 Archers Court, Castle Street, Salisbury SP1 3WE
HORTON, MR P.R.G, OBE, Hedge End, West Grimstead, Salisbury SP5 3RF
HOWELLS, Jane, 7 St Mark's Rd, Salisbury SP1 3AY
HUGHES, MR R G, 60 Hurst Park Road, Twyford, Reading RG10 0EY
HULL, MR J L F, Sandown Apartments, 1 Southerwood Drive, Sandy Bay, Tasmania 7005, Australia
HUMPHRIES, MR A G, Rustics, Blacksmith's Lane, Harmston, Lincoln LN5 9SW
HUNT, MS S, 24 High Street, Bradninch, Devon EX5 4QL
INGRAM, DR M J, Brasenose College, Oxford OX1 4AJ
JAMES, MR & MRS C, 18 King Henry Drive, Grange Park, Swindon SN5 6BL
JAMES, MR J F, 3 Sylvan Close, Hordle, Lymington, Hants SO41 0HJ
JEACOCK, MR D, 16 Church Street, Wootton Bassett, Swindon
JELLICOE, RT HON EARL, Tidcombe Manor, Tidcombe, Marlborough SN8 3SL
JOHNSTON, MRS J M, Greystone House, 3 Trowbridge Road, Bradford on Avon BA15 1EE
KENT, MR T A, Rose Cottage, Isington, Alton, Hants GU34 4PN
KITE, MR P J, 13 Chestnut Avenue, Farnham GU9 8UL
KNEEBONE, MR W J R, Rose Cottage, Barbican Hill, Looe PL13 1BB
KUNIKATA, MR K, Dept of Economics, 1-4-12, Kojirakawa-machi, Yamagata-shi 990, Japan

LANSDOWNE, MARQUIS OF, Bowood House, Calne SN11 0LZ
LAURENCE, MISS A, 1a Morreys Avenue, Oxford OX1 4ST
LAURENCE, MR G F, Apt 312, The Hawthorns, 18-21 Elton Road, Clevedon BS21 7EH
LAWES, MR G, 48 Windsor Avenue, Leighton Buzzard LU7 1AP
LODGE, MR O R W, Southridge House, Hindon, Salisbury SP3 6ER
LOWE, MRS P, Sunnymead, Old Storridge, Alfrick, Worcs WR6 5HT
LUSH, DR G J, 5 Braeside Court, West Moors, Ferndown, Dorset BH22 0JS
LYONS, MAJ GEN A, CBE, Stoke Farm House, Beechingstoke, Pewsey SN9 6HQ
MARSH, REV R, 67 Hythe Crescent, Seaford, East Sussex BN25 3TZ
MARSHMAN, MR M J, 13 Regents Place, Bradford on Avon BA15 1ED
MARTIN, MR D, 21 Westbourne Close, Salisbury SP1 2RU
MARTIN, MS J, 21 Ashfield Road, Chippenham SN15 1QQ
MASLEN, MR A, 8 Alder Walk, Frome, Som BA11 2SN
MATHEWS, MR R, P O Box R72, Royal Exchange, NSW 2000, Australia
MATTHEWS, CANON W A, Holy Trinity Vicarage, 18a Woolley St, Bradford on Avon BA15 1AF
MATTINGLY, MR N, Freshford Manor, Freshford, Bath BA3 6EF
MILLINGTON, MRS P, Hawkstone, Church Hill, Lover, Salisbury SP5 2PL
MOLES, MRS M I, 40 Wyke Road, Trowbridge BA14 7NP
MONTAGUE, MR M D, 115 Stuarts Road, Katoomba, NSW 2780, Australia
MOODY, MR R F, Fair Orchard, South Widcombe, East Harptree, Bristol BS40 6BL
MORIOKA, PROF K 3-12, 4-chome, Sanno, Ota-ku, Tokyo, Japan
MORLAND, MRS N, 33 Shaftesbury Road, Wilton, Salisbury SP2 0DU
MORRISON, MRS J, Priory Cottage, Bratton, Westbury BA13
MOULTON, DR A E, The Hall, Bradford on Avon BA15
NAPPER, MR L R, 9 The Railway Terrace, Kemble, Cirencester GL7 6AU
NEWBURY, MR C COLES, 6 Leighton Green, Westbury BA13 3PN
NEWMAN, MRS R, Tanglewood, Laverstock Park, Salisbury SP1 1QJ
NOKES, MR P M A, Wards Farm, Ditcheat, Shepton Mallet, Somerset BA4 6PR
O'DONNELL, MISS S J, 42 Wessington Park, Calne SN11 0AU
OGBOURNE, MR J M V, Dale View, Redmire, Leyburn, N Yorks DL8 4EH
OGBURN, MR D A, 110 Libby Lane, Galena, Missouri 65656, USA
OGBURN, SENIOR JUDGE ROBERT W, 317 First Avenue, Monte Vista, CO 81144, USA
OSBORNE, COL R, Unwins House, 15 Waterbeach Road, Landbeach, Cambridge CB4 4EA
PARKER, DR P F, 45 Chitterne Road, Codford St Mary, Warminster BA12 0PG
PATIENCE, MR D C, 29 Priory Gardens, Stamford, Lincs PE9 2EG
PERRY, MR W A, Noads House, Tilshead, Salisbury SP3 4RY
POTTER, MRS J, 6 Round Chimneys, Glanvilles Wootton, Sherborne DT9 5QQ
POWELL, MRS N, 4 Verwood Drive, Bitton, Bristol BS15 6JP
RADNOR, EARL OF, Longford Castle, Salisbury SP5 4EF
RAYBOULD, MISS F, 20 Radnor Road, Salisbury SP1 3PL
ROGERS, MR K H, Silverthorne House, East Town, West Ashton, Trowbridge BA14 6BE
ROOKE, MISS S F, The Old Rectory, Little Langford, Salisbury SP3 4NU
SHELDRAKE, MR B, 28 Belgrave Street, Swindon SN1 3HR
SHEWRING, MR P, 73 Woodland Road, Beddau, Pontypridd, Mid-Glamorgan CF38 2SE
SIMS-NEIGHBOUR, MR A K, 2 Hesketh Crescent, Swindon SN3 1RY
SINGER, MR J, 49 Bradwall Road, Sandbach, Cheshire CW11 1GH
SLOCOMBE, MR I, 11 Belcombe Place, Bradford on Avon BA15 1NA
SMITH, DR C, 102 Calton Road, Linden,

Gloucester GL1 5DY
SMITH, MR P J, 6 Nuthatch, Longfield, Kent DA3 7NS
SNEYD, MR R H, Court Farm House, 22 Court Lane, Bratton, Westbury BA13 4RR
SOPP, MR G A, 70 Steve Place, Sequim, Washington 98382-9547, USA
SPAETH, DR D A, School of History and Archaeology, 1 University Gardens, University of Glasgow G12 8QQ
STEVENAGE, MR M R, 49 Centre Drive, Epping, Essex CM16 4JF
STEWART, MISS K P, 6 Beatrice Road, Salisbury SP1 3PN
SYKES, MRS M, Conock Manor, Conock, Devizes SN10 3QQ
SYLVESTER, MR D G H, Polsue Manor, Ruanhigh Lanes, Truro TR2 5LU
TAYLOR, MR C C, 11 High Street, Pampisford, Cambridge CB2 4ES
THOMPSON, MR & MRS J B, 1 Bedwyn Common, Great Bedwyn, Marlborough SN8 3HZ
THOMSON, MRS S M, Home Close, High St, Codford, Warminster BA12 0NB
TIGHE, MR M F, Strath Colin, Pettridge Lane, Mere, Warminster BA12 6DG
TOMKOWICZ, MRS C, 2 Chirton Place, Trowbridge BA14 0XT
TSUSHIMA, MRS J, Malmaison, Church Street, Great Bedwyn, Marlborough SN8 3PE
TURNER, MR I D, Warrendene, 222 Nottingham Road, Mansfield, Notts NG18 4AB
WAITE, MR R E, 18a Lower Road, Chinnor, Oxford OX9 4DT
WALKER, MR J K, 82 Wainsford Road, Everton, Lymington, Hants SO41 0UD
WARNEFORD, MR F E, New Inn Farm, West End Lane, Henfield, West Sussex BN5 9RF
WARREN, MR P, 6 The Meadows, Milford Hill Road, Salisbury SP1 2RT
WENDEN, MRS P, 21 Eastern Parade, Fareham, Hants PO16 0RL
WHORLEY, MR E E, 190 Stockbridge Road, Winchester, Hants SO22 6RW
WILTSHIRE, MR J, Cold Kitchen Cottage, Kingston Deverill, Warminster BA12 7HE
WILTSHIRE, MRS P E, 23 Little Parks, Holt, Trowbridge BA14 6QR
WOODWARD, A S, 28-840 Cahill Drive West, Ottawa, Ontario K1V 9K5, Canada
WORDSWORTH, MRS G, Quince Cottage, Longbridge Deverill, Warminster BA12 7DS
WRIGHT, MR D P, Haileybury, Hertford SG13 7NU
YOUNGER, MR C, The Old Chapel, Burbage, Marlborough SN8 3AA

UNITED KINGDOM INSTITUTIONS

Aberystwyth
- National Library of Wales
- University College of Wales

Bath. Reference Library
Birmingham
- Central Library
- University Library

Brighton. University of Sussex Library
Bristol. University Library
Cambridge. University Library
Cheltenham. Bristol and Gloucestershire Archaeological Society
Coventry. University of Warwick Library
Devizes
- Wiltshire Archaeological & N.H. Soc.
- Wiltshire Family History Society

Dorchester. Dorset County Library
Durham. University Library
Edinburgh
- National Library of Scotland
- University Library

Exeter. University Library
Glasgow. University Library
Leeds. University Library
Leicester. University Library
Liverpool. University Library
London
- British Library
- College of Arms
- Guildhall Library

Inner Temple Library
Institute of Historical Research
London Library
Public Record Office
Royal Historical Society
Society of Antiquaries
Society of Genealogists
University of London Library
Manchester. John Rylands Library
Marlborough
Memorial Library, Marlborough College
Merchant's House Trust
Savernake Estate Office
Norwich. University of East Anglia Library
Nottingham. University Library
Oxford
Bodleian Library
Exeter College Library
Poole. Bournemouth University
Reading
Central Library
University Library
St Andrews. University Library
Salisbury
Bourne Valley Historical Society
Cathedral Library
Salisbury and South Wilts Museum
Sheffield. University Library
Southampton. University Library
Swansea. University College Library
Swindon
English Heritage
Swindon Borough Council
Taunton. Somerset Archaeological and Natural History Society
Trowbridge
Wiltshire Libraries & Heritage
Wiltshire and Swindon Record Office
Wetherby. British Library Document Supply Centre
York. University Library

INSTITUTIONS OVERSEAS

AUSTRALIA

Adelaide. Barr Smith Library, Adelaide University
Crawley. Reid Library, University of Western Australia
Melbourne
Baillieu Library, University of Melbourne
Victoria State Library
Sydney. Law Library, University of New South Wales

CANADA

London, Ont. D.B.Weldon Library, University of Western Ontario
Ottawa, Ont. Carleton University Library
Toronto, Ont
Pontifical Inst of Medieval Studies
University of Toronto Library
Victoria, B.C. McPherson Library, University of Victoria

EIRE

Dublin. Trinity College Library

GERMANY

Gottingen. University Library

JAPAN

Osaka. Institute of Economic History, Kansai University
Sendai. Institute of Economic History, Tohoku University
Tokyo. Waseda University Library

NEW ZEALAND

Wellington. National Library of New Zealand

UNITED STATES OF AMERICA

Ann Arbor, Mich. Hatcher Library, University of Michigan
Athens, Ga. University of Georgia Libraries
Atlanta, Ga. The Robert W Woodruff Library, Emory University
Baltimore, Md. Milton S. Eisenhower Library, Johns Hopkins University
Bloomington, Ind. Indiana University Library
Boston, Mass. New England Historic and Genealogical Society
Boulder, Colo. University of Colorado Library

Cambridge, Mass.
Harvard College Library
Harvard Law School Library
Charlottesville, Va. Alderman Library, University of Virginia
Chicago.
Newberry Library
University of Chicago Library
Dallas, Texas. Public Library
Davis, Calif. University Library
East Lansing, Mich. Michigan State University Library
Eugene, Ore. University of Oregon Library
Evanston, Ill. United Libraries, Garrett/Evangelical, Seabury
Fort Wayne, Ind. Allen County Public Library
Houston, Texas. M.D. Anderson Library, University of Houston
Iowa City, Iowa. University of Iowa Libraries
Ithaca, NY. Cornell University Library
Las Cruces, N.M. New Mexico State University Library
Los Angeles.
Public Library
Young Research Library, University of California
Minneapolis, Minn. Wilson Library, University of Minnesota
New Haven, Conn. Yale University Library
New York.
Columbia University of the City of New York
Public Library
Notre Dame, Ind. Memorial Library, University of Notre Dame
Piscataway, N.J. Rutgers University Libraries
Princeton, N.J. Princeton University Libraries
Salt Lake City, Utah. Family History Library
San Marino, Calif. Henry E. Huntington Library
Santa Barbara, Calif. University of California Library
South Hadley, Mass. Williston Memorial Library, Mount Holyoke College
Stanford, Calif. Green Library, Stanford University
Tucson, Ariz. University of Arizona Library
Urbana, Ill. University of Illinois Library
Washington. The Folger Shakespeare Library
Winston-Salem, N.C. Z.Smith Reynolds Library, Wake Forest University

LIST OF PUBLICATIONS

The Wiltshire Record Society was founded in 1937, as the Records Branch of the Wiltshire Archaeological and Natural History Society, to promote the publication of the documentary sources for the history of Wiltshire. The annual subscription is £15 for private and institutional members. In return, a member receives a volume each year. Prospective members should apply to the Hon. Secretary, c/o Wiltshire and Swindon Record Office, Bythesea Road, Trowbridge, Wilts BA14 8BS. Many more members are needed.

The following volumes have been published. Price to members £15, and to non-members £20, postage extra. Available from the Wiltshire and Swindon Record Office, Bythesea Road, Trowbridge BA14 8BS.

1. *Abstracts of feet of fines relating to Wiltshire for the reigns of Edward I and Edward II*, ed. R.B. Pugh, 1939
2. *Accounts of the parliamentary garrisons of Great Chalfield and Malmesbury, 1645-1646*, ed. J.H.P. Pafford, 1940
3. *Calendar of Antrobus deeds before 1625*, ed. R.B. Pugh, 1947
4. *Wiltshire county records: minutes of proceedings in sessions, 1563 and 1574 to 1592*, ed. H.C. Johnson, 1949
5. *List of Wiltshire boroughs records earlier in date than 1836*, ed. M.G. Rathbone, 1951
6. *The Trowbridge woollen industry as illustrated by the stock books of John and Thomas Clark, 1804-1824*, ed. R.P. Beckinsale, 1951
7. *Guild stewards' book of the borough of Calne, 1561-1688*, ed. A.W. Mabbs, 1953
8. *Andrews' and Dury's map of Wiltshire, 1773: a reduced facsimile*, ed. Elizabeth Crittall, 1952
9. *Surveys of the manors of Philip, earl of Pembroke and Montgomery, 1631-2*, ed. E. Kerridge, 1953
10. *Two sixteenth century taxations lists, 1545 and 1576*, ed. G.D. Ramsay, 1954
11. *Wiltshire quarter sessions and assizes, 1736*, ed. J.P.M. Fowle, 1955
12. *Collectanea*, ed. N.J. Williams, 1956
13. *Progress notes of Warden Woodward for the Wiltshire estates of New College, Oxford, 1659-1675*, ed. R.L. Rickard, 1957
14. *Accounts and surveys of the Wiltshire lands of Adam de Stratton*, ed. M.W. Farr, 1959
15. *Tradesmen in early-Stuart Wiltshire: a miscellany*, ed. N.J. Williams, 1960
16. *Crown pleas of the Wiltshire eyre, 1249*, ed. C.A.F. Meekings, 1961
17. *Wiltshire apprentices and their masters, 1710-1760*, ed. Christabel Dale, 1961
18. *Hemingby's register*, ed. Helena M. Chew, 1963
19. *Documents illustrating the Wiltshire textile trades in the eighteenth century*, ed. Julia de L. Mann, 1964
20. *The diary of Thomas Naish*, ed. Doreen Slatter, 1965

21-2. *The rolls of Highworth hundred, 1275-1287*, 2 parts, ed. Brenda Farr, 1966, 1968

23. *The earl of Hertford's lieutenancy papers, 1603-1612*, ed. W.P.D. Murphy, 1969
24. *Court rolls of the Wiltshire manors of Adam de Stratton*, ed. R.B. Pugh, 1970
25. *Abstracts of Wiltshire inclosure awards and agreements*, ed. R.E. Sandell, 1971
26. *Civil pleas of the Wiltshire eyre, 1249*, ed. M.T. Clanchy, 1971
27. *Wiltshire returns to the bishop's visitation queries, 1783*, ed. Mary Ransome, 1972
28. *Wiltshire extents for debts, Edward I - Elizabeth I*, ed. Angela Conyers, 1973
29. *Abstracts of feet of fines relating to Wiltshire for the reign of Edward III*, ed. C.R. Elrington, 1974
30. *Abstracts of Wiltshire tithe apportionments*, ed. R.E. Sandell, 1975

31. *Poverty in early-Stuart Salisbury*, ed. Paul Slack, 1975
32. *The subscription book of Bishops Tounson and Davenant, 1620-40*, ed. B. Williams, 1977
33. *Wiltshire gaol delivery and trailbaston trials, 1275-1306*, ed. R.B. Pugh, 1978
34. *Lacock abbey charters*, ed. K.H. Rogers, 1979
35. *The cartulary of Bradenstoke priory*, ed. Vera C.M. London, 1979
36. *Wiltshire coroners' bills, 1752-1796*, ed. R.F. Hunnisett, 1981
37. *The justicing notebook of William Hunt, 1744-1749*, ed. Elizabeth Crittall, 1982
38. *Two Elizabethan women: correspondence of Joan and Maria Thynne, 1575-1611*, ed. Alison D. Wall, 1983
39. *The register of John Chandler, dean of Salisbury, 1404-17*, ed. T.C.B. Timmins, 1984
40. *Wiltshire dissenters' meeting house certificates and registrations, 1689-1852*, ed. J.H. Chandler, 1985
41. *Abstracts of feet of fines relating to Wiltshire, 1377-1509*, ed. J.L. Kirby, 1986
42. *The Edington cartulary*, ed. Janet H. Stevenson, 1987
43. *The commonplace book of Sir Edward Bayntun of Bromham*, ed. Jane Freeman, 1988
44. *The diaries of Jeffery Whitaker, schoolmaster of Bratton, 1739-1741*, ed. Marjorie Reeves and Jean Morrison, 1989
45. *The Wiltshire tax list of 1332*, ed. D.A. Crowley, 1989
46. *Calendar of Bradford-on-Avon settlement examinations and removal orders, 1725-98*, ed. Phyllis Hembry, 1990
47. *Early trade directories of Wiltshire*, ed. K.H. Rogers and indexed by J.H. Chandler, 1992
48. *Star chamber suits of John and Thomas Warneford*, ed. F.E. Warneford, 1993
49. *The Hungerford cartulary: a calendar of the earl of Radnor's cartulary of the Hungerford family*, ed. J.L. Kirby, 1994
50. *The Letters of John Peniston, Salisbury architect, Catholic, and Yeomanry Officer, 1823-1830*, ed. M. Cowan, 1996
51. *The Apprentice Registers of the Wiltshire Society, 1817- 1922*, ed. H. R. Henly, 1997
52. *Printed Maps of Wiltshire 1787–1844: a selection of topographical, road and canal maps in facsimile*, ed. John Chandler, 1998
53. *Monumental Inscriptions of Wiltshire: an edition, in facsimile, of* Monumental Inscriptions in the County of Wilton, *by Sir Thomas Phillipps*, ed. Peter Sherlock, 2000
54. *The First General Entry Book of the City of Salisbury, 1387-1452*, ed. David R. Carr, 2001
55. *Devizes Division income tax assessments, 1842-1860*, ed. Robert Colley, 2002
56. *Wiltshire Glebe Terriers, 1588-1827*, ed. Steven Hobbs, 2003

VOLUMES IN PREPARATION

Early vehicle registration in Wiltshire, edited by Ian Hicks; *Marlborough probate inventories*, edited by Lorelei Williams; *Wiltshire papist returns and estate enrolments, 1705-87*, edited by J.A. Williams; *The Diary of William Henry Tucker*, edited by Helen Rogers; *Crown pleas of the Wiltshire eyre, 1268*, edited by Brenda Farr; *The Hungerford cartulary, vol.2: the Hobhouse cartulary*, edited by J.L. Kirby; *The Parish registers of Thomas Crockford, 1613-29*, edited by C.C. Newbury; *Index to the Salisbury Diocesan probate records*; *The Wiltshire hearth tax returns*, edited by Lorelei Williams; *Wiltshire rural industry organiser surveys and reports, c. 1938 - c. 1957*, edited by John d'Arcy; *William Small's Notebook*, edited by Jane Howells and Ruth Newman. The volumes will not necessarily appear in this order.

A leaflet giving full details may be obtained from the Hon. Secretary, c/o Wiltshire and Swindon Record Office, Bythesea Road, Trowbridge, Wilts. BA14 8BS. Details may also be found on the Society's website: www.wiltshirerecordsociety.co.uk.